About th

JOYCE MOULLAKIS is a senior journalist and columnist whose career has spanned Australia, the Asia Pacific and the United Kingdom over more than two decades. She was a finalist in the Citigroup business journalism awards and has written for the *Australian Financial Review* and *Bloomberg*, and she is currently a senior banking reporter for *The Australian*.

CHRIS WRIGHT is an award-winning journalist and author based in Singapore. He has been Asia and Middle East editor of *Euromoney*, editor of *Asiamoney* and investment editor of the *Australian Financial Review*. He is proprietor of the freelance writing consultancy Chris Wright Media and a founding partner of Resonate Global, and he is author of the books *No More Worlds to Conquer* and *Rum & Coal*.

Praise for
The Millionaires' Factory

'A fascinating account of how a successful financial institution with a global footprint can grow through good and bad times because of the quality of its people.'
Don Argus AC, Bank of America Australian Advisory Board Member

'It's billion dollar (New South) whales!'
Clive Horwood, former editor of *Euromoney*

'Joyce and Chris have brilliantly captured and woven together an exceptional account of an Australian and global financial success story. Its uniqueness, its opportunism, its stealthiness and its depth of human capital are all brought together in a balanced and memorable account of a continuing Aussie business icon.'
Steve Harker AM, former CEO of Morgan Stanley Australia

'*The Millionaires' Factory* is a fascinating insight into how very smart people have been innovators in financial services worldwide. The Macquarie Bank story should be required reading for all ages as it displays clearly that innovation, lateral thinking and hard work are the keys to success in business and life.'
John Symond, founder of Aussie Home Loans

THE MILLIONAIRES' FACTORY

THE INSIDE STORY OF HOW
MACQUARIE BANK BECAME A GLOBAL GIANT

JOYCE MOULLAKIS and CHRIS WRIGHT

ALLEN&UNWIN
SYDNEY·MELBOURNE·AUCKLAND·LONDON

First published in 2023

Allen & Unwin
Cammeraygal Country
83 Alexander Street
Crows Nest NSW 2065
Australia
Phone: (61 2) 8425 0100
Email: info@allenandunwin.com
Web: www.allenandunwin.com

Allen & Unwin acknowledges the Traditional Owners of the Country on which we live and work. We pay our respects to all Aboriginal and Torres Strait Islander Elders, past and present.

 A catalogue record for this book is available from the National Library of Australia

ISBN 978 1 76106 715 0

Map by Guy Holt
Index by Chris Wright
Set in 12/17 pt Minion Pro by Midland Typesetters, Australia

10 9 8 7 6 5 4 3 2 1

Joyce

This book is dedicated to my family, and Jesse,
for their unwavering encouragement
through this process
and for supporting my inquisitive streak

Chris

This book is dedicated to my children, Chyna and Quinn,
for tolerating a lockdown with their parents
whose vocal projection on Zoom calls could penetrate
concrete

CONTENTS

NOTE

There is a lot to say about Macquarie—more than there was room to accommodate in this print edition. We compiled 25,000 words of additional notes. Some of this material relates to sourcing, or precise legal titles and additional numbers, but it also includes whole other stories, quotes, anecdotes and people.

To allow for the maximum book length and to accommodate as much of this additional material as possible, we have hosted these notes on a dedicated website, www.millionairesfactorynotes.com, which you can access by scanning the QR code below.

Perhaps you may wish to read this with both the book and the site open on your phone, a far easier way to view the notes as they arise than flipping back and forward in a book.

PROLOGUE

Texans won't soon forget the winter storm when their electricity bills went up a hundred times over in a week as their temperatures dropped lower than Alaska's.

In mid-February 2021, snow fell deep on America's central and southern plains. It ripped across Texas and Oklahoma in blizzards the like of which they'd never seen and for which they were wholly unprepared. Dallas, Houston and San Antonio suffered their coldest ever days.

Oil and gas wells froze solid. Ice draped the wellheads and the derricks. It became too cold for wind turbines to move. Power grids failed under the strain of heating demand they had never before been expected to provide.

At the worst of the storm, on 15 February, four and a half million Texans were left without electricity. And when the blackouts started to ease, thanks to a quirk of the free-market Texas energy industry that sets its rates on real-time prices in the wholesale markets, some ordinary people faced bills of thousands of dollars for a few days of supply.

■

One week and 14,000 kilometres away in Sydney, Australia, as the temperature nudged 30 degrees centigrade on a day of scattered low cloud, Macquarie Group lodged an earnings update to the Australian Securities Exchange.

Chief executive Shemara Wikramanayake had good news. Where previously Macquarie had expected a year-on-year drop in net profits for its 2021 financial year as banks worldwide reeled from the impact of the COVID-19 pandemic, now it would instead come out ahead, by 5 to 10 per cent: a swing of about A$270 million. It would be a record year.[1]

The source of this bounty? A huge boost from Macquarie's Commodities and Global Markets division, and, more specifically, demand for a niche business it had built to ship gas across North America through a network of leased pipelines.[2]

The connection between these two apparently disparate events tells us a number of things that help us to understand Macquarie, an institution that has not only spent more than half a century being unique, but has reinvented itself so often along the way that it is unique in a completely different way every decade or so, usually in order to get ahead of a trend that hasn't even happened yet.

It's not just a caterpillar that turns into a butterfly. It's a caterpillar that turns into a butterfly and then turns into a bee because it thinks there's a better outlook for bees.

■

The first thing the story reminds us is that Macquarie is everywhere. Formally born in Sydney in 1985 out of the Australian arm of a British merchant bank called Hill Samuel & Co that began operations in

Australia in 1969, the bank with the Holey Dollar logo has long since taken on the world and won. As of 31 March 2022, only 25 per cent of its total income comes from Australia and New Zealand.[3]

The Americas, at 48 per cent, account for by far the biggest chunk, but don't just picture some high-octane New York trading floor accounting for all that. Across the country and the continent, and the world for that matter, Macquarie is on the ground, in the weeds, in the game.

Later in this book we'll take you on that most American of adventures, a roadtrip, in a roughly straight south-to-north line from the mouth of the Mississippi through Texas up to Canada. We will be about as far from Australia as it is physically possible to be. Along the way we will visit waste managers, airlines, freight terminals, fund managers, energy providers and telcos right through the middle of this real America, the one away from the coasts where the tourists don't go.

The one thing that binds these businesses is that Macquarie owns, manages or advises them all. One of these businesses, just one, is that gas distribution business that delivered so strongly in the midst of the Texas storms.

We could repeat the exercise in the UK, South Korea or a host of places in between and experience the same thing. As an investment bank, a commodities player or a world leader in infrastructure fund management, Macquarie has inserted itself into your life somewhere, no matter where you're reading this book.

There are parts of the world where every time you turn on a tap, you're enriching Macquarie. In others, it's when you drive your car down a toll road, or catch a flight from one of its airports, or source energy from something it has backed. You can do it half a dozen times in a day without knowing it.

■

The second thing the Texas story tells you is about a unique Macquarie trait: the ability to spot a niche few others can see, and then to give a handful of individuals an exceptional level of trust and support to exploit it.

The reason Macquarie was able to turn decline to growth through the Texas winter storm was because Macquarie has become one of the world's biggest players in the business of moving gas and power from one part of the USA to another, taking a commission as it does so. And the root of how it gained this apparently obscure position is a classic Macquarie story, played out time and again across the years, across products and across the world.

This one dates back to two men, Andrew Downe and Nick O'Kane, believing they could find an edge in the US energy industry and setting out to do it by acquiring a little-known Los Angeles energy marketer called Cook Inlet in 2005.

Macquarie lives and breathes a risk management system that has been known throughout its history as 'loose–tight', and later 'freedom within boundaries', which one might explain thus: if you have an idea, and if you can stand it up to the satisfaction of the bank's leaders and its absurdly smart risk professionals, then they will give you the keys and tell you to go and do it.

They won't tell you how. That's your job, because it's your idea. You will be encouraged to fail along the way. Sometimes you will fail a few times before you get it right. But provided you don't blow things up with something downright stupid (and the risk parameters will have made sure you never had enough dynamite to do any serious institutional damage anyway), you'll be backed.

And Downe and O'Kane did fail at first, losing money on developing the business organically, before they bought Cook Inlet and built on it, giving it transformational heft by adding the Houston-based trading books of Constellation Energy in the depths of the global financial crisis. Little by little, they became one of the leaders in gas marketing in North America, almost without anyone noticing.

Along the way, as just one tentacle of this burgeoning new empire, O'Kane had been systematically building a matrix of leases over gas supply pipelines and electricity transmission networks, renting the access without owning the infrastructure, until Macquarie was more powerful than anyone at moving energy and fuel quickly from one part of the USA to another.

When the earnings upgrade came that warm February day in Sydney, most journalists, and probably some analysts, were largely unaware this business existed. It was just there, waiting, built quietly, doing its thing, unnoticed. It made modest returns and did its job until, all of a sudden, the unexpected happened and in the blink of an eye it was delivering a one-off windfall of several hundred million dollars. Except it wasn't a windfall, because it wasn't there by accident.

If Macquarie's a tree, then that gas distribution network is a shoot on a twig on a branch on one of several arms off the trunk.[4] It has dozens of these shoots, tightly defined businesses like this one, growing: call options, you might say, on circumstances that might never arise—but when they do, Macquarie will be ready.

The whole point of Macquarie is the vast variety of its engines, diverse in product and geography, which add up to a collective that always seems to have an edge. Intuitively, that ought to represent unmanageable risk. But instead, it's an innovator whose implosions are rare and contained. Being both visionary and inherently conservative is the trick that has got Macquarie to where it is today.

And the architects of its best ideas get very rich along the way. Downe had moved on by the time of the Texas storm, but O'Kane? Well, he earned A$26.3 million, nearly A$5 million more than his chief executive, Shemara Wikramanayake, that year, and A$36.2 million the year after. And investors don't mind that a bit, because at

Macquarie, you get rewarded for what you deliver, not your title or your reputation, and you have every chance of being absurdly well paid when you get it right.

■

The third thing our Texas tale tells you is that making money isn't always pretty.

Macquarie is not the price-setter in this story and it did not gouge American consumers. It's just got a well-placed role in a flawed free-market mess that it didn't invent, and that it is the responsibility of Texas and other affected states to amend. But still, making a bonanza profit out of millions of Texans freezing in the dark is not a good look. Indelicate, let's say.

Macquarie insiders will tell you, with genuine pride, that they originate and develop the renewable energy projects that will drive a sluggish world towards carbon neutrality; that the Macquarie Foundation has contributed half a billion dollars to community causes. Both of these things are admirable and true.

But it's also true that Macquarie is seldom on the wrong side of the deal, and that the markets are no place to be squeamish.

If you're a shareholder or an employee, of course, Macquarie is probably the finest friend you could have. The total shareholders' equity of Macquarie is about A$31.3 billion.[5] At the time of writing its market capitalisation is about A$70 billion.[6] The difference between these two numbers is the value Macquarie has created for its shareholders along the way out of thin air, with nothing more tangible than innovation, people and a stoic work ethic. Its leaders— and there have been only seven[7] in more than half a century, if you count the Hill Samuel Australia days—are exceptionally good at what they do.

This is the story of how Macquarie got here: how a few like-minded souls in 1970s Sydney positioned themselves at exactly the right time, banking rising forces like Frank Lowy, as Australia deregulated its banking sector and the country found its economic and financial voice on the world stage. Macquarie joined that voice, and before long it was the one doing much of the shouting.

This is the story of a place that has never gone outside its own ranks to recruit a chief executive in 53 years, where it's nothing special to work there for two or three decades, and where people have no problem with a remuneration structure that only makes them rich if they commit to years of loyalty.

This is the story of a bank that is both admired and attacked in its home market. It is the homegrown self-made powerhouse that went around the world and beat the field without ever abandoning its home base, an Aussie champion abroad. But it is also the clearest illustration of Australia's tall poppy syndrome, accused of greed every time its executives' compensation appears in the papers, of being the place that takes the nation's finest minds and turns them into money machines.

This is the story of how an Australian bank that's not just Australian and not just a bank can deliver a record profit in the middle of a pandemic on the back of a biblical storm in Texas. Of a place that can turn every market calamity into an opportunity even while rumours abound of its own demise; that has so many siloes and niches that maybe a few dozen people truly understand its full scale of operations at any given time; that is unique globally, and has thrived as many institutions that have sought to impersonate it have gone to the wall in the effort.

This is the story of Macquarie: the Millionaires' Factory.[8]

Chapter 1

BEGINNINGS

It was on a 26-foot Thunderbird sailboat in Sydney Harbour in 1971 that Christopher Castleman made his move.

Castleman was on a charm offensive. A Cambridge-educated[1] executive of Hill Samuel & Co, a London-based merchant bank which traced its roots to 1831–32,[2] he was a forthright chain-smoker often found in a pinstripe suit, who liked to cap an evening meeting with a tumbler of iced Cointreau or Kummel.

The targets of his charm that day were two young bankers from Darling & Company, a 29-year-old called David Clarke and 30-year-old Mark Johnson. The pair had attended Harvard Business School before joining James Wolfensohn[3] at Darling & Company, and were making their mark in Sydney's merchant banking scene.

Clarke and Johnson were already familiar with Castleman: the trio played bridge and socialised frequently. But this time, on the Thunderbird, Castleman wanted to broach a tricky subject, and after several cold beers on the harbour, he made his pitch. How would they feel about running the Australian operations of Hill Samuel when he returned to London?

It was a hard sell and he was peppered with questions. But Castleman was used to hard sells: he was known for his boundless energy, his stamina in closing a deal, and his ability to manoeuvre through complex and tough takeover negotiations. Johnson and Clarke were taken aback, but they knew the value of listening to an offer, so they agreed to keep the discussion going.

They had their reservations, because although Hill Samuel & Co was a storied name in the City of London, that didn't translate to Australia, where the firm was just taking its first steps in 1971 to chip away at a nascent investment banking market.

So, they agreed to a number of subsequent meetings to clarify the level of support Hill Samuel would provide its Australian offshoot, and the level of autonomy they would have. For two experienced but still youthful bankers, the opportunity to run their own advisory and markets shop eventually proved irresistible.

Castleman got his targets, but not without a delay of several months. Johnson felt he needed to stay a little longer at Darling & Company to help with the fallout of the collapse of Mineral Securities.[4]

After that clean-up, Johnson and Clarke were free to start their new challenge and joined to take the tally of employees at Hill Samuel Australia to fourteen.

In later years, Clarke would ponder the fortuitous consequence of them joining together.

'We avoided the unlucky number of thirteen employees because two of us joined together,' he said. 'So the whole reason for our success is that we had good karma'. (This comment, and many others in this book, are taken from a series of interviews Clarke recorded as he was close to death in 2011. Permission to relay parts of the interviews was kindly provided to Joyce.)

When they turned up at 60 Martin Place in Sydney's central business district, where Castleman inducted his new top recruits, the idea of what this business would eventually become would have seemed absurd. Hill Samuel Australia was not nearly big enough to have its own lease; it had first bunkered in with its inaugural chairman before subletting space on level 23 from prominent law firm Dawson Waldron.

Feeling some apprehension on day one, Clarke and Johnson's first task with Castleman was to review something called the 'work-in-hand sheet', basically a green paper document that listed Hill Samuel's work under way and specifically identified clients. There was at least one promising early sign: there were multiple sheets of paper.

'On the green paper, after you went through the first sheet you turned it over to the second which meant, at least, there was some business there,' Johnson says. On the early years of Hill Samuel Australia that followed, he says: 'We were scurrying around in the undergrowth of the big regulated institutions, trying to make a buck.'

■

The two men were joining Hill Samuel at a rather dour time in Australian banking, although it wouldn't stay that way.

Investment banking and finance were dominated by a clutch of powerful stockbroking firms and some fragmented, largely state-based, banks. The climate was one of heavy regulation in the post-war era. The Reserve Bank of Australia, the country's central bank, kept a tight grip on the banking sector and the currency.

In 1971, US President Richard Nixon had abandoned the US dollar's link to gold and the Bretton Woods system of fixed exchange rates was unravelling. The fluidity of the situation saw Australia change its currency peg to the US dollar from the British pound sterling, around the same time the pound was floated.[5]

Australia didn't, though, join other advanced economies in freeing its exchange rate, as it had a still fledgling financial sector and the nation's trade, fiscal and monetary policy was largely internally focused. Not only did Australia not yet have businesses thriving internationally, it had very few that could really be considered national: the life insurance group AMP and the building materials firm CSR were among the rare exceptions.

So, in 1971, the opportunity was modest: banking services and corporate finance. Hill Samuel Australia did also offer what it called international finance, but all that really meant was foreign currency loans.

Nevertheless, there was good business to be done for classic merchant bankers who knew how to build relationships, and when Clarke and Johnson joined, the man who had laid the foundations and become the new firm's public face was chairman Stan Owens.

You can find a portrait of Owens in the 1976 annual report: not a photograph but a painting, looking suave and at ease with one leg crossed over the other, right arm slouched over the back of a chair, spectacles dangling from his fingertips. He looks as you might imagine a 1970s chairman of Rolls-Royce Australia would, which was among his many roles: indeed, he would drive one of these fine cars around Sydney.

Owens was a distinguished chartered accountant and revered communicator who had served in the Middle East and New Guinea during the Second World War. Despite humble beginnings in his formative years in Mungindi, near the state of Queensland's border, Owens had gravitas in Sydney's burgeoning financial district. In addition to Rolls-Royce, he would compile a roster of other board seats including as the first chairman of satellite company AUSSAT and chair of tiles group Monier.

Owens took the reins as inaugural chairman in 1969, after being sought out to submit a detailed proposal to Hill Samuel in London on the merits of the outpost and the best way to execute the plan. The piece of work for Hill Samuel came after Army Minister and then Minister for Education and Science Malcolm Fraser—who would go on to become Australia's Prime Minister between 1975 and 1983—had drafted Owens to compile reports on the coffee and cacao markets in New Guinea.

With a blueprint for Hill Samuel Australia and Owens at the helm of its board, the new entity was formed. Soon after, and somewhat reluctantly, Owens installed a phone at his Avoca Beach house north of Sydney, to ensure he could field frequent calls from London when he was away from his city home.

Hill Samuel would provide initial capital of A$1 million to make the foray work. The first employees to the Australian offshoot were former accountant and renowned networker Blair Hesketh, who was seconded from Hill Samuel UK, and Eton College educated Hill Samuel executive Paul Bowman, who joined the board. Soon after former accountant Geoff Hobson would join too.

Owens wasn't always present at Martin Place—he kept an office close by at Gold Fields House—but staff could often tell when he visited given his bustling walk and habit of acknowledging all employees he encountered, even briefly, by first name. A classic relationship man, he set about making introductions and made sure the new institution hit the ground running in Australia. He would open a lot of doors for Johnson and Clarke in the formative days of Hill Samuel Australia, working his connections and facilitating meetings. Chartered accountants were considered trusted business advisers back then, and were very influential in Australian business circles.

He was a great help to the two new recruits, who were representative of a policy Castleman had settled upon: that in order to make a dent in the Australian market, Hill Samuel Australia would require local leaders who would provide longevity and stability. This was in contrast to shipping in bankers from overseas for a few years at a time, which had been the approach of other major banks: send in international executives on three- to five-year contracts and then rotate.

Castleman wanted locals like Clarke and Johnson as an important selling point to Australian companies as they made themselves known to them in Sydney, Melbourne and the other capital cities.

But it was a hard slog in the early days, both winning the business and finding the people. The first year of operations led to a loss of about A$40,000. But, in an example of creativity that would become a hallmark in years ahead, a management fee was charged back to the parent and swung the Australian entity into profit. They were in the black, on their way, and now they had credibility as they pounded the pavements to pitch their wares around town.

'It was an agreement concluded between Hill Samuel Australia and Hill Samuel UK. I think Hill Samuel UK met the fee out of part of their transaction fees,' Johnson says. 'You had to convince people. If they asked, you had to show them the balance sheet.'

Hill Samuel UK had set the operation Down Under a four-year target to hit profitability. This fee meant they met it in one.

■

It wasn't long, though, before the firm was in the black of its own accord, as the year ending 31 March 1972 brought some early success and a profit of A$110,000. Drawing on the merchant bank's UK relationships and a personal local connection through Owens, Hill Samuel Australia won a mandate to manage a syndicate of Australian and international banks to provide a US$60 million loan to corrugated iron provider John Lysaght.

At the time, John Lysaght was partially owned by Broken Hill Proprietary (BHP), the resources behemoth whose various acquisitions and fundraisings would become a core source of work for the team and their successors in the years ahead. The deal itself was the largest single fundraising to date for an Australian industrial company in the eurodollar market and was highly significant for the new team: they had shown they could win business and deliver.

Owens had also rolled up his sleeves to help the firm win the role of manager on a A\$12 million loan facility for STC Finance, a division of International Telephone and Telegraph Corporation. Deals like this mattered greatly, and made it much easier to hire more talent to fill out the ranks. And from the outset, Hill Samuel Australia had a distinctive approach to recruitment that would become renowned, even notorious, as it grew into Macquarie Bank.

Clarke had studied economics at the University of Sydney, and Johnson law at the University of Melbourne. Both were highly intelligent with a thirst for more knowledge and business experience.

Clarke and Johnson went to Harvard Business School, where their paths crossed, and the two-year prestigious course left a firm impression on their views of markets and management theory. In the field of organisational behaviour, they were particularly interested in Douglas McGregor's exposition of Theory X and Theory Y, which advocated a new approach to tapping the potential of staff. It reflected a shift from pre-war techniques of mass production to changes driven by a growing knowledge economy.

It worked like this. Theory X was underpinned by the premise that employees dislike work, and therefore required coercion and control within an organisation in order to achieve goals.

Theory Y thought more highly of employees, and held that companies should draw upon goals and an employee's interest in work, their independence, problem-solving, responsibility and creative capacity.

Johnson and Clarke were firmly Theory Y. They believed that giving employees responsibility was the best approach. Their philosophy was to give employees as much latitude as possible, while remaining consistent with safety and controls. That meant encouraging employees to take their own initiative and get on with it, rather than controlling them from the top.

This attitude is just as true more than half a century later across Macquarie Group as it was in the early 1970s at its tiny predecessor. If Macquarie has stood for anything in all of that time, it has been the entrepreneurial empowerment of the individual.

Other influencers from Harvard included Professor Colyer Crum and Professor C. Roland (Chris) Christensen.[6] Clarke once said Christensen taught him the importance of success not coming at the expense of breaching or compromising ethical standards. Crum instilled in him the merit in questioning everything in business.

In assembling their senior corporate advisory team, Johnson and Clarke would scour the ranks of Harvard Business School graduates annually to seek out highly intelligent and collaborative employees.

A psychometric test—another key Macquarie screening technique to this day—would generally follow the first rounds of the interview process to provide additional feedback on the candidate's suitability to join. Recruitment firm Chandler Macleod administered the early versions of the testing, which weren't for the faint-hearted given they took about six hours to complete. The psychometric testing is now overseen by Korn Ferry and includes assessments spanning numerical ability, behavioural style and verbal and logic skills.

Johnson says: 'These tests were much more aimed at teamwork, collaboration, and to show that you didn't have any sort of wild aberrations; you could write and you were numerate. David Clarke was the advocate for testing. To allay my scepticism, David took the tests himself, and gave me his results.'

Former Macquarie Capital boss Michael Carapiet says while the process isn't foolproof, there was value in the intense level of testing and screening. 'David Clarke believed in it quite a lot,' he says. 'What I found is that not everybody who did well was a guaranteed success. But if you didn't do well, you never did well.'

Coupled with the interviews, this system set a high bar for entry and found some very impressive people. One of the earliest targets was Tony Berg, a Harvard graduate who had worked at Loeb Rhoades & Co[7] and Schroder Darling. Landing him was an example of Castleman's refined sales technique, using what they knew about Berg to attract him to join. Johnson and Clarke convinced him that Hill Samuel Australia would be an exciting option as the embryonic firm was set to scale greater heights, while they also persuaded Johnson's wife Sandra to talk to Berg's soon-to-be wife Carrol, since both women were American. Berg joined in 1972.

Around the same time, Hesketh was again on the move and shifted to Melbourne to set up a Hill Samuel office at 500 Collins Street.

The team was starting to take shape. Their Sydney digs were basically one large open boardroom with a string of square and circular desks. Johnson and Clarke shared an office and those who entered recall it as being filled with a haze of Cuban cigar smoke from about 10 am onwards.

Although his role would diminish over time, Owens was central in the early days, and not just in deal-making. He helped set the tone of the new firm's culture as well. Owens was known to lecture staff relentlessly about confidentiality.

If anyone doubted how seriously he took this, it was made very clear one evening when the deal team, working late, left reams of papers around the table at Martin Place. When they returned the next day, the deal documents had disappeared.

Sensing they were being given a lesson, the team trudged to Gold Fields House, where Owens had taken the documents. They had to apologise repeatedly and explain the lesson they had learned before

Owens was prepared to return the papers so they could get on with the deal.

They didn't make that mistake twice.

■

More milestones came along, and one involved the most Australian of specialties: the Chiko Roll.

The Chiko Roll,[8] created by a Victorian boilermaker called Frank McEncroe in the 1950s, is by any objective measure an acquired taste, but it is an iconic Australian cultural food. McEncroe saw an opportunity to create fried Chinese-style chop suey rolls with an Australian twist, making them larger and firmer with a crispy outer layer.

When a leading political figure once described it as 'fat encased in fat' he provided considerable ammunition to the opposition, who considered his views un-Australian, notwithstanding the fact that they were completely accurate.

In any event, by the 1970s McEncroe's publicly traded company was selling 40 million Chiko Rolls in Australia annually while selling a further million, inexplicably, to Japan. This success attracted US conglomerate IT&T, which made an audacious bid to buy the company.

Today, Australians rail against their mines and farms being sold to China. In the 1970s, they bridled at the idea of a foreign house buying their savoury snacks, and the bid, led by IT&T's Harold Geneen, sparked a public relations furore. Some of McEncroe's shareholders strongly opposed a foreign firm encroaching on a high-profile Aussie brand.

It was a tricky proposition for Hill Samuel Australia, which was advising a subsidiary of IT&T on the takeover tilt.

The fiery debate led to the formation of Australia's Foreign Investment Review Board, to help advise the federal treasurer on the operation of policy, and to the passage of the *Foreign Acquisitions and Takeovers Act 1975*. From Hill Samuel Australia's point of view, the commotion was not entirely unwelcome: there was good profile to be had in being in the middle of a deal that everyone was talking about and that shaped national policy.

While deals like this were very promising, the broader economic environment was darkening, and Owens would frequently use his chairman's foreword in the annual reports—tiny and quaint documents by today's standards, often twelve to fifteen pages including the covers in the early days—to bemoan what he was seeing.

In his 1973 write-up he spoke of 'stagnant capital expenditure and hence little demand for new fund raisings'; in 1974, one of the extremely few years in the history of Hill Samuel Australia and Macquarie when profits actually declined year on year,[9] he observed: 'We are now in a credit squeeze more severe than anything that has been experienced in Australia since 1960.' By 1975: 'Conditions in Australian financial markets in the past twelve months were the most difficult since at least 1960–61, and possibly the most difficult in the post-war period.'

There was also a pointed message to the government of the time: 'Until the government shows that it understands the need for adequate company profits and until it clearly indicates that it sees the business sector, long term—and I emphasise long term—as an important partner in the development of Australia, the country will not regain the drive and momentum of prior years.'

Hill Samuel Australia had been returning a profit and growing very well, but there was a problem. Inflation was heading relentlessly up, and that meant it wasn't enough to just grow. In 1975, for example, the firm made a net profit of A$352,000, but, as Owens said: 'It is an inadequate return in the highly inflationary conditions now prevailing in Australia.' To keep pace with the erosion of shareholders' capital by this inflation, he wrote, they really needed to be delivering a rate of return approaching 20 per cent.

A year after that, despite a record after-tax profit of A$668,000, the firm made a provision of A$135,000, not for any specific default but for 'uncertainties which may arise in the future.'

To get to the targeted rate of return, the team was already striving to grow and reinvent. By the mid-1970s, Banking Services had come to include money market, loans administration and treasury. Corporate Services covered lending, issues and placements, public flotation, mergers and acquisitions and reorganisation, among other things. Hill Samuel became the first merchant bank in Australia to set up advisory and finance services for the property industry, and launched a dedicated project finance unit.[10]

And the strategy was working. The firm was luring some big-name customers beyond the ones that had come from the London parent or Owens's connections.

In 1977, one of Hill Samuel Australia's star bankers, James Graham,[11] led a key mandate for Wesfarmers. John Bennison-led Wesfarmers, then with A$20 million in market capitalisation, would become one of the grandest names in corporate Australia, and Hill Samuel and Macquarie would work with them all the way up. But this is where it started: with an advisory role on a transformative A$60 million bid for fertiliser group CSBP[12] & Farmers. At stake was control of the manufacture of superphosphate in the state of Western Australia, and the bid, announced on 25 October 1977, would lead to an epic two-year tussle, the largest Australian takeover of that time.

■

Johnson and Clarke had another key Hill Samuel recruit on their target list. He was a Harvard Business School graduate, just like them, and completed the course with high distinction. He was smart, if a touch awkward, and had an offer from a Wall Street firm up his sleeve.

His name was Allan Moss.

By this stage, Clarke had developed a tradition of combining an annual skiing holiday in the USA with a recruitment effort. It was not an unpleasant pilgrimage, combining as it did the brightest available minds and the Colorado slopes, and on his 1977 trip, flanked by Berg, he used it to persuade Moss.

Moss was not easily convinced. He was weighing his options but was not sure about returning to Australia.

He agreed to join in 1977, but not before flying to meet the team in Australia to assess whether to sign on the dotted line. As a short-term insurance policy, he left some of his belongings in the USA. Suffice to say, it wasn't long before a friend shipped them out to Sydney.

'I was impressed when I got to Sydney,' Moss recalls. 'I just felt the fit was right, I felt that people were impressive.'

It was one of the most important hires the firm would ever make. Moss joined an enterprise that now had 50 employees, and he was set up with an adjoining desk in Corporate Services to Richard Sheppard, who had joined two years earlier.

Another key name had to be coaxed, not from Harvard but from Meares Michell Elders, a stockbroker, wool processor and exporter among other things. There, Philip Gardiner had been developing a system to effectively match two companies around their exposures to a foreign currency, which was a useful idea given the rigidity of the Australian currency market of the time. This would allow exporters, importers, borrowers of foreign currency and Australian investors based elsewhere to manage their currency risk.

One of Gardiner's earliest transactions was brokered via a US dollar payment being made by Consolidated Press for programming that the media group was importing to Australia for its television station. On the other side of the transaction was high-profile entrepreneur Alan Bond and an iron ore mining venture he owned called Robe River. Depending on which way the US dollar moved, one of the parties would have to pay the other, and there were multiple contracts built into the transaction, which stretched out about eighteen months.

As it turned out, Robe River owed funds to Consolidated Press, as well as Meares taking their cut. Getting that payment and cut was not straightforward: the payment was dragged out over several weeks and Bond's lieutenant, Peter Lucas, was called in for lunch to discuss the matter with the Meares board. The money eventually came through.

Once Gardiner had his business up and running, it started to capture the attention of others in the market, leading to more than a handful of offers from rival firms. One of them came from Hill Samuel Australia. Clarke asked Gardiner to a meeting in Sydney, followed, as things tended to be when deal-making in the 1970s, with two further lunches.

Clarke wanted to get involved in the hedge business and bolt it into the burgeoning firm, and his timing was good. Gardiner had become concerned about plans at Meares to include proprietary transactions in the hedge business, whereby the firm itself would be on one side of the deal rather than just brokering it. Gardiner was against this idea: it raised issues of conflict of interest, and he preferred to broker transactions between two other parties at arm's length.

This led Gardiner to agree to join Hill Samuel Australia in 1978, negotiating to bring his Meares point person Louise Burney with him.

'They were entrepreneurial and saw niches in the market. They probably didn't fully understand what really was then called the hedge market, or the grey market, but they had that ability to recognise Phil was pretty smart,' Burney says.

She was one of the first women hired by the merchant bank's Australian operations. By the 1980 annual report she was one of six senior females employed by the firm, out of some 65 key staff.

Clarke met with Burney ahead of her start date but he didn't make her sit the notorious psychometric test, something she shares with Allan Moss and very few others who were hired into Hill Samuel Australia or Macquarie.

It is a sign of progress in an offshoot when head office becomes so impressed that it starts stealing the top staff and bringing them back to the mother ship. So perhaps it should be seen as a compliment that Hill Samuel took Mark Johnson to London in 1977 to lead the merchant bank's international division.[13]

The move meant a shifting of the deck chairs. David Clarke became sole CEO of Hill Samuel Australia, with Tony Berg promoted to be his deputy. By this stage, Stan Owens had relinquished his executive responsibilities, although he remained chairman, becoming steadily more belligerent in the annual reports as he complained about the various governments and policies for the remainder of the 1970s.

They were growing, and changing. An office was opened in Brisbane, Queensland, in 1978, a year in which the team advised on 22 publicly announced takeover bids worth more than A\$300 million between them. After-tax profit rose year after year,[14] yet there was evidence of great prudence too, with provisions for uncertain events rising to A\$406,000 in the 1978 financial year.

Despite Owens's editorialising, one can see a growing confidence in the annual reports themselves. Increasingly, an identity was being expressed. In 1977, cartoons appeared for the first time, including one that provides a useful window into the way both Hill Samuel Australia and the nation itself engaged with the world back then.

It showed bundles of many different foreign currencies falling into a funnel before going through a strange mechanical contraption and producing a load of vibrant little Australias onto a conveyor belt at the other end.

By the following year, the report had become positively arty, and would become progressively more so for the next fifteen years.[15]

The team had come a long way since the start of the decade. As the 1978 report noted, the staff headcount had gone from six to 95 in eight years.[16]

That said, London still exerted a degree of influence. Trading limits were set by Hill Samuel in London, with communications between parent and the offshoot typically conducted by phone or telex. A telex operator would arrive at the Hill Samuel Australia office in the evening and type up sheets of questions and information, often seeking approval regarding financial exposures. Responses would arrive back from London via the telex by the morning.

International phone calls were closely monitored and scrutinised, given the expense.

'Even interstate phone calls had to be made through the Hill Samuel operator, so that the expense could be tracked, which was quite irritating really, but that's the way it worked for quite a while,' Moss recalls.

By now, though, Hill Samuel Australia didn't need the strictest of guidance on trading limits and risk management, for it had developed an increasingly refined and sophisticated set of policies that would stand it in good stead until the present day. If a dealer exceeded limits, it was reported to the board and was considered a serious matter that could lead to the person's employment being terminated.

Clarke was methodical about process. He ensured there were written memos to document decisions and ideas. Tony Berg, his deputy, was equally focused on having an iron-clad risk assessment process, and taking a measured approach to lending. Moss, further down the ranks, would go on to make his name in risk management.

To get a loan approved through Berg, a banker really had to conduct rigorous analysis and plead a case.

'To get a loan approved through Tony, you really had to run the gauntlet. We had a long list of people during the seventies and early eighties that we absolutely refused to deal with,' Sheppard says.

There are some who, to this day, think Berg was too cautious. But there are others who think his fastidiousness around risk would later save the bank. That was still to come.

■

As the end of the decade approached, Hill Samuel Australia was profitable, growing and confident. After pushing into trading gold and foreign exchange, by 1979 it had expanded to a team of ten dealers in its money market division and was a floor member of the Sydney Futures Exchange.

It was trading actively in government bonds, bills of exchange, promissory notes and negotiable certificates of deposit. In a characteristic that the enterprise would show time and again in its future, it had developed the skill of spotting a niche early and then getting into it effectively and efficiently. An example was the development of a function to offer short-term unsecured funds to approved corporate borrowers, from an overnight to a 180-day basis.

By 1979, profits had crossed the million dollar mark and the deposit book in the money market division stood at more than A$89 million. They had built another skill that would become a Macquarie buzzword—that of spotting an adjacency, something close to an existing business that could be easily exploited in order to spur growth—and they had learned how to fight for business when in many ways they appeared out-gunned.

The Commonwealth Bank slogan of the day was 'Get With The Strength.' It featured elephants to illustrate the big bank's heft. But it was a running joke among the Hill Samuel Australia crew that they were fast natives able to get out of an elephant's way. Being nimble would prove to be one of the greatest assets in Hill Samuel Australia's, and then Macquarie's, future.

There were changes, in the firm and in Australia. Castleman, whose hiring decisions had set the whole thing in motion, was elevated to the top job of Hill Samuel's global operations in 1980, aged 38. And Johnson had parted ways with the institution, for the moment at least.

And, as the decade came to an end, deregulatory forces were gathering momentum. The Australian Financial System Inquiry was conducted in 1979, delving into the levels and methods of government intervention in the Australian financial system, a process that would lead to the landmark Campbell Report in 1981.

The 1980s were approaching, and they would be a time of enormous disruption and opportunity. Few in Australia would prove themselves as equipped to deal with this change as that team, two of whom had made the decision of their lives aboard a sailboat on Sydney Harbour a decade earlier.

Chapter 2

CHANGING WINDS AND THE OPPORTUNITY OF A LIFETIME

The monopoly in banking given to Australia's handful of private and public banks has produced the most conservative banking community in the world. Entrepreneurial banking is foreign to these institutions. They will play no ambitious or adventuresome role in the development of this young nation's massive mineral endowment . . .

One wonders what the answer to this problem is. Perhaps it is the opening up of the banking licences in Australia to world banking competition so that some of the smug executives in Australian banks will have to get out and compete instead of having their business given to them on a plate by the provisions of the Banking Act.[1]

The man speaking earnestly to Australia's federal parliament in Canberra was a fiery 33-year-old with a sharply parted haircut and a hell of a lot to say. It was 1977 and Paul Keating was in opposition, with a shadow cabinet portfolio for minerals, resources and energy.

It would be years before he would be in government and able to act on his convictions about the state of the nation's financiers. But he would.

Keating was right. Australian banking was flaccid and there was no motivation for it to be otherwise. Hill Samuel & Co was proving that one could do very good business out of the mundane corporate finance opportunities of the day, and to an extent it benefited from regulation that kept the big trading banks, like Commonwealth Bank and ANZ, out of the business of non-banks like them. 'For Hill Samuel, regulation resembles the apple in the Garden of Eden,' David Clarke once said.[2] 'We were enticed by it, and thoroughly enjoyed it while it lasted.' But even in the 1970s the firm's bright young team were thirsting for new horizons.

'The environment was much, much more regulated than it is today,' recalls Allan Moss. 'The Australian dollar hadn't floated. Stockbrokers couldn't be owned by companies. There was strict bank regulation. Almost all business was very domestic: it was a state-by-state business environment for most companies. And apart from the commercial banks, the whole financial services industry was tiny, by today's standards. Really, really tiny.'

Keating was far from the only one to notice the problem. The Malcolm Fraser government[3] and its treasurer John Howard—like Keating, a future Prime Minister of Australia—appointed a committee to review the domestic financial system in January 1979,[4] chaired by Keith Campbell, chairman of Hooker Corporation. It had a mandate to study the efficiency, competitiveness and stability of the financial system and to suggest what to do to improve it all.

It took until September 1981 for this 835-page study[5] to thud onto Howard's desk. Mercifully, given its length, you didn't have to get too far into it to get the gist. 'The most efficient way to organise economic activity is through a competitive market system which is subject to a minimum of regulation and government intervention,' it said in its very first paragraph. That meant removing controls and allowing a handful of foreign banks to compete.[6]

In practice, the Fraser government would implement little of the Campbell Report: Howard did set about inviting tenders for new foreign licences in January 1983 and Hill Samuel Australia set about applying. But that government wouldn't last long enough to see it through.

The idea was still reasonably fresh in the memory when Bob Hawke won the 1983 election and installed Keating, now a rising star with a growing reputation for articulate and sometimes vicious flair in parliamentary debates, as treasurer. As Troy Bramston's definitive biography of Keating[7] reveals, within days of the election Keating was meeting with Reserve Bank chair Bob Johnston with two things on his mind: the floating of the Australian dollar and deregulation of the financial sector. He said he wanted to revisit the Campbell inquiry and asked that a working party be formed to do so.

This review group, chaired by a businessman called Vic Martin,[8] came to similar conclusions to the Campbell Report. 'Campbell was the roadmap to the financial markets,' Keating said. 'The Martin report gave me a storyline to take to the caucus.'[9]

Convincing that caucus was not straightforward: this was a Labor government, and Labor policy had not normally been about strengthening the hand of big business or banks. But, as always, Keating had a turn of phrase to shift the doubtful. 'If we are going to get blood to the muscle of the economy, it's got to come through the major institutions, and if the major institutions can't attract the deposits, can't manage the bigger proportions of credit in the economy, we are not going to achieve our objectives,'[10] he said.

He got his way. The floating of the Australian dollar and the abolition of most exchange controls, a team effort involving both Hawke and Keating, came first, on Monday 12 December 1983.[11] Then Vic Martin's report was released on 22 February 1984, supporting most of the Campbell recommendations.

Some of the changes, such as the abolition of fixed-rate commissions in stockbroking and a new facility for brokers to become corporate entities, were introduced that April. But letting foreigners in was a bigger deal, and Keating spent a brief spell stating his case to media in his usual brazen style.

'All the regulations we've had for years . . . in the banking area have produced nothing except a great clutch of merchant banks and building societies,' was one typical remark of the time. By June he was doing the same with the NSW Labor Conference in Sydney Town Hall. 'It's time the privileged, comfortable and dozy position of our banks is livened up by some real competition,' he said.[12]

In a cabinet submission in August 1984[13] he proposed inviting domestic and foreign interests to apply for a limited number of banking licences, the rationale being that foreign banks would bring greater competition to existing stalwarts and the benefits would flow to the community and boost employment. On 10 September, Cabinet agreed and Keating announced it the same day. Australian banking was about to change forever.

■

While all of this was happening, Hill Samuel Australia had been quietly going from strength to strength. Its annual reports, whose increasingly brazen motifs and messages seemed to be a statement of growing confidence in their own right, had begun to show charts, and no matter what the underlying metric—after-tax profits, return on shareholders' funds, asset base—the direction was relentlessly upwards.[14] 'We're always pushing hard to stay in front,' was the headline on the 1981 report, filled with pictures of (white, male) athletes. (The first picture of a woman in an annual report came in 1983—not an executive but someone milking a cow, supporting some analogy between banking innovation and the vaccine for smallpox.)

The headcount was growing, too. At the 1980 year-end,[15] after more than ten years of operations, the staff had grown from a handful to 142, requiring a move to a new office at 20 Bond Street in Sydney.[16] By 1987 the number would hit 675.

That meant some adjustments. 'The culture had to change somewhat over time because you wanted to keep the best parts of the culture: short lines of communication, bright people, highly competitive,' remembers Richard Sheppard. 'But as it got bigger, you had to overlay that with systems and structure which wasn't required in those early days.'

But one of the skills of the team was that they managed to keep their edge while growing, all without any significant stumbles. By 1980, their track record included mandates for Telecom Australia, STC, Monier, Blue Circle Southern Cement, Bundaberg Sugar and Wesfarmers, among others.[17] In the 1981 financial year, the banking division acted for twenty of the top 100 listed companies in Australia. Around this time, shopping centre group Westfield and its co-founder Frank Lowy were turning to Hill Samuel for advice[18] too.

But it wasn't just Australia-based companies. A growing relation-ship with Heinz explains the otherwise incongruous appearance of a full-page photograph of a bottle of tomato ketchup in the 1980 annual report. Hill Samuel Australia had arranged and managed a syndicated credit facility, short-term financing, a fixed-rate term loan and advised on various acquisitions, often making submissions to the central bank and the Foreign Investment Review Board.

Every year brought new niches, divisions, products. In 1981, for example, they introduced specialised property leases, long-dated promissory notes, and the management of underwritten facilities for those notes. In an unusual step for the time, they launched an investor relations service within the corporate securities division, to better communicate with the people they were selling to. And the international division, which had started out doing nothing more than sorting out foreign currency loans, was by now a sophisticated risk management shop.[19]

An economics department was established, and the firm's monthly Banking and Capital Markets Report started to gain circulation. The project finance team had found another niche, one with major ramifications for the firm's future, raising over A$1.3 billion by 1982 for everything from cement plants to paper manufacturing mills, coal loading facilities, communication satellites and shipping.

The first subordinated convertible notes; a new relationship with Goldman Sachs to help bring Australian borrowers to the New York commercial paper market; a new leveraged lease packing business:[20] everything the firm touched seemed new and often lucrative.

Two ventures in particular stood out.

One was gold bullion. The firm had started out with the launch of a bullion department back in 1979 and by the early 1980s was offering two-way quotes for gold and silver. During the 1982 financial year it began making a market for bullion as a principal, and eventually the firm would become the largest single buyer of Australia's gold output. Its presence in this market saw it build relationships with every major producer, refiner and industrial user in the country—and beyond, with dealing networks in Hong Kong, London and New York.

The architect of Hill Samuel Australia's bullion and commodities operations was Clive Carroll,[21] who was recruited into the firm by Phil Gardiner in 1978. After a stint helping to manage the futures business, Carroll had the idea of pushing into gold futures. He discussed it with Gardiner and then made a strong case to Clarke, and was granted a small limit to give it a try.

When he did, it was clear there was considerable money to be made. 'The price of gold on the Sydney Futures Exchange was very much different to the international price. So, we started arbitraging,' Carroll says. 'We were really one of the first to start to do that.

'Then when the gold price buckled within a couple of days, we'd made millions of dollars. So that basically catapulted us into respectability within the financial marketplace. We were marketing arbitrage to clients as well because it was a very high yield: it was more than double what you could get elsewhere in the financial markets.'

In a manner that would later become characteristic of Macquarie, it took a subject and hit every possible angle of it: buying, selling, supplying, delivering, storing, hedging, offering derivatives, servicing every end of the chain. It served the miner, the investor, everyone in between and then made another buck out of the volatility in the price.

In another distinctive step that would be demonstrated time and again over the next 40 years, Macquarie developed a habit of running towards a market when everyone else was heading the other way.

Hill Samuel Australia had been a pioneer of cash-and-carry transactions, where physical gold was bought and simultaneously sold forward at a premium exceeding the carrying costs. Others saw the market and moved in. When market conditions changed in 1980, most of them left again; Carroll and the team promptly moved into physical bullion dealing and hired specialists to fill gaps the exit of their peers had left. The firm was Australia's leading bullion dealer by 1983,[22] which was also the year of deregulation of foreign exchange: the skills they had learned around bullion were priceless and gave the firm a springboard to build a lucrative commodities business which, at the time of writing, 40 years on, is the bank's most powerful engine.

Having achieved a leadership position, the firm was forever trying to find ways to stay ahead of the competition. Later in 1983, they realised that their gold producer clients were struggling with a significant unknown: the price they would obtain for their gold once they'd got it out of the ground. So, Hill Samuel Australia agreed to buy the production of several gold producers for up to twelve months at a guaranteed minimum price, meaning that the producers still got the benefit of any increase in gold prices but were protected from falls by a floor. Hill Samuel took a cut in exchange for the protection and the certainty.

'We were buying physical gold from the refineries and from the producers, and we were also doing forward sales with them,' Carroll says. 'Then we were doing other gold-backed financing businesses as well, such as forward sales and gold loans.'

He recalls in the early years of the business buying the first bar of gold produced by the Ok Tedi mine, which mining group BHP co-owned with the Papua New Guinean government.

'We lost money on the deal; it was a show pony deal,' Carroll says. He also recalls a young fellow named Jodee Rich working the overnight shift on the bullion desk. Rich would later start telecommunications group One.Tel, which spectacularly collapsed in 2001.

Bullion aside, one of the most successful products in the bank's history appeared in December 1980 when the Hill Samuel Cash Management Trust (CMT) was launched.

This idea came from an entrepreneurial financer and corporate adviser by the name of Keith Halkerston,[23] who also served on the Campbell Committee. Like everything else the firm did, it filled a gap they (or at least Halkerston, who sold the idea to them and took a success payment) had been clever enough to spot: the absence of a money market fund that offered security, liquidity and yield to small investors. Investors needed A$5,000 to buy in, and increments of A$1,000 thereafter.

Clarke formed a panel to discuss the idea, which included Corporate Services director Robin Crawford and head of the Money

Market unit, Tim Rossi. The panel was also closely monitoring developments offshore where Merrill Lynch, Pierce, Fenner & Smith had in 1977[24] launched a cash management account that blended traditional banking services with stockbroking accounts. It was growing at a rapid clip, and other firms in the US market were jumping on the bandwagon.

Rossi—who by this stage had been nicknamed 'Rocket' Rossi for his trading prowess—was headed to the USA on a skiing trip and decided he would drop in at Merrill to ask a few detailed questions. Not long after, they decided to start preparing for a launch and brought in David Adams,[25] who would play a big role in marketing, branding, administration and getting the Hill Samuel Cash Management Trust up and running.

So what had they seen ahead of starting Australia's first CMT?

'There was a big gap between the wholesale rates and retail rates. As had been the case for America,' Clarke said in 2011. 'We said, "Well, if it works in America it will work in Australia."'

Moss explains the underlying dynamics: 'The idea was that there was a very big arbitrage in the deposit market between bank bills and retail deposit bonds. It was huge. And the idea of the CMT was to arbitrage that.' The trust would buy bank bills, which were paying a high yield in those days, and could consequently offer a much higher rate of interest to 'mum and dad' investors than they could ever get in a bank deposit. It could do so through a pooling mechanism— the secret sauce to the whole idea—that brought together enough money from small investors to give them access to securities they could never normally purchase, and liquidity to get the money back out again when they needed it.

'Okay, we weren't a bank then,' says Moss. 'But effectively, we were offering bank security, because we were only investing in bank bills or Treasury notes. And it just took off hugely.'

As the team ironed out the structure, conditions became less favourable. Rossi remembers that Clarke was very strategic about when the CMT would launch.

'David very cleverly would say we should only do it when rates are starting to rise, and we've got a really good story to tell,' he says. Rossi and his teams watched leading indicators to assess the potential for rises in the cash rate, and Hill Samuel soon after pushed the button on the CMT.

The trust was up and running, hitting A$140 million[26] in its first five months of operations and A$800 million by early 1983, by which time it had become a source of considerable pride. 'Without doubt, the most public known example of Hill Samuel's particular brand of fresh thinking is our Cash Management Trust,' wrote Owens.[27]

The same section of the annual report notes with similar pride the great innovation of 'a telephone redemptions and a security code system' and 'our word-processing facilities [of] almost 1 megabyte of CPU memory', but however antiquated that seems today, it was working. In 1983 the CMT held 35 per cent of the entire market for such funds and it would hold that edge longer than anyone could have expected: in twenty years' time it would top A$10 billion under management.[28]

Success brought some challenges. 'It was just frantic, because we had not anticipated the rate of growth,' Moss says. 'This is when computers were in their infancy. So we just took over another floor in the building and threw bodies at it. Honestly, people were working literally night and day, sleeping under their desk.'

That's if they could find room to do so amid the piles of paper as the infant computers struggled to gain traction.

'You could walk in that room and you could just smell the perspiration,' Moss says. 'But they got it done. And gradually they got automated and they got out of the piles of paper.'

The rapid growth in income stemming from the CMT also caused some friction in the months after its inception, as the revenue splitting and transfer pricing—where units charge each other for services—had to be figured out.

Competition between the units was often fierce as each lobbied and argued for their slice of the earnings. Adams and Rossi pled their respective cases. The tussles were sometimes jovial but otherwise long and protracted, and Clarke would start to lose his patience. When he started to flap his tie about, most bankers knew it was a sign the arguments needed to stop, and Clarke would go away and rule on the matter.

Both bullion and the Cash Management Trust reflected an emerging philosophy at Hill Samuel Australia that would continue to be reflected throughout Macquarie's history: be open to numerous ideas without ever betting the farm on any of them.

'Basically, we had this mantra if there was an idea, you could employ one or a few people on that idea, and it didn't require much investment to pursue,' says Tony Berg.

'If the new idea worked within six months, then you had a new business that could grow very large like the bullion business. If it didn't work you could close it down with very little cost.

'The way I put it, it was an option. If it worked, you had endless upside. If it didn't, you would write it off to experience. The risks and rewards were asymmetrical.'

Johnson, present in the same interview, adds: 'That became the whole ethos of the bank. If people had a good idea, they had the mechanism to start to explore the possibilities.'

As the firm grew bigger this would perplex new outside directors, who assumed that capital allocation was decided from the top and would wonder what the process was. 'And, in fact, there wasn't really very much of a capital allocation process, because it was going on by stealth, out of the operating budgets down at the lower level,' Johnson says. Leadership at Hill Samuel Australia, and later Macquarie, would never really be about the top telling people lower down what to do. It would be about listening to the people in the trenches and giving them the tools to make their ideas work.

■

It's no surprise that a team as astute and ambitious as this was watching the shifting sands of national policy and eyeing the main chance. Clarke would later say that the process of planning for a deregulated environment 'was certainly well advanced by late 1980, well before the period of real change in the competitive environment.'

As soon as the Campbell Report was released, efforts redoubled,[29] and in the 1982 annual report Owens made it clear the team wanted in to this brave new world.

> We believe that our record of success in Australia as a competitive and responsible institution, together with the professionalism and experience of our staff of over 250, makes Hill Samuel a leading candidate for a banking licence.[30]

Owens had set in motion an ambition that would transform the firm. Sadly, however, he would not be around to see it.

Owens had secured a coveted board seat at the Bank of New South Wales,[31] which became Westpac in 1982 when it merged with the Commercial Bank of Australia. As Hill Samuel Australia was pursuing the path to become an authorised deposit-taking bank, Owens couldn't sit on both boards and had decided to step down from that of the merchant bank.

His foreword to the 1983 annual report—a pretty stylish one, with a cover showing an inverted globe with Australia at the top, with classic Escher artwork scattered throughout—is dated June 1983. It is poignant, for it includes this line: 'After thirteen years as Chairman of Hill Samuel Australia, I will be stepping down from this position later this year.'

It must have been among the last things he ever wrote. He did not live long enough to enjoy a long stint on the prestigious Bank of NSW board, for he died unexpectedly on 3 June 1983, aged 66.

■

Following the loss of Owens, David Clarke became executive chairman[32] and Tony Berg became managing director, or in today's equivalent the CEO. In practice they worked together, and they had differing approaches. Clarke was a smooth and process-driven business administrator and a lateral thinker who could see the adjacent in everything, but could be indecisive on big issues. Berg was a sharp, conservative brain who took Clarke's risk management discipline and elevated it to something of an art form. But the two fitted together most effectively.

'Tony and David sat in the same office,' recalls Graeme Samuel,[33] who joined in 1980–81. 'They were partners. They played off against each other very well. David was a flamboyant ideas man, out there in the social world, a networker. And Tony was that careful manager, very, very tough on risk. And they had the right roles.'

Others recall Clarke would often join the after work 'cool-down sessions', which at times included fierce table tennis competitions, and a steady flow of drinks.

Samuel remembers an instructive moment that stays with him more than 40 years on. Having formed the opinion that Berg was stifling the firm's lending and that it was becoming a problem, 'I went in one day, and I said: "Look Tony, why wouldn't we co-underwrite this? After all, Potter Partners[34] are underwriting."'

'And I'll never forget this, because he really ripped into me. He said: "Don't ever let me hear you say something like that again. Whatever they do is their business. We'll assess our own risks." And he was absolutely right.'

To this day, it's a Macquarie hallmark not to be looking to competitors for guidance but to assess risk and reward on its own merits, every time.

In truth, Owens had been a non-executive figurehead for years; Clarke and Berg, plus a growing bench of ability beneath them, were running the show, and both were across the idea of seeking a licence if the opportunity arose.

When Keating began talking about new banking licences in 1983, he first spoke of issuing six. This provoked mixed opinions among the Hill Samuel Australia team: it was exhilarating that new market opportunities might arise, but there was no way on earth they could see a path to being one of six foreign banks to win a licence.[35]

'When Keating announced he had in mind six new banking licences, that was scary for us, because we could count on it that we wouldn't be one of the six,' says Berg. Bank of America was probably a shoo-in, plus maybe Citibank and Bankers Trust, they reasoned; probably one of the Japanese, like Mitsubishi Bank, probably a European, certainly UBS, maybe NatWest or Lloyds. 'Very quickly you could get to six names without us being there. We were a minnow. And we thought: my God, if these guys get banking licences, we're going to get killed.'

Berg was on the board of the Australian Merchant Bankers Association—its very title tells you something about how Australia had become mired in a bygone age of banking. Through that association, he was able to have a meeting in Canberra with John Stone, who had served as Secretary of the Treasury. While Stone and Keating had a changeable and increasingly antagonistic relationship, particularly over the float of the Australian dollar, the two men were closely involved in banking reform.

'I took him aside at that meeting and said: "You know, John, this is potentially very difficult for us,"' Berg recalls. '"We don't know how we are going to exist under this new system. Can't we get a licence too?"'

Not as a foreign house, they couldn't: Hill Samuel & Co, the London-based parent, was massively out-gunned compared to some of the other obvious contenders. But there was another way.

Stone, a serious intellect and nobody's fool, gave Berg a clue. 'He said: "Well, you're smart merchant bankers. It shouldn't be beyond your wit to work out a structure that will work,"' Berg recalls. 'And he basically said: "The treasurer has announced there are going to be six foreign bank licences, and if you want a licence, you're going to have to get one without being a foreign bank."'

What Stone was alluding to was the idea of a new domestic bank licence, and for a precedent, they could look to a familiar name. Mark Johnson had not lasted particularly long in his London posting to parent Hill Samuel & Co, and had left to set up Australian Bank, which when it launched in 1981 was the first new domestic bank to obtain a licence in Australia for more than 60 years. It didn't exactly flourish, being too small, but it did show a new domestic licence could be achieved.

'We'd seen Mark do it,' Allan Moss recalls. And if it could be done, the team wanted to do it.

But why was it so important?

For years the team had been trying to work out whether merchant banking was the place to be in the mid- to late eighties, and whether they might be better off as a trading bank if the opportunity arose. Clarke would later describe the decision to seek trading bank status as 'based on both defensive and offensive reasons'.

On the defensive side, deregulation would mean competing directly with the banks. So if banks were allowed to pay interest on cheque accounts for the first time, that would have impact for the Cash Management Trust, for example. 'In lending and deposit-taking our view was that we should either compete effectively with the advantages offered by a licence, or be out of those activities altogether in an exclusively investment banking role,' Clarke said. This remains a characteristic of the bank today: be among the leaders or find a specific angle in a particular niche, or don't bother.

On the offensive side, they had realised that being a trading bank would mean they could use the CMT—truly a golden goose for the firm by now—and draw cheques against it. They could offer a full range of services to clients and could be as good in lending as they were in corporate advice. It would also help with another problem.

'We wanted a licence because it was so prestigious, and also because it would help our dealing room,' Moss recalls. 'The big problem in the dealing room was not actually shortage of capital. It was inward limits, which were, as the expression suggests, limits that other people would mark on us.' Here, they ran into the problem that their parent, Hill Samuel & Co, was middle-ranking in London and 'internationally nowhere,' Moss says. 'So we couldn't get the limits we needed. We felt that the prestige of being a licensed bank and being regulated by the Reserve Bank of Australia would assist us a lot with inwards limits, and it did.'

Being experienced innovators by now, they got around it for a while.[36] But it was a problem that needed a licence to solve.

That wasn't the only issue. 'David and I genuinely believed that we wouldn't be able to keep the team together unless we went down this road,' says Berg. 'Our employees would see better opportunities elsewhere, and everything we were building up would just implode.'

One option was to acquire another bank that already had a licence, and the team was sufficiently emboldened to make an attempt to buy Bank of Queensland around this time. David Clarke, in an interview recorded weeks before his death, recalled it as 'a pretty amateurish attempt'; Tony Berg today says he only vaguely recalls it, 'as a way of getting our hands on a licence, a reverse takeover. But Bank of Queensland in those days was very small, and they weren't interested. I suspect there were a hundred of those sorts of things we looked at.' A whole new licence was the better way to go.

The stakes were high, and everyone could see it. Moss was by now an executive director in corporate finance, one of the most senior positions. 'By 1983, David and Tony had been thinking about the banking opportunity for a year or two and it was clear that we had to get serious if we were going to do it,' he says. 'So I volunteered to head up the project to write the submission for the licence.'

Berg and Clarke assembled three internal workstreams. Moss led one alongside the Corporate Services division's Bruce Watson and Harvard graduate Lisa Warshaw to craft the submission, while academic and economist John Hewson[37] consulted on the project. When it came to the execution phase, operations banker Julian Beaumont was responsible for converting functions to fit the new bank and technology manager Gail Pemberton (then Gail Burke) played a key role in sorting out the technology.

'I got total freedom, and very little guidance,' Pemberton recalls. 'But because I was a structured person, coming from the background that I came from, I just went about finding, working out what technology was required, putting a team together, recruiting and building the platforms.'

There was one considerable problem in the plan to get an Australian licence: Hill Samuel Australia wasn't Australian. It was based in Australia, its staff were Australian, its ideology and its prospects were Australian, but it was owned and subject to control by London.

'We weren't really Australian,' says Moss. 'We just weren't. So we had to persuade Hill Samuel & Co to sell down.'

■

Moss's working group would toil away full time for eight months on the bank licence application, while a much larger working party was involved at various times throughout.[38]

The team divided its tasks. Clarke took charge of negotiations to persuade the parent to sell, and Berg and Moss set about striking a deal with Keating and Stone, as well as other key players such as Lyle Procter at the Reserve Bank of Australia.

To qualify for a local licence, the bank could be no more than 10 per cent foreign-owned, which Hill Samuel & Co was never going to agree to. So instead the team came up with the idea of the London parent keeping a 30 per cent stake, but with voting shares below 10 per cent, and hoped they could sell that idea to the politicians. Berg remembers going to John Stone with this structure and that 'basically, in a nice bureaucratic way, he gave us encouragement.'

So how to talk the Londoners into it? It wasn't an easy sell. 'We were the star in their firmament,' says Berg. 'You can see why they wouldn't want to lose it.' Worse, the UK was facing the Big Bang financial reform[39] that would ultimately obliterate every British merchant bank bar Rothschild & Co. Australia was really one of the parent company's only promising paths to growth.

Clarke is no longer here to recall his pitch, but those who were around him remember it clearly. Firstly, and being somewhat cruel to be kind, it needed to be pointed out to Hill Samuel & Co that it was no great shakes on the world stage. It had Australia, South Africa, a presence in South Korea and a modest New York outpost, but that was about it; in truth, the Australian operation was the only successful one of the lot. 'So, it wasn't like partially divesting their Australian presence was an aberration in an otherwise successful international network,' Moss says. 'They didn't have a network.'

With that established, the pitch was that the Australian operations—and Hill Samuel & Co's stake in it—would lose momentum if nothing was done. In Sydney, the team could also sense they had outgrown the London-based parent and it was time for more independence. 'David said to them: look, we need this licence, and really it's better for you to have 30 per cent of something really good than 100 per cent of something that's going to struggle,' says Moss.

Berg adds: 'If you don't do this, you may end up with nothing, because we are just not going to be competitive. That was the approach. And they were not easy meetings that we had in London. There was still a sense of colonialism in London: these gung-ho Aussies trying to steal their business.'[40]

But it worked.[41]

And so to Canberra. Berg and Moss recall the negotiations differently. Berg doesn't recall having any significant dealings with Keating, instead working almost entirely with John Stone and the Reserve Bank; Moss remembers one key meeting with Keating and found it very positive. 'I have to say he was great,' Moss says. 'He was supportive because he was keen to encourage competition and innovation in Australian banking, he was enthusiastic, he was frank, he was very down to business.' The key meeting took half an hour in Parliament House.

Moss remembers the most difficult meetings—and many of them— as being with George Pooley[42] at the Foreign Investment Review Board. 'George had the problem that we clearly weren't within the rules,' says Moss. 'No-one was meant to own more than 10 per cent of a domestic bank. Thirty per cent was just hugely outside the number.' In the end it was probably Stone on the Treasury side who got the deal over the line.[43]

The next challenge was to raise A\$43.7 million of capital from Australian institutional shareholders to buy the parent out.[44] Richard Sheppard, by now in the Melbourne office, remembers 'trawling the streets of Melbourne with Robin Crawford,[45] trying to sell Macquarie Bank shares at A\$1.83[46] per share.' Macquarie's earliest major shareholders included NRMA Investments, Prudential Assurance, the Queensland Electricity Supply Industry Superannuation Board and the Melbourne and Metropolitan Board of Works Superannuation Scheme.[47]

'That was actually quite difficult,' says Berg, with a smile; at the time of writing, Macquarie's market capitalisation is about A\$70 billion, its shareholder equity A\$31.3 billion. 'It was a lot of money in those days.'

Also, the Australian executive directors committed to purchase 9.9 per cent of the voting capital, and were given the chance to participate in a partly paid share scheme. 'Management participation has been, and is expected in future to be, a critical element in retaining and attracting committed top executives,' potential institutional buyers were told.[48] Skin in the game, partial ownership of the bank and the sometimes preposterous riches that could come from these arrangements are still hallmarks, and often controversial hallmarks, of Macquarie today.

■

The 1984 annual report was the last as Hill Samuel Australia and the first with a chairman's review not by Stan Owens but David Clarke. And on the very same page that it marked the passing of Owens, the firm introduced a new brand to the world: Macquarie Bank Limited.[49]

At the time Clarke's foreword was written, it was not yet clear if they would be successful: they had instead received an indication from Keating that the application looked good, albeit in rather more ponderous terms.[50] But Clarke and his team were already planning ahead.

'We intend that the characteristics which have marked the development of Hill Samuel Australia—our commitment to innovation, competition, hard work, professionalism and successful achievement for clients—will also characterise the new bank.'

But that name, Macquarie: what was that about?

Hill Samuel had made it clear during discussions that the new bank could not use their name, which suited the team just fine. Throughout early discussions, they called themselves Newbank, but they were going to need to do better than that. So they set about thinking what they wanted to evoke in their name.

After an internal staff competition yielded inadequate and sometimes silly suggestions, it was time to get serious. Watson was given the task of finding the prospective bank a suitable name, and it would begin with a pile of research and grunt work. He liaised with Berg.

'Our whole mantra was that we were innovative, exploring,' says Berg. 'My idea was we would name ourselves after one of the great Australian explorers.'

Watson made a trip to the Stanton Library in North Sydney and borrowed a host of books on the founding fathers of many of Australia's cities, towns and coastline. This was due diligence of a different kind for Watson, who had to cull many of the names of frontier-spirited legends from the list.

'Matthew Flinders was running a close second but obviously some names got cut out by me straightaway,' Watson recalls.

Flinders—who is credited with being the first to circumnavigate and chart Australia's coastline[51]—was eventually ruled out given he'd been imprisoned for almost seven years in Mauritius by the French

governor. He'd stopped for repairs to his vessel there as the Napo-
leonic Wars were raging and had been deemed a spy.

Berg says: 'What we found was that they were either rogues, or
they came to terrible ends. Leichhardt died in the desert. So did
Burke and Wills.'[52]

Clarke told the same story for laughs, including at a speech to the
Australian Business Economists at Sydney's Menzies Hotel in June
1984.[53] 'Once we had embarked on the theme using the name of one
of our pioneering ancestors as the centrepiece for the bank's name,
it was really quite difficult to find a single person who was neither
caught with his hand in the till nor was killed in tragic or unseemly
circumstances.'

Finding no reputation with which they could be happy associating,
Watson looked elsewhere, and turned at last to Lachlan Macquarie,
one of Australia's first governors.

'Governor Macquarie, he ticked every box,' Watson recalls. 'He'd
instigated the Bank of NSW, developed the colony and died in noble
service back in Scotland, without a whiff of scandal. I remember putting
it up to Tony, and he just said: "Oh, I think you found us a name!"'

But there was a final hurdle for Watson to overcome. He'd found
a dormant company, named Macquarie Finance, and set about
tracking down the owner in Tasmania, paying the fellow a small sum
to change its name.

There were compelling reasons to take the name. Not only did
Governor Macquarie establish Australia's first bank,[54] he also introduced the country's first domestic coinage, and it had a story attached
that spoke to creativity and innovation, exactly the attributes the
team wanted to represent.

Initially, a shortage of coin in the new colony of New South Wales
had led to a barter economy, one in which the most valuable unit
of monetary exchange was rum. Nothing good tends to come from

booze as a medium of exchange, so Lachlan Macquarie imported Spanish dollars and punched a hole out of the centre of each coin. Thus, he created two units of currency: the Holey Dollar, as the outer coin became known, which was given a value of five shillings; and the dump, as the centrepiece was called, worth 15 pence.

It was ingenious. In one stroke he had created two clearly identifiable coins out of one, and, through their being unique, restricted use of the coins to the colony.

'Finally,' Macquarie Bank says by way of explanation in the 1985 annual report, 'as the combined value of the two new coins was six shillings and threepence against the original dollar's value of four shillings and ninepence, Macquarie had made a profit.'[55]

It was a solution to a challenging problem that delivered a profit from innovation. Clarke, Berg and the rest felt an affinity with Lachlan. Macquarie they would be.

∎

Finding a name made a difference. 'It was very interesting to notice how the tone of discussions changed after we had a name,' Clarke said. 'The fact that people were working for a tangible goal and thinking of themselves as Macquarie bankers helped to create a team spirit.'[56]

It wasn't as if they were working off a blank sheet of paper as the opening date of early 1985 approached. They knew what they were good at: corporate finance, funds management (through the beloved CMT), and dealing operations such as currency hedging and precious metals. Funds management, in particular, should get stronger with bank status because they would have access to the overall banking payment system in Australia.

They could also see the immediate low-hanging fruit that a licence would bring them, mainly in lending. Trading banks were already their biggest competitors, but Hill Samuel Australia had suffered from a higher cost of granting credit because their deposit base was smaller and the deposit rates higher. Bank status would give them a level playing field.

And they could see where they could go next: letters of credit, acceptances and guarantees, for example.

But what they also got from a bank licence was momentum and true independence. As 1985 approached and as they built the Holey Dollar logo into their brand identity, they were an experienced and successful team of bankers, young enough to be hungry, with their own money committed to its success. There was a sense of a great deal of deregulated and uncharted territory to fight for.

Chapter 3

DEALS, HORNS AND THE CRASH

From its inception, Hill Samuel Australia and Macquarie's leadership championed the idea of the adjacent business: an area the firm could naturally push into from an existing position in order to boost revenue. That way risk was curtailed, given some existing knowledge of the business area, but the upside for Macquarie could be great if it worked.

The theory of adjacencies and dominant market positions was in overdrive in the latter half of the eighties. Macquarie's banking licence and growth blueprint was throwing up all sorts of opportunities for the firm. Clarke and Berg were pursuing their aspirations to grow rapidly at the same time as they navigated a highly competitive environment.

In this vein, the Macquarie foreign exchange unit—led by executive director Peter Taylor, who had joined as a trainee straight out of university in the seventies—was by 1985 looking at how to capitalise on the increase in overnight customer orders.

Macquarie's foreign exchange troops were reluctant to pass the orders to a competitor, or even to blue-blooded merchant bank Hill

Samuel in London, which remained a sizeable shareholder but was culturally a very different beast.

The foreign exchange team was seeking its own solution. They thought setting up a foreign exchange office in London might work well, and Taylor soon found himself on a plane over there to conduct his own on-the-ground cost-benefit analysis. His time in London, however, pounding the pavement and speaking to treasury types at Hill Samuel, led him in the opposite direction.

Taylor soon came to the conclusion the expense of establishing and running a London bureau for Macquarie at this point in time was too prohibitive.

It would be more viable to operate the foreign exchange unit around the clock out of Sydney.[1] Macquarie then established night shifts, which marked a first for an Australian firm on currency spot pricing, forwards and options.

'We did have enough business to run it 24 hours out of Sydney, and we got more business,' Taylor recalls. 'Because if you were in the middle of the night, and you wanted to do something, it was so much easier to ring the Macquarie night desk than to have to ring London or New York.

'As a result of the 24-hour foreign exchange service, it led to an increase in business during the day as well.

'It was infinitely more profitable than being over in London and just trying to compete with all the big London banks.'[2]

This was an example of Macquarie's business adjacencies theory, as staff looked at how to move deeper into existing markets and traverse new ones that made some strategic sense.

The tax and structuring bankers were, for example, scouring local and overseas markets for financing and leasing opportunities.

That team—which then sat within corporate advisory—structured among the first major leveraged plant and equipment leases, to a joint venture for Ashton Mining Group, which was involved in the Argyle diamond mines. The mines, in the rugged and remote east Kimberley region of Western Australia, have been a key global source of rare pink carats and stones that would be highly sought after—and perhaps purchased by Macquarie bankers with their share of profits in later years.

The leasing and tax unit also worked with then domestic carrier Australian Airlines the following year on a US$300 million plane financing facility,[3] which drew in staff spanning leasing, tax advisory and corporate finance.

At the same time, however, Macquarie's lending business was coming up against the challenge of official interest rates in the order of 15 per cent.[4] In 1986, it was making 'slower progress' than expected as borrowers were dissuaded by the high interest rate climate, while competition for customers was intense.

■

Macquarie was making its presence well and truly felt in deal advisory, amid rampant and often debt-fuelled takeover activity during the rough and tumble of the eighties. It was a frenetic time for dealmakers and the available fee pool was even more lucrative as bankers scurried around seeking a piece of the action. It was a time of sharp elbows and questionable tactics in the corporate world, but also a great opportunity for a hungry team of bankers with an innovative state of mind to make their name.

By 1986, twelve months after becoming a bank in March 1985, Macquarie had handled takeover and merger transactions for more than a quarter of the top 100 Australian companies and managed and underwritten 30 share issues for customers that raised A$1.5 billion.[5]

At that large end of the market, it wasn't long after BHP's acquisition of Utah International from General Electric—one of Macquarie's most prestigious deal mandates to date—closed in 1984, that the bank was once again in the throes of a fierce fight.

This time, BHP chairman James McNeill required a hard-headed tactical adviser as the big Australian resources group came under sustained and multiple attacks from high-profile entrepreneur Robert Holmes à Court.

BHP was already a mainstay of the Australian bourse and a blue-chip stock held by institutions and mum-and-dad investors alike in the post-war period, when investment options remained extremely limited. Via mining, production and marketing, BHP operated in iron ore, bauxite, coal, silver and oil markets.[6]

John Rendle, a director in Macquarie's Sydney office, had led the advisory work for BHP on Utah, a complex assignment that included the acquisition and sales of joint venture interests and a major issue of shares. But this time, a different set of skills was required.

McNeill had a plan. He picked up the phone to Melbourne-based Macquarie director Graeme Samuel—who was known as an aggressive operator, the sharpest of legal minds and not lacking in the confidence stakes—and summoned him to a meeting.

'I went around there and saw him. And they said, we want you to act,' Samuel recalls of the meeting. 'It was just reputation.'

Samuel meant Macquarie by this stage was well known in the Australian corporate community for its advisory work on mergers and acquisitions and capital raisings. But this latest gig would prove a relentless and tough assignment.

Samuel joined Macquarie in 1980–81 after fielding a call from David Clarke and meeting him and Tony Berg not long after for a discussion at the Hilton Hotel in Melbourne.[7] Samuel, who was then at Melbourne law firm Phillips Fox & Masel,[8] running its corporate arm, and was a leading practitioner on legal work in takeovers, took some convincing to make the jump to merchant banking.

He went over the Macquarie offer with a fine-tooth comb with the help of his accountant, including a quasi-employee incentive share structure colourfully referred to as Disneyland. Samuel realised he was ready for a new challenge.

As BHP was locking in Samuel and Macquarie, Perth-based Holmes à Court was building an empire and using audacious bid tactics[9] in an attempt to wrest control of one of the nation's most lauded companies in BHP. First, Holmes à Court used small firm Wigmores before he changed tack and employed larger takeover vehicle Bell Resources.

There was also an agreement on the quiet with Adsteam's John Spalvins, involving options and share purchases.

Spalvins was among Australia's most powerful and ambitious corporate titans at the time. Adelaide Steamship Group owned a spate of well-known Australian household brands, including Four'N Twenty pies, Bodalla cheese, Pura milk, Peters ice-cream, Birds Eye frozen foods and Nanna's frozen apple pies.

In the cut and thrust of the BHP contest, Melbourne-based broking and advisory house Potter Partners found itself on the nose with the mining group. It had been concurrently advising the company and also brokering many of Holmes à Court's purchases of BHP stock.

This made McNeill furious and Samuel didn't miss a beat, even though he was up against a formidable and strategic opponent in Holmes à Court.[10]

Macquarie—now a seasoned operator in the takeover space— drafted in a senior team led by Samuel and including Robert Johanson, Alastair Lucas and Simon McKeon as the battle for BHP played out. The youngest member of the deal team was Peter Yates, who was called on for his computer modelling and spreadsheet skills.

'I learned how to program, do computer modelling in Japan on a device called a Wang, which was a computer, and using a spreadsheet called Lotus 123,' Yates says. 'I got my job at Macquarie because of that skill. I always laugh about it because I think Graeme Samuel thought it was a kama sutra position.'

McKeon recalls the significance of that role: 'That BHP mandate was not the first big transaction that Macquarie had done, but it was a very, very significant step up. Macquarie put a lot of resources into it.'

Samuel knew how to bring together his team and also recruited well-known mergers and acquisitions lawyer Aleco Vrisakis to assess legal action against Potter Partners. Yates had carefully compiled trading activity in BHP's stock on his trusty spreadsheet and was able to identify some anomalies.

The defence team spearheaded by Samuel was also strident in fighting against the use by Holmes à Court of a partial-bid technique aimed at BHP shareholders. 'They would bid for 50 per cent of everyone's shareholding but would take more if people didn't accept. And it was a clever trick and later banned,' Samuel recalls.

'What happened was the small shareholders didn't accept, some of the institutional shareholders accepted for 100 per cent of their shareholdings knowing that maybe 75 per cent to 80 per cent would be accepted.

'And they always knew that once the takeover was finished, because only 50 per cent was owned by Holmes à Court, if it succeeded, they'd be able to buy back in. It was a great arbitrage.'

Holmes à Court eventually amassed a BHP holding of about 30 per cent and sent Australia's business community into a frenzy over his tactical use of exchange-traded options. In the USA, too, he was capturing attention as an acquirer after snapping up stakes in petroleum group Texaco Inc and steel and energy firm USX Corporation.

There was, however, a further twist in the tussle for BHP, because the miner and Samuel had kept a few tricks up their sleeves while manoeuvring in the background.

Melbourne-based raider John Elliott—who had been undertaking his own takeover spree—executed a quick-fire raid on BHP's shares through Elders IXL using debt and a complex cross-shareholder agreement with BHP.

A two-pronged takeover defence strategy was in play against Holmes à Court, in what was a much-vaunted alliance between BHP and Elders. Both companies were this way protected through blocking stakes from Holmes à Court's clutches, and eventually a ceasefire was declared.

It was an odd alliance, but it worked. Elders—another high-profile Australian company[11]—had traversed industries including wool, livestock, metals and merchant banking. Elliott, via a merger with jam and foods group Henry Jones IXL and a spate of other acquisitions, had created a sprawling conglomerate.

From BHP's chieftains there was a collective sigh of relief as Elliott and Holmes à Court put down their deal-making weapons. But the intensity of that takeover defence was one of several reasons Samuel parted ways with Macquarie not long after the cessation of that work.

'That battle had been an exhausting experience. I spent a year and a half, probably every day and night up at BHP's headquarters, working Saturdays, working Sundays. I was just tired,' Samuel says. 'I didn't think that there could be anything that would surpass that in terms of involvement.'

Samuel went on to work for a cashbox[12] and then two years later jointly established boutique and independent advisory firm Grant Samuel[13] with his former Macquarie colleague and executive director Ross Grant. From 2003 to 2011, Samuel headed the Australian Competition & Consumer Commission.

■

The 1987 share market crash put the final nail in the coffin of Holmes à Court's plans for BHP and several of his other targets.

These were the heady days of corporate raiders, leverage and frenetic takeover activity. Holmes à Court was in a different league, though, from another group of Aussie buccaneers looking to make their mark in the eighties who would also hit the wall in the later years of the decade, or soon after.

In 1986, a flamboyant Christopher Skase bought into the Sheraton Princeville in Hawaii.

Skase had already amassed a sizeable media and tourism group, benefiting from an era of easy credit.[14] His corporate vehicle Qintex collapsed in 1989 with ballooning debts, with Skase duping shareholders and declaring himself bankrupt two years later. He subsequently fled Australia to the Spanish resort town of Majorca, never to return, citing ill health.[15]

Rambunctious Australian businessman Alan Bond was able to pull off a historic victory in the America's Cup in 1983,[16] taking the trophy from the USA for the first time in 132 years. That won the hearts of Australians and even prompted then Prime Minister Bob Hawke to label any employer not giving their staff a day off to celebrate 'a bum'.

But Bond's world would also soon come unstuck.

He agreed early in 1987 to acquire media mogul Kerry Packer's television station the Nine Network in a bumper A$1 billion deal that would later spur Packer to say: 'You only get one Alan Bond in your lifetime, and I've had mine'.

That was after Packer—who had a penchant for gambling but a strong and ruthless business acumen—bought back Nine for one-quarter of the price, as Bond was left floundering in debt[17] and was eventually declared bankrupt.

And after building one of Australia's largest conglomerates,

Spalvins saw it come crashing down in 1991, as lenders moved in on the company's mounting debt pile.

Macquarie under Berg's risk-averse stewardship was carefully sidestepping dealing with or having large exposures to many of those colourful and sometimes bizarre Australian corporate characters. But Berg's position on avoiding working with some of the busiest entrepreneurs in that period was controversial and meant Macquarie was sacrificing income.

'In the mid-to-late eighties you did have Bond, Skase, Holmes à Court all doing deals, making takeovers, raising huge amounts of loan money and so on. They had, how do I put it, dubious ethics, and the question was, would we bank those people? In terms of giving them advice, and or lending them money,' Berg says. 'My feeling was, no. These were people that, you know, this was dangerous. These were people that you shouldn't be dealing with.'

Mark Johnson, who helped put in place the foundations of Hill Samuel Australia, believes it was Berg's meticulous attention to managing risks and trawling through detail that helped Macquarie ride out the 1987 crash and subsequent turbulence.

'Tony may well have saved the bank after the 1987 crash, because he's also a detail freak. He wouldn't allow any new product or service to be introduced unless he understood it fully,' Johnson says. He also cites the structure Berg put in place as ensuring the prudential arm of the bank, which included credit approvals and internal and external limits, was independent and reported to the managing director.

Macquarie's approach to minimising risk and its individual exposures persists today as it constantly evaluates hundreds of deals and mandates. The firm conducts a granular assessment of the worst-case scenarios and seeks out chunky investment returns accompanied by a risk profile that is kept in check.

Risk management was, and remains, a hallmark of the Macquarie model that is a key differentiator for the group. There have been notable slip-ups along on the way, several casting a pall over the group, but Macquarie applies a thorough risk lens to everything it does. That has served the firm well in navigating severe market events, recessions, the global financial crisis and the COVID-19 pandemic while still posting annual profits.

■

For the year ending 31 March 1986, Macquarie booked another record profit.[18] All of the operating divisions were in the black, despite branch banking—a condition of the licence—posting a loss in its first year of operation.

With a new banking licence and name the firm was forging its own path and wanted to take employees with it on the journey. Competition for the best and brightest staff across deal advisory and money markets was fierce, and the firm had not been immune to the poaching efforts of rivals.

David Clarke and Johnson had put in place the foundations, but a burgeoning Macquarie business now wanted a formal iteration of its purpose and aspirations to ensure it retained a distinctive culture. The top echelon realised the growth in income and headcount warranted a formal articulation of the firm's ethos, principles and expectations.

Knowing this was no small task, in early 1986 Clarke and Berg had called upon McKinsey & Company to assist. Enter McKinsey's head of Australia Fred Hilmer and lieutenant Helen Nugent to collaborate on the discrete Macquarie work, which would end up being a multi-year project.

Both Hilmer and Nugent would separately later go on to have stints on the Macquarie board.[19]

Hilmer and Nugent, flanked by Clarke and Berg who were driving the process internally, had the difficult task of taking the pulse of disparate units within Macquarie to help frame the new corporate ethos.

'It [the existing policy] was motherhood stuff and Tony and David were very deeply perceptive and they argued that really wasn't going to cut it,' Nugent recalls of Macquarie's overarching framework when she arrived to help steer the project. 'First of all, we did a survey of all of the staff to try to articulate what the values were of the organisation itself.

'We actually asked what were called horns of a dilemma questions. In this situation, what would you do? And that was really important to tease out.'

The horns of a dilemma scenarios put Macquarie staff in perplexing situations and provided multiple options to choose from that could be viewed as equally challenging. Macquarie employees were no doubt feeling the pressure of being impaled by either of the bull's horns.

The work Macquarie and McKinsey were doing came against the backdrop of simmering tension between the operating divisions. The bullion and money market teams had dubbed the corporate services and advisory bankers the 'plastic men' due to their perceived lack of personality. In turn, some of the corporate advisory bankers used to rile up their bullion and foreign exchange colleagues, questioning their work ethic as the markets types disappeared to long lunches with a bottle of wine or two. A lot of the office friction and competitive banter went back to the Hill Samuel Australia days and the creation of a newsletter called 'The Whisper', in which teams parodied each other including with pointed cartoons, mostly by Beaumont.

It wasn't only the divisional cultures that differed. The trading divisions also made markets as well as serving customers, so there were many considerations to take into account. Hilmer and Nugent, in consultation with Berg and Clarke, had to mobilise a working group of Macquarie people who held opposing views on some of the principles and framework being worked up for the firm. That group included Richard Sheppard, John Caldon[20] and David Adams.

It was an in-depth process that involved figuring out how best to compile and structure the new document in consultation. That process took the best part of a year and a lot of back and forth among the camps.

'There was a huge amount of contention around the divergent views,' Nugent says. 'We basically got them to work through the issues, to develop the chapters and to sign off on it.'

After much consternation, and at times heated debate, in early 1987[21] Berg, Clarke, McKinsey and the team landed on a 'Goals and Values' document aimed at sustaining a 'cycle of success'.

It was dubbed *Macquarie Bank: What We Stand For*, and the 26-page document[22] spanned a number of areas including the firm's objectives, how it dealt with external partners and how internal operations would be managed, including the behaviour expected of staff.

The document outlined two tests for the firm's success. The first was qualitative and related to earning the respect of existing and potential customers; the second set a quantitative goal linked to superior returns and growth opportunities.

Macquarie put a stake in the ground to achieve a return on shareholders' funds 'well above' the industry average, and that over an undefined period, it would be among the best of its peers. It also targeted a growth rate in profit, revenue, equity and staff numbers that was 'sustainable and manageable', providing staff with the incentive to stay and participate in growth of the business.

The document—although viewed by some employees as a wasted exercise and a joke given many believed they were already working within that ethos—instilled early on some of the key tenets of Macquarie's culture.

'We encourage our staff to experiment in developing services and products. The rate of change in financial markets makes this vital . . . We hold our staff accountable for developing a service or product to its full potential,' the document said.

'We do not hesitate to discard a service or product that is likely to damage our reputation or provide an inadequate return.'

To get key Macquarie people behind the document and to underscore its importance, McKinsey dispatched its culture and organisational structure guru, Jon Katzenbach, to Australia. The aim was to emphasise the importance of a company's DNA and cultural settings, and it was felt a global heavy hitter would have significant sway with the senior Macquarie staff.

The first hurdle was to get Macquarie's then eighteen or so executive directors on side.

The scene was set on a weekend at the nineteenth-century Milton Park Country House in the Southern Highlands of New South Wales. If the majestic surroundings in the secluded woodland estate, complete with its own manicured gardens, didn't help the executive directors agree on the contents of the Goals and Values document, nothing would.

Not everyone was open-minded, though, and most of the attendees drove their own cars in case they needed a quick escape from fiery clashes.

Despite this trepidation, the sales pitch and the contents of the document were enough to win the executive directors over and they signed off on the blueprint at Milton Park that weekend.

Berg and Clarke then embarked on the next phase of the pitch, rolling out 'Goals and Values' to the entire Macquarie workforce. The pair issued a personal invitation to every person in the bank, from executive assistants to executive directors, and there was a launch in every city.

That document became a key part of Macquarie's lengthy induction process along with the famed—but often dreaded—psychometric testing.

Berg recalls: 'It's obviously a lot better for me to say: look, clearly this doesn't fit in our goals and values, than for me to say my gut tells me that this is a wrong thing to do.'

Nugent adds: 'It's probably the most seminal piece of work I ever undertook in terms of client impact.'

In 2011, Clarke said of the document and its various revised iterations: 'We spent a lot of time on developing *What We Stand For* and it's stood the test of time . . . some of the wording, wordsmithing has maybe changed a little bit, but not a lot.'

The Goals and Values document would provide important insights into how Macquarie was approaching a number of key areas, including pay, promotion, risk management, accountability and behaviour.

It specified no tolerance for deliberately exceeding trading limits and even went as far as telling employees never to publicly denigrate a competitor. Staff would be compensated 'at or above levels' of peers and rivals and there was a preference for promoting existing staff to senior positions over looking for staff externally.

Risk management flowed through the document's core.

'Entrepreneurial flair should be tempered by due regard for risk,' the Goals and Values document said. 'We expect staff to take a pro-active approach to risk management. Financial Management should be informed of deals with significant credit risk. Further, staff are encouraged to share problem transactions with management rather than conceal them.

'When the bank is acting as agent the client relationship must come ahead of the house account,' the document said, noting that when Macquarie was trading as principal the 'highest ethical behaviour' was expected.

The benchmarks and standards were set, but that didn't mean they would always be met; investment banking and trading came with inherent risks and challenges.

Several years after that Goals and Values document, Macquarie approved detailed procedures to manage and resolve potential conflicts of interest between the bank's divisions and its customers. That issue would go on to plague the entire global investment banking industry, and Macquarie at times, as it pushed into doing principal deals from its own balance sheet.

In spite of the documented goals, rules and processes, Berg was still often coming to verbal blows with senior staff over his conservative risk appetite.

Head of bullion and commodities Clive Carroll vividly remembers almost being fired by Berg for taking his division to the South Pacific island of Noumea in New Caledonia for a Christmas party.

'Tony Berg found out about it and I nearly got the sack. He felt it put too many people at risk, but I'd actually organised for myself and another key guy within the division to fly on a separate plane,' he says.

Still, Berg's decisions and tight leash on Macquarie's operations in those years positioned the firm well to withstand the mammoth share market crash of 1987, and a wave of aftershocks that ensued in corporate Australia.

Macquarie's 1987 annual report, released after it ruled off its financial year on 31 March, held pertinent clues about looming risks on the horizon.

'A number of the worldwide financial markets have been experiencing boom conditions in 1986–7. This has unfortunately led to a number of excesses—some of which have already become clearly evident—notably in respect to trading and credit risks and ethical standards,' Clarke said in the chairman's statement. 'We believe such developments to be a cause for considerable concern.'[23]

Reading the tea leaves, Berg in late 1986 tasked an intern to compile research on events surrounding the US share market crash of 1929 and its fallout.

'Blind Freddy could see that there was a bubble developing in the stock market,' he recalls.

Leading into the chaos of late 1987, Macquarie, in partnership with McKinsey, had also conducted research on the nation's twenty or so busiest—but often highly controversial—corporate raiders and the firm's appetite to do business with them. Issues and clashes around that list and how much, if any, business to do with those entrepreneurs was causing immense unrest within Macquarie and, in one observer's words, was 'tearing the place apart'.

Needless to say, the lion's share of those names didn't emerge on the other side of the 1987 crash, and the recession that enveloped the Australian economy in the early 1990s.

The lending and credit policies of many banks were loose in Australia in the eighties as deregulation spurred lenders to pursue faster growth and more market share. High levels of corporate leverage were not uncommon. In the USA, concerns were mounting about a widening trade deficit and a controversial tax bill on takeovers.

Macquarie was about to face its biggest test yet.

■

It was early in the morning of 20 October 1987 and Allan Moss, head of risk management and domestic markets at the time, was driving his car to Sydney Airport en route to Brisbane. As he navigated the traffic, a radio news update caused Moss to shudder.

After a five-year bull run Wall Street was hitting the skids, plummeting about 23 per cent overnight and sending shockwaves through global markets.[24] Investors and financial markets were roiled by a deluge of selling that was exacerbated by program trading, as computerised orders were triggered during the rout.

Moss quickly came to the realisation that as head of risk management he couldn't get on that flight, but continued as calmly as he could to Sydney Airport. On arrival, he told his travel companion—future star investment banker Michael Carapiet, then a commercial lending manager—the trip could not go ahead.

Moss then made his way promptly to Macquarie's Bond Street office. An immensely challenging day lay ahead for Macquarie as local traders braced for how the Australian market would fare in light of the massive global ructions.

In the lift at Bond Street Moss encountered a banker from a rival firm who was citing the morning's newspaper suggesting an absurd daily market drop of 10 per cent. Moss set the employee straight: Wall Street was down more than 20 per cent. There was a stunned silence.

Moss emerged into the anxious dealing room. There was trepidation in the air as traders worked through their positions. This would be a momentous but excruciating day. Macquarie was a market-maker in equity options and that book was being more closely assessed than all the others.

'It was pretty eerie because we were seeing all of that action that took place in a different time zone. We were in the tail end of it,' says Clive Carroll.

Sensing the mood of anxiety in the trading room, Berg realised he had to act, climbing onto a desk to address the troops. He sensed he needed to calm the nerves of those on Macquarie's front line.

'Tony was saying: "Look, we've lost some money but it's business as usual. Just keep doing what you're doing, I've got every confidence in everyone", or words to that effect,' Peter Taylor recalls. 'As opposed to some banks who cut limits and activity, Macquarie just kept trading.'

Berg and others had decided the best course of action was to keep the dealing room operating as usual and refrain from cutting trading limits, albeit some of the pricing being put to customers reflected the highly uncertain environment.

The crash that October day dealt a heavy blow to financial markets around the world and stoked fears of a recession or, even worse, another economic depression. In the USA that market rout became known as Black Monday, and in the Australian time zone Black Tuesday, as the local market plunged 25 per cent.

It was unprecedented. Some A$65 billion was stripped from the market value of Australia's listed companies after record one-day market falls in the USA and United Kingdom. In Japan and Hong Kong, authorities intervened in share markets as they sought to minimise the damage and smooth the volatility. Politicians around the world urged calm as contagion spread.

In some respects, Macquarie—given its close assessment of financial risks and the external environment—had seen the writing on the wall.[25] The bank had modelled and conducted scenario planning for a severe market downturn such as this, but the extreme one-day plunge sat even outside that.

Berg revisited that timely piece of work undertaken by the intern on the 1929 rout to understand what could lie ahead. In 1929, the Dow Jones Industrial Average had tumbled 13 per cent on 28 October, followed by a drop of almost 12 per cent the following day.[26]

A few weeks later the bourse had shed almost half its value.

This time was different, with a heftier initial blow to markets. At Macquarie, all eyes were on the screens as the Australian exchange opened. All hands were on deck on the trading floor.

'It was pretty clear that the [Australian] market was going to gap and it opened down 20 per cent,' Allan Moss recalls. 'This had never happened. It probably hadn't even happened in wartime.

'That was a significant market gap, because it was quite different to what had happened in the US, where it moved down 20 per cent during the day.' That is, in the USA the move was incremental; in Australia it happened in one hit at the opening.

Outside the office, the general public and investors in markets throughout the world assessed the damage, with many nursing huge paper losses.

The Australian stockbroking industry had already been riding a wave of change as automation and computers were becoming commonplace. The Australian Stock Exchange had only been formed six months earlier by combining the six independent and state-based exchanges.[27] In rather fortuitous timing, the day prior to Black Tuesday had marked the first day that a clutch of selected stocks in Australia were traded using computer terminals, via a system known as SEATS.[28]

Back on that fearful day in October 1987, after Macquarie had moved to stem initial losses in its trading book, a newspaper journalist rang the Sydney office and said they'd heard about a run on the bank.

Moss sensed he had to act quickly and explained there was no run; but, given the panic hitting markets, he figured it best to invite the journalist to visit the dealing room and Macquarie's bank branch downstairs to assuage any concerns.

The journalist was shown the reality: there was no queue of people trying to pull out money at the Sydney branch, and work was being undertaken as calmly as possible on the trading desks. The media issue was cauterised.

'Only one counterparty reduced their limit on us in the '87 crash,' Moss says.

Berg notes: 'It was a scary period. We lost money that day, but because of those controls, we didn't lose too much. In fact, the traders were pretty smart, they made it up.'

There were some losses in October across trading desks, but the volatility following that dire day helped Macquarie stem the losses—largely within equity index options—and then trade profitably soon after. Profit for the full year ended 31 March 1988 increased 22 per cent to $26.4 million.[29]

'We continued to maintain the highest prudential standards and actively managed risk situations such as underwriting and options. As a result, when the crash came we were not materially exposed,' Macquarie's 1988 annual report said.

'Minor losses in October in some trading areas were within manageable proportions. In fact, October profits were at normal levels and we earned more in the second half of the year than the pre-crash first half.'

■

The 1986–1987 period also heralded the arrival of names that would prove highly important in the decades ahead for Macquarie, including future CEOs Nicholas Moore and Shemara Wikramanayake and future aircraft leasing boss Stephen Cook. After setting up Australian Bank, which was then sold to the State Bank of Victoria given the difficulties encountered in generating enough scale, Mark Johnson returned to the Macquarie fold as an executive director and chairman of corporate services.

As the fresh new faces were getting acquainted with the Macquarie machine, the 1988 annual report summed up how the bank had navigated the market maelstrom.

'The past year will be remembered by the finance industry for its considerable excess and for the October stock market collapse,' the report said.

'The bank proceeded cautiously during the first half. We benefited from high volumes in various financial markets and from high levels of underwriting and takeover activity but we avoided increasingly marginal credit situations.'

The share market crash had ripple effects, though, and also spurred turbulence in other areas of Macquarie's business. In the same month as the 1987 rout, Macquarie listed a property trust after raising A$80 million from institutional and individual investors.[30] It traded well initially before the crash caused it to trade at a steep discount to its underlying real estate value, and soon an offer for the real estate emerged. The offer was rebuffed by the board, who relayed they were taking a longer-term view.

By this stage, the impressive Cash Management Trust had burst through A$1 billion and Macquarie was separately handling about 30 per cent of Australia's total gold production via hedging products, gold-backed financing techniques and forward sale programs.

Macquarie was also quietly looking to markets close by for growth, tentatively at this stage. It was one of only two Australian trading banks to be granted a New Zealand banking licence during that period, leading to the opening of a branch in Wellington.

In equities, Macquarie was also assessing ways it could build a business and make inroads into the stockbroking arena. The bank acquired the remaining capital in a stockbroking associate[31] and Berg lured back broking operative Bill Best from Potts West Trumbull to run a renamed Macquarie Equities business. The idea was to build it into a formidable institutional share trading brokerage, but it wouldn't be easy.

In Australia, Macquarie was up against far more entrenched players, including the storied JBWere, Potter Partners, MacIntosh and Ord Minnett. The institutional equities business would go on to build a strong position in the Australian market, but for Macquarie over the coming decades it would never be quite clear where the business should sit. At times it was a separate division or within investment banking, then it moved to Commodities and Global Markets, before returning to Macquarie Capital.

Peter Curry, who led syndication, says the equities business needs to be considered in a broader context for the benefits it delivers other parts of Macquarie.

'It's very important, and you can't look at it like a standalone business. Because it's like an octopus. It gives you an entry point and Macquarie couldn't have done half the deals they did, if they didn't have their own broking business.'

But even as Macquarie was plotting its next phase of growth and forging a path in equities, Clarke and Berg maintained some caution about the external environment.

'We are not convinced that the worst of the turbulence in the financial markets is over. The possibility of more shocks to the system cannot be ignored, which makes us determined to remain vigilant,' they said in the 1988 annual report.

Meanwhile, in 1989, Best was putting together his own plan for the equities unit and coming to the realisation Macquarie needed an offshore presence to keep pace with its broking rivals.

Best had hired Englishman Robert Goatly, a relationship broker, into his Sydney team from Kleinwort Benson Australia and Goatly had spotted an opportunity.

The offshore operations of Kleinwort, known as Kleinwort Hattersley Securities, were being dismantled and the people, leases and operations were up for grabs. If Macquarie moved quickly to pick up those operations, it would deliver the firm a European presence in equities, people on the ground in London and a smaller office in Germany.

Goatly made a recommendation to Best and up the line at Macquarie before connecting his new employer to representatives at Kleinwort in London. Very soon after, Moss and Best boarded a plane to London to scope out whether it could work, as rapid-fire due diligence was required. In Munich, Kleinwort's Germany office was manned by just two people and proved difficult to locate, but Best and Moss eventually figured out it was hidden above a shoe retailer.

The due diligence showed Macquarie could make a small calculated bet on Kleinwort that could deliver in spades for its fledgling equities business. Best and Moss soon sealed the deal, adding about nine people to the equities division and marking an important milestone as Macquarie started to dip into bigger markets outside Australia.

'If you aspired to be one of the top businesses in that [equities] area, which I think every Macquarie business did and everyone was encouraged to, then you just had to have that distribution otherwise you just couldn't communicate with the fund managers in terms of what was going on,' Best says of the Kleinwort opportunity.

'Allan was certainly for it, encouraged it and pushed it.'

The London office initially dealt in Australian stocks before adding project and structured finance, foreign exchange and metals trading.

Around the same time the Kleinwort transaction was being assessed, Macquarie showed it was prepared to quickly unwind decisions that weren't working. It transferred its New Zealand foreign exchange trading operation back to Sydney, citing a policy for only operating in areas 'where we are most effective'.

There were also changes afoot in the organisational structure. The 1989 annual report highlighted the formation of the Financial Markets division, bringing together all the operations involving trading and brokerage under Allan Moss. The other operating divisions were Corporate Services, Corporate Banking, Investment Services and Operations.[32]

This report outlined that Moss had also become deputy managing director, in a signal that succession planning was under way. After all, his empire had just been markedly expanded and Macquarie by this stage had been around—including its Hill Samuel Australia days—for two decades.

But again in 1989 external storm clouds were gathering, as underlying issues were becoming more pronounced in the Australian economy. The commercial property market was cooling, interest rates were high and there were growing concerns about the credit quality of large parcels of bank loans.

Macquarie launched a study about the outlook in November 1989 to considerable attention. Titled *A Boiling Frog? Australia's Economic Challenge and a comprehensive Agenda for Action*, the team rolled it out with seminars.[33] It made a stir, provoked debate on big issues, and placed Macquarie at the centre of them as a thought leader.

But the study and its critique managed to incense Federal Treasurer Paul Keating, spurring a harsh response.

'I don't think we felt inhibited about making those sorts of comments. Mr Keating thought it was really pretty nasty. He wrote Tony one of the most scathing letters I've ever seen,' Clarke said of the exchange.

But Clarke and Berg were still worried. 'While the Australian and world economies have been generally strong during the year, some of the imbalances have not yet been overcome,' they wrote in the 1989 annual report.[34] 'We believe difficult and unpredictable periods still lie ahead.'

Chapter 4

ROADS, FEES AND BT IN THE ALLAN MOSS NINETIES

Everyone has an Allan Moss story, but they all boil down to the same portrait: an avuncular and likeable clumsiness that masked one of the sharpest minds ever to grace the industry.

A thoroughly decent and unpretentious man, Moss's down-to-earth nature sometimes manifested itself visibly during his time at the top. In an institution full of people wearing Rolexes worth as much as a car, Moss was forever associated with a digital watch. When he travelled, he would cover his case with masking tape in the shape of a vast letter A so he could spot it on the baggage belt. Those who attended presentations early in their careers with Moss recall his adoration of the overhead projector, with its hand-drawn text on transparent film, a good decade after everyone else had moved on to more advanced technological fare.[1]

Moss used to call himself Denis, in reference to Denis Thatcher, in a self-deprecating nod to his wife Irene's[2] authority, particularly at government events. He was a man who could be counted upon to drop things or get off at the wrong floor but who has probably one of the most towering intellects ever unleashed on Australian banking.

'If you went to him with a problem over a deal, he'd sit down and listen,' says Simon Wright, head of fixed income and foreign exchange, in an account mirrored by dozens of others. 'He wouldn't say anything. He would listen for five minutes, take notes—you wouldn't know what he was writing—and put them in his top pocket.

'And then he would speak and he would cut straight to the chase. He knew exactly what the problem was and exactly how to solve it.

'He was a man to be respected. I was pretty young at that time and sort of awestruck by his intellectual prowess. But he was so disarming: anyone who got in the lift with him, he would know their name and what they were working on.'

A story from Irene O'Brien is illustrative. She was in communications at the Australian Securities Commission (ASC)[3] when the Simon Hannes scandal (see Chapter 5) kicked off, and her path had crossed with Moss briefly while keeping a dialogue between him and ASC head Alan Cameron. Several years later, and having done a whole other job at the Australian Broadcasting Corporation (ABC) in the meantime, she joined Macquarie in corporate communications in what would become the Banking and Financial Services group.

'On my first day at Macquarie, I was in the lift and Allan Moss walked in,' she says, 'And he said, "Hello, Irene." I was like: Oh my God, I've had a job in between then and now, and he still remembers me.

'He came across as being the muddle-headed professor, but that man had a brain that was so sharp. If he thought something was a bad idea, he told you, nicely, but you wouldn't want to go against that. There was this underlying sense of: Allan knows what he's doing and I'm really not going to argue with him.'

■

By the early 1990s, a feeling had begun to develop in some divisions that Tony Berg might be holding Macquarie back from its true potential. Nobody doubted that Berg's discipline had protected the bank in the '87 crash; it just might have saved it. And the rigour he instilled around risk management continues to be visible, and essential, in the bank today.

Nicholas Moore recalls: 'Tony used to say the one thing you get sacked for is bottom-drawering an issue.' Moore used this approach throughout his rise to the top. 'If there's problems, you bring them out and you put all the resources on it that you can to fix the issue . . . We want to fix problems and set things right.' That approach of facing a problem head-on was instrumental to Berg's approach.

Bill Moss, who joined under Berg and would go on to drive Macquarie's real estate business, says: 'Tony was constantly testing your temperament, your ability to reason, your ability to convince.

'A lot of people used to say: I hate going to see Tony, he wins all the time. Whereas I found Tony brilliant. He would draw the best out of you.'[4]

But Berg's discipline was also keeping them out of some new businesses and locations.[5]

Berg had articulated this position in the 1990 annual report, a renowned contribution to the Macquarie visual canon fronted by an image of the shape of Australia cut from a Jaffa cake. (Consensus has it that the nadir—or zenith, depending on your point of view—of this visual extravaganza was the 1991 annual report, which looks for all the world like a King Crimson album cover, filled with celestial orbs and comets and an oceanic land slipping down waterfalls into space. Others think the mouse-on-an-escalator motif of 1993 takes some beating for obscurity.) The point of this confectionary theme, articulated in the now-customary laboured analogy of the introduction, was that in a world of 'mouth-watering toffees from England . . .

heavenly chocolates from Switzerland . . .' it was just fine to be a good old Australian Jaffa.[6]

It went on: 'In an age fixated with globalisation, the concept of country specialisation at first appears to be an anachronism . . . Macquarie bank will continue to capitalize on being the Australian specialist, even through the international offices it now operates.

'And it sincerely believes the challenge for a successful country specialist is not to seek opportunities in markets where it lacks a home town advantage, but to broaden its Australian expertise and to resist the "global" temptation for as long as possible!'

The problem was, not everyone internally wanted to resist that global temptation. Australia didn't feel like the goldmine it once had. The 1991–92 recession in Australia and the property crash[7] that came with it hit the industry hard, with Westpac almost collapsing in 1992 as its property loan losses ballooned. That recession led to Macquarie's first-ever decline in after-tax profits[8] and the writing off of some A$10 million in loans, increasing the sense that there could be more to do overseas.

You couldn't really argue with Berg's results—that year brought a fifth consecutive record operating profit as Macquarie Bank,[9] and the year after would bring a sixth—but a growing sense had emerged that Macquarie could be missing out on new horizons that wouldn't necessarily involve undue risk.

In some sense, one could understand his position. The track record of Australian financial services businesses going overseas was lamentable then and has become even worse since. Also, the idea that Berg was dead against international expansion is reductive. 'It was the one issue which Allan and I had not agreed on, but I want to put it in context,' Berg says today. 'I was a great devotee of the concept of competitive advantage.' So he was against Moss's idea, from the markets business, that there was headway to be made in taking options trading overseas to Frankfurt, for example, because he could see no edge; but he believes he would certainly have backed infrastructure going overseas had it been sufficiently advanced to do so under his years. 'I like to think I would have recognised that opportunity.'

Also, several people recall an agreement that Berg would have backed an overseas office if any three divisions wanted to be there, a position that would have made sense of the overheads; it's just that, in those days, there were hardly any countries where more than two business areas could see an opportunity.

That would change, as some enterprising teams were taking shape. The Financial Packaging Division, a structured finance advisory group, had emerged under John Caldon's corporate services group, and Nicholas Moore would make his name here, becoming an executive director in the 1990 financial year and joint head of the division the following year.[10] It would become a magnet for some of the institution's bigger names: the Yates brothers, Oliver and Peter, would work here, as would Stephen Cook, Anthony Kahn, Michael Carapiet, Garry Farrell, Peter Salisbury, Michael Price and John Roberts.

'There was a lot of Big Four accounting influence in the way of systems and processes: people who came from professions rather than bankers, that was my recollection,' says Roberts, who joined the division in 1991. 'It was a really talented group who were challenged to innovate and differentiate their services.

'Macquarie had no balance sheet capacity to underwrite risk, no significant brand or even an essential reason to exist: what was it that you were selling? You didn't have money to lend.' The team was selling advice and trying to position it as more valuable than services from lawyers, accountants or other bankers. 'But that required you to start with a blank sheet of paper and work out how you could become relevant. You had to go out to the business world and create, and

persuade people to pay you money for an idea.' That was what financial packaging was about: starting with variations on basic finance
leasing products, it would go on to be the engine room of infrastructure and morph into one of the defining forces of the whole bank.

Peter Salisbury, who was hired into the team by Caldon in 1990,
recalls the work ethic of the place. 'John's big thing was always new
ideas,' he says. 'If you went out to see a client with last week's product,
John would get the shits with you. What's the incremental benefit if
you're just offering something that's already known?

'That culture of trying to be different to the other guys and
presenting something that nobody else has got: that all goes back
to John. He was insane, he worked so hard, but it was just continual
improvement.'

From early on, it was a success story, completing A$2 billion
worth of structured international and Australian financings in the
1991 financial year, and by 1992 was considered a leader in developing and implementing innovative financing techniques, and
perhaps the largest structured finance group in Australia.[11] But it was
international in scope, and this began to collide with the domestic
intentions of the top management.

'If you look around all of the Macquarie international offices,
every single one was started with structured finance,' says Oliver
Yates. 'Japan started with structured finance. Germany started with
structured finance.'

Much of this business had started with Jim McMeckan, who had
been raising bonds for Australian Airlines, and a moment of classic
Macquarie opportunism. Stephen Cook was also steering efforts on
the business side, and this leasing operation would grow immensely
in the years that followed.

Babcock & Brown, an investment and advisory firm whose path
would often cross with Macquarie's over the years, together with

Allco Finance Group, had cornered the market in Japanese cross-border leases, which was a very successful business.[12]

By chance, Peter Yates and McMeckan had been in a waiting room before a meeting at Australian Airlines where a group of Japanese were discussing a cross-border lease that was rapidly going wrong and how they were going to save it, with no idea that Yates, who had attended university in Japan and was fluent in the language, could understand every word. He told McMeckan what they were discussing; McMeckan, seizing the moment, told the airline Macquarie would come back the next morning with a revised proposal. This was news to Yates, who had never modelled a cross-border lease, but they did it overnight. 'So we went back in the following day, never having done a Japanese cross-border lease in our life, and told Australian Airlines that we would rescue that deal.'

And with that, Macquarie's Melbourne office had pioneered a new line of business, and Peter Yates would spend so much of the next five years flying in and out of Japan on alternate weeks that he became one of the top ten frequent flyers for Qantas in each of those years, to the considerable annoyance of his wife. They then did Hong Kong leases, and US leases. Nicholas Moore, seeing this success, then broadened the horizons beyond aircraft to mining equipment and telecommunications.

Peter brought in younger brother Oliver, who had just finished his undergraduate degree and was due to do a law degree next, to assist with modelling one summer. Suffice to say, Oliver never went back to law: he worked out how to apply the same techniques to shipping containers, offering container companies financing at a cost below bond rates. Before long they were doing a lease for Genstar Container Corporation[13] to do a cross-border lease from Japan into the USA that had nothing whatsoever to do with Australia. 'For the first time ever at Macquarie there was no Australian client, no Australian bank and no Australian equity,' says Peter.

But by now this international, entrepreneurial flair had hit opposition. Oliver recalls Genstar was done 'against the wishes and an explosive response from our managing director at the time [Alastair Lucas]. What the hell were we doing running and getting international mandates?'

Oliver also recalls David Clarke coming to the new UK office, set up in 1991, with that famous orange Jaffa annual report to present to UK staff and clients. 'And he stood up in the meeting and said: you know, the thing about Macquarie is we're just the Australian specialist, and we don't want to do anything overseas.' Macquarie already had about a dozen staff in London doing nothing but international transactions. 'Everyone said, are you kidding? The growth is all offshore, it's not onshore. The bank was running behind what the staff were doing, which was growing very rapidly overseas.'

By this stage Berg was looking around anyway. 'By the early nineties I had started to think about the future,' he says. 'I was by this time in my mid-forties. The way I saw it, I could have stayed at Macquarie for another ten years, but I decided that was not a good idea for me, or the bank.' He says he spoke to Moss, by now the deputy managing director, around 1991. 'I had a discussion with him, and said: "Allan, if I moved on, would you want to be the CEO?" And in no uncertain terms, he said yes.

'So I said: "Okay, I will look for another position".'

Berg was linked with several positions, including Commonwealth Bank of Australia, and had been urged by Mark Johnson, during a beachside Wollongong stroll at an off-site, to wait for the AMP top job to come up, but ended up going to Boral. 'For me it was an interesting challenge,[14] totally different from Macquarie Bank,' he says.

It was an amicable handover. 'Everyone understood his decision to take that role,' says Moss, who had been deputy managing director for four years by the time Berg formally stepped down in 1993. And

Moss, of course, was next: apart from his experience as deputy, he had spent six years in corporate finance, written the submission for the bank licence, and been head of risk management, head of lending and head of the whole dealing room at one stage or another.

A point of view continues to exist among some former staff that Berg was urged towards the exit, with the international issue a clear point of internal pressure. But for his part, Berg says it was time to go and that he had given his word to Moss, and Moss presents it as a smooth and well-managed internal transition.

Whatever the circumstances, Berg's departure fitted with a theme that continues to resonate with Macquarie to this day: that it seems to end up with the right CEO for the right time. As we will discover, Moore was the right CEO to take Macquarie through the financial crisis and reinvent it. Wikramanayake was the perfect person to be in charge amid a global pandemic, and to front the necessary response to climate change. And Berg was the right man at the helm to keep growth sensible and sustainable through the 1987 crash. 'Tony was a fantastic CEO, but would the organisation be what it is today if he hadn't jumped ship to Boral?' asks one who worked with three different chief executives.

And Allan Moss? He would be the right guy for the boom years.

■

Big Al, as subordinates like Moore and Carapiet had come to call him, took the helm at a good time. His first financial year, to March 1994, would be marked by a record profit[15] and recognition by the global banking magazine *Euromoney*[16] as the best bank in Australia. It was the top bullion dealer in Australia, more often than not the leader in equities, top in research and development syndication, cross-border leasing and the biggest arranger of public infrastructure finance.

Moss took on a bank with 21 distinct divisions from corporate advice and futures trading, areas of strength since the Hill Samuel days, to mortgage securitisation in Australia and options trading in Hong Kong.

Moss's ascent to the top coincided with an evolution of the Australian economy. Protectionism was on its way out. Exports into East Asian growth were the theme of the day. Against that backdrop, Australia's banking system was becoming more developed, sophisticated and vigorously competitive. There was a sense of a bank and a nation evolving in unison.[17]

'I'd have to say I was lucky,' Moss says. 'Roughly around when I became CEO, things started to really look up globally. There was deregulation from almost the very beginning of my career to the end, and significant growth.'

A shift that's worth remarking upon was that by the time Moss took over, fees had risen in the income mix over interest margins and trading income. Fees would become central to the Macquarie story. Sometimes they would become too central.

Moss assumed control of a business with 1500 employees across Australia plus London, Munich, Wellington, Johannesburg and Denver. Plans were under way for Macquarie Equities—which had become a separate entity in 1991—to open in New York, and for Private Client Investment—created in 1993—to do so in Hong Kong. There was a sense of new horizons from business to funding: a new offshore debt instrument program allowed it to use international debt markets.[18]

Moss resists the temptation to see his style as a significant departure from the past. 'Tony and I got on very well, and we were pretty much on the same page on just about everything, particularly risk management,' he says. 'So I wouldn't say that Tony was more or less conservative than me.

'But Tony did see us as an Australian specialist. And I did not see it that way.' And, while international expansion had begun under Berg, 'it would be fair to say that we sped up the move overseas, and dramatically so after I became CEO.'

■

Shortly before Moss had stepped up to the top job, a moment of unheralded future significance occurred at a grim-looking but vital brown coal-fired thermal power station on the outskirts of Traralgon in southeast Victoria. This was Loy Yang, divided into two sections, A and B.[19]

By the start of the 1990s the state of Victoria was in considerable financial stress, with some of its banks on the edge of insolvency and the budget deficit getting progressively worse. The state premier of the time, Joan Kirner, set about trying to sell state assets,[20] among them Loy Yang B.

McMeckan, then an executive director in Caldon and Moore's financial packaging group, secured an advisory mandate for the US power specialists Mission Energy with an ultimately successful bid.[21] It represented the first major privatisation of power generation in Australia.

This was the tip of a spear. When Kirner was replaced by Liberal premier Jeff Kennett in 1992, these initial sallies into the sale of state assets would become one of the most comprehensive and rapid privatisation programs ever seen. Between 1995 and 1998, A$29 billion of state assets in gas and electricity were sold to the private sector, in addition to various other essential services and several prisons. And while no other state would go so far, others were thinking along similar lines.[22]

This normalisation of private enterprise in the business of infrastructure happened to come at the same time as a transformation in the retirement savings industry, known in Australia as super-annuation. In 1992—under now Prime Minister Paul Keating, whose influence would again be considerable for Macquarie—employer contributions to superannuation were made compulsory. It would take time, but this change would create powerful and cashed-up funds with money to put to work.[23] Over time, these super funds, as Australians call them colloquially, would become the clients, sources of capital, and co-investing partners for Macquarie.

Keating would make one other step that would prove highly significant to Macquarie. Also in 1992, he introduced a new product as a mechanism to support the development of infrastructure in Australia. In the USA, infrastructure tends to be funded by long-term municipal bonds with tax-free income. Australia had no equivalent, so Keating created the infrastructure bond, free of both interest income tax and capital gains tax.[24] And if Macquarie loved one thing, it was a tax angle.

The result of these bonds was that they effectively reduced the costs of borrowing to finance the construction of infrastructure projects, but at some cost to the government, eventually benefiting financiers more than roads.[25] 'Whatever the original purposes, they had been engineered to within an inch of their life,' says former Australian Treasurer Peter Costello now, who considered Macquarie one of the key architects of this situation. 'You've got to hand it to them. I mean, it was a beauty when you saw how they engineered this stuff. Nicholas understood the Tax Act very well, I could see that.'

Macquarie's brains trust was watching these gathering forces closely, but initially as an adviser. And then things changed. 'The inflection point,' says Anthony Kahn, whose career was about to change as a result of these themes, 'was Hills Motorway.'

Today Hills Motorway is known as the M2, a key artery linking the west of Sydney to the centre. The authors collectively have spent more time on this sunburned stretch of snaking asphalt than we would care to remember. But back in the nineties, the funding of this greenfield road project, involving the first listed toll road company in Australia, would change Macquarie forever.

Moore, Caldon and their team in the financial packaging group, which around this time was renamed Project and Structured Finance, had been chasing opportunities in public–private partnership infrastructure development for some time, 'with limited success, but learning all the time,' Moore recalls. Then the tender was announced for Hills Motorway.

The battle lines were drawn, with Leighton and Commonwealth Bank, successful bidders on the earlier M4 and M5 motorways in Sydney, among the three consortia that were forming to bid. 'We were seeking to get hired as an adviser and, unsurprisingly given we had not advised on any roads to date, it was challenging,' Moore says.

Salisbury, who had experience on toll road deals from previous jobs[26] and had asked Caldon to be put on toll roads in order to do the same at Macquarie, remembers the team preparing a twenty-page booklet analysing the potential financing for a bidder.[27] Salisbury remembers taking the booklet to talk to the three consortia, while all the players were working out who best to team up with. 'As you go around the forming consortium in this early stage, it's a bit like your first high school dance,' Salisbury says. 'The music starts and the girls are over there and the boys are over here and you're sort of milling around working out who you want to dance with.' They all took the booklet, but it appeared nobody wanted to dance. One of the Leighton executives told Salisbury: 'We're not going to hire you guys because Macquarie doesn't do project finance.'

But then they found their way in. A construction business called Abigroup had set up a fourth consortium with GHD, a contractor and engineering firm.[28] Abigroup was accomplished at building roads—and cheap—but had negative shareholders' funds and, although listed, was tiny. 'Abigroup had their own challenges, having recently emerged from administration,' Moore recalls. 'But they had an excellent road paving group. We signed up together and were viewed as the outsiders.'

So far, so good, but at this stage Macquarie was only doing what it always had: corporate advisory. But then the institutional brain-power of the bank began to come to the fore. A former Westpac banker called Nick James had joined the team, and he was an extremely advanced computer modeller for the time. Combining that with the deep-seated tax structuring expertise already in the business, the team came to realise that there was some value they could create.

Without disappearing too far down the rabbit hole of infrastructure finance, the way that the M4 and M5 had been structured was that the equity in the projects was not considered to have any value in its own right, and was effectively given to the Commonwealth Bank on the M4, and Leighton on the M5, free. Since nobody had a clear view on the future cash flows of the roads, nobody really ascribed value to the equity. 'The practice up until that time was that the financial markets would only provide debt on what was considered the most certain revenue,' Moore says. 'Thus the project size was limited to the amount of debt the project could bear, as the equity risk was considered unbankable.'

After crunching the numbers, Macquarie found it had an edge. 'We brought value to the table by being able to put a dollar value on the equity,' Moore says; he remembers the pitch as being that out of a A$500 million contract, the equity was worth A$120 million.

'So by us saying that, effectively we increased what we could deliver to the road project, and thus the community, by A$120 million.

'And that changed the game, in terms of road projects in Australia, because we were putting value on something that hadn't previously been valued.'

More than that, it hadn't been built, which was also new. 'Traditionally, we'd raise money for existing businesses,' says Bill Best.[29] 'This was very different.'

The other innovation Macquarie pushed for was to list the company, rather than it being private, in order to improve the value of that equity portion. This was not straightforward: although the company was fully funded, it had not yet made a cent of revenue, so the whole premise of the listed company would be based on projections. In fact, its 1994 listing would come three full years before the opening of the motorway on 26 May 1997.[30]

Macquarie's own equities business underwrote this A$155 million initial public offering (IPO), a considerable risk for a wholly untested model, and the first equity risk Macquarie ever took in infrastructure.[31] It didn't quite fly out the door. Moore recalls: 'As with some new deals we ended up with quite a shortfall on it.'[32]

But it was worth it. 'The net result of it was that it changed the way people looked at patronage[33] infrastructure assets, particularly here in Australia,' Moore says. Beforehand, it had been viewed as a government asset, a liability, a question of future cost.[34] 'You don't see it as an asset, it's a liability,' Moore says. Macquarie was able to change that view with Hills Motorway: showing that even if future revenues were uncertain, they still had value.

The message still took time to come through. 'The value of infrastructure as an investable class, particularly for patronage assets, took a while to be accepted globally,' Moore says, particularly when technology investments were providing such strong returns and promise. 'It took five or even ten years for major institutions to set aside funds for infrastructure as a separate asset class.'

But they would. And in the meantime, Macquarie would figure something else out.

When the deal got done, there was a lot of internal pride at the structural brilliance[35] but also an uncomfortable truth. 'When we sat back and looked at it, we thought: for all this applause, we haven't made a huge amount of money,' says Salisbury. 'So who made all the money?' They concluded that the answer was Abigroup. 'They had a cagey old guy called John Cassidy and he'd been around government tenders forever and he knew how to skin that old cat.' They calculated that Abigroup, as a developer, had made multiples of what Macquarie had made.

Salisbury remembers Caldon saying: 'We've done all this fantastic stuff. We've done half a dozen financial innovations nobody has ever seen before. And we made, like, four or five million bucks.' Even in the nineties, that was considered small fry for Macquarie relative to the potential.

On the back of their M2 success, Caldon and Moore swiftly put Macquarie's own advisory fees up for infrastructure financing, which certainly helped with the revenues; by the time Melbourne's City Link project came along, Michael Carapiet and Salisbury were able to pick one bidding consortium meeting each—they were held at the same time—and go with the one that met the greatly increased asking price first (Carapiet won that one).

But there was a dawning sense that the real money resided in being like Abigroup: a developer. They needed, ultimately, to shift from being an adviser to being a principal. And to pull the capital together, they needed to build a fund to invest in the development of infrastructure projects.

It was an idea that would change the bank.

■

The year 1996 brought a landmark: the listing of Macquarie.

It was an odd sort of a listing, in that it didn't involve raising any cash. 'We didn't need money at that time,' says Moss, 'though the fact that we could raise money would become very significant later. The real drive was that the shareholders wanted it. They had committed their money since 1984 and they had been a long time without liquidity.'

In the meantime, there had been a few changes of institutional ownership. The biggest was when Hill Samuel reached the point where it was obliged, under the terms of the original deal with government, to sell down a significant chunk of its stake. Macquarie introduced Hill Samuel to the Brunei Investment Agency, a deal that required Moss to meet the Sultan of Brunei in the royal palace in Bandar Seri Begawan. What was the Sultan like? 'He was giving me money, and I tend to like most people giving me money.'

A grey market had existed for Macquarie shares, but nothing with anything like stock market liquidity. But listing wasn't a straight-forward decision. Berg had been dead against the idea.

'It took us a while to do it, for good reasons, not just mucking around,' says Moss. 'Internally there were sincere misgivings, because there was a feeling that there might be more pressure to produce short-term results.' Around 1994, for example, Macquarie had had to accept a hit to profits[36] in order to expand overseas, which had been unquestionably the right call, but precisely the sort of thing that might have been harder to get past shareholders in a listed company. There was also a concern that the profit-sharing scheme, 'which was definitely absolutely fundamental and central to the Macquarie culture,' could also be problematic, Moss says. 'So there were concerns that it might be a bit of a distraction.'

Set against that, by now about a quarter of the staff in the company held options. Having a share price to look at would engage them more closely with the bank, its performance and its strategy. 'It would be fair to say most people below the senior level were a bit vague on the bank as a whole,' Moss says. 'But once we listed and the share price started to respond, it was actually very educational. Everyone was reading the financial newspapers getting to understand what each of the groups was doing. It was an upside we hadn't anticipated.'

Richard Sheppard ran the listing project under Moss's direction; he remembers the close on the first day at A$6.50 a share. When we speak to him, not long after an event to mark the 25th listing anniversary, it's at around $200.[37] Macquarie listed on the Australian Stock Exchange (ASX) on 29 July 1996, entering the ASX All Ordinaries Index on 30 October.

There wasn't much fanfare. Nobody seems to recall a bell. After all, no money had been raised.

But the listing gave an exit, if required, to those who had bought in to the business a decade earlier when it gained its Australian banking licence. Anyone who had put A$1,000 in in 1985 was worth more than A$14,000 that day. But there was much better to come for those who stayed in.

■

Macquarie Bank was not the only entity to be listed that year. Monday 16 December 1996 brought the listing of Infrastructure Trust of Australia (ITA), which raised A$300 million, was heavily oversubscribed and swiftly climbed by 30 per cent.

ITA was the result of the Project and Structured Finance team's realisation that they could be doing a lot more as infrastructure asset owners and developers beyond being merely advisers. The fund was sold as a way to allow both institutional and retail investors to make small and liquid investments in infrastructure, something that had previously been impossible because the sums required were too big for retail and too illiquid for anybody who wanted to get in and out. Also, institutions quite liked the idea of retail investors being in a listed fund: they create liquidity.

It was one of the clearest examples of Macquarie's theory of adjacencies, and Shemara Wikramanayake still uses it as an example today. Macquarie went from merger and acquisitions and debt financing advice, to taking part in that financing, to being a developer, to creating funds for the assets it was developing and then operating those assets over the long term for investors. Always the next logical step. 'It was just an example of responding to changes, with patient adjacent growth,' she says now.

Getting to this point had not been easy. Even Macquarie's own asset management group of the time had blanched at the idea of a fund for infrastructure assets, baulking at the levels of gearing involved, which could be as much as 90 per cent on some Macquarie deals. The asset management team did at least help their project finance peers to organise dozens of meetings with institutional investors, but the 'instos'[38] wouldn't bite at the idea of a cashbox without knowing for sure where the money was going to go. 'Come back when you've got some seed assets,' Salisbury remembers being told.

So Macquarie set about tapping contractors in the existing toll roads, by now well-known to them, to see if they could buy their equity. For example, it bought the Hills Motorway/M2 stake from its consortium partner, Japan's Obayashi. Upon listing, ITA's assets included stakes in both the M5 and M2 motorways in Sydney, Melbourne's City Link project, Sydney's Eastern Distributor and, after flotation, an interest in Loy Yang A.[39] Infrastructure Funds Management, a newly established Macquarie division,[40] would manage the vehicle.[41]

Also—and this was significant—Macquarie sought not only to buy equity stakes in existing infrastructure but also to become developers in their own right. The first step on this path was Brisbane's Airtrain, a commuter railway line from Brisbane to the airport, which was a highly mixed experience. 'That turned out to be probably the worst deal we've ever had the pleasure of working on,' says one who was involved, recalling that it had so many moving parts between state government, Queensland Rail, Treasury, a state-run airport and even Westfield, that it took years to conclude. 'It was horrendous. But it would have brought one of the biggest profits, in terms of fee multiples, ever for Macquarie. It was an enormous fee earner relative to the size of the deal,' this banker says.

'And everyone thought: well, if we can get these done, we've got to keep doing these developer roles, because you can make a fortune.'

Making a fortune would become a characteristic of Macquarie's infrastructure funds. This same banker estimates that ITA, a A$300 million IPO, probably made about A$30 million of fees.[42] (See the footnote for a more detailed accounting, by author L. Solomon, that makes that estimate look frugal.) The model, in these early days, was to take the infrastructure assets—already monopoly businesses, in the main—put them in the funds and load them with debt. After bundling and securitising the infrastructure into these diversified portfolios, they would sell them on, taking fees at every possible turn.

Later, Macquarie would find itself having to move to more independent and arms-length arrangements, but at first, different bits of Macquarie would advise on the deals, arrange funding for the deals, execute the deals, manage the funds, find new assets, take a cut on selling the assets when the time was right, and also handle anything like swaps or forex or lending that was needed along the way. Timed correctly, Macquarie could get a fee for advising the public sector body that wants to build or sell an asset, another for arranging the financing, another for underwriting that financing, a management fee (typically 1.5 per cent) on the fund the asset goes into, a performance fee on top of that (usually 20 per cent over a pre-agreed benchmark), and eventually fees on selling the asset too.

As Macquarie was coming to realise, it could get away with this because of the emergence of infrastructure as an asset class that they were helping to create. Pension funds, like the rapidly growing Australian superannuation sector, were beginning to see infrastructure as a lucrative alternative to fixed income, such was the predictable and dependable nature of the underlying cash flows, and the typical strength of the yields Macquarie could still generate on an infrastructure fund even after skimming as many layers of fees from it as possible. Where private equity could shoot the lights out with returns but would be volatile and erratic along the way, Macquarie was offering exposure to regulated assets that weren't suddenly going to suffer from wild gyrations in cash flow or an unpredictable outlook for success or failure.

■

In coming up with this listed fund idea, Macquarie had a well of experience to draw from: its own property team. This had been one of the first arms of the business to demonstrate the Macquarie ethos of learning from failure and refusing to give up.

Macquarie had tried to launch a listed vehicle, the Macquarie Property Trust, back in 1987, underpinned by a Lonsdale Street building in Melbourne. The 1987 crash and the cratering of the Australian property market put paid to that.

Bill Moss (no relation to Allan), who would lead the property business for several decades to come, saw opportunity in the tumultuous real estate market and troughed prices of the early nineties. He thought it was the perfect time to start acquiring assets that would increase in value in the next cycle.

Moss had been hired in 1984 by Phil Cave, who had sold his leveraged lease packaging business to Hill Samuel and stayed on. Tony Berg had asked Cave to re-establish a property division, and Cave, looking for someone with the right experience and skills to spearhead the bank's efforts, found Moss at Beneficial Finance, where he was the NSW state manager.

Moss was not immediately impressed: Cave's pitch involved a base pay rate about A$10,000 less than what he was already earning. But Cave sold the idea of building a business and the right to participate in the profit share structure. Moss, he said, would earn many multiples of his current base rate if he performed. And oh, he did.[43]

Moss had his reasons for wanting to take a risk. He had been given a shock diagnosis of a muscle-wasting disease, FSHD.[44] Already walking with a slight limp, he had been told by doctors he would likely be wheelchair-bound by 50. Wanting to supercharge his earning capacity while he could, he was ready to move.

'I didn't see that [the FSHD diagnosis] as a major problem,' Cave recalls of the discussion. 'I actually spoke to him about it and he said: look, it's a degenerative disease but I'm fine and it doesn't affect my thinking.'

Moss recalls: 'They just looked at what they thought I could do rather than any impediment. I don't think they saw the impediment. But today, I think in our society, people see the impediment.'

Cave left Macquarie in 1986 and would go on to start the private equity and turnaround firm Anchorage. The way was clear for Moss, who several former colleagues describe as sometimes difficult to deal with, but who had considerable drive and ability. He was made an executive director in the 1988 financial year, joined the powerful executive committee at the heart of the bank in January 1997, and would build a property empire for Macquarie that by 2006 was worth A$43 billion, including direct and joint investments. At its height, the property business housed nine listed trusts and 26 unlisted investment funds.

After real estate prices bottomed in 1993, the strategy gathered momentum and started going global, first in China, then Malaysia and Hong Kong. Moss also convinced Macquarie it should set up the Industrial Property Trust of Australia (IPTA), a joint venture with Lang Walker's development group, Walker Corporation. Walker, which was also a Macquarie client, had built a portfolio of projects in the nineties including Sydney's Broadway Shopping Centre, the King Street Wharf, and student housing spanning several capital cities including Melbourne and Brisbane.[45]

This time around, Moss and others wanted to take a more targeted approach to a listed property fund. They thought they could better tap into investor interest if they created sector-specific trusts, around industrial and warehouse buildings, for example, or commercial office buildings. This approach, they thought, would also help them compete against bigger rivals GPT and AMP.

The IPTA listed in late 1993, but again it would prove a hard slog for the new property fund, as capital was scarce and real estate prices slow to recover.

By this time, Richard Sheppard and Moss, flanked by mortgage operatives Tony Gill and Frank Ganis, had helped Macquarie push into securitising mortgages. This approach, which involved bundling lots of illiquid assets (in this case mortgages) together and turning them into securities that could be sold and traded, had been taking place for some decades in the USA but was relatively new in Australia.

Moss had a friendship with Aussie Home Loans founder John Symond going back to his days at Beneficial, and the duo formed a partnership that would see Macquarie securitise the fledgling non-bank lender's mortgages. Symond came to be known as 'Aussie John' and traded on a man-in-the-street image, promising to save borrowers thousands of dollars and get them a better deal. His advertising catch-cry—'At Aussie, we'll save you!'—became synonymous with the company, and also a larger push by non-bank players to shake up Australia's staid banking sector, and the cosy relationships between the nation's biggest banks.

Macquarie used a subsidiary called PUMA to bundle up the mortgages and sell them as bonds to investors, and it began accepting Aussie home loans before providing securitisation to a broader set of lenders. By 2007, ahead of a freeze in funding markets, Macquarie had securitised more than A$50 billion in home loans across Australia, Europe, Canada and the USA.

Once again, Paul Keating's path would cross with Macquarie's. Bill Moss had had a quite public spat with Prime Minister Keating about Sydney Airport flight paths over his home suburb of Hunters Hill, but after that had become acquainted with Keating and grew to like the sharp-tongued politician. After John Howard won office in 1996 and Macquarie was looking to push into securitisation markets in China, Moss thought Keating might be able to help.

'I contacted Paul Keating and I said: "Look, do you want to come and do some work for us as a consultant?" So he did, and he was so well connected to China,' Moss says.

'He got me in front of [Chinese premier] Zhu Rongji. We went in to talk about securitisation and sat there for a couple of hours and these two talked about world issues. Everything from Taiwan to US politics.'

Moss's book *Still Walking* outlines the internal resistance at Macquarie to hiring Keating: after all, he was a Labor politician. But Moss persisted as he saw the value in what he could bring to Macquarie as it expanded its property and securitisation business into Asia.

'Watching him in action was a remarkable experience; he is a brilliant, charismatic communicator and motivator,' Moss says.

■

The IPTA listing and growth trajectory, however, was taking longer than expected. Moss urged patience but, despite his assurances, Walker decided to bail, selling his share of the management company to Macquarie.

Moss was playing a longer strategic game. Real estate businesses are closely tied to the prospects of the property market and the macroeconomic environment, which explained the early sluggish performance of the fund. Thinking ahead, Moss sought to diversify the property division in an attempt to better protect it from the next inevitable sharp downturn in valuations. Getting into assets such as university housing, conversions of commercial buildings to residential and later owning childcare centres would see his division earning more stable income and annual funds management fees. In later years he would go further, launching a leisure trust managing assets including bowling alleys, marinas, theme parks[46] and fitness centres. At one point Macquarie also moved into disability taxi services, but this venture was sold off in 2008 due to the stranglehold established taxi players had in the industry.[47]

Just two years after the IPTA IPO, Macquarie's property unit established the CountryWide property trust, focused on shopping centres, raising A$123 million.[48] It was the start of an onslaught. The North America-focused Macquarie ProLogis would follow, and in the unlisted space, the China Housing Investment Fund. Another unlisted fund, Bermuda-headquartered Macquarie Global Property Advisers, was jointly owned by Macquarie and the staff who had bought themselves out of Lend Lease.[49]

In the late nineties, the bank's stable of sector-specific property funds was rebranded to include the Macquarie name. The bank joined with wealthy investors to set up a residential investment program for developments in China's housing market.

As the empire developed, so too did the structures. Macquarie became the first property fund manager to introduce performance fees,[50] which kicked in above a threshold rate of return. These fees would become a hallmark of Macquarie funds from property to infrastructure, and would be adopted by the broader industry too, with a fair amount of controversy along the way.

Next came a new bout of deal-making: mergers between existing trusts. The landmark event here would come in 2000 when the Macquarie Industrial Trust was merged with the Goodman Hardie Industrial Property Trust, creating the largest owner of industrial assets in Australia.

■

Over in another part of the business, a group of Macquarie bankers was conducting a piece of work for Sydney Water that would lead to an odd coupling between the bank and Australian golfing great Greg Norman,[51] the 'Great White Shark'.

Tony Fehon, a former Macquarie auditor at Pricewaterhouse-Coopers alongside Greg Ward (who would also join Macquarie), had come on deck with the bank in 1994 and was soon advising Sydney Water on the best use of the Botany wetlands that flanked the city's airport. Fehon and the team surveyed a raft of options and came to the conclusion that if the golf courses in the area were brought up to championship level, they could create a more attractive gateway to Australia's best-known city.

Somehow word got out, and their work piqued the interest of Norman's right-hand men, Bart Collins and Bob Harrison, who

had joined the golfer in 1988 to work on strategic business opportunities and golf course design. It wasn't long before Bill Moss and
other Macquarie executives were attending a meeting with Norman's
entourage and trying to get a sense of how serious he was about
course development.

By 1996 Macquarie and Norman had negotiated a joint venture
called Medallist,[52] and together they compiled a detailed list of at
least 50 potential projects. Two years on, however, not a lot had
emerged from the grand plan of designing and developing top-notch
golf courses, and Bill Moss was getting frustrated.

He turned to Fehon to get to the bottom of the US delay, sending
him to Florida[53] to find out why the team was not executing on
deals. Fehon led the team to whittle down the list and prioritise the
projects, starting with two.

He didn't hold back in what one of his colleagues dubbed the
'pineapple' meeting—meaning he was fearful of getting hit with
the 'wrong end of the pineapple' if decisions and action on the golf
courses weren't forthcoming.

The signing of the two initial deals had the desired effect and the
team was soon teeing off.

Medallist's first deal was in Pelican Waters, in Australia's Sunshine
Coast in Queensland. It was also perhaps a sentimental decision for
Norman: the sunshine state was where he grew up.[54]

Next came the first home building joint venture at the eighteen-
hole championship courses at the Tiburón Golf Club in Naples,
Florida, in the USA.

Moss's book cites inspiration from Norman: 'His mottos, Attack
Life and Tough as Nails, were phrases I could relate to because when
I met Greg I was living these phrases.'

By 2000, Macquarie's annual report showed Medallist was developing projects worth A$550 million. Ultimately, ten golf course

projects and three Norman developments were completed during the bank's putting days across the USA, South Africa and Australia. Macquarie's real estate empire would, however, face its biggest test during the global financial crisis—but more on that later.

■

In federal politics after the 1996 election, privatisations were also firmly in the spotlight as the new John Howard government moved to sell one-third of telecommunications and infrastructure group Telstra. It was a politically charged deal but a chance for Macquarie to nab a role in a selldown worth more than A$14 billion. While it missed out on a marquee role as a joint global coordinator,[55] Macquarie took a lead manager spot on the portion being sold into the Americas.

Allan Moss had been involved in Macquarie's pitch alongside Alastair Lucas and others. Goldman Sachs pulled out all the stops, even flying out then global co-chief executive Jon Corzine and father of the modern initial public offering Eric Dobkin[56] to help the head of its Australian office on the pitch.

Not that Goldman's Australian boss was short of confidence. His name was Malcolm Turnbull, and he would later switch to politics and become Australia's 29th Prime Minister.

■

In 1998, Anthony Kahn, who had been working for Macquarie in North America, was called back by Caldon and Moore to run the infrastructure funds management business. ITA was, at the time, the only listed infrastructure vehicle Macquarie had.[57]

The stars were aligned for infrastructure as an asset class. Interest rates were on a long downward trend, increasing the value of infrastructure assets as yield became more scarce from bonds. And then there was demographics: Kahn had been deeply affected by a book called *Boom, Bust and Echo* that had followed the evolution and power of the Baby Boomer generation. 'I was very much of the view that demographics were driving at least 70 per cent of what we do, and 30 per cent was uncertain,' Kahn says. 'We were also lucky: all the trends were in the right direction.'

Government, too, was getting on board. Public–private partnerships (PPPs) were gathering momentum around the world, led by the UK with Australia close behind (Macquarie had nothing to do with the origins of this particular structure, aligning itself with an existing idea). PPPs were, and remain, controversial from a political perspective. On the plus side, they provide governments with the capital to build or refurbish more infrastructure than they could otherwise afford, and transfer risk to the private sector. On the other hand, they are associated with questions about accountability and transparency, and the public tends to get very angry when they result in increased costs, particularly on infrastructure once considered public.

Bob Carr had become New South Wales premier in 1995, and would adopt the public–private partnership model for two landmark projects, the Lane Cove Tunnel connecting the M2 motorway to the approach roads to the city of Sydney, and an east–west cross-city tunnel. What he liked about it, in the cross–city tunnel in particular, was that '[t]here was not a cent of taxpayer contributions. There was a toll, but it wasn't much more than the price of a cup of coffee to get a dramatic saving in your travelling time. And its great advantage—the killer argument—was that it shifted risk: if it didn't achieve the traffic numbers and toll revenue that were expected, the loss of revenue would not fall on the state budget, it would fall on the private sector,' Carr tells the authors. On that one, he even managed to get the winning bidder to contribute A$100 million for roadworks elsewhere, so that far from being subsidised, the private sector was itself subsidising road improvement. 'This is a project so pure in the PPP sense that it simply would not have been built if it had required state government revenue.'[58]

That wasn't a Macquarie deal—and was, in financial terms, an absolute dog for the winning consortium[59]—but the principle was important: state government seeing the merits in the model. 'Macquarie was part of this process,' Carr says. 'They were an active bidder, they mobilised capital, and sometimes they won a contract, sometimes they lost.' He recalls Macquarie proposing an extension of the Bondi rail link to Sydney's landmark Bondi Beach, which the two sides got as far as investigating and costing, although eventually the fares required to compensate the consortium for the outlay were considered prohibitive and the idea was shelved.

Also, while Macquarie had developed a reputation for pushing the tax concession laws absolutely to their limit, their relationship with government was not as fraught as one might think. 'I never found Macquarie argued after the event,' says Peter Costello, who became federal treasurer in 1996 and often crossed swords with Macquarie, and more specifically Nicholas Moore, on arcane matters of tax. 'It was: "these are the rules of the game, we exploited them to the full. If you want to change the rules, we'll abide by whatever the new rules are." And you knew that they would exploit the new rules to the full as well.'

Costello sees a certain gamesmanship in all of this—'they were very entrepreneurial, and sometimes too entrepreneurial, and had to be pulled back'—and is, on balance, a great admirer of the innovation Macquarie took on Australia's behalf to the world. 'They engineered tax breaks to within an inch of their lives, and I had to close them down [the infrastructure bonds]. But it gave rise to an industry that went overseas and I always thought that was good for Australia.

'I didn't like my tax system being gamed, but I wasn't so worried by them doing it to other countries.'

Macquarie's infrastructure advisory and funds management teams set about finding more assets, and were drawn increasingly to those outside of Australia, where they could apply the expertise learned at home to new markets. In 1999, ITA was renamed the Macquarie Infrastructure Group (MIG). We will meet it, and Macquarie's burgeoning listed infrastructure business, again shortly—in Canada.

■

In the summer of 1998, something happened in Russia that would have an unexpected and transformational impact on Macquarie's future.

That year, a perfect storm of circumstances hit the Russian currency: an artificially high fixed exchange rate, a vast fiscal deficit, the economic aftermath of war in Chechnya, declining national productivity, the Asian financial crisis, declining foreign exchange reserves and a dismal failure in financial management generally.

This was the Russian financial crisis, which led to an International Monetary Fund bailout and eventually the devaluation of the ruble and the Russian Central Bank defaulting on its debt.

Among the financial victims of all of this was Bankers Trust (BT),[60] which had built a large position in Russian government bonds.

Seizing the day, Germany's Deutsche Bank stepped in and agreed to purchase BT for US$10.1 billion, finalising the deal on 4 June 1999. There was plenty Deutsche liked about BT, but among the things it felt it didn't need were the bank's impressive operations in Australia, apparently because Deutsche at the time already had a good business there.

'I always remember, when my business was acquired by Macquarie, we had a meeting at the Wentworth across the road from BT's head office with [Deutsche chief executive] Rolf Breuer,' remembers Cathy Kovacs, who was a salesperson at BT. 'And this big German man with his pocket handkerchief told us how much he loved our business.' There were Swatch watches for staff.

'And then the executives came down from their office in Grosvenor Place to our dealing room, looked under the hood, and said: we don't want it. And the next thing we knew we were being sold to Macquarie.'

For the time being, Deutsche decided to keep BT's asset management division, which would end up going to Westpac some years later. But the investment banking arm? Well, that was up for grabs.

It was quite the prize, and Macquarie's bankers had the respect for it that one boxing champion has for another. 'BT in Australia was an outstanding organisation,' says Allan Moss. 'They were our number one rival. We always thought they were our most formidable competitor.'

Over at BT, the feeling was mutual. 'I'd been at Bankers Trust for thirteen years, I was a loyal BT person,' remembers Murray Bleach. 'I absolutely hated Macquarie. They were the enemy, and I was going to get them.' He's smiling: he would go on to run the Americas for Macquarie.

'We were always competing against Macquarie,' adds Kovacs. 'Whether it was equity brokerage, futures brokerage, derivatives brokerage, the warrants market, we competed with them. They were arch-rivals.'

Acquiring BT Australia? Taking all of that competitive zest out of the market and instead bringing the whole force of them onto your own team? Macquarie's top brass were seduced by the idea. 'The idea that you could be buying your major competitor . . . how fantastic!' says Greg Ward, Macquarie CFO at the time.

It looked a good fit and, better still, it wasn't at all obvious who else might buy it. Post Asian financial crisis and Russian crisis, the usual global candidates were bruised and conservative.

By now, Macquarie had form for acquisitions, though none so bold as this one. 'We had a long history of buying businesses when people had invested in the good times, then sold out in the bad times,' says Moore. It was a process that began after the 1987 crash and the subsequent recession, most prominently with the acquisition of Security Pacific Australia Limited in 1992.[61] Being strong enough through the business cycle to seize opportunities when they presented themselves would be an enduring Macquarie trait, never more so than after the global financial crisis.

Below the top level, enthusiasm for the BT idea was more restrained. Gail Pemberton was in London recruiting, and suffering from flu, when Moss called her saying the BT deal was back on. She flew back immediately and recalls a meeting with business leaders a few day later in which Moss argued that this was a one-off opportunity that they should grasp. In her recollection, in that whole group of people, 'the only person who expressed the slightest amount of enthusiasm was Nicholas Moore. Everyone else was: I think it would be a lot of trouble and a distraction.'

Moss got his way, but he did intuitively accept that Macquarie should not be over-eager. 'We really, really wanted it, but we didn't want to pay too much for it, because we knew we were probably going to have to pay twice, in a sense,' he says—once to Deutsche and then one way or another to retain the BT staff.

Moss reasoned that the price would fall, which it did. Deutsche had an equation to consider: if they just closed the place they would have to pay redundancies to everyone. At a certain point it would make greater financial sense to sell for a bargain price to someone who wanted to keep the staff or would pay for those redundancies.

'Eventually they got to a point where they really didn't want it after about nine to twelve months,' Moss says.

'Allan wanted to wait for the call,' Moore says, 'and he was right, it came before too long.' He and Moss went to see Ken Borda, who ran Deutsche in Australia, and basically agreed the deal there and then.[62] The details have never been disclosed, but Moss recalls 'we basically got it at book value'.[63] It is thought that Macquarie paid about A\$100 million, which is nothing for a truly transformational acquisition.

■

When news started to spread, and interviews commenced, the BT loyalists gathered. Murray Bleach got together with his friend Andrew Hunter. 'I remember us saying to my wife: we couldn't look ourselves in the face if we went to Macquarie, right?'

That attitude barely survived the weekend. Bleach saw Nicholas Moore the following Monday; Moore reminded him of a deal Bleach had beaten him to on South Australian railroads, and said he wanted Bleach to come across, bringing a key trams and trains deal with him. 'So in a matter of hours, we were card-carrying Macquarie boys, proud as punch. Never missed a beat.'[64]

Others had deep-seated preconceptions that had to be dealt with. To Andrew Low, who had been at BT since 1991, 'Macquarie was the arch-rival, the silver-tail, Harvard crew, and we were the kids from the other side of the track.' Alastair Lucas and Simon McKeon were enlisted to talk him round. 'It took some convincing. But obviously it was a terrific thing, for me and for pretty much all the people that came across.'

Tim Bishop, initially sceptical, recalls a town hall Allan Moss gave to BT staff, which he says convinced much of the group it was a good move.[65] 'We were won over by his humble nature and the genuineness of his words: the way it came across about how valued we would be.' But it was Moore's enthusiasm that stuck with him. 'Nicholas was up to his neck with passion,' Bishop says. 'A big part of Nicholas's brilliance is his ability to draw out the key elements from something complex.'

Another who was convinced was Alex Harvey, who had been in investment banking at BT and would go on at various times to be head of Asia, head of Telecommunications, Media and Technology and CFO at Macquarie.

It's also striking how many would go overseas and be successful: Bleach would run America, Andrew Low and Alex Harvey would both be heads of Asia at different times, Andrew Hunter would end up running London, and John Walker would build the South Korea business. In Australia, in the years after integration, Tim Bishop would head for the top of Macquarie Capital globally and Michael Cook would lead client coverage, while Mary Reemst would become CEO of Macquarie Bank Ltd following a change to the holding company structure after the global financial crisis. Bishop would also end up taking over from Bleach as head of Macquarie in the USA, and went on to become the first BT executive to join the Macquarie Group executive committee.

'As it turned out,' Low says, 'it was mostly the BT crew that powered Macquarie to take over the world.'

Oddly, the most senior, Peter Warne, did not immediately come across; he was made redundant, marking a theme of his engagement with Macquarie, which had rejected him for a job back in 1980. But much later Warne would be invited to join the board in 2007 and would be chairman from 2016 to 2022.

In fact, only two of the eleven members of BT's management committee, Rowan Ross and Michael Cook, moved across, which was perhaps significant. 'There's a bunch of senior folk who didn't become part of the Macquarie story,' says Tim Bishop. 'But you go down one rung, to people of my generation, I think there was a great sense of freedom for us.' Bishop had just made his name at BT with a real estate deal for what would become Goodman Group. Macquarie, upon acquiring BT, therefore told him to go and hire some people and build a real estate advisory business. 'That would never have happened for me at BT. At Macquarie I was given freedom and confidence to explore and build something.'

And even if BT's top brass didn't come across, that didn't dilute the ability of those who had worked for them. 'The quality of people that came across was first rate,' says Bill Best.

Integrating a deal of this size was not straightforward. Greg Ward, then CFO, remembers it as one of the first great challenges in his role, running due diligence and integration with Moore, who was the transaction lead. 'It was a very big undertaking at the time. Their balance sheet was bigger than ours.' Thus, Macquarie's balance sheet more than doubled[66] and risk-weighted assets went up 70 per cent to A$8.5 billion, though a series of capital raisings kept the capital adequacy ratio intact.[67]

The situation was further complicated by the fact that Macquarie was in the middle of fitting out its brand-new offices at 1 Martin Place, in a tower placed above Sydney's old General Post Office building[68] that deftly maintained the gorgeous Sydney sandstone of the nineteenth-century facade. 'We had to restack floors in Martin Place, because we went from two dealing floors to four, and dealing floors are very technology-intensive,' says Pemberton. She and her team had to interview individually a large proportion of the 900 BT people to establish if they would join or not (530 jobs were offered and 450 joined[69]), find the right place for them to be, and create temporary network connections between Martin Place and Bond

Street. This did, though, have the advantage that absolutely everyone was starting in a new dealing room at the same time.

In terms of personnel, there was not quite the difference people were expecting. 'Culturally I think they were very, very similar in terms of the quality of individuals,' says Ward, noting that many of them went on to have successful careers at Macquarie. 'It was just a wonderful acquisition. I think for most people, after some initial trepidation because it was us against them and they were joining the competitor, it was a great marriage where one plus one really added up to a lot.'

An effort was clearly made at the top not to be too them-and-us. Kovacs recalls being 'in the BT dealing room, minding my own business. And all of a sudden Allan Moss was standing next to me, in his unassuming kind of way, saying to everyone: hi, I'm Allan.' It occurred to Kovacs she had never seen the head of BT in the dealing room. But further down in the trenches, it wasn't quite the same. 'It was very us and them for a long time in the business I was in. You were definitely made to feel like you were the new kid on the block and you had to prove yourself.'

She recalls no formal process of integration, but simply an attitude: 'they would say, the most important thing is the talent that walks out of the business every day.' Like Bleach, having been so competitive with Macquarie, she had expected to serve out the minimum required before moving on. 'But I ended up staying for ten years.'

For Bleach, who had been so against the whole idea of moving, he was pleasantly surprised both by Moore's accommodation and by the similarities in ethos. 'Both organisations were growing, hungry, fighting,' he says.

Low remembers that when the BT team arrived at Macquarie's offices, they were mixed up to avoid a sense of BT people being in one corner, Macquarie in another. 'They also didn't fudge the hard questions about who's in charge, which is the mistake that people make, particularly in professional services.'

Others do recall crucial differences, though. Warne notes that Australia was home and head office for Macquarie, whereas BT bankers in Sydney had always reported to New York, which was a significant shift for them.

For Mark Johnson, attitude to risk was an issue. 'We found that the BT dealers exceeded their limits almost as a matter of nonchalance,' he says. 'Because they had a big brother behind them who hadn't enforced this discipline. In Hill Samuel and Macquarie, all limit breaches were reported to the board.'

And Oliver Yates thinks there was a sinister change that came with the acquisition. 'The organisation was politics-free until we bought BT,' he says. 'That was a very significant structural change in the organisation.

'Many of those people who had grown from the Macquarie side hadn't needed to play politics. Then the BT staff arrived, who were very good at playing politics, and the old Macquarie family were completely blindsided by this game, because we'd never played it. It was kind of like they infected us with a virus which most people had no idea how to defeat.'

Be that as it may, Yates has one of the best stories about the BT acquisition. He was in his home in Scarsdale, New York state, one day, when his neighbour who worked in the same area said: you've got this whole team arriving from BT.

This was news to Yates, who checked it out, and it turned out BT Australia owned a bullion book[70] whose traders were in New York.

'When they worked that out, Deutsche Bank started going around with a kill disk.[71] So I told everyone to unplug their PCs, throw them in cars, and come up to our office, which they did.'

So many of them arrived that the office couldn't cope with the heat from all the computers; in a typical Macquarie just-deal-with-the-problem move, Yates ripped out the glass from the retaining windows ('there's no-one to do any of this stuff in New York, you just do it yourself, I came in on the weekend and did it'). With sufficient circulation of air to stop the whole set-up from exploding, Macquarie got the live bullion book, before returning the computers to Deutsche three weeks later. 'That actually grew the office quite significantly.'

Some took time to find their niche. John Walker had been a government official who had been headhunted into BT to spearhead government relations. He wasn't sure about Macquarie: he had meetings with Shemara Wikramanayake, Michael Carapiet and Kerrie Mather but was undecided about where best to go. 'Allan Moss heard that I was undecided, so he set up a meeting.'

Walker told Moss he had concerns about the ability of Macquarie, which had a reputation for being siloed, to work together. Moss told him: 'John, let me put it this way. We make a lot of money.' Walker stayed for another twenty years.

■

The result of all of this was 450 people joining, transforming Macquarie's niche debt markets business into one covering the whole gamut of debt finance, and bringing with it a whole new agricultural commodities business. Partly because of the deal, that year the international network of offices grew to include Chicago, Vancouver, São Paulo, Tokyo and Cape Town.

One future star who was a close observer to the process was a young Michael Silverton, now head of Macquarie Capital, but then working in a role directly for Allan Moss. His window seat to the whole thing was valuable. 'BT in 1999 was the big turning point,' he says now. 'We got hundreds of people who came in and they all had more of a global mindset than many of the Macquarie people did. We were all yearning to expand our horizons and go offshore and thought we could compete.'

BT would prove to be helpful in that respect. 'Taking over BT there was quite a sibling rivalry,' says Silverton. 'The similarities were far greater than the differences, but they were more worldly than we were. It was a really critical juncture for us.'

Chapter 5

ROGUES AND SCANDALS

Macquarie's ascendancy to the top ranks of Australian takeover advisers and respected trading house by the mid- to late 1990s was not without controversy or, at times, scandal. Investment banks seem to court controversies, and Macquarie has had its fair share. Simon Gautier Hannes, Macquarie's then youngest-ever executive director[1] and a sharp mind, was on extended leave from the bank when a deal dubbed Project Tennis—discussed further below—was entering its final set.

Hannes was described by former colleagues to the authors as super smart and a prodigious banker, particularly as he led several banner transactions for Macquarie. But coupled with those traits he was seen as a bit of a loner with odd mannerisms and at age 36 still lived with his parents in the leafy north shore suburb of Roseville, Sydney.

In 1995, Hannes led Macquarie's efforts on a much larger transaction than Project Tennis, advising John Uhrig-chaired mining group CRA Limited in its protracted and complex A$27 billion merger negotiations with UK-based RTZ Corporation. The complexity of the transaction was underscored by reports at the time saying at one point there were almost 100 lawyers working on the deal and around the clock.[2] Sleep and personal relationships were put on the back-burner as fleshing out the deal took precedence.[3]

Those negotiations would eventually be sealed with CRA merging with RTZ and becoming a dual-listed company, trading on the Australian and London exchanges, through a nil-premium marriage of equals. That was among the first times in Australia the structure had been implemented, and the joint entity was initially called RTZ-CRA. Not too long after, the company rebranded to one of the world's most recognised mining names: Rio Tinto.[4]

Hannes had been lauded within Macquarie for helping to shepherd that deal through and also providing a secret fallback plan to CRA's Uhrig should the dual-listed structure not see the light of day. Hannes was flanked on the deal by Ed Gilmartin, who had joined the firm from Hill Samuel in the UK and ended up marrying colleague Shemara Wikramanayake, the current Macquarie Group CEO.

Back to Project Tennis, though, which was a A$2 billion takeover of transport group TNT by postal and telecommunications firm Royal PTT Nederland, known as KPN. In mid-1996, Macquarie's bankers were in the thick of discussions between TNT and KPN as the parties deliberated over whether they could find common ground.

Macquarie was acting for the target, TNT—which was a long-standing client—and had in July that year also placed TNT on an embargoed list of stocks that staff were prohibited from trading. Hannes, as an executive director, had signed a copy of the embargo list that included TNT, and had also that month attended a dinner meeting at a Japanese restaurant of his division's executive directors. That dinner included going through a key document that mentioned

Project Tennis, and it was followed by a weekend trip in the Mt Buller ski fields in Victoria for Macquarie's senior bankers to talk through the potential fee haul for deals under way. A slide outlining Project Tennis showed a possible fee of A\$5 million to A\$10 million.[5]

What happens next is a torrid and confusing tale about how one of Macquarie's most senior takeover bankers lost his way.

■

Hannes had fitted Macquarie's criteria to a tee, being academically talented and quickly able to learn how to execute deals. He'd been the recipient of a Sydney Grammar scholarship in his earlier years and became a Macquarie executive director at just 29. Separately, Hannes's broader family was doing well in business through photographic firm Hanimex.[6]

But despite Hannes's pedigree, in September 1996, as juries at the NSW District and Supreme Courts would later find, he made a series of suspect cash and bank cheque withdrawals from a spate of banks.[7] Some of those were made using a disguise, which was later seized as evidence from Hannes's home. The bulk of the transactions were below the threshold of A\$10,000 that requires reporting to the financial crimes regulator. While on extended leave from Macquarie, but still with access to the office and available to consult where required, Hannes opened a cash management trust account with broker Ord Minnett using the pseudonym M or Mark Booth. Oddly, his sister Mignon's married surname was Booth, but Hannes used a mailbox address in the north shore suburb of Mosman in Sydney and was never formally identified by the stockbroking firm.

Court documents from the trial draw on evidence that Booth was asked for a passport but claimed he had forgotten to bring it when picking up documents from the Ord Minnett foyer. When a tax file number was requested, Booth told the broker he was in the process of applying for one.

One of the phone numbers he provided Ord Minnett was for the Intercontinental Hotel in Sydney where Hannes claimed Booth—a marketing consultant from the UK—was staying. The other was later found to be for the NSW Department of Health.

Hannes's version of events centred on him joining an investment syndicate, which meant he personally had nothing to do with the decisions taken. The court ruled otherwise, essentially finding that Hannes was in fact Booth, and that he had requested Ord Minnett invest A$90,000 in TNT options. At the time, those A$2 options looked highly opportunistic when the company's shares were trading much lower at about A$1.50. Choosing options provided Hannes the scope for a much bigger pay day over buying TNT shares, and each option contract was for 1000 shares.

Hannes asked then Macquarie junior Duncan Murdoch—working on Project Tennis—what his valuation range on TNT had come in at and the young banker told him the range was A$2.25 to A$3.27. The more senior operative then questioned whether the valuation was too lofty. Murdoch purportedly said it may have been on the high side, but justified by TNT's European operations. That probing question, along with accessing the Macquarie office late at night in the months prior to the deal being announced, would contribute to Hannes's undoing.

The TNT takeover was announced on 2 October, pegged at A$2.45 per share, and sent the target's stock soaring, making Booth aka Hannes a tidy sum of about A$2.04 million.

But the sheer scale of the options transactions had quickly piqued the interest of the Australian Securities Commission (ASC), which promptly opened an investigation, and within days started court proceedings against Booth and to freeze the proceeds.

As the net was beginning to close in on Hannes—still going by the name Booth—he told his Ord Minnett broker he realised there was suspicion of insider trading in TNT. Hannes provided a statement outlining the general information that had led him to believe TNT shares would rise. He denied he had any inside information but the following month faxed Ord Minnett and said he would forgo the proceeds from the transactions as he did not want the investors he bought the options from to suffer losses.

Around this time, pictures of Mark Booth in a bank branch were circulating and there was confusion and mystique about who this curious fellow was.

As one former Macquarie banker recalls, around this time Hannes was again in the Sydney office and they were chatting about something innocuous when David Poole, one of the lead advisory bankers on the TNT deal, walked past. The banker turned to Hannes and said: 'Oh, I wonder if he's Mark Booth?' He was asking in reference to Poole. He was unaware that the real culprit was even closer at hand.

■

In mid-January 1997, authorities were on the cusp of an arrest.

When Australian Federal Police officers and the ASC raided Macquarie's Bond Street Sydney digs, advisory staff still beavering away on deals were shocked. They were told to move away and wait in one side of the office, as authorities seized material from Hannes's desk and the surrounding area.

'There was a bit of disbelief: maybe it's a mistake or they've got the wrong guy. It was just such an aberration,' says a person on the fateful Macquarie floor recalling the events of that day.

Around the same time a search warrant was executed at Hannes's Roseville, Sydney, home and a range of items were also seized.

An arrest and charges soon followed and the banker—who had just recently been at the top of his deal-making game—was now himself a target having to frame his own defence.

Meanwhile, Macquarie would have to manage the enveloping crisis.

It was summer holiday season in Australia, and CEO Allan Moss was taking advantage of the quieter time to attend a meeting in the Gold Coast with a colleague and a Macquarie customer. Given the relaxed mood he had failed to switch on his phone after landing in Australia's sunshine state, and it wasn't until he arrived for the meeting that Moss got the message to call Sydney urgently.

He was told he had a message to call ASC boss Alan Cameron[8] and didn't waste any time doing so. That conversation threw up the shocking information that Hannes had been arrested for alleged insider trading and several other charges. Moss was soon on a plane back to Sydney and convening an emergency meeting with then-head of corporate advisory Alastair Lucas and about six other senior staff.

Cameron says the regulator felt an obligation to let the bank know of the Hannes arrest.

'We just thought it would be appropriate that the boss of Macquarie should know that one of his executive directors had been arrested, because we didn't know what authority he had inside the bank.

'Macquarie otherwise had quite a good reputation for compliance.'

He says the size of Hannes's trades raised the alarm with the ASC, and the transactions were eventually triangulated with the bank withdrawals to pinpoint Hannes.

'By trading in the numbers and the quantity that he did it just stuck out, it was always going to have to be investigated,' Cameron recalls.

The ASC's national director of enforcement at the time was Joe Longo,[9] who was cutting his teeth at the regulator by liaising almost daily with the Director of Public Prosecutions on pending and active cases.

After the meeting with senior Macquarie staff, Moss decided he should be the one to make contact with the accused while the bank drafted a press release for investors and the media.

'It wasn't disruptive but it was distracting,' Moss recalls of the chain of events. 'I could not have been more surprised if Simon had been struck by a meteor in Pitt Street Sydney. I said that to other Macquarie leaders and I actually meant it.

'He was a really bright guy. We had thought that he was a really ethical person.'[10]

Hannes wasn't immediately available to take Moss's call on the day of his arrest, but they spoke hours later in a phone call that would be recounted and used as evidence many times as the case and various appeals played out in court.

Hannes told Moss it was a friend who had conducted the TNT options trades and that he would not identify that person. Moss said it would be difficult for anyone to believe Hannes without him divulging the identity of his friend.

Court documents show that Moss said Hannes replied: 'My friend is blameless and I really don't want to involve him in this whole thing because he is blameless and it would be unfair to involve him in it.'

Moss wrapped up that conversation and told Hannes a press release would be forthcoming. There was an impromptu, rather than a formal, meeting of board directors, including Moss and David Clarke, and the press release was approved for distribution.

Macquarie's shares fell 31 cents to A$8.44 on the day that announcement went public in January 1997. Bankers were quickly on the phone to explain this was the alleged action of a sole banker and that Macquarie's systems and processes were robust. The bank wanted to ensure customers had faith in it and to highlight that, if Hannes was in fact guilty, he was a solitary bad apple.

Former Macquarie executive director John Green recalls being called into a high-level meeting to discuss how the bank would communicate with staff and corporate customers on the imbroglio.

'We thought it was a life-threatening moment for the organisation because it's corporate finance,' he says. 'Our entire business was dealing in confidential information and maintaining trust, so to have it alleged that one our most senior people was not just abusing the trust, but doing it illegally, was shocking.

'We had all the staff come in eight o'clock on the Monday, to tell them what was going on. Their faces were white.

'Then we divvied up our clients to ring them so they could hear it from us before they read about it in the newspapers.'

Green recalls speaking to then St George Bank boss Jim Sweeney to let him know about the incident and the stain on the Macquarie name. But after explaining the situation, Green remembers Sweeney remarking: 'Oh is that all?' Sweeney made the point that incidents like this were commonplace in financial services and Macquarie had been fortunate not to encounter one, until now.

Reports at the time said Hannes—as a highly regarded executive director at Macquarie—would have been earning in the order of a tidy A$1.6 million sum annually.[11]

A document written by Hannes but not admitted as evidence in the first trial showed that he was assessing the pros and cons of visiting the ASC to explain his version of events. Among the cons was that Macquarie might take his A$1 million in the dividend reinvestment plan as penalty if he was found to have acted inappropriately. There was also the issue of why Macquarie's Chinese walls—which are meant to protect deal confidentiality—were perhaps not as robust as they should have been.[12]

The pros included establishing his innocence and that it was the right thing to do, but for Hannes it was vital Mark Booth attend as well.

The high-profile arrest and the subsequent NSW District Court hearing caused a media frenzy. The jury, the press and the public were seeking to understand whether there was another party involved as Hannes was claiming, or otherwise what drove a successful and highly paid banker to try to game the system.

Did he just believe he was so clever that he could get away with it? Was he—given the extended leave he had taken—planning a career change and wanting a big pay day on the way out? Or was there an underlying issue that caused the lapse of judgement and the idea to trade TNT options? Was Hannes really protecting a co-conspirator who he never gave up? To this day, former Macquarie colleagues can't understand what motivated Hannes to make those fateful decisions.

■

Whatever the motive, Macquarie's reputation was dealt a blow by Hannes's actions. During this period insider trading and market manipulation cases were not uncommon, but they were something firms constantly pitching their trusted advice around town wanted to avoid.

In 1998, a landmark case saw Australia's Federal Court—via Justice Ronald Sackville—find that a London-based Nomura arbi-traging team engaged in false and misleading trading relating to the Australian Stock Exchange and Sydney Futures Exchange. The activity related to stock manipulation and buying shares from itself.

That came after the spectacular demise of Barings Bank in 1995 due to the ballooning losses of rogue futures trader Nick Leeson.

Even esteemed bulge-bracket firm Goldman Sachs had been entangled in controversy in the eighties.

A long-running scandal that hit Wall Street hard uncovered an insider trading ring. Among the casualties was Robert M Freeman,[13] Goldman Sachs's former head of arbitrage, who pleaded guilty to a mail fraud in 1989, relating to an incident of insider trading.

In Hannes's initial trial the prosecution called 45 witnesses, including three experts, while the Hannes camp had two witnesses, including its own expert. The prosecution's argument drew on a handwriting expert and technology specialist and also presented the court with Hannes's notebooks, a diary and files accessed from his computer. Evidence included four deleted files from a floppy disk seized by police, which were retrieved by the technology expert.

Hannes chose not to give evidence at the trial and became known for playing a daily game of cat and mouse with photographers tasked with getting snaps of one of Australia's most notorious bankers for their news pages. Eventually the snappers got their pics of Hannes, but only after one day placing their cameras on the ground and letting him escape as a show of respect for the lengths to which he went to evade them.

Bank tellers who served Hannes were required to give evidence, as were a long list of his Macquarie colleagues including Poole, Lucas, Mark Johnson, Geoff Joyce, and Susan Rousselot.

Research reports from stockbroking analysts suggesting TNT was a takeover target were used by the Hannes camp to point to general information in the market at the time, noting the company could become the subject of an acquisition.

The court documents made an interesting reference to a draft Macquarie research report on TNT that had changes made to it before publication, following a discussion between the analyst and Poole. The mooted takeover value in the report was amended to

A\$2.25 from A\$2.05 and the words 'TNT is vulnerable to a takeover' were removed, as were any references to KPN as a potential buyer.

After the twists and turns of the court hearing and lengthy deliberations by the jury, Hannes was found guilty of one charge of insider trading and two charges of breaching of the *Financial Transaction Reports Act 1988*.

The District Court in September 1999 imposed a sentence of two years and two months in prison and a fine of A\$100,000, but a non-parole period of eighteen months. It was the first time the regulator had secured a guilty verdict via a jury against a person who had defended insider trading charges.[14]

Hannes's first appeal in October 2000—just two months and nine days out from the end of his eighteen months jail time including time served—saw the convictions quashed and a retrial ordered.[15] The NSW Court of Criminal Appeal saw merit in the prisoner's argument that the prior trial judge had made errors in her directions to the jury, but noted a retrial was warranted.

But the retrial went a similar way to the first and the jury found Hannes guilty of the three charges. The presiding judge re-imposed the fine and sentence for insider trading, but ruled that Hannes couldn't serve the four-month sentence for the reporting offences concurrently. That meant his total sentence, not including the parole period, was extended by a further two months and he returned to prison. Hannes declined to be interviewed for this book.

Nick Minogue—who was at the bank from 1993 to 2009, including a stint as head of risk—recalls the Hannes incident prompted Macquarie to revisit its insider trading controls. He notes when other institutions suffered compliance woes the bank would also closely analyse the exact scenarios internally.

'Everything that happened in another institution, be it Nick Leeson or whatever, we always assumed that it would happen to us,'

Minogue says. 'We would want to know why it wouldn't happen and how fast we would catch it is usually a question in a trading context,' Minogue says, citing possibilities ranging from fat finger mistakes in trading rooms to all sorts of frauds that banks are susceptible to.

'From time to time we did discover slight gaps in our process which might have lent themselves to some sort of problem. There were things that we didn't expect to find in our trading systems and we would take very prompt action indeed.'

■

Macquarie would suffer further embarrassment at the hands of recalcitrant staff or former employees during the 2000s.

Former Macquarie banker Ian Chalmers, known to those close to him as 'Rocky', had already left the company when he got caught on the wrong side of the law. But references to his time at Macquarie were everywhere after criminal charges against him became public.

Rocky was hired by Richard Jenkins due to his experience in markets and stockbroking, and it didn't hurt that his psychometric test had shown exceptional results, facilitating his entry to Macquarie in 1996.

The nickname came about in the mid-eighties when Chalmers was working in the open outcry trading pit,[16] and his then colleagues thought his shouting sounded a lot like the voice of Hollywood star Sylvester Stallone. By that time, the *Rocky* movies starring Stallone as champion boxer Rocky Balboa had released a fourth sequel.[17]

In 2007, not long after leaving Macquarie as an executive director in equities, Chalmers was sentenced to prison when a jury found him guilty of being 'knowingly concerned' in the importation of a commercial quantity—in this case, 30 kilograms—of cocaine.

He was also sentenced for participating in the supply of 4.45 grams of ecstasy. It was a disturbing chain of events for those following the case at Macquarie. Chalmers had been a successful equities sales operative, despite some qualms about his behaviour.

The prosecution's case alleged Chalmers was involved in a scheme in which a courier would travel from Australia to a South American location to collect the cocaine and on return to Sydney ensure they travelled domestically but on a leg of an international flight. That would allow baggage handlers who were in on the plot to divert the suitcase and remove it from Sydney Airport, avoiding customs inspection.

Chalmers was involved in booking and paying for flights for long-time family friend, Sean North, who was never arrested or found after the events—a police arrest warrant is outstanding for Mr North but no charges have been laid—implicating Chalmers in the criminal activity. He was known for some excessive behaviour even while at Macquarie, including his expense account, and was understood to have mutually parted ways with the bank after deciding to take a period of extended leave.

For some staff, getting caught up in the high-intensity Macquarie world wasn't a positive experience. As one employee who was there around the time of Chalmers's arrest recalls: 'The culture in a nutshell was work hard, party hard—but on steroids.'

But Chalmers's drug-taking had begun while residing in London before he joined Macquarie, according to court documents.[18]

In May 2007, he was sentenced to five and a half years in prison for conspiring to import a commercial quantity of cocaine, with a non-parole period of three and a half years.

The prosecution appealed that sentence and in December that year Chalmers was dealt an even longer stay in jail. The three presiding judges increased Chalmers's sentence to a non-parole period of eight years and sentence of twelve years.

Recalling the imbroglio, Chalmers doesn't think the high-octane investment banking and stockbroking culture contributed to his run-in with the law in any meaningful way, and he maintains he was not a beneficiary of the drug importation, with authorities viewing him as a 'high-profile target'.

'Are they [bankers and brokers] out there playing hard and working hard every day? Of course, they are. I would have expected statistically that you would have had a lot more disasters,' he says.

'But I think addiction, drug use and alcohol abuse, would appear on the face of it to be a problem across the board. It doesn't matter where or who you are.'

On his sentence, Chalmers believes it was excessive given his supposed role in the drug operation. His version of events has him repaying a debt to his friend by purchasing the ticket to South America.

'I got more time for purchasing an airline ticket than people got for manslaughter and sexual assaults. So I lost a lot of comfort in the whole legal system.'

He recalls his first day in jail ,when a prison officer told him there was good and bad news.

'I said you might as well give me some good news because I'm not hearing any at the moment. Well, the good news was because of all the publicity in the newspaper, none of the inmates were going to think that I was a rock spider. I asked: What's a rock spider?

'He said that's a paedophile. But the bad news was because of the publicity in the paper, he was going to have to put me into the protection-type area. I found out later, that's even worse. It's basically where paedophiles and others like that get put anyway.'

Chalmers says various friends and former Macquarie colleagues showed him kindness and compassion through those years, and on his subsequent release. 'I never went to jail for being a professional crook,' he adds.

It wasn't just the seasoned Macquarie bankers getting into trouble with authorities. In 2005 young Macquarie employee Sean Clifford, then 23, found himself in hot water after a Sydney colleague came across a backpack beneath his desk stuffed with A$50 and A$100 bills amounting to more than A$110,000. The incident was reported to police who, upon investigating, found another A$150,000 in a safety deposit box and charged Clifford with larceny by finding.

He pleaded guilty in relation to the charge after saying he found the loot in a Sydney street in the heart of the city.[19] He dodged jail but was handed an eighteen-month good behaviour bond, with the sentencing magistrate making it clear to the youngster that if he'd handed the money in to police—given it remained unclaimed— he'd have been allowed to keep the cash.

Then there was Macquarie private client adviser and broker Newton Chan who was entangled in action with the Australian Securities and Investments Commission (ASIC) about five years later.

Chan pleaded guilty to several charges of market manipulation and one charge of providing false information to ASIC, relating to trading in Bill Express, the listed electronic payments company that collapsed in 2008 under A$250 million of debt.

Chan was convicted and sentenced to twenty months in jail, of which four months was to be served immediately.[20] He had artificially propped up the Bill Express share price by using accounts under fake names.

The Bill Express scandal also embroiled several of the payment firm's executives and board directors.

A judgment transcript by Supreme Court of Victoria Judge Terence Michael Forrest credited Chan, although he was still dealt a conviction, with assisting authorities with their broader enquiries.

'Your income was very high—in excess of half a million dollars per annum. In July 2005 you were made an associate director of MEL [Macquarie Equities Limited] and in 2008 you were made a division director,' the judgment said.

'On 14 July 2008 you were invited to Mr Ian Christiansen's [Bill Express CEO] house. There he gave you a computer memory stick with in effect "your script" for answering future questions put to you by investigators. It is to your credit that you did not stick to that script and in fact supplied that memory stick to investigators together with an account of the circumstances in which you acquired it. I regard this as strong, if slightly belated, evidence of contrition.'[21]

But one of the weirdest scandals to rock Macquarie involved its private wealth division and allegations that two advisers drugged a colleague with Valium and laxatives and then circulated photos of him passed out.[22]

The Sydney Morning Herald report showed several pictures, including one with a moustache and smiley face drawn on the victim's face. One of the emails circulated included the words: '. . . Chilean style, don't fark with me, u end up down the rabbit hole'.

The alleged incident occurred on a trip to Chile, with a news report at the time saying Cleveland Mining managing director David Mendelawitz, also a client of the firm, reported the Macquarie advisers to ASIC in relation to the claimed conduct in 2011 and 2012.

The controversy also drew out allegations of irregular share trading in the mining stock, but a threatened class action against Macquarie never eventuated.

At the time a Macquarie spokeswoman said the company had investigated the lawyers' allegations of price manipulation 'and categorically rejects that this occurred in relation to Cleveland Mining, and in relation to other small-cap companies suggested by the law firm'.

'We have informed clients that we have found no evidence of inappropriate conduct of the type the lawyers are claiming.'

Given Macquarie has more than 19,200 staff—at the time of writing—the company is bound to have issues flare up in the future.

But so far, perhaps its risk management focus has protected the firm, helping it avoid large rogue trader issues that have plagued European banks including UBS and Société Générale in the past two decades.

Considering the number and diversity of people working at Macquarie, Wikramanayake says it will inevitably have 'idiosyncratic incidents' every now and then. 'There have been individual incidents that are just not pertinent in the overall life of Macquarie; idiosyncratic things where typically one individual is involved. But we haven't had any systemic, big issues in our 53 years.'

That may be true in trading, but Macquarie did run into systemic issues within its private wealth division. More on that later.

Chapter 6

TAKING ON THE WORLD

When you look at a Macquarie operational briefing or result presentation these days, there will always be a stylish little pie chart telling you how much income comes from each part of the world. Lately, the Americas have become the most powerful force by far, driven by exceptional returns in the Commodities and Global Markets division out of Houston; in the most recent annual results before this book was published, to 31 March 2022, 48 per cent of profits came from the Americas. Australia, these days, is just a quarter.[1]

It's easy to forget how recent a development this is. Twenty years ago, in 2002, international income—the whole world put together—was 26 per cent of the total, Australia 74 per cent. It wasn't until 2006 that there was enough global income to bother breaking it down by region and, back then, Asia was the driving force.[2] Only in 2007 did Macquarie start making more from the rest of the world than it did from Australia.[3]

As we learned earlier, much of Macquarie's initial engagement with the world came through tax-based cross-border leasing structures.

In many markets, there was a modest equities business early on, and sometimes, as in Hong Kong, private wealth would prove to be the bridgehead. The forerunners of today's Commodities and Global Markets (CGM) business, such as foreign exchange and commodities trading in bullion and base metals, also took Macquarie on some of its earliest forays overseas.

In fact, international operations dated back to the 1970s and the Hill Samuel days,[4] and Macquarie had gained a New Zealand banking licence in July 1987, with the acquisition of the London and Munich broking operations of Kleinwort Hattersley Securities into Macquarie Equities coming in the 1990 financial year. But it wasn't really until a few years into Allan Moss's stewardship, and particularly the influx of worldly talent that came with the BT acquisition in 1999, that Macquarie's global voyage really gathered speed and heft.

Initially, the drive was modest. 'Allan would pay for a desk,' says John Green, who spent thirteen years at Macquarie from 1993. 'If you thought your business had something to offer in an offshore market, he would pay for your first foothold. After that, it was up to you.'

Macquarie, these days, is everywhere: the 2022 results briefing identifies 62 distinct overseas offices, from the world's major financial centres to the relative obscurity of Braintree, Essex, Boise, Idaho, or Hsin-Chu, Taiwan. If one counts employees within businesses owned by Macquarie's funds, the group employs 212,000 people internationally, compared to about 15,000 in Australia.[5]

We don't propose to tell the story of how Macquarie ended up in all of these places and what they did when they got there: there just isn't room. Instead we'll give you a few stories. Elsewhere, you can read our roadtrip across the assets and businesses of the USA. And in this chapter we will take you to some quite distinct places that tell us much about how Macquarie takes on the world and, usually, wins: South Korea and Canada, with a trip to Europe in between.

■

Seoul Searching

You land in Korea's Incheon International, the modern island airport that serves Seoul, and you catch a taxi in to the city.

Maybe you take the northern route, the airport expressway over the Yeongjong Grand Bridge, from which as you cross the sea you can see mountains to your left, the North Korea border winding invisible amid them. Or perhaps you take the newer route south to beat the traffic, over the Incheon Grand Bridge, at 12.3 kilometres the longest in the country, a grand cable-stayed design that speaks of national ambition. Either way, you've already crossed paths with Macquarie well before you've got to your hotel, and you'll probably do so again when you hit the toll roads on the mainland.

There's a lot we can learn about Macquarie's international approach and distinct internal culture from South Korea. Whether you call it a rise and fall or a practical streamlining, Macquarie's 25-year journey from nothing to a 400-staff powerhouse back to something half that size is a microcosm of how the Australian firm does things, and approaches new ideas.

It's also useful to look at as a reminder that, in the early days of expansion, Macquarie focused quite logically on the part of the world that was closest to it. The bank opened in Hong Kong in 1994, China in 1995, and had project finance offices in Singapore and Jakarta by the mid-nineties; some of the bank's biggest future names, including Shemara Wikramanayake and Nick O'Kane, would spend time living and working in Malaysia, where the bank held a joint venture with AMMB, also known as AmBank.[6]

In March 2004, when it bought the Asian equities business of ING Bank in a deal so preposterously good Macquarie appears to have been paid to take it on rather than giving any money to ING, it brought a region-wide presence of 450 staff in cash equities sales, trading, execution, research and equity capital markets across ten Asian nations, and it felt like this was the future. Macquarie became the largest issuer of equity derivatives in Hong Kong, and top for listed warrants in Singapore, where it would launch an Asian regional hub for fixed income, currency and commodities.[7] As an investment bank it would be bookrunner on some of Hong Kong's true landmark IPOs, such as Agricultural Bank of China, China Minsheng Bank and China Zhongwang Holdings.[8] By 2010, Macquarie was—briefly, as it turned out—using the phrase 'Asia-Pacific' a lot and bracketing Australia within it.[9]

But that presence was trimmed and refocused. Today, when one looks at those income pie-charts and sees Asia at just 7 per cent of the total, the first question is always: why isn't Asia bigger than this? But we'll come back to that.

A brief primer on modern South Korea: after the Korean war ended in 1953, the South rebuilt through a policy of industrialisation based on exports, and driven through a clutch of family conglomerates called *chaebol*. These are groups like Samsung and Hyundai that, even today, are so diversified it seems there's nothing in modern Korean life they don't touch.

Powered by manufacturing, South Korea developed from a wartorn husk to a modern developed country between the sixties and the nineties, and for a time was the world's fastest-growing economy: the miracle on the Han River, as they used to say.

But then, in 1997, came the Asian financial crisis—the IMF crisis, as they still call it in Seoul, leaving no doubt whom Koreans blame for it—and the collapse of the currency hammered the country afresh. A change was needed, and while government would remain at the core of pretty much everything, the state decided to move from central planning to something more market-oriented. They wanted a shift to high technology industries, they wanted more exports, and they wanted more infrastructure to help it happen.

Enter Macquarie.

'What other firm says: post-currency crisis Korea wants to retool its economy and is going to need better ports, roads, bridges and tunnels to be the building blocks of economic growth, so I'm going to get a plane over there and create a business around building and operating those assets?' says Ben Way, now head of Macquarie Asset Management and for several years Macquarie's head of Asia. 'We didn't have any other presence in Korea, and we didn't have anyone that spoke Korean, but we're going to get up and go and do it.

'It was genuinely innovative and groundbreaking and not without risks.'

In 1998, in the aftermath of the Asian financial crisis, Macquarie did have a cross-border leasing presence in South Korea but not much else.[10] One of the first people to be sent up to do something about it was John Walker, a government relations specialist who had come across in the BT acquisition.

Struggling to find a niche after joining, he attended a mid-year conference in which Nicholas Moore said that being dominant—as Macquarie was in many Australian businesses—was a very bad place to be. Inspired, Walker walked right up to Moore and told him he wanted to go and build a business. They settled on Korea, where he could use his government relations skills. Walker visited briefly on a global tour, and a few weeks later moved there on a one-way ticket.

'At one point there was a rumour going around that if the phone rang in Sydney and you didn't recognise the number, don't answer it,' says Walker. 'It might be John Walker and you might end up like him, on a one-way flight to Korea, divorced, with your life changed.'

Macquarie started out by forming joint ventures—more of them than they ever created in any other single country.[11] They did so with a lot of local institutions that were actually in competition with one another, but managed the process by doing different ventures in different areas. So they struck a deal with Kookmin on treasury in 1998, with IMM Asset Management on funds management in 2000, and later Woori Bank on equity and commodity derivatives in 2003.

'Macquarie was a no-name in this market, so the best way to penetrate into the market was to have joint ventures with big local names,' says Eric Kim, senior managing director in Seoul and head of the office today.

The most significant of these ventures was with a leading local bank called Shinhan, and the two agreed to look at infrastructure together.

This was a classic example of taking what Macquarie knew at home and trying it out somewhere else. There was no real culture of private sector ownership of infrastructure in Korea, and initially Macquarie didn't get its assets from the state but from construction companies, which would participate in toll road deals as equity investors and receive long-term off-take agreements and revenue guarantees from the government. When those construction companies wanted to free up some equity to bankroll whatever their next project was, they would sell It. 'So, it was a no-brainer for us to step in and invest in all the good toll roads at the time, including the road you probably drove in on,' says Kim.

To Walker, it was a perfect example of the 'freedom within boundaries' terminology that was adopted in about 2002, an evolution of Moss's 'loose–tight' philosophy. 'You felt as though you were an entrepreneur, but with support,' he says; he could call Moore or Carapiet for help at any time. 'And the fact that the company had a bias for saying yes was really important.' Walker recalls an occasion when the Grand Incheon Bridge was up for tender, and a British developer thought they had the deal stitched up only for it to fall through.

Walker and colleague Hajir Naghdy[12] held a meeting at the Grand Hyatt with the stakeholders, phoned Carapiet after the meeting, and a week later had approval for A\$200 million of Macquarie's balance sheet in order to take part. 'At the signing ceremony the local banks couldn't believe it,' Walker says. 'And it just came down to that discussion between me and Michael. Being able to move with that agility really put us ahead of people.'

The importance of local cooperation is perhaps particularly important in infrastructure, an early learning of Frank Kwok, then a rising star and now the head of Macquarie Asset Management Real Assets for Asia-Pacific. 'When you invest in infrastructure, you can never move that infrastructure, so it is where it is,' he says. 'And the thing that you need to manage is stakeholders, because an infrastructure asset is there to serve the community. So if the community doesn't want you there you're not going to make a good investment. You really need to understand the local dynamics.'

In 2003 the team founded the Korea Road Infrastructure Fund, unlisted and a great novelty at the time, and made their first investment into a road in Gwangju. By the end of that financial year, they had secured exclusive or preferred positions in six other toll roads in South Korea. A year later they had achieved a third close, with commitments of A\$714 million, and had added the Baekyang Tunnel and Machang Bridge to the pile.

They were able to do all this through a combination of circumstances. Walker in particular had experience working with governments. They built a team of locals who understood the market: Kim, who runs the business today, was hired by Walker in 2002. The team knew how to run infrastructure. And they also had experience of talking institutional money into wanting to be infrastructure investors.

Korea has a strikingly powerful and increasingly sophisticated pension fund sector—today, its National Pension Fund is on track to be the biggest of its kind in the world—and even then, its demographics were exceptional: a young population in a growing economy with increasing wealth and a state that wanted to ensure there were mechanisms for them to be financially secure in later life.

Macquarie tapped into Shinhan's relationships with Korean 'instos', explained the long-term nature of infrastructure and why it was perfect for pension funds, and away they went. 'Most of the investors we got money from, more than 90 per cent, were domestic investors in the Korean market,' says Kim. 'We were pioneering in educating them about infrastructure: that this was a really good cash-yielding business and asset class, perfect for insurance companies and pension funds, with long-term asset-liability matching solutions.' Korean funds were soured by the experience of the Asian financial crisis, but the stable characteristics of infrastructure, as sold by Macquarie, resonated.

'We had a slow start in the beginning,' Kim says. 'We had to explain what Macquarie was, why an Australian bank was here, what was our speciality, why infrastructure.' But he recalls a 'big bang when everyone was jumping in,' after which they never looked back.[13]

Walker adds: 'It was a little bit seat of your pants. We didn't have a compliance officer. Later on people became more sceptical of the adventurous model, but it worked.'

Macquarie was trying plenty else besides, in its usual manner of empowering people to try out new ideas and see if they worked. The rest of the industry looked on, bamboozled.

'We used to see them just running around, trying everything they could think of, just crashing into each other around town, and think: what the hell are these people doing?' says a banker at a leading international bank in Seoul. 'Who are they? But now I realise that's what they were doing. Trying new ideas to see what worked.'

Sandra Interdonato was on the Korea staff in the early days. 'There was such an energy about what we were doing, such a buzz,' she says.

'Well before we listed MKIF [Macquarie Korea Infrastructure Fund], we were the first real infrastructure players in Korea. We were paving the way, speaking to regulators, accountants and lawyers.'

With so little policy and regulation in place for this emerging industry, Macquarie worked with third parties to help put it together, in some sense designing the very framework within which they would thrive.

'We were all working incredible hours,' says Interdonato. 'But we loved what was going on. Putting your mind to something and going after it. Not seeing problems or roadblocks as hindrances and blockages but working with people to get it done.'

Nick van Gelder, a key figure in the Macquarie infrastructure story in Asia, would make his name here before dying tragically young. David Russell and Adam Ballin, who would go on to earn a fortune after establishing their own renewable infrastructure firm, Equis, also spent crucial years in the Macquarie team in Seoul.[14]

Korea was getting noticed by head office. By 2005, the Incheon Expressway graced the front cover of Macquarie's whole annual report.[15]

It was not always easy. South Korea has its moments of flamboyant corruption, and is politically charged to a degree that makes Canberra look like a yoga retreat. Korea has complex relationships between national, provincial and city governments, and no culture of lobbyists. Every time the government changes, a host of senior figures either on the other side of the political landscape or in major companies that were considered to be friendly to the old guard, end up in jail. Most *chaebol* have had a chairman or two imprisoned, and nobody seems much surprised when it happens, least of all the chairmen.

For Walker, this meant trying to convince Macquarie's compliance department to allow them to bank convicted felons, because if they couldn't, then there wasn't really anyone major left to advise.

'How do you advise a company on an M&A [mergers and acquisitions] deal when the chairman's in jail?' he says. 'One of Macquarie's great strengths is compliance, so how do we manage to work with so many groups where the chief executives were convicted criminals? I was flying to Sydney virtually every month to meet compliance.'

And in practice the bank did get on some big deals through Macquarie Capital, notably advising SK Telecom on its US$3 billion acquisition of Hynix Semiconductor in 2012, a marquee deal, and helping another *chaebol* company, Daewoo International, sell down Kyobo Life Insurance for US$1.1 billion.

Walker's relationships with government were so good that they were able to draft the legislation that allowed Macquarie to list its own fund. It also tried to support the government in its efforts to develop the capital markets, travelling around the world with the Financial Supervisory Service (FSS) regulator, speaking at its events. Walker made sure to make it clear to the government Macquarie had their back: he got into an on-stage dispute at New York's Plaza Hotel with LoneStar, the controversial foreign raider that spent years trying to buy Korea Exchange Bank. Walker took the government's side on stage, but didn't hesitate to be outspoken in private.

Moore had spoken to Walker about the idea of cultural generosity, of ensuring that others like government would share in the success. With this in mind, there was once an occasion where Macquarie had won a sell-side advisory mandate to a group that was selling a toll road. But the creditor bank wanted Macquarie, as a foreigner, squeezed out. Walker said he understood the man's impossible position and, to the considerable chagrin of Sydney, waived the million-dollar binding fee. 'My guys wanted to kill me.'

'Later that day, a cheque for a million dollars came. He paid us the fee anyway, the most honourable business practice I've ever seen. It was about communication.'

After Macquarie took over ING's Asia equities business in 2004, bringing in a securities team, the Korean business was humming. It peaked at a staff of about 400, frequently doubling profits annually. 'From 2002 to 2007, we were growing greatly every year,' says Kim.

Walker would be brought on to the global analyst calls and results briefings. Real estate got involved, listing the Macquarie Central Office Corporate Restructuring REIT (real estate investment trust) on the Korean Stock Exchange in 2004. The toll road fund was rebranded Macquarie Korea Infrastructure Fund (MKIF) and listed both in Korea and London in March 2006, while another unlisted infrastructure fund, Macquarie Korea Opportunities Fund, was started the same year. They launched a private equity joint venture with a group called Ilshin Investment Management.

They bought roads, subways, broadcast communication assets, energy companies, water treatment plants and a container terminal in the southern port of Busan. If one considered all the contractors and operators on underlying assets, over time Macquarie must have had 40,000 people working for it, in construction, ticket collecting, you name it. It was a responsibility. 'We used to talk about that a lot,' says Walker, 'reminding people that we are using real money, money from mums and dads.'

MKIF was a big step. 'The listed infrastructure fund was maybe the moment the market recognised us as a serious player,' says Kim. 'Listing a fund on KOSPI [Korea Composite Stock Price Index] for the first time in history. People were like: what the hell is that? And how have they become so successful?' Being listed, it would also bring Macquarie a local retail following: today the fund has almost 160,000 individual investors.

But then something seemed to change. Most of the joint ventures had run their course by now, either being unwound or bought out. The asset management joint venture with IMM had been sold to

Goldman Sachs in 2007, a decision that had brought Walker to cross purposes with Allan Moss, who used largely the same argument as when he had persuaded Walker to join all that time ago: 'It's a lot of money.' It was rumoured to be 32 times book value, an offer they couldn't refuse, but Walker didn't like what it said about commitment in a nation where that matters considerably.

'I pushed back against the sale of the IMM joint venture,' Walker says. 'I had a run-in with Allan Moss about it. We were going around the world talking about the fact that we were building a business, and then we sold the business. So it was very difficult.'

When Walker had to go in to explain himself to the deputy governor of the FSS, he was greeted with this. 'Mr Walker, there is this Korean proverb. I'm walking along the street, and a *gachi* [Korean for magpie] shits on me. And I think, what's happened? Why has the *gachi* shat on me? What's happened is you sold your licence.' Walker reflects. 'It was a very difficult meeting.'

And this represents another key Macquarie theme: the minute a business is no longer attractive, it's out. It's ruthless but effective, but the jury is still out on whether it works universally. In many Asian nations in particular, you don't get to flip in and out of businesses and their local employees and then expect to be welcomed back in again. It would be interesting to be a fly on the wall next time Macquarie wants an asset management licence in South Korea.

The global financial crisis didn't hit Asia's financial services industry anything like as badly as the rest of the world, but it did hit Macquarie's Korea operations. Kim estimates that 'a majority' of those in advisory within Macquarie Capital at the time were gone after the GFC. Worse, the same perception Macquarie had been dealing with at home and elsewhere in the world—that it found a way to take fees from every possible angle on every deal, and that it had conflicts—was playing out in Korea too.

Macquarie did grow again after this in other areas. By 2010 it had a banking services licence and was offering corporate and foreign exchange services to big local clients; it became the top name in listed warrants, only for the regulator to shut down that business after an inconvenient rule change.

And missteps were starting to appear. In 2014 Macquarie bought ING Investment Management Korea,[16] bringing A$24 billion in assets under management into the fold and becoming the largest foreign asset manager in Korea. But it never really integrated, and only moved into Macquarie's building in the final year before it was sold to a local private equity fund without ever having been absorbed.

Worse, it had serious problems internally: illegal bond trading, parking bonds at brokerages, or not properly recording their purchases, all of which happened before Macquarie bought it, but the mud stuck regardless.[17] 'Unfortunately that was not one of our better acquisitions,' says Megan Aubrey,[18] who heads external fund managers for Macquarie. 'The business we had acquired had some historically poor trading practices.' The FSS imposed a three-month partial suspension and a fine of ₩100 million (A$106,000 at current exchange rates) on the Korean arm of the funds group.

'We lost quite a few institutional clients because of that regulatory sanction,' says Aubrey. 'It felt like a local owner would be a better owner.'

The headcount is roughly half what it used to be. Walker left eventually, and the senior team is almost entirely local now, though all remember Walker, not least because of his double life as a local musician. He even released an album, complete with artwork demonstrating his double life—one picture in a suit with a binder, another in bleached jeans with a guitar. He named the record Twelve Bridges and filled it with rock tropes about highways, which seems a fitting combination of his two existences.

'Twelve bridges? That's a lot of tolls, even for Macquarie,' quipped *Euromoney*.[19]

But in infrastructure, Macquarie is as potent a force as ever. Today, as with much else in the Macquarie world, the direction is towards renewables and private equity.[20] When you go to Macquarie's office in Seoul's slick Centropolis building (fellow tenants: Credit Suisse, Carlyle, Deutsche) the Green Investment Group (GIG) logo sits next to Macquarie's in the lift lobby; GIG had a large team in Korea which is now being integrated into Macquarie Asset Management. Their work spans waste to energy, offshore wind and hydrogen, among other things.[21]

Kim, who has seen it all now, thinks the culture has changed a little. 'Macquarie is very agile, in terms of making decisions, but I think we have become a little bit more patient than before,' he says. 'Since 2009 I can feel that we are longer-term investors.

'Before then, when you had a call with the leadership team, the first question they would ask is: how much would you make out of this opportunity? Now it's: what does it mean for our investors? Is it going to hurt our reputation in the market? Looking back over the last ten years, that's how we have maintained our trust from our investors and business partners.

'But we still have that DNA that if we think it's not going to work, then we have to move quickly rather than sit on failures and do nothing about it.'

In aggregate the Korea story represents a lot of Macquarie themes. Verena Lim, today the head of Asia and a Korean-Australian herself, thinks of Korea as 'a good case study for how to build a business in a new geography and make sure that it's sustainable.'

'A lot of the growth strategy was an option play,' adds John Roberts, whose connection with Macquarie and infrastructure spans over 30 years.[22]

'Post the Asian debt crisis there was a culture in Korea which was different to many other regional countries. If you wanted decisive action to grow a business and be successful, you were better off being in Korea than I would say just about anywhere else in Asia. They have a culture of making things happen.'

■

O Canada

To the north of Toronto there is a toll road that infrastructure specialists speak of with such reverence you would think it were the Road to Damascus rather than the Road to Clarington, Ontario. Some of them get genuinely emotional when they talk about it.

'I've seen a number of toll roads in my time, and it is still hands down the best one that you would want to own,' says Michael Smerdon, Macquarie's first local executive hire in Toronto. 'If you had only one toll road to own for your life, that would be it.' Peter Salisbury, who set up the Toronto office, is similarly emotional. 'The 407 is the most beautiful toll road you've ever seen in your life. If there's a better toll road in the world now I haven't heard of it.'

Within and beyond Macquarie, they line up to praise it. 'It's a great road,' says Frank Kwok, now head of Macquarie Asset Management Real Assets for Asia-Pacific, but part of the Toronto team early in his career. Leo de Bever, former head of infrastructure at Ontario Teachers' Pension Plan: 'The reason I made one of the most advantageous investment decisions in my life is that no-one at the time really understood Highway 407.' Alina Osorio, founder and president of Fiera Infrastructure, and a Macquarie Canada alumnus: 'It's really an amazing example of value for time.'

Well, having driven it, it's a bit dull after all that praise, to be honest, but then again infrastructure specialists aren't in these things for the view. The 407 is a road of some significance for Macquarie, because it is at the heart of the group's international expansion in infrastructure. It would prove a difficult opportunity that it took Macquarie two attempts and several years to get into, but the relationships formed through those years would be enduringly important to the Macquarie story internationally. Equally significantly, the way those relationships evolved—sometimes negatively—would tell its own story about the Macquarie culture and how it needed to change over time.

The story really starts with Peter Salisbury, who had been part of the Hills Motorway deal, going to a toll road conference in Denver in 1997, for the International Bridge Tunnel and Turnpike Association, which sounds like the sort of party you really wouldn't want to miss.

Salisbury had been on the lookout for international toll roads that might present an investment opportunity for Macquarie, and realised he couldn't find any privately owned toll roads in the USA. He gave a presentation on the subject, armed with his knowledge from Australia, and afterwards an American came up to him and said: 'Son, you're a freak show. You're like the bearded woman. We don't have privately owned toll roads in America: we think it's very strange and we don't like it.' It left such an impression he would later incorporate the freak-show motif into his presentations with some pride, replete with images of people draped in pythons or sawn in half.

There was a reason for this American attitude: muni bonds. In the USA, infrastructure such as roads is usually funded with tax-effective municipal bonds that give a very low cost of finance, meaning America has not typically needed to reach out to any other form of capital to get their roads built.

Rather than being discouraged, Salisbury was inspired, shooting his mouth off to Nicholas Moore about just how Macquarie could clean up in the USA if privatisation of roads ever took off. Eventually

Moore, perhaps to get rid of him, told him: 'If you reckon you can do 300 toll road deals in America, why don't you go and do it?'

Salisbury had bitten off more than he could chew. 'I came to understand later on that the politics around this were astronomical,' he says. 'I think the privatisation of these things is probably going to happen in maybe 2150.' Salisbury's close friend Murray Bleach would go on to succeed in some US road deals in Chicago and Indiana, but neither of them ended well (see Chapter 7).

After banging his head against a wall in the USA for some time, Salisbury realised there were better opportunities to be had further north. It would come to seem like providence: when he and Michael Carapiet went to Toronto for the first time to have a look around, it turned out that ice hockey legend Wayne Gretzky's last ever match was happening that night at the Maple Leaf Gardens rink, and they went along.

Gretzky notwithstanding, the most useful thing to understand about Toronto was its geography. With Lake Ontario a natural frontier to the south, the city stretches out in the other directions, and was dissected both by a clogged foreshore route through the city and a toll-free highway further north called the 401, which, despite having as many as twenty lanes at certain points, was jammed with trucks and commuters even by the 1990s.

Further north still was a newer road, the 407, a modest four lanes at the time, which opened in 1997. By the late 1990s, Ontario's provincial government had decided to sell the road to the private sector as a toll road, with the bidders being required to commit to expand it in both length and width.

Salisbury and Carapiet set about some rudimentary research by driving the 401, which was horrendous, and the 407. As they drove, they did some simple sums. If a twenty-lane highway is at capacity and traffic is growing at 5 per cent per year, you need a new lane of traffic every year, which logically would go to the 407. 'Where on earth can you find a revenue stream that's going to grow like that?' Salisbury asked. 'So we're thinking, this is the best road we've ever seen anywhere in the world, and the prospects of this are astronomical.'

On the strength pretty much of that drive, Salisbury and Jim Miller[23] moved to Toronto in July 1998 to put a bid together, initially in combination with Bank of Nova Scotia. Others, including Anthony Kahn, would come at intervals during the bid to work on it, since the logical place for the road to go if they won it was Macquarie Infrastructure Group (MIG). Nick James, the nuts and bolts man from Hills Motorway, would also come over to present.[24]

Macquarie began hiring. Salisbury teamed up with two people from Tony Ferguson's natural resources M&A (mergers and acquisitions) team to rent an office and buy furniture. By the time Alina Osorio joined from RBC Dominion Securities some years later, she noticed that none of the desks matched, a sign of that early furore.

It was clear from the outset that the required extension of the 407, which today is 151 kilometres long,[25] was going to require a ton of money, and much more than Macquarie and Bank of Nova Scotia were going to be able to put together.

The other thing that became rapidly clear was the power and sophistication of Canada's pension and sovereign wealth funds. Ontario Teachers' Pension Plan (OTPP) and Ontario Municipal Employees' Retirement System (Omers) in Toronto, and Caisse de dépôt et placement du Québec (CDPQ, often colloquially called The Caisse) in Montreal all had billions of dollars of assets to deploy and an enlightened attitude towards the idea of new asset classes.

Salisbury is not your typical alpha Macquarie banker, with none of the swagger of some of the other leading lights who came through the system, but he did seem to connect well with Canadians, who have a particular way of doing things in which personal relationships and trust are enormously important. More than twenty years on, the biggest names of the era speak fondly about their early interactions with Macquarie, even if in many cases they would later sour.

One was Leo de Bever, who had the curious title of head of research and economics at Ontario Teachers', but was actually in charge of setting asset allocation and quantifying risks in various places and asset classes. Leo de Bever[26] is considered one of the key architects of Canadian pension engagement with infrastructure around the world.

'The status quo is a formidable opponent,' he says. 'And the status quo had no box for infrastructure.' Macquarie would help him out with that.

Leo de Bever's interest in the idea of infrastructure coincided with Salisbury opening an office for Macquarie in Toronto. 'Peter is as honest as they come, and he and I hit it off,' says de Bever. 'We struck a deal. You guys in Australia became familiar with infrastructure before we did. I want to learn from you, start investing in infrastructure, and we will provide a lot of the initial capital. And the fact that we are on board will help you to market infrastructure in Canada.'

Another key figure was Michael Nobrega, who had set up Borealis, an in-house infrastructure investor and asset manager at Omers, in 1997. When the 407 came up, 'that's when we joined with Macquarie, because we needed somebody with that type of toll road experience,' he says. 'We were not looking to them for money, but expertise: how to structure deals, working on a timeline that was 24/7.

'They were very good at that: smart guys and they worked very hard.'

A third was Ghislain Gauthier, who was in charge of infrastructure development at CDPQ, although it wouldn't be until late 2000 that infrastructure would emerge in its own right from the broader private equity division there. Salisbury came to see him in Montreal in 1998 to talk about the 407 and the toll road sector. 'I still remember, the first presentation by Peter was an eye-opener for the business,' he says. 'I remember meeting with my boss afterwards, and saying: we have an interesting project. He was looking at me like: what the hell are you talking about? But this is where it started at CDPQ.'

With the customary jostling as three major bidding syndicates came together, some of these people would end up being opponents and some partners on the 407 bid. Gauthier, having enjoyed several presentations from Salisbury, Jones and others, would phone up sheepishly some weeks later saying CDPQ was joining a bid with SNC Lavalin, the Québécois engineering and construction company, with which it routinely worked closely. Ferrovial, the Spanish infrastructure specialists, would also join that consortium.

Macquarie would eventually align with Omers and the British Columbia Investment Management Corporation (BCIMC, now known as BCI), a public sector money manager headquartered in Victoria, on Vancouver Island. Both institutions put themselves on the line for the bid. Nobrega went before his board for approval to commit up to C$1.2 billion of equity.[27] 'They looked at me and said: are you crazy? We're going to put C$1.2 billion not just in one asset class but one asset, and we've never done this before?' Omers/Borealis would eventually underwrite C$750 million of the bid, a staggering number for the time.

At BCIMC, Doug Pearce, then the fund's CEO and chief investment officer, was also on a learning curve. 'We didn't have an allocation to infrastructure at that stage,' Pearce remembers. 'But we were interested, because one of our standing attributes was that we were long-term investors. We wanted something that would provide a good solid return, a real asset.' BCIMC came in for C$250 million; Pearce would tell Salisbury it was the largest private investment they'd ever done.

For its part, Macquarie put in C$200 million to the bid through Macquarie Infrastructure Group (MIG), and Nicholas Moore later stepped up for C$150 million of subordinated debt after an expected provider pulled out. 'You've got to say, that was an incredible thing for Nicholas to do, and he did it over a weekend,' says Salisbury. Many people have a similar Moore story.

The work was absolutely intense. Smerdon had joined in December 1998 and had gone home for Christmas to Vancouver, then got a call from Salisbury saying the data room for the deal was to open on Boxing Day and he needed to come back. It was an appalling winter even by the exemplary standards of appalling Toronto winters, with the worst storms for 70 years, the city in lockdown and private vehicles banned from the roads; the army was called in and Salisbury remembers getting snowdrifts *inside* his house. Not that any of them were ever home. 'From Boxing Day straight through until the bid went in in April '99, we had one day out of the office, some random Sunday,' Smerdon says. 'Every other day it was eighteen, nineteen, twenty hour days.'

The government had deliberately made it a short timetable; Nobrega remembers it as three months from issuance of the bid invitations to deadline. There is a place at which Toronto's major bank headquarters all meet at roughly the same intersection; he remembers that at two o'clock in the morning people would go down to have a smoke—all bankers smoked in the late nineties—and would look across and see the bankers for the rival bids across the street doing the same thing.

For a time, Macquarie and its partners appeared to be in the box seat. The market rumour was that they had the most equity—about C$1.5 billion—and were going to win, and that the competitors were struggling to raise the necessary funds.

But just before the final bid day, Salisbury was on his way to visit someone and was going up an escalator from the underground when he saw SNC Lavalin Capital's chief, Pierre Anctil, and a senior colleague, Jean Daigneault. Believing their bid to be in trouble but wanting to be civil, he gave them a wave and asked: how's it going? They gave him broad smiles, ear to ear, and chuckled.

'I went back to the bid room and said: guys, we're in trouble.'

They were. The SNC Lavalin-Ferrovial-CDPQ consortium had gained a billion dollar equity commitment from Cintra, Ferrovial's toll road division. They won the bid.

The Macquarie team was devastated. 'To work that hard and then to fall short was just gutting,' says Smerdon. Salisbury recalls: 'We sulked for a week and went to the pub for lunch every day.' Kahn, who had spent a bitter winter in Canada working on the deal, was not thrilled either. The fellow bidders were stoic. 'You work three months 24/7, and then you lose,' remembers Nobrega at Omers. 'So you go to the pub. Have drinks. Drown your sorrows.'

There was a solemn moment when Macquarie had to give all the equity back: it had been a hard-money deal, in which the moment the winner was announced they were expected to give the government the money, so the whole C\$1.5 billion of equity was sitting in cash on deposit on an account. A young woman who was in Toronto from the Sydney office had to send all the money back to the equity investors in the morning before flying home to Sydney that afternoon. The team wryly reflected it would be in keeping with the mood of the day if she just took it all and ran off to Rio.[28]

Salisbury told everyone to take some time away, then regrouped. Moore had asked him if he wanted to pack up and come home or stay and keep trying to build something, and on reflection they decided two things: that there would be other things to do in Canada, and that even if they hadn't got into the 407 at the first time of asking, who was to say they couldn't get in later?

This was a fairly classic Macquarie attitude. What does failure mean? It just means you learn from it and have another go. Fail to succeed, as Moore used to say: indeed, when he became head of corporate finance, Moore had run a presentation on failing.[29] 'It was about celebrating failures,' remembers John Green, who attended. 'About learning from failures. He got people who had tried things and failed, to stand up and say this is what we did and this is where it went wrong, but this is what we learned.' Toll roads were among the stories that were told.

But at this stage it's worth asking just what was so damn special about this road.

Smerdon describes it as a combination of several things. One was geographical location, as Salisbury and Carapiet had discussed: nothing could be built in the south because of the lake, the excess traffic in Metro Toronto was growing, and so was the city itself.

Then there's the size of it. 'It's pretty rare to be able to get a road that is 140, 150 kilometres long that you can toll,' Smerdon adds.

Then there's the concession agreement. Usually these deals are about 30–35 years, but this one was 99 years. Osorio, who would join Macquarie in 2003, was at RBC and advising the government at the time, and remembers the debate about whether it should be 25 years, 99 or even in perpetuity; the decision was that 99 years was long enough to get significant value from the private sector but without transferring ownership forever. Today, it looks a generous deal to the private sector; anyone buying it knows that, held indefinitely, it will remain a productive asset in the portfolio beyond their career.

And the last key point is tolling regulation. Usually a toll road has tolls that must be linked to consumer price index (CPI), or some other inflation-like measure. 'But because the whole idea around it was to relieve congestion off the 401, the government built in a mechanism into the tolling arrangements to keep it flowing,' Smerdon says. 'So if traffic levels on the road hit a certain level, you're basically allowed to keep increasing tolls to keep it free-flowing.' The tolls also adjust in real time, varying by time of day and section of the road.

That, of course, sounded like manna from heaven to Macquarie bankers; imagine a deal where you were encouraged to put tolls up to the point where it started to take congestion *off* the road! Not just permission to charge the Ontarian motorist more from time to time, but explicit encouragement to do so!

'You can appreciate,' says Osorio, 'why to people on main street, maybe that's not the most popular solution.[30] But from a value for money perspective for the operator, it's fantastic.'

So for various reasons, Macquarie decided it wasn't going to take no for an answer. SNC, CDPQ and Ferrovial had the equity, Smerdon says. 'So we said, let's go and see them, with the cunning plan of saying: hey, do you want to sell any?'

It wasn't always smooth: one of the first meetings was with a high-flying line-up from Ferrovial, and the team took their guests to a seafood place in Toronto, only to find that the most senior member of the Ferrovial team had a seafood allergy. Undeterred, the team kept plugging away, phoning Ferrovial and its toll road subsidiary, Cintra; bugging CDPQ; haranguing SNC Lavalin. Macquarie's projections and modelling told them there was still huge potential value in the 407 even at a higher price, and so they kept going back to the equity owners, time and again, saying: how about this price? How about now?

Eventually, they wore them down. 'The price had gone up significantly,' remembers Gauthier at CDPQ, a recipient of a hell of a lot of phone calls from Macquarie over the previous years. CDPQ still didn't have an infrastructure benchmark, instead housing the asset in its private equity portfolio, which had tougher targets. 'So for portfolio reasons we said: we have a very good price, so why don't we take our money back? And that's what we did.'[31]

'So after two years,' says Smerdon, 'they agreed to sell us some. It was just persistence.'

As it happened, having lost out with much heartbreak in 1999, Macquarie ended up owning stakes in the 407 from two different directions. And for this part of our story we must leave Canada and turn to Europe.

London Calling

While all of this was happening, Kahn and his team had gradually been building up Macquarie Infrastructure Group (MIG), and much of the action was taking place out of the UK.

Steve Allen, who would go on to serve as MIG's CEO and later the chief risk officer of all of Macquarie, had been involved at a junior level in the development of infrastructure in Australia before telling Moore he wanted to go to try to do the same thing in London. Moore, characteristically, had presented various obstacles to Allen in order that he think everything through, and then had given his blessing to go to join the modest London office.[32]

While Allen had tried to get things rolling, in 1999 he was approached by a UK company called Kvaerner, a construction group that had run into financial trouble. It had a portfolio of assets in the UK and Western Europe ranging from stakes in Lisbon toll bridges[33] to a waste-to-energy plant in Dundee, but its most striking holding was a concession for a toll road to be built called, at that stage, the Birmingham Northern Relief Road.

The UK's M6 motorway is a notoriously traffic-clogged artery linking the south of England to the northwest via the Midlands, upon which one of the authors, being from Liverpool and with family in the Midlands, would conservatively estimate he has spent a cumulative period of several weeks peering into the back of stationary articulated trucks in traffic jams big enough to make the national news. Kvaerner's concession[34] allowed it to build a toll road to the north of the M6—quite an unusual conceit in the UK, where bridges and tunnels might carry tolls (the author has spent even longer stuck in the tolled Mersey Tunnel than on the M6) but motorways never do. But if ever there was a need for a relief road in the UK, this was it.

MIG bought the Kvaerner assets for A$230 million, paying much of the cost of it by selling assets it didn't want to take on, and swiftly realised that the M6 relief idea had struck a chord. 'It caught the imagination of our investor base,' Kahn says. 'They were enthusiastic, and supported us, and MIG started its ascendancy.'

It felt like a landmark, and one that had been hard won. Kahn and the Macquarie Infrastucture Group (MIG) team had made enormous efforts in investor education around infrastructure. They had their own investor relations people, own media relations representative, their own lawyers, their own risk management people. They did roadshows in every Australian capital city and when they ran out of capitals they took the show to regional centres like Toowoomba.

Kahn remembers watching Cathy Freeman win the 400 metres at the Sydney Olympics that year and feeling a definite sense of momentum and pending change. The truth is, Midlands Express-way—as the relief road would come to be known—never really hit the traffic expectations they had had for it, as it turned out stoic Brits would rather be grumpy in traffic than pay four quid[35] to alleviate their own misery.

'But MIG and its investors did very well out of it. The acquisition, and subsequently building the road, captured the imagination and gained the confidence of investors, and the MIG share price rose.'

Better still, Kvaerner was full of experts. 'Nicholas, as I, was keen to grow in-house expertise,' says Kahn. 'We took the guys from Kvaerner who knew how to build roads and negotiate contracts. We knew what we didn't know.' Airport and telecommunications experts would follow. That has been a hallmark of Macquarie from Sydney

Airport to Minneapolis oil trading: you don't overestimate what you know yourself, you hire the best people who definitely know.

Moore, who tends to resist the urge to over-hype acquisitions, likes this one as a classic Macquarie story. 'So the globalisation of our infrastructure business was very much driven by the fact that Stevie went to London, built a team, and the opportunity came along with Kvaerner to buy their rump development business. And then we were able to use those assets to really start a global infrastructure business offering a unique portfolio of development assets.'

It was against this backdrop that Ferrovial, which had beaten Macquarie to the 407 in 1999, approached Macquarie in London with a proposal in January 2001. Ferrovial had over-reached on a project in Chile and had hit financial difficulties. It knew, thanks to Salisbury's incessant badgering in Canada, that Macquarie knew the 407 better than anyone, and might be a suitable partner. Would Macquarie like to buy a stake in Cintra, the toll road vehicle?

'I don't know how we kept the process quiet,' says Kahn. For about nine months the team did due diligence, completing the deal to acquire 40 per cent of Cintra for €816 million in September that year.[36] Cintra held stakes in fourteen toll roads in Spain, Portugal and Chile . . . and the stake in the 407. MIG's stake in Cintra gave it 24 per cent of the road. Finally, *finally*, it was in.

To fund the deal, MIG—not Macquarie Bank, the fund itself— launched a A$1.55 billion equity raising, through an accelerated rights issue brought to the bank by UBS, which joint led the deal with Macquarie's own equities team. In the end it raised A$1.7 billion in three days, Australia's largest share capital funding exercise for a listed company.[37] Three months later it was raising another A$800 million to buy out another 20 per cent stake in the 407 from CDPQ.

MIG had found its voice[38] and was delivering for the mother ship, giving A$69.2 million to the bank in management fees in the year to

30 June 2001. And this was just the start. The European infrastructure business that would grow from these beginnings under John Roberts had, by 2019, launched six iterations of its Macquarie European Infrastructure Fund (MEIF) vehicle, the last of which raised €6 billion on its own;[39] Macquarie would, in the years ahead, buy airports, water utilities, communications and renewables all over Europe, eventually becoming strong enough to buy the UK's Green Investment Bank. It all, in some sense, started with the Kvaerner and Cintra deals.

■

Back in Canada, Macquarie had been keeping busy while trying to fight its way into the 407. Having built relationships with big institutional investors, the team set about partnering them on a range of smaller electricity deals, particularly in hydro.[40] But they were pretty feeble. Salisbury remembers calling Carapiet and saying: great news, Carras, we've got a two million dollar mandate. Carapiet was delighted: a $2 million fee would cover the team's overheads for the next twelve months. 'Then I had to break it to him that wasn't the fee, it was the enterprise value.' The fee was a success-only $20,000. 'At which point, there was silence.'

Still, Carapiet and Moore let them run with it in the hope that all this effort would lead to grander sums, which eventually it did, because Macquarie was still really without competition in infrastructure advice in Canada. Miller returned home, but a strong team including future infrastructure stalwart Frank Kwok and utilities expert Warren McNabb remained. 'And we just worked our way up the tree of bigger and bigger electricity deals,' Salisbury says. Provincial governments were moving towards privatisation and there was a decent business in advising them, firstly on rate-setting and dividend policies, then on M&A.

One deal with potential took them to the Province of Alberta, where TransAlta was selling a transmission business, AltaLink, serving 60 per cent of the province.[41] Macquarie teamed up with SNC Lavalin, their former opponents from the 407 bid, Ontario Teachers', and another group from the USA that had pledged equity. Two days before final bid, that other group dropped out. Leo de Bever at Ontario Teachers' stepped in and agreed to cover for the dropout, underwrite the entire debt package, A$700 million, as well as taking 25 per cent of the equity in the C$850 million bid.

That done, he took Salisbury aside, and told him: I want you to understand the importance of a relationship in Canada. If we have a good relationship with you, this is the stuff that we can do. 'I've never seen any financier do what he did,' says Salisbury. 'It was astounding, but classic Leo. There's never been a deal so complex he couldn't analyse, nor a faltering project that he couldn't stabilise.'

This would prove to be a crucial but troubled relationship, and Macquarie did not really take heed of what de Bever was trying to tell it. 'It was hard to get across to Australians how important Ontario Teachers' is in the world of pension funds,' Salisbury says. 'Simply doing business with them as a deal partner or an investor gave Macquarie a significant credibility lift with North American and European pension funds.' Ontario Teachers' was very highly regarded in its industry, Salisbury says, 'whereas Macquarie was not well known in those markets then.'

Up to about 2003, this would be a mutually beneficial relationship—follow the footnote for a list of Teachers' contributions to Macquarie funds and deals.[42] Teachers' was the biggest name, but generally the Canadians were becoming an enormously useful constituency of capital for Macquarie: the big three pension funds, the newer CPPIB,[43] and the sovereign wealth funds. Before long, Macquarie felt confident enough to launch its own fund in Canada, to be called Macquarie Essential Assets Partnership, or MEAP.[44]

This would be Alina Osorio's job as CEO of the new fund. Having set up an office—in the spirit of governance, they moved it across the lobby into a separate room from the advisory team, who were over with accounting—the next job was to raise capital, which brought the usual challenges. 'So usually the conversation started: who's Macquarie? How do you spell that? How do you pronounce that? What do you want? And what's the fund,' Osorio smiles. 'It was really fun.'

The pitch, put simply, was that it was the right time to marry this emerging acceptance of the asset class by the powerful pension funds, with the mood of deregulation in Canada, creating a growing investment opportunity. Altalink seemed a natural asset to seed the fund with. Salisbury had Ontario Teachers' in mind as the C$150 million cornerstone for the new fund, which was one of three separate deals de Bever took to the board, getting approval for all three.[45]

But around about now, de Bever's view of Macquarie began to dim. 'The problems began to emerge relatively quickly,' he says. 'I got approval from the OTPP board, and after I did, Macquarie changed the deal out of Sydney.' For example, he says, Teachers' had negotiated the ability to make large co-investments in exchange for the large amounts of capital it was providing. 'And then Sydney said, well, that's interesting. But the fees on co-investments are the same as they are for primary investments, which clearly is not the case. And this repeated itself over time.'

Part of the problem from de Bever's point of view was that 'they would trade on our name. They would ask for help in introducing me to other investors in infrastructure. And the next thing we knew, because those investors were bigger, instead of being grateful and rewarding us in some way, or at least treating us as fair as anybody else, the new investors got a better deal.' The clearest example of this was ABP, the biggest Dutch fund; de Bever is Dutch, speaks the language and for years was on the investment committee at ABP, but feels his reward for the introduction 'was to be cut back on participation in certain deals, which is not the kind of thing I would do.'[46]

He remembers being called in the middle of the night on a weekend because Macquarie needed $50 million in order to close a deal, which de Bever said Teachers' would provide in exchange for some reward, either in terms or access; either way, 'I never got paid for that privilege.'

The CEO of Ontario Teachers' at the time, Claude Lamoureux, began to form a similar view. 'Initially, they were really nice to deal with,' he says. 'We really helped them to get in business. But eventually, we literally stopped doing business with them.' Partly it was all the layers of fees, but the bigger problem was this sense of going back on a deal. 'We would be offered a deal, we'd say: yes, we'll do it, 100 per cent. Three weeks later you'd get a phone call saying we'll cut you to 50 per cent.

'Eventually you realise they're using your name to say to other people we've got full subscription, so we want more fees.

'These guys are the best in the business. They were the best partner. But eventually they became too greedy.'

Moreover, some of the big instos had begun to develop suspicions about the whole Macquarie fund model. Gauthier at CDPQ recalls: 'Macquarie was very aggressive, and at some point in time at the big pension funds it became a topic where even before looking at the deal you would be saying: tell me about the conditions and how it will work, and how long you will stay, and will you want to sell off your investments too soon so you end up making more money on management fees.

'At some point in time it was more challenging for Macquarie to interest us in deals.'

One problem was that Macquarie's funds had limited terms, and at the end all the assets would be sold. Leo de Bever thought it would be better for all the anchor investors to just take out their participation in kind through the shares that they owned, rather than having to sell only to reinvest in similar assets and incur the costs all over again.

But at a deeper level, there were the fees. 'These things have a two and twenty kind of structure[47] in terms of fees,' says de Bever. 'But what was not so clear was that Macquarie had a number of ways they could earn additional income from these funds. They became the champions of continuous re-gearing, meaning that over time, as the valuations of some of these assets went up, they would put additional leverage on to bring it back to where it was in the beginning.' In principle, there was nothing wrong with that, 'except that they did it in a way that was particularly beneficial to Macquarie in terms of additional services that were being provided. And it was not always clear that they were being provided at market rates.'

Ontario Teachers', which probably committed more capital than any other investor in the world to Macquarie deals in the aftermath of 9/11, pulled out of MEAP over Macquarie's approach.[48] In the short term it didn't matter: BCIMC became the cornerstone investor with a C$100 million contribution, and Doug Pearce recommended the fund to CPPIB, which committed C$200 million.[49] The British Columbians were not blind to Macquarie's sharp-elbowed nature. 'The Australians were a little bit more aggressive,' Pearce says. 'We had long discussions about fees and governance. But they also brought some very smart people into our market, and we followed them internationally.' BCIMC, too, would eventually decide to move away from Macquarie funds. 'There were layers of fees which we didn't like, I don't think they were transparent about it, and related parties was an issue also,' says Pearce. But for now, it worked. CPP, the newer pension name on the infrastructure scene, would later come in with a still bigger contribution, C$200 million, and Alberta's AIMco sovereign fund would also take part.

Macquarie veterans had their own concerns. Osorio says the culture was part of the problem. 'It didn't quite start out this way, but it was a place where you maxed out the last penny,' she says. 'People are cutting edge, driving to maximisation of profits, and sometimes short-term maximisation at the expense of longer-term relationships.'

But to her, it was the related-party transactions that were problematic. 'As CEO of the fund I was responsible for some thoughts and ideas about moving assets between funds. Investors hate that. It brings up a tonne of issues of fair value accounting or valuation, but also related-party conflicts.' Also, because advisory was Macquarie-owned as well, fee structures in each deal had to be approved by investors along with any related-party issues. 'So it became apparent to them what the fee structures were. I wouldn't say the fees were egregious for the time. However, the related-party nature proved challenging for some investors and the resulting impact on long-term relationships. On some occasions, many layers of fees were starting to creep into the equation.'

Smerdon, too, saw an evolution happening in Macquarie's relationship with Canadian capital, and it was not a good one. At first, 'they definitely saw Macquarie, I think correctly, as the innovators in this space, and people they could learn from,' he says. 'Even to this day, when I think of the great training grounds for new people where you're going to get the most innovative thinking and the best quality of deal execution, Macquarie is still high on the list.

'But these people were looking for a relationship, and an enduring one, whereas at the time Macquarie was a very transactional shop. It was always about: who's best placed to help us win this deal and earn this fee? And you might have been the best partner for the last deal but that doesn't mean we're going to sign up with you on the next one.' That just doesn't wash in Canada. 'It was not a good cultural fit.'

That transactional nature led to the attitude of 'how many different ways can we get fees out of a single transaction?' And investors began to ask him: if I'm in this fund, why do you always use Macquarie as your adviser? Why is there never a different debt arranger? 'Which were valid questions. But Macquarie saw this as a process: you keep everything in-house to maximise the chances of winning the deal.'

Issues like this were by no means unique to Canada: Chapter 8 explains the furore that arose around Macquarie Airports, Sydney Airport and the consequent impact on the Macquarie Communications Infrastructure Group (which, it turned out, would later be bought by CPPIP), for example. MIG had to oust a member of its investor relations team called, appropriately, Dennis Eager for ill-judged comments about the ability to toll the M6 relief road in 2003.[50]

But none of this stopped the Canadian fund being a success. MEAP would become Macquarie's first unlisted infrastructure fund in North America when it reached close in 2004 with five under-lying investments, and would be something of a quiet landmark, for this was the future: unlisted rather than listed vehicles, though the theme would not really reach its peak until the global financial crisis. It would perform exceptionally well and, by any estimation, delivered for its investors, with a 22 per cent rate of return. 'It was an incredible, entrepreneurial environment, hiring people as we went,' says Osorio. 'Even today, it was one of the best performers in the Macquarie fund family.'

All told, the Canadians would prove essential to multiple international funds too. When Macquarie European Infrastructure Fund (MEIF) was launched in 2004, CPP would be the biggest investor at €200 million. BCIMC and AIMco would both participate in various MEIF fund iterations, as would CDPQ, while the British Columbians would also take a US$100 million stake in Macquarie Infrastructure Partners, an Americas-focused unlisted infrastructure fund. Ontario Teachers', despite de Bever's growing concerns, would be the cornerstone for Macquarie Airports Group, as well as providing the introduction to ABP, which would be the largest investor in MEIF. Salisbury estimates that Macquarie had raised over C$40 billion from Canadian pension funds up to 2022.

Macquarie's boom days in Canada ran their course. Smerdon remembers there being five people in the Toronto team when he joined but estimates the headcount in Canada peaked at about 1200; he doubts there are more than 40 in Toronto now (in fact, arguably the more important Canadian presence is the Calgary office housing the commodities team Macquarie acquired from Cargill, within the Commodities and Global Markets business).[51]

MEAP has since been liquidated, having reached its term; today, no infrastructure funds are run from Canada. Osorio had wanted to do a MEAP 2, but seeing that the funds were going to be run out of New York instead, she crossed back to the pension side and joined OP Trust before founding Fiera. Osorio is one of a quite extraordinary set of alumni from that Toronto office: Smerdon is now head of infrastructure at Canada Post's pension plan, Frank Kwok is among Macquarie's most senior infrastructure figures in Asia-Pacific, Kevin Warn-Schindel is managing director at HarbourVest in Boston,[52] and others pepper the senior ranks of pension funds and private equity across Canada, the USA and the world.

But the big years, particularly around the 407, would be enormously influential for Macquarie. 'It was one of our first forays into infrastructure outside Australia, and it made me realise that this was an asset class which would have institutional support, which at the time didn't really exist in Australia,' says Frank Kwok.

Macquarie would call upon the Canadians again during the global financial crisis, and since then an equilibrium has been reached: where once the big Canadian pension funds bought into Macquarie's infrastructure vehicles, today they see them as direct co-investors, a model of partnership rather than client. It seems to work well for everyone.

■

What do we learn from the Korean, British and Canadian experience? That nobody is quite like Macquarie at spotting a gap no-one else can see, throwing resources at it with patience and backing, and a tolerance for getting things wrong initially on the path to getting them right. That, in the pre-financial crisis days at least, it could push too far, be too transactional for the appetites of the institutional money it was chasing. That it had extraordinary success in taking learnings from Australian infrastructure and taking on the world with them. And that its lust for the very last fee dollar would come at a longer-term cost.

The stories also remind us that from the very earliest days, nobody has ever sat there as a CEO or in an executive committee meeting and said: I think Macquarie should go and launch in this country. That is simply not what happens. Macquarie's expansion has been about people on the ground wanting to take a chance and say: I think there's a gap there, I think we've got an edge.

'It's really hard to grasp, over that period in the late nineties and early 2000s, just how many options were evolving,' says John Roberts, who was part of the UK growth story. 'You're sitting around going: gosh, this is a blank sheet of paper. There is no script. What are we going to do? But there was this MacCap [Macquarie Capital] energy to drive, originate investment opportunities with a belief we'll find the capital.'

He remembers how quickly the business turned from knocking on doors in North America and Europe looking for work, to suddenly gaining traction everywhere: joint ventures with Old Mutual in South Africa, Shinhan in Korea, the State Bank of India, the World

Bank, Abu Dhabi Investment Corp. 'And then the business suddenly starts to credentialise itself.'

But Macquarie took on the world, not with a fastidious plan, but a fearless attitude built on boisterous self-confidence. 'You're not talking about a well-oiled machine which has been doing this for 100 years,' says Roberts. 'You're talking about a bunch of people who are making this up and figuring it out along the way.'

Chapter 7

AN AMERICAN ROADTRIP

CHRIS WRIGHT

From the southern bank of the Mississippi, where the river makes a series of languid turns before shaping the city of New Orleans and flowing out to the Gulf of Mexico, you can look across the water and see a cluster of dozens of cylindrical white and grey storage tanks on the other side, linked by a riot of pipes to waiting ships berthed on a wharf.

We're looking at the St Rose Terminal, one of nineteen owned across North America by a group called International-Matex Tank Terminals, or IMTT. The company started out around here back in 1939 when it purchased the nearby Avondale terminal, on the southern side of the river just a little further downstream.[1] Today IMTT handles the storage of bulk liquid products across North America, be it petroleum or vegetable oil, from Placentia Bay in Newfoundland through the St Lawrence river system and the Great Lakes to the Mississippi.

In 2006, it caught the attention of Macquarie. Murray Bleach was head of the Americas at the time, with a mandate to build an infrastructure business across the continent, and he'd run into a problem: there just wasn't that much infrastructure in the USA that was for sale.

'We couldn't buy airports. There were negligible toll roads,' he says. 'So we were thinking: what else is infrastructure? And one day it dawned on us, what about those bloody big tank farms? So we went about tracking down who owned them.'

So that's how it works? You spot an alluring bit of infrastructure, and then you go and knock on the door and say: can I buy it?

'Absolutely. Absolutely.'

And what do they say, in a place like that, when you knock on the door?

'Well, probably the first person to knock on the door gets the best deal,' Bleach says. 'But it doesn't take long for everyone else to start chasing these things.'

Thus did Macquarie's engagement with American infrastructure proceed: not purely through the careful sifting of a thousand opportunities, but by spotting things on various riverside horizons and asking nicely if they were for sale.

'Necessity is the mother of invention,' says Bleach. 'When you haven't got anything, you're like: shit, what can we buy?

'The deal environment is, you've got to do a deal, right? Well, that looks like an infrastructure asset. And we're going to buy it.'

Bleach, a raconteur with a larrikin streak, is underselling Macquarie's due diligence for the sake of a good yarn: of course there was more to it than that.[2] But Bleach is not joking about how the deal started: with shoe leather and gumption and a big smile.

Macquarie Infrastructure Corporation, the New York Stock exchange-listed infrastructure fund, acquired 50 per cent of IMTT in 2006 for US$250 million, then bought the remainder of it in 2014 for US$1.025 billion.[3] Along the way IMTT went from having ten storage terminals to 19, seven of them in a single swoop with the acquisition of Epic Midstream in 2017, which MIC funded.[4]

And then, when the time was right, Macquarie[5] sold it to Riverstone Holdings[6] for US$2.685 billion in 2020. That's how it works. Macquarie's moved on: profit made, fund matured, job done.

■

We are starting a journey here, where America runs out of room and reaches the Gulf of Mexico. We are both making a voyage and making a point. We will describe a roughly northward arc through the middle of America before crossing to Canada and finishing on more well-trodden coasts, and in doing so we will try to demonstrate just how frequently one crosses paths with Macquarie, even here, as far as it is possible to be from Sydney. (See picture insert for map.) Frequently we will be enriching Macquarie; sometimes we will be encountering its history, and often, no doubt, its future.

We're heading, first, for Houston, but on the way there we'll take a diversion further north in Louisiana to Pineville,[7] a town of 'faith, tradition and pride ... a safe, family-friendly city where southern hospitality abounds and family values are honoured,' as the town's website says.

Macquarie found itself in this community of Baptist churches and memorial park cemeteries when MIRA teamed up with British Columbia Investment Management Corporation and others to buy Cleco Corporation, a Pineville utility holding company that owns Cleco Power, in 2014.[8] Macquarie put it into Macquarie Infrastructure Partners III.[9]

There's a couple of things we can learn from Cleco. One is the benefit of being local, and also the work involved in being so. David Fass, head of real assets for the Americas at Macquarie Asset

Management, says there's probably somebody from Macquarie down in Louisiana every week, 'doing something, having dinner in the local restaurants, staying in the hotels, and that's how they know what's going on there.'

Partly that's a matter of staying in touch with a key asset, but it has a peripheral benefit too. 'They're not down there necessarily looking for the next utility to buy. But they're part of the community, and they sit on the board with twelve other people who are local to Louisiana, and they chat over breakfast lunch and dinner about what else is going on.' Perhaps, Fass says, hypothetically, they hear that the patriarch of a local family who owns the railroad has died with no obvious successor. And perhaps that leads to a call or a meeting. 'If you took out the map of the United States and put a bunch of pins in it, you'd find we're in a lot more places than you think we are,' Fass says. So that, really, is how Macquarie finds its infrastructure opportunities off the beaten track: by being there already.

This is also a good place to mention David Agnew, a genial figure from South Carolina who once worked for the mayor of Charleston and then Barack Obama's White House. Agnew was the Director of Intergovernmental Affairs, an office that exists to try to get things done in coordination with governors, mayors and tribal leaders across the country.

'Nothing happens in a straightforward way for the US government,' he says. 'It's layer upon layer and all sorts of nuance about who's responsible for what. Most of the time, there is tension.' Recognising the impact of this troubled dynamic upon the purchase of infrastructure, Macquarie hired Agnew into a then-new role in 2014 to build relationships across this complex system.

'It's knowing how the federal, state and local governments work together—or don't work together,' he says. 'How a governor's office works, or a mayor's office, and helping us as investors and private sector actors negotiate all that.'

A fan of the local and the small-town, Agnew loved working on the Cleco deal and reckons he's done something similar in about 25 states while at Macquarie. 'There's a whole set of interesting people that you get to meet, and the dynamics between big city politics and rural state politics are completely different,' he says; we meet him in New York but sense he'd rather be in Pineville.

He works closely with all of Cleco's public stakeholders—governor, mayor, city council members, community—and has strong relationships with Louisiana's governor and senators. And, just like Fass, he sees adjacencies that arise from the effort. At the time of writing Cleco had recently announced a federal grant for the study of a major carbon capture project in Central Louisiana.

'That's a great example of Macquarie working with a portfolio company, and then coming together with all the stakeholders at a very high level to making something happen,' he says.

'And you have to work on that. It's not something you can just pop in and do, create those relationships, create that trust. But if you work on the relationships that come with the investment, opportunities like that come along.'

We cross into Texas on the 10 Interstate and before long are in Houston. It is April, an interesting time of year in America when you can get any kind of weather; we'll see snow in Toronto and a tornado in Kansas before we're done, but here in the south, it's heating up.

Houston is enormously important to Macquarie and home to one of its most prized divisions and ideas. When Nicholas Moore was chief executive, if you ever asked him to give an example of what he thought was the Macquarie story in action, with all its ideas of individual empowerment and backing and accountability, he would talk about Andrew Downe and Nick O'Kane's development of the

North American energy business, starting with the acquisition of a small boutique in Los Angeles called Cook Inlet in 2005, then a much bigger Houston-based business that had been hit by the global financial crisis, Constellation Energy, in 2009.

Somewhat to the chagrin of the Californians, O'Kane made the decision to combine the whole operation in Houston, where today it occupies several floors of One Allen Center—just across the street from where Enron used to be, some of whose alumni now trade for Macquarie.

The whole of North American energy commodities is covered from here. Take gas: by 2019, Macquarie was active on 50 of the 61 major interstate gas pipelines, leasing capacity rather than buying the pipes. Power and gas are where the business made its name but as you make your way across the 31st-floor trading hub you see LNG, oil, emissions and more being handled, while others focus on commodity finance and structuring.

There is a meteorologist on this floor, Peter Sciola, his screen different from everyone else's and filled with shifting weather patterns. His is a vital job and he gets to speak first at the morning meetings. Nobody here has forgotten the February 2021 winter storms and what they meant socially, logistically and profitably: this is where our book began.

There are screens here showing, live, similar floors in Minneapolis and Calgary, dating from the purchase of Cargill's oil trading business in 2017. Together these businesses have, in recent years, been perhaps the most important engines of Macquarie profitability and have elevated Nick O'Kane to most likely successor when Shemara Wikramanayake decides to go. O'Kane's no longer here—he relocated back to Sydney two years ago, which some think is partly in order to put him in the right orbit for the top job one day—but there's still a black Macquarie surfboard in the office where he used to sit, apparently originating from California. O'Kane got them made when Macquarie bought Cook Inlet, sensing some common ground, Australia to California, surfer to surfer. 'It was my way of saying: we're like you,' O'Kane says.

■

It's time to hit the road again and we drive three and a half hours north through a green springtime Texas to Plano, a rather non-descript corner of the sprawling Dallas/Fort Worth conurbation. There are two places of interest here. One is Atlantic Aviation, which is not the corporate jetting business it sounds like but a network of what's known as fixed base operations (FBO), providing fuel and hangars to private aircraft at 69 locations across the USA. The key figures: Macquarie bought it for a reported US$238 million in 2004, sticking it in the Macquarie Infrastructure Corporation listed fund; it sold it to KKR for US$4.475 billion in 2021.[10]

How do you make a return like that? One of the key people on that deal was Michael Dorrell, who would go on to create Stonepeak, an alternative investment firm specialising in infrastructure and real assets with a lot in common with Macquarie (and which continues to attract the elite of Dorrell's former employer, most recently Macquarie Capital co-head Daniel Wong).

'Because there was no infrastructure equity market in the US, you were competing with private equity buyers who want 25 to 30 per cent return, which is a big gap from what infrastructure returns were in Australia or Europe,' he says. 'Nobody was trafficking in this traditional infrastructure risk-return market.'

In the absence of that competition, he recalls Macquarie was able to buy Atlantic Aviation for about eight times EBITDA,[11] then set about buying other FBO businesses across America and rolling them in. 'We were in for about five or six times EBITDA, post-synergy.'

CEO Louis T. Pepper helped, 'a really dynamic customer-oriented CEO who brought a lot of pizzazz to Atlantic,' Dorrell recalls. 'He wanted to service private airports almost like a five-star hotel.'

Then, in the time Macquarie held it, great growth took place in private aviation in the USA. But the biggest reason for the outsized returns was being in first. 'Because the capital that comes in later is in a more competitive environment, return expectations become normalised,' Dorrell says. 'So those who got in early get outsized returns.'

Plano is also where we find Aligned Data Centers, a developer and operator of hyperscale data centre facilities that Macquarie bought into in 2018.[12]

Aligned's particular twist on the data centre theme is that it invented a technology called Delta Cube that deals with one of the most pressing problems of this growing industry: heat. The technology removes heat at source rather than trying to cool it later. Just keep them and their business in your mind: we'll be meeting them again.

Continuing north we enter Middle America, crossing first to Oklahoma—where Macquarie owns Lagoon Water Solutions, and a network of wells and pipes across the Anadarko Basin[13]—and then Kansas.

As we drive, the political iconography turns red. Along the interstates, American flags the size of tennis courts flap above auto dealerships. On the smaller roads, Trump photos appear along with strident pro-life ads. *What's the cost of an abortion? One human life.*

As we approach Kansas City at night, an ominous warning from a woman in a gas station: 'get somewhere safe.' Crossing the Missouri river the forked lightning turns the black night sky a vivid and crackling pink. Wind rocks the car. These are the great central plains.

Kansas City, unexpectedly, is home to Macquarie's fifth-largest office in the USA, and that's because of the acquisition of Waddell & Reed into Macquarie Asset Management in April 2021.

Our lesson from Kansas: that acquisitions bring you local complications. The Waddell & Reed deal is pretty universally considered a good one for Macquarie, filling in gaps in the legacy Delaware Investments business it had acquired in Philadelphia in 2010, but it did involve a lot of redundancies, which makes sense from any macro bottom-line perspective but goes down like a lead balloon locally.

On the corner of Baltimore Avenue and West 14th Street in Kansas City is a stylish building occupying a full city block. It looks ready for business, but its doors are boarded up with ugly plywood.

This fine location was built for Waddell & Reed as the anchor tenant, but when Macquarie bought in, it refused to move there, to the chagrin of the mayor.[14] Instead what's left of the acquired team remains in the neighbouring city of Overland Park about twenty minutes' drive away, where the office looks somewhat like a university campus with a lake next door and several geese strutting around in apparent indifference to this sensitive civic matter.

■

From here, slap bang in the middle of America, we could go anywhere.

We could strike due north to Minneapolis and across into Canada to Calgary, where the two main offices Macquarie bought from Cargill are located. A growing Canadian natural gas business is evolving up there on the Albertan prairies; we've already seen it, on a direct video link to Macquarie's trading floor in Houston.

Or we could go west and find connections from the top to the bottom of the West Coast; from the Long Beach container terminal, one of the assets of which Macquarie Asset Management chief and top-job potential heir Ben Way most adores, to Puget Holdings and its subsidiary Puget Sound Energy, an electric and natural gas utility in Washington state that Macquarie likes so much it has now bought it twice.[15] Most recently, it did so in February 2022[16] alongside Ontario Teachers' Pension Plan. The experience of having to sell then return is part of the reason Macquarie is now developing perpetual funds with no hard time horizon.[17]

In fact, we could go further west still until we hit Hawaii; Hawaii Gas was the final asset to be sold from the listed MIC fund. Its sale to Argo Infrastructure Partners,[18] announced in June 2021 and completed in August 2022 concluded MIC's life as a public traded company[19] and, with it, almost ended Macquarie's once-ubiquitous ownership of listed infrastructure funds.[20]

But instead we will head east across Missouri through the soybean fields.

The radio, in the brief gaps between country music, ZZ Top and the Bible, is full of weather. Last night, a tornado ripped through parts of Kansas and there is heavy damage to property. There are ads for buying local, for leasing tractors, for litigation against unsuccessful hernia surgery. Dogs lean out of the windows of 4x4 pick-up trucks. Maybe they're sick of the radio.

Although we can't see it, we are accompanied on our journey by fibre cable that tracks our route across the state and much of the mid-west, sneaking into Iowa, Oklahoma and Tennessee. It's owned by a company called Bluebird Network, headquartered in Columbia, Missouri, and represents one of an increasing number of businesses in digital infrastructure that Macquarie has built in recent years.[21] We'll be hearing more of that in Philadelphia.

We cross the Mississippi north of St Louis—where Macquarie owns yet another data centre facility—and enter Illinois, still accompanied by the Bluebird fibre as we head northwest towards Chicago. We are on the outskirts of the city when our paths seem to repeat.

There are tank storage facilities at Joliet and Lemont on the Des Plaines River. Both belong to IMTT.

When we reach Chicago, it is time to join some toll roads. They come in quick succession: the Chicago Skyway and the Indiana Toll Road, and unfortunately their proximity is not all that bonds them in the Macquarie story.

Macquarie bought into these assets in 2005 (Chicago) and 2006 (Indiana), and did what Macquarie tended to do with assets in those days: leveraged the hell out of them and put them in a fund.

Both of these assets attracted a fair amount of attention from the local financial and political press at the time, and provided grist to the mill of those who thought there was something seriously awry with the Macquarie model. It is assets like these that first set Jim Chanos off on his very loud mission to prove that Macquarie was some sort of pyramid scheme, which would become a profoundly damaging allegation during the global financial crisis as Macquarie's share price collapsed. But we tell that story elsewhere (see Chapter 10).

Macquarie used to say that stories about the failings of the Macquarie model represented an inability to understand that model rather than a structural flaw. The problem was, those stories had a point, and Chicago and Indiana were where it would be proven. Both projects hit financial trouble, one filing for bankruptcy, and ended up under new ownership.

From the outset Macquarie's appearance in these toll roads had baffled Americans, who were far less used to the very idea of private ownership of roads than their Canadian neighbours. Still, the philosophical struggles were swiftly compensated for with what seemed remarkable largesse: it is said that the US$3.8 billion bid Macquarie and Ferrovial made for the Indiana Toll Road was a billion higher than any other bidder and double what officials in the state had expected to achieve.[22]

Today Macquarie considers these deals as lessons learned. 'Those assets were demand-driven, where you took full exposures to volume and rates,' explains Luke Chenery, who was drafted in as CFO of both roads when they were already in trouble as the global financial crisis bit in 2009, and was powerless to redeem them.

'Their undoing was that during the GFC, the trucks just really disappeared. We didn't have enough revenue to support the debt, which in these assets are typically highly leveraged. And so the debt had to be restructured.' Chenery now runs another Macquarie asset, the Goethals Bridge between New Jersey in New York, and we'll be meeting him there directly; suffice to say this time he's gone for a project with no exposure to volume or rates.

'The lesson learned was we just put too much debt on an asset that couldn't handle it,' says Louis Paul, not involved in either deal, but today focused on transportation assets for Macquarie Asset Management and the MIP funds.

That's true, but it was also a quite specific form of debt, somewhat notorious these days, called the accretive swap. This meant starting out with a low debt payment that would rise over time no matter what happened with the business. From a Macquarie perspective, it sounded great: they could borrow more, as the credit metrics looked better early on as a result of the structure. 'The accretive swaps were a great innovation to match the cash flows of the Indiana business to the financing,' says Bleach, a key figure in the Indiana deal. But the debt burden grew as the trucks stopped rolling.

With the benefit of hindsight the whole contention looks outlandish; indeed, we've seen presentations in the industry highlighting the two deals as case studies of 'financial engineering gone too far'. On the Indiana deal, for example, US$3 billion of that purchase price was borrowed from banks, with Macquarie's contribution just $374 million. But the result of the accreting swap was that by 2012 the road had US$5.8 billion of debt, which was US$2 billion more than the initial purchase price despite having had eight years of toll collection accrue in the meantime. *Fortune* calculated that on Skyway, Macquarie would pay interest of just US$129,000 on $961 million of debt in 2007, but would owe US$480 million on the same debt in 2018. 'That's not a typo,' the magazine felt obliged to point out.[23]

Macquarie thought it would be protected by easy credit markets and the relentless enthusiasm of the American consumer for driving. 'If you looked at a graph of traffic anywhere in the USA from the time that the car was invented through 2007, it went up every single year,' says Paul. 'And the mistake we made was to apply a capital structure to those assets that relied on that trend continuing.' When it didn't, the whole structure toppled. 'The recession knocked the cash flows around so the business was unable to meet the financing requirements,' Bleach says. Macquarie says it no longer takes leverage on that scale and that it always plans for the worst and mitigates accordingly.[24]

There was another problem too, one that would have lasting consequences. Both roads were originally bought by Macquarie Infrastructure Group (MIG), the listed toll road business, but the interest in both of them was then sold to Macquarie Infrastructure Partners, the private infrastructure vehicle for North America. It was exactly the sort of opaque intra-company deal that investors were coming to dislike—the more so when the deals went bad. There is an argument that these transactions, more than any other, resulted in Macquarie's infrastructure asset management being separated from the investment banking business.

The roads have taken us east across Indiana—and, as it happens, from one Macquarie real estate asset (Logistics Property in Chicago) to another (RHP Properties in Farmington Hills)—and once more we have a choice. We could continue east into Ohio, where Macquarie bought Cincinnati Bell in September 2021, took it private and put it into Macquarie Infrastructure Partners V. But instead we'll move north into Michigan, passing through Ann Arbor and Michigan Electric Transmission,[25] another Michael Dorrell deal, and in to Detroit, where we want to show you a tunnel.

∎

The towns of Detroit, Michigan, and Windsor, Ontario, have a lot to do with one another but are separated by two things: a river and a national border. Between them is a tunnel that, frankly, feels very much like it might collapse on you when you go through it, but in normal circumstances has a lot to recommend it as a business case.

It was a small deal—Macquarie put in something like US$12 million of equity in a deal with a US$60 million enterprise value, which the bank would scarcely bother with today. But it was the first successful infrastructure deal of the Toronto business, which would go on to be much more important to Macquarie than is widely understood, a tale we tell in Chapter 6. So it had significance.

The fun part of this story is the business case. The two cities are very highly integrated for a range of reasons around everything from manufacturing to healthcare, culture, gambling and alcohol.

Michael Smerdon, who was closely involved in the deal and oversaw the asset around the turn of the millennium, says that auto manufacturing in the Ford, General Motors and Chrysler plants in Michigan is so integrated with Ontario that a single vehicle will cross the border multiple times, either as parts, as a vehicle that needs painting, or one that needs assembly. Healthcare professionals commute from Windsor to Detroit every day.

That's a key part of the premise for the tunnel, but equally central to Macquarie's projections for traffic was the fact that people can drink at the age of 19 on the Canadian side but 21 in the USA, and that there was a casino on the Canadian side, guaranteeing a steady toll-paying flow of American teenagers wanting to get drunk and Americans of any age wanting to lose their money. In the other direction, the major league baseball and hockey stadiums for Detroit are both downtown close to the tunnel, which was appealing to Canadians wanting to watch a game. 'There is a lot of traffic,' Smerdon says, 'that is entertainment-related.'[26]

Macquarie sold it many years ago, which is just as well. COVID-19 shut the tunnel completely and then Canadian truckers did their best to barricade it in their odd freedom protests of 2021. Even in April 2022 the bus route through it was suspended. None of this undermines the relief of getting out of the thing and emerging into Canada.

It is time to go to see the holy grail of infrastructure: the 407 toll road around the north of Toronto. The previous chapter explored the significance of this deal and the almost biblical reverence infrastructure professionals seem to hold for it.[27]

For the purposes of our road trip, though, we're only interested in driving it, from which we learn the following. One, it's damned long, starting way before anything that looks remotely like Toronto and ending a long way after anything that looks much like Toronto either: about 130 kilometres in total, very long for a toll road.

Two, approaching it from the lakeside south gives a useful demonstration of why it is in such a commanding position: its loop around the north of the city can't ever be mirrored or competed with by an equivalent to the south, because that would be right in the middle of Lake Ontario, which, among other things, is considerably deeper than most ocean continental shelves.[28]

Our drive on the 407 is smooth—the surface is immaculate—and, for the most part, unimpeded by many other people at all using the road. But, as we've learned, the tolling system is such that the owners can push the tolls to eye-watering levels in order to keep the road free-flowing, and it works: when our tolls finally reach us via a disgruntled car rental agency some weeks later, they amount to C$68.75.

Towards the middle of the 407, we see its future. Toronto is a hugely congested city that is spreading steadily north, and what was rural when the road was developed twenty years ago is no longer so. The market for the 407 is developing around the 407 itself. The future is promising. You can see why Macquarie fought so hard to get a foothold in the road after losing its initial bid.

We decide to test the desirability of the 407 by driving the other way on the free alternative, as it is known in the trade: the 401. Rush hour is kicking in and it is packed. There are places where the road runs eight lanes each way, and it's still miserable. So the 407 isn't cheap, but it speaks to an equation every Torontonian driver must consider: what matters more to you, time or money, and where precisely does the equilibrium between them fall? The 407, which is probably worth at least US$30 billion these days, serves that mental and emotional calculation.

The 401 has completely ruined our afternoon, and we eventually abandon it—past the offices of Ontario Teachers', as it happens—for the relative serenity of the 407 again. As we reverse our steps and move west we are struck by the fact that by the time you get to the end of its considerable length, you are not that far from Niagara Falls and the US border. What the hell. Let's go see the waterfall and go back to America.

■

At the other end of New York state from the falls we could, of course, go to New York City, and Macquarie's offices on West 55th Street,[29] around the corner from Carnegie Hall and a couple of blocks from Central Park, where energised Macquarie bankers run the surprisingly hilly ten-kilometre loop before or after their working day and probably sometimes both. (COO Jennifer Coyle recalls one particularly alpha-minded recruit who came in one day saying he'd just done a running loop. 'Central Park?' she asked. 'No. Manhattan.' A work ethic like that is going to go places at Macquarie.)

Much goes on here, across many different business lines, and Michael Silverton's role as global—not regional—head of Macquarie Capital in New York carries some significance as a representation of Macquarie's growing heft in North America. (It is somehow reassuring that even the Americans call Silverton 'Silvo', some of them even adopting something of an Australian accent as they do so.)

But the spirit of the trip instead keeps us on the other side of the Hudson to see two assets in New Jersey.

First, we meet Luke Chenery, who, having survived the experience of the midwestern toll roads, has been the driving force of the first new bridge in New York in about 80 years.[30] This is the Goethals Bridge, and no simple acquisition: the bid Macquarie won was to replace an ancient and decrepit existing bridge from New Jersey to Staten Island by building two new bridges right next to it and demolishing the old one while progressively transferring the traffic from one to the others. At the time we meet, Chenery has been on the project for eight years, running it from an office hidden underneath the spans on the Jersey side ('When you work in infrastructure, the hardest thing is sometimes finding the front door,' says Louis Paul), which is a considerable improvement upon the construction trailers they all lived in for the first five years.

The scale of this endeavour is quite something. The two-span cable-stayed bridge cost US$1.5 billion and is used by 32 million travellers per year. At the peak of construction there were over a thousand people working on it, and twelve different 400-foot cranes in use, their height at the ceiling of what could be permitted in light of its closeness to Newark Airport. Design and engineering cost US$100 million alone. It involved the jurisdiction of two states, crossing the New Jersey Turnpike and a major rail line on one side, and protected wetlands on the other.

'The old bridge was 90 years old. It was functionally obsolete,' says Chenery. 'It could just no longer carry the loads and the capacity that it was originally designed for.' The new bridge opened in 2018.

How does Macquarie decide that the risk and economics of a project like this stack up?

'You start with the underlying physical reality,' says Louis Paul. 'In this case, simply, there is a river, and people need to cross the river.'

The traffic numbers on the old bridge clearly state the case, and then it's a question of working out all the stakeholders, starting with the Port Authority of New York and New Jersey, which was procuring the project. In a marked difference to previous projects like Chicago Skyway, on this deal Macquarie would never be exposed to the accuracy or otherwise of their traffic projections: what they were actually bidding on was cash flow from the Port Authority, which basically means the cash amount it repays. So Macquarie invests the money upfront, and under a long-term contract with the Port Authority, gets that capital returned over time, plus some more. Macquarie's bid was for the quantum of that return, and theirs was the lowest bid.

'On the risk-return side, we're effectively getting a payment authority from the Port Authority, which is backed by the two states, and that's a credit question,' says Paul. 'Are the states of New Jersey and New York going to continue to operate the way that they have been, is the tax base going to change, is the Port Authority as a quasi-government going to have sufficient capital to make those payments over time? And then it's execution.'

This security has prompted Macquarie to leverage to its customarily eye-watering levels: somewhere around 90 per cent on the bridge, but secured by the cash flow.

'Making sure that you don't put our investors in a position of ruin is the first thing,' Paul says. 'And the second is putting our investors in a position where we can make a reasonable return for the risk we are taking.'

Part of the Macquarie skill in these things is to hire the right people and then leave them alone unless necessary. 'They are not involved in my day to day, they leave that to me, and I think that's appropriate,' says Chenery. 'They are certainly involved in risk and governance and the things that drive their investment thesis.'

As Chenery drives us over his bridge with considerable pride, we can see another crossing in the distance, the Bayonne Bridge, which looks, from a distance, as if someone had taken the Sydney Harbour Bridge and hoisted its road deck up in the air like someone pulling their trousers up to their midriff and anchoring it there with a belt. This will be relevant to the next place we visit.

Right next door to Newark Airport, our next stop is the Maher Container Terminal in Port Elizabeth, New Jersey. Waiting for us there is Gary Cross, the CEO and something of a legend in New Jersey and the port world; in fact he'll be inducted into the International Maritime Hall of Fame the week after we meet.[31]

Maher Terminals is one of five container terminals in the port of New York/New Jersey, and is the largest privately held marine terminal in North America. Unlike its Maersk-owned neighbour, it's independent of any shipping line. 'We're the largest in the port and we're the largest terminal in North America,' Cross says, from an office with a balcony where we can look over the whole terminal. 'And we handle a whole lot of containers and a whole lot of ships and a whole lot of trucks every day.' Fifteen hundred unionised workers and a vast floating force of truckers assemble here.

Macquarie's engagement with Maher is interesting for its opportunism. Initially a family business founded by a breakbulk stevedore called Michael Maher in the 1940s, Maher's sons sold the company to a subsidiary of Deutsche Bank in 2007.[32] 'They were a reluctant owner,' says Cross. 'They really didn't want to be in this business. And from day one, they probably had one foot out the door.'

Macquarie came to sense the opportunity in this after Deutsche had already poured a great deal of money into a preposterously daring project.

Three of the port's terminals sit west of the Bayonne Bridge, and Maher is one of them, which didn't particularly matter to anyone until ships started getting bigger, culminating in the Ultra Post Panamax class. The technical term is air draft, but in simple terms, the new ships were way too tall to get under the bridge.

For years, a wild idea was talked about: if bigger ships can't get under the deck of the Bayonne Bridge, why not just lift the deck? 'It had been talked about for years,' says Cross. 'But quite honestly, nobody believed it would be done. Number one, there's never been anything engineered like that ever before. And two, in this area, it takes forever sometimes to get things done.'

Still, Cross and his colleagues spent long enough in New Jersey's state capital of Trenton to come to believe that it would happen, which it eventually did, a remarkable feat of engineering. Although it sounds like exactly the sort of don't-tell-me-it-can't-be-done thing that Macquarie would involve itself in, the bank had nothing to do with the bridge, but the awareness that the project was actually going to happen, plus an understanding of Deutsche's predicament at the group level in those years, got the Australians interested.

Macquarie already liked the basics: container terminals are driven by the US consumer buying goods that are made outside of America, and if you believe in that consumption habit, you have a base to start from. On top of that, New York is one of two places[33] in the USA where there are about 50 million people within 200 miles. Maher's independence, being therefore open to all shipping lines, was also appealing.

But the lifting of the bridge was a game-changer. If that happened, the other advantages of the three terminals west of the bridge would step up: they were better places for trucks to get to than terminals closer to the ocean, and they also had better rail links.

Truckers are actually very powerful in this equation—Cross calls them an unofficial marketing force—in that they can influence where cargo goes, and truckers much prefer Maher to some other terminals because it's cheaper and quicker to get there and the process is extremely efficient when they do.

'The question was when it would be finished, as opposed to if it would happen,' says Paul. So Macquarie set about wooing Deutsche. 'We were literally walking down to Wall Street and knocking on Deutsche Bank's door from the middle of 2015.'[34]

Driving around the port, Paul and Cross point out some of the ways capex from Macquarie has since been deployed. Among them are things called straddle carriers, which move the containers around the terminal and if they look oddly familiar, it is rumoured that George Lucas modelled his AT-AT walkers in *The Empire Strikes Back* after seeing some in a port. Anyway, most straddle carriers are capable of lifting three boxes high; now Macquarie is investing in carriers that are capable of lifting four boxes high, meaning a third more boxes can be stacked in the terminal.

On this asset, Macquarie unarguably has volume risk, but it seems to have learned its lesson from more debt-stacked deals like the Indiana toll road. It has less than 20 per cent leverage on an enterprise value basis.

'We talked about ITR and Skyway when we were underwriting these assets,' Paul says. 'The investment committee said the whole way through: we're happy to take a lower equity return on the basis that the fundamental capital structure that we're investing in is lower risk.' COVID-19 was perhaps the proving ground for this revised philosophy: in the uncertain months when everything shut down, the finances weren't stretched and in fact Macquarie was able to put in more capex for when things picked up.

■

It is time to head south to our final roadtrip destination. As we cross the Benjamin Franklin Bridge over the Delaware River from New Jersey to Pennsylvania, the Macquarie logo is visible on a building in the city. And this is significant.

Brand recognition among ordinary people doesn't really matter to most of Macquarie; it couldn't much care if it's a household name in many of its markets because its businesses can be so esoteric and niche. Provided the right investors and clients know who they are, it's all good.

There are two exceptions to this. One is Australia, where the Banking and Financial Services division clearly needs a powerful well-known brand. And the other is right here in Philadelphia.

The acquisition of Delaware Investments, discussed in Chapter 11 about rebuilding after the global financial crisis, was in some respects transformative for Macquarie ('transformative is a strong word,' protests Moore, but hear us out). It brought Macquarie considerable heft in the US mutual funds world, and with it, a need to be known.

As we discuss elsewhere, for about six years after the acquisition, Macquarie let Delaware be Delaware, though it gradually imposed its own culture. In 2016 the Delaware name was dropped from everything except some individual funds, and the Macquarie name[35] replaced it.

The clearest expression of this quest for mainstream recognition is Macquarie's proud new building on Independence Mall. It doesn't look much from the outside but the interior was designed with something of a blank sheet of paper, and it is undeniably impressive and creative, stewarded by Ilysse Pratter, who guides our tour today.

Like many a Macquarie office worldwide, it has an internal stairway, for something the bank colloquially calls the bump factor: Macquarie would rather you got between floors on the stairs than the lift because you're more likely to bump into a colleague and have your particular aura of Macquarie-ness rub off on a peer to the betterment of all. The same holds true in offices in Sydney and London, among other places. (There was much discussion about the colour appropriate to an asset manager's stairway banisters. Ilysse doesn't know the precise name of the colour they deployed on the rails, so we'll christen it Sober Clay).

From the roof terrace you look down on the history of America. You can actually see the Liberty Bell in its glass-fronted housing at the street level; the US constitution was signed in Independence Hall, over to the right. It is a storied address and Macquarie is very proud of it, seeing in it a commitment mirrored by its decision to make Philadelphia its global headquarters for asset management on the public market side, with Shawn Lytle here the global CEO for the business.

There is another side to this: Patrick Coyne, who headed Delaware before, during and after the Macquarie acquisition, preferred the old place near the railway station, on the grounds that that's where actual people are, and it's easier to get fund managers on the train from New York to visit you where they used to be. He remembers with some pride Nicholas Moore telling him that the office cost per foot was lower in Philadelphia than anywhere else for Macquarie worldwide. But Macquarie wants to make a point with its new address, and that point is: just look at us.

The final instalment of our trip takes us to a building in Philadelphia that today is home to Netrality Data Centers, which Macquarie Infrastructure Partners bought in 2019. Netrality operates what you call a carrier hotel, a central point of connectivity.

'If you think what the US is from a connectivity perspective, there's about twelve national networks that cover the US, about 100 cable companies, eleven high-level telephone companies, thousands of fibre companies, and they all need to connect with each other,' explains Anton Moldan, a senior managing director at Macquarie and the firm's North American brains trust on all things related to data centres.

Netrality's Philadelphia building has over 90 different network providers connecting into it. Among other things, Netrality allows different customers to communicate directly with one another through fibre, rather than having to go through some other intermediate point.

And it is quite the building: office manager Natalie Kidd can narrate its story right down to its 228 foundational footings. Originally known as the Terminal Commerce Building, it was built on top of an existing rail depot by the Reading Railroad, opening in the 1930s. 'The rail tracks came in underneath the building,' says Kidd. 'They could offload the goods and take them to a single floor in the building where you had your entire operation, instead of having to warehouse out in North Philadelphia.'

This history has proven to be oddly relevant almost a century later. When there was manufacturing happening in the building, it was important it didn't vibrate every time a train came in. So it was built with incredible stability, with 7600 tonnes of structural steel. Modern data centres need the ability to maintain the weight needed for equipment, generators and cooling.

'The bones of the building have really lent itself to what it has become,' says Will Schultz, Netrality's VP of technology.

The building is far bigger, at 1.3 million square feet, than the data centre operation needs: the business model doesn't require a lot of people and, aside from the mighty back-up generators we see in the basement, its equipment load is smaller than you would think.

So there's room to lease to other tenants. Among them: a life sciences company called Biomeme, which specialises in advanced DNA diagnostics and real-time disease surveillance; and, on the ground floor, a quite extraordinary gaming complex run by Nerd Street, with hundreds of top-end computers taking advantage of the building's low latency data connectivity.

Any attempt to understand data centres is an education. People say things like: 'Fibre is just moving light at the terrestrial level,' (Moldan), and 'light travels faster through fibre than it does through air' (Netrality CEO Gerald Marshall), and we nod accordingly. Among other things, this tour yields the news that the US army has a division dedicated to gaming.

But it is perhaps enough to know that it's big business. Marshall says 'probably 80 per cent of our customers come to us like fish jumping into a net.' Sales the business did last year were up 30 per cent year on year. 'That's just the beginning of what we think is a pretty material growth,' Moldan says.

So what does a company like this want from an owner? 'They're a great sounding board, because we don't always have the answer to every issue that comes with one of us,' says Marshall of Macquarie. The level of knowledge—Moldan talks about the industry like an insider—also helps. And capital? 'We've funded it internally through cash flow and increased out debt a little bit. The plan is there will be more equity available, but we haven't had to tap it.'

Businesses like this are hard to find: this is one of the only independently held platforms of scale that owns both the land and the building. They don't come up that often.

But they link. Everything links with Macquarie. Netrality's data centres are in Houston, Kansas City, St Louis, Chicago and Indianapolis; we've been past pretty much all of them on our roadtrip. And when Marshall talks about other providers he works with, they include Bluebird, the fibre network in Columbia, Missouri; and Aligned Data Centers in Plano, Texas. They're both Macquarie businesses and we went through both of them on our tour.

It feels like we've gone full circle. Not that it was ever in doubt, we have learned this: Macquarie is everywhere, and it's all connected.

Chapter 8

AIRPORTS AND BAD PRESS IN THE 2000s

'Macquarie: what a bunch of bankers.'

Say what you like about Richard Branson and Virgin, but the man knows how to drum up a bit of publicity. This was the slogan that appeared on Virgin-sponsored billboards, and briefly in the livery of a few Virgin Blue[1] aircraft, in a dispute with Macquarie over access to Sydney Airport in 2002.

Given sufficient time, pretty much everyone would probably end up on the sharp end of a Virgin slogan at some point in their corporate existence, so in isolation one shouldn't read too much into it.

But it wasn't in isolation. All of sudden, everywhere Macquarie looked, there was bad press.

Alan Jones, the obtuse and thunderous radio broadcaster who by the early 2000s had become one of the most powerful (and loud) voices in Australian society, had Macquarie in his crosshairs. Allan Moss's temperate nature was being tested by endless questions about the moral justification for just how much money he was earning. There were doubts about the whole Macquarie model, about governance in its satellite funds, about behaviour around coal mines and airlines and related-party transactions. It got to the point where Warwick Smith, a former government minister who had joined in 1998 with a dual mandate for telecoms banking and to build out the communications function, set up a daily morning council that the comms team openly referred to as a war room.

'Every morning we would sit down with senior management and say: here's the story, how are we going to deal with it?' says Matthew Russell, a member of that war room. 'How do we get ahead of the news cycle?'

Something had happened. Unmistakably, Macquarie had gone from being seen as a scrapping homegrown underdog battler to that uniquely Australian phenomenon: the tall poppy. And as Bob Hawke,[2] or at least a film version of him, had it: 'We have a way of dealing with tall poppies in this country: we cut their heads off.'

How had this happened?

■

It had all been going exceptionally well. With BT bedded in, and the world increasingly in Macquarie's sights, the whole thing was levitating. Every year of the 2000s until the 2009 financial year, the one that includes the global financial crisis, would be an all-time record, each one eclipsing the last, sometimes by as much as 60 per cent or more year on year.[3] Moss was presiding over a fearless and hungry enterprise that believed it could do anything.

Never shy of an internal restructuring, Macquarie had reshaped itself yet again in 2001. An investment banking group was formed, merging the Asset and Infrastructure group (which itself had previously been the Project and Structured Finance group and before that the Financial Packaging group) with Corporate Advisory and the Institutional Stockbroking group. This whole thing would later become Macquarie Capital, which would mean that in theory one could have worked for divisions with five different names[4] over the course of a decade or so without ever changing jobs or desks. The greater significance of it all was that it would elevate Nicholas Moore to pole position to succeed Allan Moss, while sidelining corporate advisory doyen Alastair Lucas.[5]

A few months earlier, the Equity Markets Group was formed, carved out of (but crucially different from) the Equities Group, which was itself quite separate from the equity capital markets division, which was instead part of Corporate Advisory and Institutional Stockbroking (institutional stockbroking having previously been a distinct division within the Equities Group), which you'll remember would go on to be merged into Investment Banking.

There was, no doubt, a robust internal logic for all of these things, but it did cement Macquarie's growing reputation for an almost perverse complexity, something that would become a problem when it turned out nobody could really understand the bank during the global financial crisis. The place became siloed even by the usual standards of investment banking, and no matter how much the top brass said about seamless cooperation for the good of the client, there was vibrant internal competition that would sometimes turn to open contempt.

'There was a healthy mistrust of each other,' says Simon Wright, head of fixed income and foreign exchange. 'It was siloed, a kind of sibling rivalry, very strongly so during the nineties and noughties, though less so today.

'People who were hired in the eighties and nineties were quite different animals to what they are today, and now people play nicer,' says Wright, who says that today hiring is conducted quite specifically to encourage a collegiate collaboration. Not then. 'Previously, you would hire people to be hungry animals.'

So one banker recalls the irritation in the commodities business towards investment banking. 'The MacCap guys thought they were the kings. They were the guys in flash suits talking loud in the lifts.' Another, in corporate services, recalls: 'The only thing that united the groups was hatred of the Property Group.' A third: 'I think the group heads would happily have ripped each other's heads off.'

The early 2000s would probably be the nadir—or zenith, depending on your love of a good scrap—of this situation. There was a dark humour to it. At the top, Allan Moss would project an unflappable serenity. Throughout the 2000s, as the maelstrom of a fabulously complex and successful business broiled beneath him, it was quite commonplace to see him strolling up the pedestrianised concourse outside the new office. 'You'd see him walking up and down Martin Place like he didn't have a care in the world,' recalls one. 'He just came across as calm and cool and not really fazed by anything.

'And then you'd see the group heads and they would be fighting each other tooth and nail every single day. I mean, they were all just horrible to each other.'

Beneath the chief executive, Macquarie's next significant tier is the Executive Committee, or Exco. In the early 2000s, this broke down thus: Nicholas Moore (and later Michael Carapiet) for the investment banking group, Andrew Downe for treasury and commodities, Ottmar Weiss for equity markets group, Bill Moss for the banking and property group, David Deverall[6] for the funds management group and Peter Maher for the financial services group.[7] There are some extraordinarily strong personalities in that group, including one who was widely rumoured to own a crossbow. Maher's perspective, as an outsider drafted in from Westpac to build a retail business within Macquarie, is interesting. 'I had some of the most direct conversations one-on-one with other group heads, and as they say, you don't turn up to a gunfight with a feather.'

Michael Silverton, who today is head of Macquarie Capital in New York, had a window seat to Excos of this era in a role working directly for Moss early in his career. He's diplomatic. 'The camaraderie wasn't very evident back then,' he says. 'It did seem like far more of a federation of businesses that happened to come together once a week.' He searches for the right words. 'There were some moments, I would say.'

It's important not to picture Allan Moss as someone who was blind to this commotion; he was relaxed about people competing, given a natural overlap between some businesses. 'It was never a problem,' he says now. 'Around the edges, there's always a little bit of friction. I didn't spend my days worrying about the relationship of one executive committee member to another.

'I always had the view that really good investment bankers are often a bit difficult. And I always felt that aggressive energy could be pointed outwards.'

And Moss could be as firm as was necessary. 'He could be quite a tough figure when he wanted to be,' says Matthew Russell, who worked closely with him in corporate communications in the 2000s. 'He didn't get angry often but when you saw it, it was obvious.'

Russell recalls a time when Macquarie, which had been mandated on an advisory deal for Australia's defence force, lost the mandate after a breach of insider trading rules. 'Allan personally interviewed everyone on the deal team,' Russell recalls. 'He wanted to eyeball them all one by one. He was confronting in his approach to that, forensic. One of his phrases was: loyalty is a two-way street.' That was powerful, perhaps the more so for his decent nature. 'You just didn't want to disappoint him,' says Russell.

There are even some who wonder if the avuncular clumsiness might just have been an exaggeration, a way to get people comfortable. Jo Spillane remembers an MBA recruiting presentation where halfway through Moss dropped his slides on the floor and was scrambling around trying to pick them up, while never pausing on delivering his message around Macquarie's unbroken record of profitability. It sticks in her mind that when she went to speak to him at the break, she was trying to put a brochure in an envelope, and he took it from her and helped her. There was a humility here, but it also served a purpose, putting her at ease. 'Macquarie was different, it wasn't brash,' she says now. 'It was an uncanny mix of confidence with humility, and a fearless willingness to grow and evolve. It's hard to describe.'

It was noticeable, for example, that Moss was a far better public speaker than his everyday bearing and nature would suggest. 'I remember he got up and made a speech at one of the executive director dinners,' says Tony Fehon, who spent almost thirteen years at Macquarie from 1994.[8] 'And it was incredibly humorous. There might have been a shyness, I don't know, but there was this evolution and suddenly he was actually a great speaker.'

Several people also say that, although he rarely expressed it, Moss became frustrated with David Clarke's attitude to being chairman. Moss would spend a month preparing for an annual general meeting, turning the pages with the communications and investor relations team, who would be tasked with compiling a thick document of every possible question he might face, all of which he would learn pretty much verbatim. Moss was notorious for asking for an extra presentation slide: 'Can we pull a slide together about every person that's working on every asset in the world, by tomorrow?' was an internal joke about Moss's commitment to try to explain as clearly as possible to the world what this complex institution was doing.[9]

That was essential, because Macquarie was just growing in all directions: geographically, by product line, by size, by profits. It must have been exhilarating, we say, to have all these engines of growth delivering, but with so many spinning plates, there must be a point at which you can't be on top of everything all the time?

'It was always very positive,' Moss says now. 'I did have a lot of trust [in people running the divisions] but you don't rely on trust, we had systems. As Michael Bloomberg said: "Trust, but verify".'

Moss had come up through risk management and in some measure invented the modern incarnation of that system. He felt 'we had established a culture of responsibility and integrity . . . it was in everybody's interest to be sensible people who recognised that risk management was a value-added function. We knew what we were doing.'

∎

The reasons Sydney Airport became a magnet for public opprobrium were varied. Some were structural; some about market perception of value. Some were the distinct emotional connection people seem to have with the infrastructure they use, a curious phenomenon Macquarie would have to learn to deal with all over the world.

Airports had been a natural extension of Macquarie's burgeoning infrastructure theme, and grew the same way roads did: by starting with advice and then moving on to development and ownership. In the 1999 financial year Macquarie advised on the A$467 million acquisition of airports in Adelaide, Coolangatta and Parafield, as well as the Airtrain city link to Brisbane Airport and a A$1.9 billion borrowing program for Sydney Airports Corporation.[10]

'I'd also been doing some work for the airlines, looking to liberate their airport infrastructure,' says Kerrie Mather, yet another member of that 1986 intake who would go on to be instrumental in the bank's future. 'To understand their value, you needed to understand the value of the airports.' Gradually Mather began handling assignments for the airports themselves, and came to understand that the Australian government, as well as others around the world, was looking to privatise them. 'It was a new asset class with very similar fundamentals to roads: capital-intensive, good cash flows, but with many more levers and more customer-facing businesses than toll roads.'

In October 2000, Macquarie bought a British advisory firm called the Portland Group, which specialised in developing business plans for airports to maximise their commercial revenues. Martyn Booth, who was the co-founder of Portland, was then hired as a specialist adviser. With Booth's assistance, Macquarie bought 50 per cent of Bristol Airport and later 24.1 per cent in Birmingham Airport; in between the two, Macquarie established Macquarie Airports Group (MAG) an unlisted investment vehicle seeded with Bristol with a mandate to make equity investments in airports in OECD countries, focusing on Europe and the UK. Finally, Macquarie listed Macquarie Airports[11]—the listed vehicle would be known as MAp, and the unlisted vehicle in which it invested, MAG, making yet another contribution to Macquarie's soup of confusing acronyms.[12]

All of this had been preparatory work around a broader goal: Sydney Airport. The government had commenced a formal sale process, and Macquarie reasoned that having a listed vehicle would be a useful way to provide consortium investors with an exit when they needed it. The idea of owning Australia's true gateway airport transfixed the city: there were about twenty expressions of interest that eventually coalesced into three serious bidders involving, between them, pretty much every bank, law firm and accountancy house active in Sydney.

But then came the 9/11 terror attacks in 2001. Several Macquarie staff escaped the World Trade Center towers, among them economist Rory Robertson, who was at an economics conference on the ground floor of the complex and wrote a truly extraordinary email about his experiences in the immediate aftermath.[13] 'I was maybe 250 yards from the WTC when I looked up and saw the second plane fly directly—maybe 150 yards—above me,' he wrote. 'Instantly, I knew it was going to hit the tower. I didn't watch. I didn't see it hit. I just ran.'

But beyond the many human horrors of that day there was an immediate challenge for Macquarie, in that it was in the market with a A$500 million capital raising at the time. 'It was big, and of great strategic significance, because we wanted it in order to be able to buy assets in the infrastructure business as seed assets for new funds to be listed subsequently,' says Allan Moss. 'And I got a phone call at about midnight from one of my colleagues saying two planes had hit the World Trade Center in New York.'

Moss met with Peter Mason of JPMorgan, the joint underwriter, at seven the next morning to decide whether or not to pull the deal, given that Wall Street, in the immediate debris zone of the fallen towers, was shut for the foreseeable future. JPMorgan had doubts about pushing ahead. CFO Greg Ward remembers going through market risk-loss analysis to understand the exposures and potential losses from what was happening, a fast-reaction exercise that would prove useful experience when the global financial crisis came along seven years later. Richard Sheppard came into the office and drafted a memo to cancel the capital raising, assuming that was what would happen.

They opted to go ahead. 'It was a dreadful day,' Moss says. 'In every dealing room in every country in the world, the TV just had that ghastly scene of the towers falling all day. That was the backdrop to the deal.'

Sheppard recalls that the book had been filled[14] overnight but the overseas investors all pulled out. 'We had enough friends and supporters to complete the capital raising,' he says. But it had been a frantic process to get there. Executive directors in equities including

Peter Curry and Rocky Chalmers have different recollections of helping to get the deal across the line. Large Australian shareholders were primarily called on to maintain their support for the raising, albeit at a lower price, although some international investors also participated; four institutions committed to stump up for the lion's share of the raising. There were also phone calls with the exchange and government representatives about whether the Australian market would open, given the USA was still reeling from the attacks.

'The market needed to remain open otherwise the institutions couldn't price or transact or commit to anything if the markets were closed,' Chalmers says. 'I'd received a lot of phone calls over the weekend from major investors in the bank. At that stage they were all very supportive. They said they were not going to walk away, they wanted us to reprice it.'

Moss recalls it as the only capital markets deal that was done in the world the day or for several afterwards (although follow the footnote for an account of a key transaction Macquarie handled for QBE in the following days, and other activity[15]). 'We thought it was the right thing to do,' Moss says. 'Morally it seemed like one shouldn't give in to terrorists if one doesn't have to. But that wasn't the reason for doing it, we were doing it because we were able to and it was a sensible idea.'

The 9/11 attacks had an immediate impact on the aviation industry, and in Australia they were followed in a matter of days by the collapse of Ansett, Australia's second airline at the time. After that, the government shelved the Sydney Airport sale; with a team of 40 people now available, Mather and her team turned their focus to the creation of the listed Macquarie Airports vehicle, floating in a two-instalment partly paid structure (we'll come back to that) in April 2002.[16] Mather was its CEO.

By then, the Sydney Airport sale was back on, and the delay may have worked in Macquarie's favour, along with a requirement that

Australians hold at least 51 per cent ownership. 'Macquarie Airports may have been the silver bullet, because Australian equity was a scarce resource and whoever had the most of it was going to win that bid,' Mather recalls. Macquarie's Southern Cross Consortium[17] went big with its pitch: A$5.6 billion, believed to be $600 million higher than the next highest bid,[18] joltingly so after a period when it had been publicly trying to talk the price down. In June 2002,[19] Macquarie and its partners were named the winning bidders, securing a 99-year lease in what then-Finance Minister Nick Minchin called 'the biggest government trade sale in Australian history.'

It was a day of internal celebration. Macquarie had thrown everything at getting the bid ready and watertight and Moore still looks back on it with pride as an illustration of the bank's application of maximum possible resources to a task. 'Here in the building I'm in right now [1 Martin Place] is where we did the bid,' he says. 'We had like 60, 100 people in the bidroom. We left no stone unturned.'

But that day was also, in the words of one who worked in investor relations, 'the beginning of the end for about five years. I remember 2002 as a terrible year, our annus horribilis.'

Why?

It started with a perception that Macquarie had overpaid—which, with the benefit of hindsight, is the easiest complaint to debunk. Twenty years later,[20] and long after Macquarie had moved on,[21] the airport would sell again for A$23.6 billion (this time with Macquarie advising the buyer).[22] Nobody internally, having studied the numbers so closely, was particularly worried about it. 'A lot of it was: have we overpaid? Would we ever be able to make a return from the investment?' remembers Stuart Green,[23] who joined the airport fund in October 2002 in the immediate aftermath of the bids and was immediately dealing with worried investors. 'But nothing ever made us waver in terms of the quality of the asset. It was the gateway to Australia.' But this overpayment idea was accepted as an unarguable truth in commentary of the time, and that was problematic.

The noise around the deal was amplified by a matter of timing: the fact that just three weeks to the day after the Commonwealth government announced the winning Sydney bid, MAp announced an A$842 million deal to acquire a stake in the concessions to run Rome Airport.[24]

In isolation, it looked a really good deal; raising capital for both at once looked overwhelming. As John Roberts in London, involved in the deal, recalls now: 'When we bought our shareholding in Rome, it was like putting oil on the fire of an already under pressure Macquarie Airports share price.' He adds wryly: 'Being 12,000 miles away in the UK was a relief.'

Moore recalls it as an issue of timing: the funds had the money ready for the Sydney commitment, but then Rome, which had been on Macquarie's radar for a long time, suddenly became available, and would not wait. 'So we needed to make a call: do we let this opportunity pass?' asks Moore. 'Or do we go back to the shareholders and say: look, this is a really good opportunity as well, and the metrics in Rome are even better than the metrics in Sydney?'[25]

Mather remembers going to Moss after the news came in of the successful bid; he advised her to go to the top ten investors and ask them, in confidence, what they thought. They liked it.

The team opted to buy both at once, which necessitated a capital raising. So MAp, with UBS Warburg alongside, set about a A$670 million institutional placement and priority entitlement offer,[26] launched to the market two days after confirmation of the Rome deal.

Now came the third problem. MAp's IPO had been raised, requiring investors to pay two separate instalments of a dollar apiece, one in April (before Sydney or Rome were on the horizon) and the other in October. The new capital raising, and the announcement of the two new acquisitions, came in between. And before the second instalment was due, the share price had started falling.[27]

Looking back, there is a school of thought that the partly paid model should never have been anywhere near retail investors.

The logic was that the funds would be raised at the time when they were needed rather than all in one hit up front. 'We didn't know how quickly we were going to be able to invest in quality assets and we didn't want to be just sitting on investors' cash,' says Mather. 'It seemed a good strategy and investors liked the idea.' It arguably transfers a project finance problem into an equity investor's problem. It worked fine in boom times, but it also exposed investors to market movements over periods of months, which was a horrible place to be if markets fell. 'That became really challenging,' Mather says of the second instalment. It also became a magnet for hedge funds playing the arbitrage. One of Macquarie's worst ever deals, the float of BrisConnections in 2008—which fell 60 per cent on debut in just the first of a sequence of disasters[28]—would use this structure (see Chapter 10), after which it was mercifully consigned to the dustbin of bad ideas.

World events weren't helping. The threat of war in Iraq was growing; in October 2002 came the Bali bombings, targeted very clearly at Australian tourists. Both impacted the outlook for aviation and therefore the fund's share price. It would get worse before it got better, with the outbreak of the severe acute respiratory syndrome (SARS) virus occupying headlines through 2003.[29] 'That first year effectively meant Sydney Airport had zero international traffic,' says Mather, 'which drives 75 per cent of revenue.'

A broader problem was that there were just too many listed entities connected with Macquarie. Another fund listing, for Macquarie Communications Infrastructure Group (MCIG), had to be scaled down considerably in August 2002 from a planned A$500 million to

A$310 million, and even after that, opened at a steep discount to its offer price at launch.[30] Macquarie Infrastructure Group (MIG) was doing much better but was raising money too; all told Macquarie and its specialised funds tapped the market for A$6 billion in funds in the ten months to July 2002. 'We've taken a lot of money out of this marketplace since March this year,' Allan Moss told one of the authors that month.[31] 'In truth we've probably taken a dollar or two too much.'

The flood of Macquarie-linked paper had become problematic as it meant fund managers were awash with exposure to either the group or its listed funds. Partly for that reason, Macquarie's own share price began to drop too. It fell from A$41 per share in September 2001 to A$25 in August 2002.

Moreover, there was growing concern about the fees going from funds to other parts of Macquarie, and what was perceived as a lack of transparency. To take one example from the era, in the 2005 financial year performance fees alone from specialist property and infrastructure funds—not base fees, nor any other advisory fees or service fees to other parts of Macquarie—were A$312 million. As MCIG was struggling its way to market, it became clear that Macquarie's advisory fees were A$70 million on that float, in addition to A$50 million on the airport float.[32]

MIG did set about changing some of its disclosure rules in the course of 2002, and also allowed the fund to pay its fees to the parent in scrip instead of cash, as did Macquarie Airports. But there was a common feeling expressed in the personal finance pages of the time, notably by now-ubiquitous TV presenter David Koch,[33] that it surely made far more sense to own Macquarie stock, as recipient of all these fees, than to own any of the satellite funds that were paying them.

Then there was the brawl with Virgin. At the heart of this was a claim that there was an agreement Virgin would be able to take over the terminals previously used by Ansett, which went into administration in 2001 and ceased operations in March 2002. After the privatisation, Virgin Blue's co-owner Patrick Corporation claimed, the circumstances of this deal—both in terms of the number of gates and the duration of the access—were changed.

Patrick's CEO Chris Corrigan had a turn of phrase every bit as punchy as Branson's: 'This is turning into a public policy disaster,' he told the ABC in July 2002.[34] 'You've got a privatised monopoly and now you've got a private owner, who clearly has paid too much for the airport, who's now trying to find new and improved ways of gouging money out of the public.

'You know you've got a parking toll, you're going to have a terminal toll, you've got landing tolls already, they're talking about baggage tolls. Soon there'll be a toll on a cup of coffee out there.'

At this point Branson was unleashed, the billboards started appearing, and the planes started landing with mockery on their fuselages. When Macquarie Airports had to hold an emergency general meeting to get approval for the capital raise, staff and shareholders came out of the meeting to find a load of Virgin flight attendants with super-soakers. (Macquarie annual general meetings would go on to become a handy forum for entertaining dissent; one year the hosts of the satirical TV show *The Chaser*[35] turned up at an AGM with a portable toll gate and started telling people they were charging $3 for access to the meeting that would go 'directly into the directors' bonuses'.[36])

Mather claims that Macquarie Airports inherited a lot of these issues, which is almost certainly true: in particular, she says that some of the charges that were levied on airlines, which went up by as much as 90 per cent prior to the privatisation, were decided under previous government ownership, not by Macquarie or Macquarie Airports.

Along the way, taxi drivers joined the fray, outraged by the way they believed they would be impacted by fees at the airport.

Jo Spillane,[37] who helped write the Macquarie Airports prospectus, remembers not wanting to tell taxi drivers to drop her at Macquarie. 'I don't have any memory of feeling terribly disturbed by it, but I had my head down,' she says.

The Branson matter would later be resolved in typically theatrical style with a preposterous performance outside an airport terminal in November 2002, in which he dressed up in a native American head-dress, accompanied by women dressed as Pocahontas, and buried a hatchet in front of the T2 airport terminal. Sydney Airports Corporation chief Tony Stuart went along with it, against the firm advice of Helen Nugent, then the chair of Macquarie Airports. 'I said to Tony: You're the CEO, it's your call, but I certainly wouldn't do this and I would advise you not to.'

Moore himself went through a bruising encounter with Alan Jones after telling the *Australian Financial Review* (AFR) in June 2002: 'I don't think anyone really cares what he thinks.' Jones certainly cared, and set about intensifying his attacks on the bank; Moss intervened, took out an apology to Jones in the same edition of the AFR that Moore's comments appeared, and reportedly went to Jones's Circular Quay apartment in Sydney to hand him a written apology from Moore. Moore gave another interview to the AFR a week later in a notably different frame of mind. 'We've never said we are infallible,' he said.[38]

Warwick Smith, who had responsibility for some of the smoothing over of bad press at this period, says: 'We made a bit of a rod for our own back during that period.' Moore, he says, 'learned the biggest lesson of his life. I know the good and the bad of the Alan Joneses of this world, but he was powerful and he was quite unique.'[39]

Eventually it reached the point where anything that happened at the airport—parking, flight delays, anything—was seen as the direct responsibility of Macquarie. And this spoke to a tricky disconnect between investors, who want the fees to go up, and users of the public assets, who want the reverse.

Macquarie had never been through anything like it and took time to find its feet. 'We definitely had a press problem,' says Moss now. 'But there was no statistical relationship between the bad press and our business performance. It was invisible in all our metrics except the share price of the affected funds.' This is true: the total annualised return of Macquarie Airports or MAp from the time of the Sydney Airport acquisition to the fund's later internalisation was 12.6 per cent, outperforming the S&P ASX 200 by 5.6 per cent per year.

So what, ultimately, was it about? Retail shareholders losing money was certainly part of it, and Macquarie did make structural and market mistakes at this time. And there is a profound public dislike of the privatisation of public assets, particularly if people perceive it as being accompanied by higher costs and lower service, whether objectively accurate or not. But there is also something distinctively Australian about attacking institutions that have grown successful enough that there is a popular mood to cut them down. That's the definition of tall poppy syndrome.

'I think, in Australia, there was a bit of a cultural cringe, particularly around the airport,' says Moss. By this he appears to mean that, with Macquarie up against the best and biggest investment banks in the world, for Macquarie to have won it must have paid too much. He describes the situations with Jones, Corrigan and Virgin as 'really unpleasant stoushes' and says it was 'really distracting for quite a few of our staff.' Moss went around speaking to people in meetings, division by division, explaining why it was a good deal, why Macquarie was confident, why it was professional.

Moss believes the noise around the airport was also the reason that MCIG, the fund based around broadcast transmission towers formerly owned by NTL Australia, struggled to get away. There had been high hopes for it. 'This is a business which, on the face of it, doesn't look like infrastructure, but actually, it's got all these really long-term 20–30 year contracts with a government counterparty,' says Andrew Low,[40] in charge of the business, referring to contracts with state-owned Australian channels ABC and SBS. 'Effectively, this is a bond.' They secured a credit agency wrap too, but it wasn't enough to save the deal from the dismal surrounding sentiment,[41] though in later years it would flourish.

'It affected the float, which was a great deal, by the way: an absolutely fabulous deal,' says Moss. 'But we really struggled to get it listed, and in the end we had to keep 30 per cent of it. We sold that residual 30 per cent later at a much bigger profit but we would still have preferred to sell it in the IPO.' In fact, Macquarie had to battle with its joint underwriters, UBS and JBWere, not to pull the deal entirely. 'That was entirely because of the doubt from the airport which of course proved to be a fantastic investment.'

There was another consideration, one that Macquarie wouldn't fully digest and act upon for some years: that retail were just not the right owners for long-dated and illiquid infrastructure assets.

Shemara Wikramanayake, a rising name in infrastructure at the time and today the CEO, can see it clearly now. 'What was going on with things like Sydney Airport is we were using listed vehicles to invest in illiquid assets, and we thought that was a good way to have these things owned to give investors greater liquidity at smaller investment sizes,' she says. 'With hindsight, it's not such a good match' if investors haven't had specialist advice on tolerating illiquidity. 'Because the biggest thing the investor needs to understand is the longer duration and illiquid nature of the assets.'

Bigger, sophisticated institutional investors of large pooled liabilities, who were just beginning to emerge as infrastructure specialists at the time (see Chapter 6 for more on this), have the stomach and capacity to commit for the long haul and worry less about illiquidity along the way. Retail shareholders are a different beast. 'And so, when the listed markets tanked, they sadly exercised their right to liquidity at the worst time for them and sold,' Wikramanayake says. So when an outcry developed that Macquarie must have overpaid—a contention clearly nullified in the years since—rather than having long-duration asset pools that stood by the assets, instead Macquarie got 'listed vehicles that were saying: I read that you've overpaid, I'm going to sell my shares, and that's going to push the price down even more.'

While more funds would follow in the years ahead, 2002 was the moment in which a crucial shift would gather pace, from listed funds filled with retail investors to unlisted funds dominated by institutions. 'The listed infrastructure business was growing fantastically, and then the listed market turned against externally managed funds,' recalls Robin Bishop, former head of Macquarie Capital for Australia and New Zealand.[42] 'You can scream at the storm, but if the market does not want to listen, ultimately, you have to change your strategy. Close them down, restructure, get the best possible outcome and go where the markets are receptive—which was the unlisted market.'

And that's what ultimately happened. At the time of writing Macquarie has two listed infrastructure funds left, MKIF in South Korea and FIBRA Macquarie in Mexico. Everything else would be sold, absorbed, taken private or otherwise removed from public listed life. It would take years to play out, and the global financial crisis would hasten it, but the writing was on the wall even then.

'It was the wrong pool of investors for the asset class—unless they have specialist advice on their capacity to tolerate illiquidity,' Wikramanayake says. 'And that was a lesson the whole industry learned. The market evolves, and our large portfolio of unlisted funds better meets the expectations investors have.'

■

There were plenty of other ideas at this time beyond airports. One of them was to take on retail. Macquarie had a track record here, with the Cash Management Trust and retail broking, and as a condition of getting its bank licence from the Reserve Bank of Australia had opened a series of branches in the 1980s.[43] But it had never really thrown the full force of the bank at it. And to this end, in 2000 it hired Peter Maher and gave him a new group, Financial Services Group, or FSG,[44] to bring anything consumer-facing under a single group and to build from there.

'It had become clear that our strengths in retail were modest,' says Allan Moss. 'But it had also become clear that there was a set of skills, very different to wholesale investment banking skills, that went with retail. So it was a very rare thing for us: we went outside to hire someone at the most senior level, and that was Peter Maher.'

Maher, who joined from Westpac,[45] was an interesting hire. He remains the only person to be appointed externally as a group head and to go straight onto the Exco. 'Macquarie tends to breed from within, so it was unusual,' he says.[46]

But Macquarie had taken this uncharted course because, Maher says, 'having had a number of attempts, they had realised that retail was a little bit different from being an investment bank. It was an area they viewed as strategically potentially attractive, but hadn't known how to crack it.' A strategic study by Accenture convinced the bank that a decent retail business wasn't going to be built instantly and would require time and investment.

This was interesting, because Macquarie in general—and certainly everyone else on that Exco—was a place with a quite rapid expectation of profits, and little tolerance of heavy costs along the way to achieving them. Maher says that from the top, he was 'given enough rope,' as he puts it. 'I'm sure there would have been some people on the inside waiting for me to stuff up because I wasn't an investment banker, and some other people who were cheering on the sidelines going: thank God, we've got a retail guy.'

Still, it would take until 2004 to make a real contribution, after which it stepped up considerably. 'There was just an unspoken pressure to get it right,' Maher recalls. 'Nobody ever shirtfronted me in the executive committee and said: what the hell are you doing? But you definitely felt the collective pressure.' That was a pressure that the environment caused you to put upon yourself. 'It's the pressure from your own aspirations and pride when you're sitting around a table and everyone is talking about how many hundreds of millions they are making. It strengthens the ambition.'

The vision had to be communicated internally within the team too. Megan Aubrey was another to join the team with experience from a bigger established name, in her case a decade at Colonial First State. 'I realised I'd joined the one group at Macquarie not making much money at the time,' she says. 'The first presentation I saw, from Peter Maher, showed the financials, and I thought: right, that's not ideal.

'But the next few slides showed the vision: here's the six things we will do. If you see that, and if you like a bit of a challenge, you are confident and you get behind it.' Aubrey would go on to build the Professional Series, which gave Australian investors exposure to leading international fund managers they would never otherwise have had access to.[47]

In practical terms, some differences were swiftly clear. At Westpac, Maher had served on the IT investment committee, where for three years in a row, a proposal to build a wrap platform had been raised. 'And it got knocked back, because with a single IT investment budget, core systems upgrades and regulatory changes took priority, and relatively small amounts for what was viewed as discretionary expenditure.' But when he got to Macquarie, he found Neil Roderick and Matt Rady were already building a wrap platform there. Maher asked Roderick how he had done it. 'And basically, they just didn't tell anybody. They figured out a Skunk Works[48] way to get it started.' From this Maher understood an attitude that pervades Macquarie today: keep as many decisions as possible close to the market and the clients, and keep centralised decisions for things like risk management.

Australia has one of the most intermediated and sophisticated personal finance landscapes in the world. Wraps and mastertrusts, in Australia, are platforms through which financial planners help individual clients to reach products, chiefly managed funds.[49] Macquarie came to this from an odd direction: most platforms had been developed by participants who already had a large linked adviser base, such as AMP, so their priority tended to be selling in-house products distributed by their own advisers, though this would change with regulation in later years.

Macquarie didn't have a big in-force adviser network; it just had the Cash Management Trust (CMT), which was widely distributed by independent financial advisers. That was the market Macquarie knew, 'so from day dot it was the most open architecture platform,' Maher says. That would turn out to be ahead of its time. Yet again, the CMT, which had been quietly shooting the lights out for the past 25 years or so by now, was delivering. 'It had given us great exposure to the broader adviser market and the insights that come out of that.'

The CMT had always had a strong service culture, and Maher tried to spread that across his new division, aided by Sheryl Weil, who had been head of service for the Brisbane operation. 'She embodied a service culture and a great client experience culture, all of which roll off the tongue easily when you come from retail, but it's not necessarily the first things you look at when you come from an investment banking background, which is very focused on deal completion and the fees.' Within a few years of CMT being rolled into Maher's division it had gone from around A$3 billion to $10 billion.[50]

Then, through the 2000s, Macquarie set about bringing its particular brand of financial engineering to the masses: through financial planners and dealer groups, but ultimately, to you and I, the mums and dads of Australia. And one quirk of this enthusiasm was that it wasn't just Maher's division, but several others, including Ottmar Weiss's[51] equities division and the funds management group, that were out there trying to build products for us.

It was big business. The eight years or so running up to the beginnings of the global financial crisis in 2007 were marked by a relentless appetite for risk, at every level from individuals to institutions.

One gets a sense of the momentum—and some problems that came with it—from a single week in May 2005.[52] That week, Macquarie launched:

- ALPS, a series of high-yielding capital-protected securities in which the yield fell each time one of a basket of stocks fell by a certain amount;
- Atlas Trust, a capital-protected unit trust similar to ALPS but with a built-in call option tied to the S&P/ASX 200;
- The sixth in Macquarie's Equinox series, which gave investors exposure to a range of global hedge fund managers;
- A margin loan with a twist, linked to property syndicates and property security funds;
- The ReFleXion Trusts, which used derivatives to give investors exposure to indices in Asia.

None of these were simple, and the desires of customers were only part of the driving force for their creation. Macquarie's bankers certainly consulted with financial advisers, and wouldn't deliver a product for which there was no appetite, but the sometimes bewildering range of products was also a function of very smart people—lawyers, financial engineers, tax specialists—trying to come up with something new.

Of course they wanted their products to deliver growth and income, befitting the hunger for risk of the era. But the other main driver of the time was Australia's fixation with tax minimisation. Australians may not be aware of it, but there is no other market in the world where the level of individual literacy around tax effectiveness is so high—which is, in turn, a function of tax itself being high,[53] and opportunities to seek deductions from it plentiful.

Channelling that consumer fixation, Macquarie's boffins would often start from the premise of: what would be tax-effective? If expense related to income was deductible, what could be done with that? What followed was a decade of products with increasingly elaborate bells and whistles, with embedded leverage and capital protection and loans and derivatives and options involved. There were products linked to wineries and olive farms and cricket bat willow plantations and the Australian film industry, primarily because of tax concessions that were linked to those things. A merry dance with the Australian Taxation Office (ATO) followed, from whom the best reward was a favourable tax ruling that could be given to investors; when the ATO wouldn't provide one, Macquarie would typically go and find a senior barrister to give an opinion instead.

Macquarie was far from alone in this, and was actually not the worst in terms of complexity: it was other companies that first thought it was a good idea to sell CDOs[54] to retail. All the Big Four retail banks[55] had divisions offering similar products, and there was an abundance of financial engineering at international investment banks, including UBS, Deutsche and ABN Amro. One of the authors ran the AFR's investment sections at the time and published a weekly column untangling the details and parameters of complex products; there was never a shortage of products to dissect.

But Macquarie was the most successful.

Across the industry, as the decade rolled on, products became so complicated they seemed almost obstructive.

Take Atlas: a capital-protected unlisted unit trust made up of two parts. One was a coupon that increased steadily but whose return diminished if any of a range of underlying stocks fell more than a certain amount from its price at the product's launch. Then there was a call option embedded in it to deliver 75 per cent exposure to any increases in the S&P/ASX200. Working out how exactly this might impact a return was the work of a mathematician; forming a cohesive investment view on how it might pan out was the task of a clairvoyant.

An issue for the market, and for the bank's own sales teams, was that Macquarie was uncoordinated in the way that it developed and timed these products. Presented with that list from 2005, a former banker observes: 'Each one of those products was designed by a different person. They were incentivised to come up with new products. And the job of the salesperson was not to say no, it was to find a way.'

The result, for end investors, was an onslaught driven by the entrepreneurial and siloed culture of the bank. And for Macquarie, it meant that its biggest competitor during this era was frequently itself, with different products being generated from different divisions in what was inherently the same space. Moss, though, was loath to intervene: let the market decide, was his attitude. Survival of the fittest, in product terms. It was the find-a-niche evolutionary spirit of the bank.

And so for several years the equities division, the equity markets group,[56] the structured tax team and various other siloes would find themselves going head to head.

It drove financial planning groups—the buyers of these products— to distraction. Who am I supposed to be speaking to, they would say?

If I'm talking to you, who was that other guy who just called me? 'Some large financial planning dealer groups got angry and said: listen, we only want one person from Macquarie speaking to us,' recalls a banker at that time. 'We need a relationship manager.'

Relationship managers did exist, but they didn't really sit across divisions, and their incentives were ultimately about the products within their own division.

At one stage Moss set up a cross-divisional committee to try to do something about it and encourage people within Macquarie to work together. It might reward, say, somebody who through their tax-effective leasing work found a likely candidate for an IPO and referred it to the capital markets team. It had some success, but it didn't change an inherently competitive internal dynamic.

What changed the picture completely was the global financial crisis.

Chapter 9

LET THE GOOD TIMES ROLL

As the 2000s rolled on, and as the troubles of 2002 were digested, Macquarie was characterised by a steadily greater ambition. There was a feeling that anything was possible.

Richard Sheppard recalls what the Monday morning Exco meetings were like during this period. 'There were lots of ideas,' he recalls. 'And there were lots of things that weren't all that successful either. A lot of the big ones are pretty public: Qantas, London Stock Exchange.'

Indeed, the spirit of those years is perhaps best demonstrated by those two deals—deals that didn't happen.

In August 2005, to widespread astonishment, Macquarie confirmed an outlandish rumour that it was considering a bid for the London Stock Exchange (LSE). The authors both worked on the *Australian Financial Review* at the time, and can still recall a moment of stunned silence when it was confirmed. 'Wait, what? It's *true?*'

Macquarie would go on to launch a £1.5 billion hostile bid for the LSE, though it never got particularly close to the finish line; Jim Craig, head of Macquarie Group in Europe, pulled the plug on it in February 2006 having been unable to agree on the value of the business.[1] The idea had not been as outlandish as it seems: as Moss says, they simply thought of it as quasi-infrastructure, 'the financial infrastructure of the world, really,' with resilient earnings over the long term.

The idea came and went within six months, and in the British context is nowhere near as important to the bank as the Midlands Expressway, Thames Water, Green Investment Bank or a hundred other deals. But people still talk about it in the UK, as a landmark moment when an interesting but niche Australian upstart suddenly crashed into the British national consciousness.

Moore is surprised by the attention given to this, but he does understand it. 'You mentioned the London Stock Exchange bid as something to cover. And to me, in the history of Macquarie, I would not even put that on the page,' he says. 'It was a nothing, it never happened. Of all the deals that we've been involved in, and there's been many, that one never happened.'

The reason it sticks in the popular imagination is the way it represents Macquarie's sense that nothing was out of reach at this time.

The London Stock Exchange is the very essence of global commerce, and speaks to 450 years[2] of Britain's involvement in that story. It's been housed since 2004 in modern premises in Paternoster Square next to St Paul's Cathedral, but in the popular imagination it is still somewhat associated with its former home next to the Bank of England in the Royal Exchange building, a grand stone structure fronted by a portico of eight Corinthian columns. There's a statue of the Duke of Wellington out the front that was unveiled when the Battle of Waterloo was in living memory: you really are taking on history when you take on the LSE.

Like it or not, the brazen ambition of it all resonated internally too. Nicole Sorbara, now a member of the Exco, remembers what that bid felt like as a cultural statement. 'It's part of the Australian culture where we think: we'll give it a go,' she says. 'The sense of: why not? It's not necessarily listening to all the reasons why you can't. It's more questioning: what are the possibilities? What's stopping us?'

But the fact that anyone knew about it at all is telling. There was a lot of noise around Macquarie, and at least some of it was generated from the inside.

'Although it was against policy, some Macquarie executives and advisers seemed open to share,' Moore says. 'People were talking about deals that had a 2 per cent chance of happening, but we were filling the pages of the newspaper every day, as a willing accomplice. The LSE was just the most iconic example.'

Another deal that didn't happen, but got a lot closer to doing so, was Macquarie's role in a bold attempt to take Australia's flagship airline, Qantas, private in an A$11.1 billion bid in late 2006.

It's hard to convey to a non-Australian just how iconic the national airline is. A kangaroo graces its aircrafts' tails. *The Spirit of Australia* is among its taglines, *I Still Call Australia Home* among the anthems attached to its advertising. Its safety record turns up in global pop culture like the movie *Rain Man*.

So it created a storm in Australia when a hefty local and international consortium including Macquarie emerged as its attempted buyer. Politicians scrutinised foreign ownership implications, several investors were staunch critics of the idea, and public hysteria, much like the airline, was in the air.

It wasn't as unlikely as it seemed. In the months leading up to the bid, Macquarie had gained a foothold in the global aircraft leasing market. It had been part of a consortium that agreed to acquire GATX Air in September 2006, a deal that exhibited several hallmarks of its approach to chunky transactions: business

adjacency and the use of partners, in this case including Och Ziff
Capital Management Group, to help lighten the amount of equity
Macquarie had to tip in.

This is how it came about. Macquarie had started acquiring
aircraft on its balance sheet in 2004 and 2005 and then set its sights
on trying to acquire AWAS, the former Ansett leasing division owned
by Morgan Stanley. Asset finance head Stephen Cook was leading
Macquarie's efforts but they missed out on AWAS and another asset
at a similar time. Determined not to miss out again, he identified
another significant opportunity.

Cook put in a call to then GATX president and CEO Brian
Kenney. He knew the New York-listed company was not enthusiastic
about its presence in aircraft leasing and thought it might be open
to divesting itself of its entire plane leasing unit, ideally without an
auction process.

Cook timed the call well: he caught Kenney when he was particularly frustrated with the aircraft side of his business, which was
predominantly a rail car investment and leasing company. 'Brian
recognised he had quite a messy, complicated business, with many
different partners and investors. I was able to convince him to sell it
to Macquarie on a bilateral basis,'[3] Cook says.

The US$1.46 billion acquisition of GATX Air cemented
Macquarie's early ambition in the aircraft leasing sector. It wasn't an
easy transaction by any measure: of the 87 narrow-body commercial
jets in the deal, 49 were held in joint venture partnerships. But it led
to the formation of Macquarie AirFinance, with the bank taking a
35 per cent stake in the new unit.

It was just two months after that deal that Qantas's Flying Kangaroo
sprang into the public arena. In fact, the deal had been in the works
with considerable planning and behind-the-scenes manoeuvring for
months, and there had even been an earlier iteration of the Qantas

bid, never made public until now, eighteen months beforehand. The airline had powerful admirers within the bank.

'It was perceived to be a robust business,' says Moss. 'We felt that we knew a fair bit about it because of our long involvement in airports.

'We felt we could contribute.' Quite apart from the airports, 'we had been financing aeroplanes for twenty years.'

There was no way Macquarie could attempt something this audacious alone, and its participation in any buy-out had to be capped, for several reasons: the size of the cheque involved, the level of risk in the deal, and debatably Macquarie's management of Sydney Airport. So the deal team assessing the opportunity, led by then head of industrials Tim Bishop, first looked for suitable bid partners.

Bishop first approached Texas Pacific Group, now TPG, given the buy-out group's experience in the aviation sector, which had included the turnaround of Continental Airlines. Texas Pacific, in turn, brought in the Canadian private equity firm Onex. That was about as much as could be done internationally since foreign ownership of Qantas is restricted to 49 per cent under the airline's constitution, and the deal would have to navigate Australia's tough Foreign Investment Review Board with a sign-off from the federal government.

They needed a domestic partner, and Bishop knew just the place: Allco Financial Group, founded by experienced dealmaker David Coe, known to all in deal circles as 'Coey'. Coe was no stranger to leasing or complicated deals, and better still, the Allco group included a cashbox private equity vehicle[4] called Allco Equity Partners (AEP); it was led by Peter Yates, who had been a Macquarie banker for fifteen years before becoming CEO of Kerry Packer's media behemoth, Publishing and Broadcasting Limited.

The problem was that Allco was in many respects a competitor to Macquarie and Nicholas Moore, Bishop's divisional boss, didn't much like the idea. 'Nicholas wasn't really happy about it, but I said I can't see another solution to this,' says Bishop. 'They were historic competitors as individuals and as firms, but my view was I couldn't see another domestic solution to it and it was somebody that we could at least work with.'

It would later transpire that Yates wasn't as sure about this bid as Coe. Having launched his cashbox after lobbying the ASX (Australian Stock Exchange) to change the rules around capital raising, he had found to his chagrin that the markets had gone crazy and there was not much available at a sane margin. 'We were really quite famous for apparently failing to win every deal because I simply refused to pay stupid prices,' he says now. 'As we got towards the middle of 2006 I got exceptionally nervous that the markets were going to crash for sure. The prices people were paying were nuts: nine times leverage, eighteen times earnings.'

But Qantas was a name of particular allure to Coe, who really wanted a landmark deal. 'David Coe had always dreamed about Qantas, and Nicholas Moore had a very solid understanding of its fundamental value,' recalls Yates. 'They believed that if it was properly split up, and you financed the aircraft separately to the properties and then spun out the frequent flyer business, there was a huge amount of latent value inside it.'

Coe and Yates would develop such radically different views on the whole idea that, the day before the bid was to be announced, Coe told Yates to resign as CEO of AEP. Yates called Moore to tell him the next morning, to Moore's astonishment. 'You're meant to be fronting this deal,' Moore told him. 'And you're resigning? No way.' The decision was swiftly reversed.

The consortium called itself Airline Partners Australia to play up the domestic representation.[5] The team pulled together a group of big-name banks to assist in the funding package. They had also sounded out Qantas CEO Geoff Dixon about how a buy-out proposal might be received, and had told him they would back him and his existing management team.

After weeks of frenetic speculation, the bidding consortium was publicly confirmed and Qantas disclosed a complex offer of A$5.50 per share in December 2006. The board rebuffed it, so they came back the following day offering A$5.60 in cash including a dividend to be paid to investors and fewer conditions.

There were various versions of the offer's finer details that followed, and, with the leverage involved, a so-called covenant-lite debt package that would provide long-term respite on hefty interest payments should Qantas endure a severe financial crisis or a pandemic-like event—both things that would later transpire.

But fund managers UBS Asset Management and Balanced Equity weren't buying it, and opposed the deal. The deadline for acceptances was extended several times in 2007, until 4 May became the drop-dead date.

The bidding group were quietly confident of hitting the necessary 50 per cent acceptance threshold, but it turned out they were complacent. As the clock ticked through the final 24 hours, the deal hinged upon an American billionaire hedge fund manager called Samuel Heyman, who refused to believe there was a hard deadline for the bid acceptance. Apparently not a man to be rushed, he went to bed and then submitted an acceptance for his 4.9 per cent stake in the airline the next morning—which was, given the time difference, after the stated deadline of 7 pm Australian Eastern Standard Time on the 4th. That, and other fund managers holding out for a higher offer, brought to an abrupt end the audacious bid for Qantas.[6]

Bishop was among the bankers licking their wounds as the bid collapsed. 'It clearly wasn't our finest hour. I'm not going to suggest otherwise,' he says.[7]

The market furore around it all was deafening, overwhelming more successful deals. At the same time much of this was happening, Macquarie was advising Wesfarmers on acquiring then-embattled Australian supermarket and retail group Coles,[8] a deal with a compelling industrial logic. That transaction had a lot of moving parts including Robin Bishop working on an under-the-radar acquisition of retail stalwart Solomon Lew's stake in Coles and then blowing a competing private equity bidding consortium—with considerable muscle—out of the water on the auction. But the Coles transaction got a fraction of the column inches Qantas had done.

■

It would be remiss to look at the deals that didn't happen and not some of those that did. For Macquarie itself, the acquisition of Cook Inlet in Los Angeles in 2005 would be a landmark, not apparent at the time, that would lead to the supercharged profits driven by Commodities and Global Markets that have characterised the 2020s (see Chapter 7 for more on this). But Dyno Nobel is perhaps the most Macquarie deal of that pre-GFC era.

The short version: Macquarie and some partners bought Dyno Nobel, the explosives manufacturer, for US$1.7 billion in 2005, sold the European, Asian and South American assets to Orica for US$685 million, then listed the remainder of it at a market value of A$1.9 billion the following April, a deal that made Macquarie about A$400 million return in seven months.[9]

That's easy to say. But think about what that deal is. 'The idea of a bunch of investment bankers from Australia buying an explosive manufacturer headquartered in Oslo and created by the founder of the Nobel Prize sounds completely unlikely,' says Robin Bishop, who was one of the deal's architects. 'We are going to separate it into two parts. We're going to run one part of Dyno where we have no economic incentive until Orica get antitrust approval in 42-odd countries, and then deliver it for Orica. And we are then going to float the remaining operation in Australia.'

He pauses for emphasis. 'There's a hundred reasons to say no to the idea,' he adds. 'But the skill of Macquarie is it does not simply say no. It doesn't say yes either, necessarily; it says what we don't like is XYZ, so solve those problems, find a solution, change the scenario, protect Macquarie from downside risks.'

Bishop recalls having his first meeting with Nicholas Moore about this leftfield idea, and found that Moore, at that stage, didn't really want to talk about the deal or the company. He wanted to talk about manufacturing ammonium nitrate, about chemical formulas and calculations, about trade flows and about movements in the index that measures US gas prices. 'This was early in the process, and Nicholas's deep pre-existing knowledge and powerful intellectual curiosity exposed our knowledge,' says Bishop. He and a colleague left and Bishop said: we've got to get this deal and make a great success of it, otherwise our careers could be over after that meeting. 'He (Moore) has always had that capacity to know more about the situation you're focused on than you did. Which was always a bit disturbing.'

Countless Macquarie bankers have had the same experience, and, frankly, so have we: in the first of our two interviews with Moore for this book, he put us through our paces for 40 minutes, throwing out questions about shareholder funds and price-to-book ratios and breaking down our idea for the manuscript chapter by chapter, then told us that before we met again we should read all 52 annual reports. (This was, as it happens, exceptionally good advice.) Once we had done so, and came to our second meeting more statistically armed, he was a totally different person: generous, articulate, incisive and even funny, for two hours.

So Moore, not unreasonably, wants people to know everything about what they are doing, and considers it the essence of proper risk management. Only when you are truly an expert in the field of your deal can you truly be across what will make it work and what will bring it down. Both as a rising banker and later chief executive, he would always conduct deal meetings like this: probe, look for the weakness, test the information, test the people.

So, crucially, in that difficult first meeting Bishop had with Moore, one thing Moore never said was: no. 'So, rather than saying no he drills you to find out: do you really know what you're talking about, do you fully understand the risks, have you done the work? And you will be supported with time, people and resources to do the work to see if you can say "yes" to each of those questions.'

The odd structure of Dyno Nobel came about partly because of Macquarie's ability to turn a problem into an opportunity. Georgina Johnson (née Georgina Lalor), now co-head of equity capital markets for Australia, got a baptism of fire when this turned out to be the first deal she ever worked on after joining. As she recalls, the idea was originally for Orica to buy it, but for antitrust reasons they couldn't take on the Australian and American components of the business. 'So we took that on the balance sheet with a group of institutional investors who would be the eventual holders in the IPO.'

Pre-IPO holdings are absolutely commonplace among institutional investors now, but they weren't in 2005: Lalor remembers Bishop having to educate the instos about how it would work and fit within their mandates, particularly since many of them were only permitted by their own internal rules to hold unlisted securities for a maximum of six to twelve months. 'And we found we had a structure that worked incredibly well for those investors, because they were the natural holders post-IPO.' Plus, Macquarie made several hundred million dollars.

Hugh Falcon, who today runs capital markets for Asia-Pacific, cites the deal as one of the best examples of a Macquarie approach. 'What Macquarie does is try to bring more ideas—transformational ideas,' he says. Falcon worked at Macquarie, left for Goldman, then came back again, so has some context on the differences between two exceptional houses. Goldman, he says, has a consistent model focused around mergers and acquisitions core advisory and capital markets businesses, with a well-honed strategy that is broadly the same globally and can be rolled out across multiple markets. Frequently, Macquarie deals don't look like anything else they or any rival have ever done before or since.

Using the balance sheet, for example, is an interesting twist, as was the case in Dyno Nobel and a later classic Macquarie deal, Quadrant Energy.[10] 'That lends a level of creativity that goes with this culture that I think built Macquarie a reputation,' says Falcon, 'for being seen as about ingenuity and quite bold transactions.'

Sometimes deals were so good for Macquarie it would later turn out to be problematic. An example here was the Beaconsfield coal mine in Tasmania.

In 2002, Allstate, which owned 51 per cent of the mine's joint venture, was struggling and went into administration; its creditors agreed to sell Macquarie (the mine's only secured creditor, thanks to an earlier A$21 million project finance facility) loans with a face value of A$77 million that Allstate had made to its own subsidiaries for A$300,000. The mine, by now under Macquarie's effective control, then returned to profit, eventually yielding Macquarie A$27 million in recovered interest and loan repayments on this and other debt.

It was an exceptional outcome for Macquarie. But then, in April 2006, the mine collapsed, killing one miner and trapping two in a narrow cage underground for two full weeks until they were rescued, during which a major global media story had developed around their plight. That, in turn, focused media attention on Macquarie's role at the mine.

It was a stretch to hold Macquarie responsible for anything that had happened at the mine; it had simply ended up owning the debt. In fact, Macquarie's bad press at the mine pre-dated the accident: the bank sued Michael West of *The Australian* for an article he wrote in March 2005 about the money Macquarie had made from the mine and the manner in which it achieved it, alleging that creditors were not given the full picture as to how rich the mine was. Macquarie eventually lost that action in the ACT Supreme Court four years later at rumoured legal costs of up to $4 million.[11]

Shortly after the men were freed, Macquarie said it would donate the remaining $48 million in intra-group debt that it held on Allstate to a trust set up for the benefit of the miners.[12] That ended up being quite the largesse: when the gold price soared in subsequent years, the debt paid off in full.

Still, today Macquarie insiders look back at that decision as a good example of the bank trying to find creative solutions to fix problems. But it also showed there were challenges that came with being so clearly the winner in a deal: the losers tend not to like it and it doesn't look great.

Another complex deal to evaluate came when the West Australian energy company Alinta came up for sale. Macquarie had been a long-standing corporate adviser to Alinta, but when several senior executives decided to attempt a buy-out and said Macquarie was considering advising them on doing so, Alinta dumped Macquarie[13] in January 2007. Macquarie presents it differently today—it became a bidder at the request of the board and had to cease being an adviser to the business as a consequence, it says—but had it failed to manage a conflict?

Later that month, Alinta said it would accept Macquarie itself as a bidder for Alinta, at which point Babcock & Brown, the closest

Christopher Castleman, who helped establish Hill Samuel's Australian operations and ran the global group from 1980 to 1987.
Source: Jane Clarke.

Stan Owens, inaugural Hill Samuel Australia chairman.
Source: Owens family.

Signing of the John Lysaght (Australia) loan agreement, August 1971. Stan Owens addresses representatives from a syndicate of international and domestic banks.
Source: Owens family.

Mark Johnson joined Hill Samuel Australia/ Macquarie Bank as joint managing director with David Clarke in 1971. He left in 1981 but returned in 1986 as chairman of Corporate Services. Appointed to the board the following year, Johnson retired from executive responsibilities in 2007.
Source: News Corp.

Tony Berg joined Hill Samuel in 1972 and led Hill Samuel Australia/ Macquarie Bank as managing director for about a decade until 1993.
Source: Macquarie Group.

David Clarke, receiving the Officer of the Order of Australia (AO) for service to business and the community in 1992, flanked by his sons. Clarke was managing director of Hill Samuel Australia/Macquarie Bank before becoming executive chairman in 1984. In 2007 he ceased executive duties and was chairman until March 2011. Source: Jane Clarke.

Phil Gardiner joined Hill Samuel Australia in 1978 and played a leadership role in the firm's hedge, foreign exchange and money market businesses. Source: Phil Gardiner.

The currency hedge market is complex enough without relying on a banker who's yet to get his feet wet.

Most of the operators now jumping into the hedge market are bound to flounder around until they get the hang of it.

Unfortunately, it's your money they'd be experimenting with. That's why Hill Samuel makes so much sense. We've spent a lot of time learning the intricacies of foreign currency hedging. And today no one knows this complex business better.

We know where the market is segmented. We understand exchange gains and loss taxation. We know how to handle the special accounting for foreign exchange. We have the experience necessary to measure a client's exchange risks.

We also have the necessary international contacts. And we can arrange your hedge in Deutsche marks, Swiss francs or Japanese yen, as well as U.S. dollars.

Moreover, we accomplish all this for you with the speed and personal service you expect from a merchant bank.

So if you're thinking of doing a little hedging, hedge a little more. Come to the experienced people. Hill Samuel. We got our feet wet a long time ago.

Hill Samuel
Australia Limited

Sydney: Philip Gardiner, Peter Taylor, Louise Burney, Warwick Gartrell. Phone (02) 232 4233
Melbourne: Geoff Cunningham. Phone (03) 614 1033
Brisbane: Claude Santucci. Phone (07) 221 0661

Quirky Hill Samuel advertisement spruiking the firm's experience in the hedge market. Source: Phil Gardiner.

Hill Samuel Australia/Macquarie Bank's Andrew Downe, Clive Carroll, Ray Hall and Mitchell Duggan dining with clients in 1986. Carroll, Hall and Downe all had stints running the firm's Commodities and Global Markets team. Source: News Corp.

Hill Samuel Australia/Macquarie Bank executive director John Caldon in 1996. Source: News Corp.

Changing of the guard in 1993. Macquarie Bank managing director Tony Berg with executive chairman David Clarke and incoming managing director Allan Moss. Source: News Corp.

Macquarie Bank executive director Simon Hannes with mining industry executive Leonard Davis and CRA chairman John Uhrig. Following the 1995 merger of RTZ and CRA (which became Rio Tinto), Davis was appointed deputy chief executive and operating chief of the combined entity. Source: News Corp.

Macquarie Bank executive director Simon Hannes after an appearance at Sydney's Downing Centre District Court in 1999. Source: News Corp.

Macquarie Bank CEO Allan Moss (right) with Bankers Trust Australia chief, Rob Ferguson, and head of investment banking, Gavin Walker. They announced Macquarie's acquisition of BT Australia's corporate finance and trading arm in 1999. Source: News Corp.

Part of the deal team involved in Macquarie Bank's 2002 purchase of Sydney Airport. Source: News Corp.

Virgin Blue airline staff during a protest outside Macquarie Bank in Sydney in 2002, amid heightened tension over the airport's acquisition. Source: News Corp.

This early Macquarie Bank annual report cover from 1986 shows a businessman's breakfast of the period (with filtered coffee) and spruiks the firm's early success. Source: Macquarie Group.

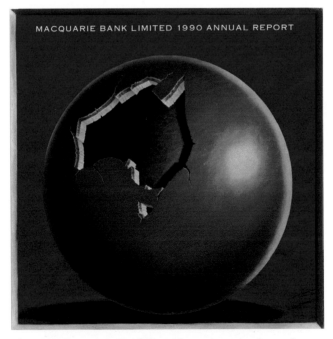

The 1990 Macquarie Bank annual report cover shows the outline of Australia cut into a Jaffa, a popular chocolate confectionery in Australia. It highlights the bank's role as an Australian finance and advisory specialist. Source: Macquarie Group.

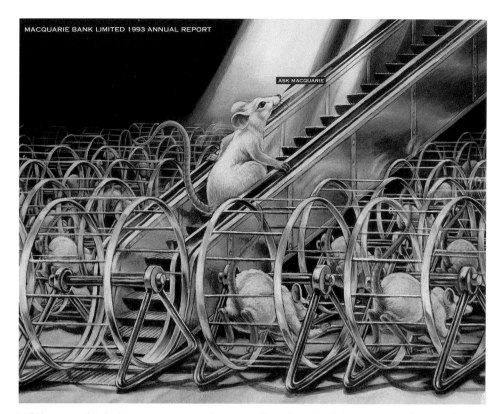

While some think the mouse-on-escalator motif on the 1993 Macquarie Bank annual report cover takes some beating for obscurity, the report considered the difference between being stuck on a treadmill or going on to greater heights. Source: Macquarie Group.

The 2005 annual report cover shows an example of Macquarie Bank's expansion into international infrastructure, the Incheon Expressway, a 40-kilometre toll road in South Korea, in which Macquarie's Korean Road Infrastructure Fund held a stake. Source: Macquarie Group.

The Airline Partners Australia consortium's board. It put forward a $5.60-per-share offer for Qantas in 2006, but the bid ultimately failed the following year. Source: News Corp.

The Major Gift Appeal's chairman Lachlan Murdoch accepted a cheque in 2006 on behalf of Surf Life Saving Australia from Macquarie Bank executive chairman David Clarke. Source: News Corp.

US President George W. Bush welcomed by then Australian Prime Minister John Howard and Macquarie Group's Mark Johnson to APEC's Business Summit at the Sydney Opera House in 2007. Source: News Corp.

Macquarie Group CEO Nicholas Moore and acting chairman Kevin McCann explain a slump in 2009 profit to investors during the fallout from the global financial crisis. Source: News Corp.

Macquarie Group CEO Nicholas Moore leaving the Royal Commission into Misconduct in the Banking, Superannuation and Financial Services Industry in late 2018. Security guards help him navigate the media throng. Source: News Corp.

Baton change. Macquarie Group CEO Nicholas Moore announces his retirement in 2018, handing the reins to Shemara Wikramanayake. Source: News Corp.

Lal Lal Wind Farms, backed by Macquarie Group, are close to the Victorian towns of Ballan and Yendon. At the time of writing, Macquarie's Green Investment Group had agreed to sell its holding in the wind farms. Credit: Joyce Moullakis.

Newcastle Port's energy precinct, glimpsed beyond the coal ships being loaded. The port is pursuing a diversification strategy that involves increasing its involvement in renewable and cleaner forms of energy. Source: Newcastle Port.

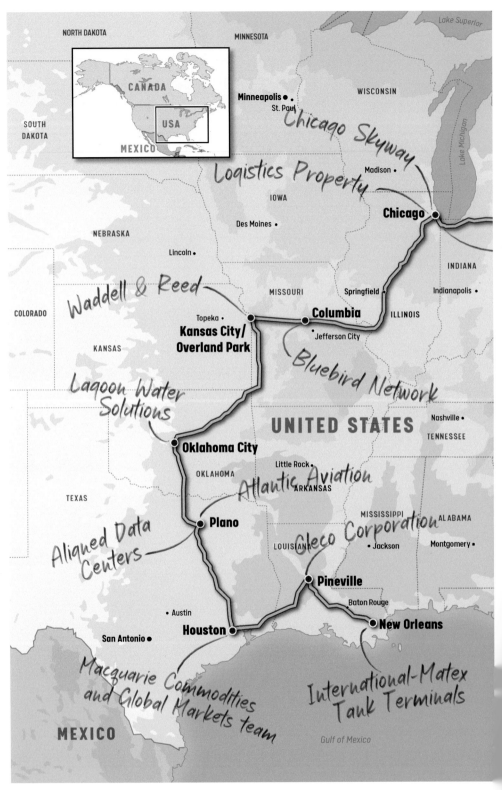

Current and former Macquarie Group assets encountered in our American road trip, Chapter 7. This is not a complete list of Macquarie assets in North America.

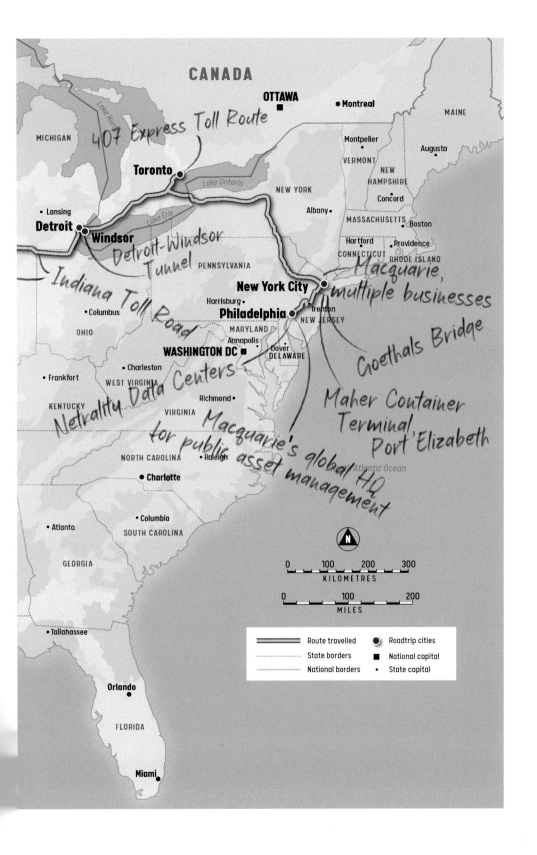

CANADA

407 Express Toll Route

Detroit-Windsor Tunnel

Indiana Toll Road

Netrality Data Centers

Macquarie's global HQ for public asset management

Macquarie, multiple businesses

Goethals Bridge

Maher Container Terminal, Port Elizabeth

MICHIGAN

OTTAWA ■

● Montreal

MAINE

Montpelier •

VERMONT

NEW HAMPSHIRE

Augusta

Toronto

Lake Ontario

NEW YORK

Concord •

Lake Erie

Albany •

MASSACHUSETTS

Boston •

• Lansing

Detroit

Windsor

Hartford •

• Providence

CONNECTICUT

RHODE ISLAND

PENNSYLVANIA

New York City

Harrisburg •

Philadelphia •

Trenton •

NEW JERSEY

• Columbus

OHIO

MARYLAND

Annapolis •

WASHINGTON DC ■

Dover •

DELAWARE

• Charleston

WEST VIRGINIA

• Frankfort

KENTUCKY

Richmond •

VIRGINIA

NORTH CAROLINA

• Raleigh

Atlantic Ocean

• Charlotte

• Columbia

• Atlanta

SOUTH CAROLINA

GEORGIA

N

0   100   200   300
KILOMETRES

0   100   200
MILES

• Tallahassee

Orlando •

FLORIDA

	Route travelled	●	Roadtrip cities
....	State borders	■	National capital
	National borders	•	State capital

Miami •

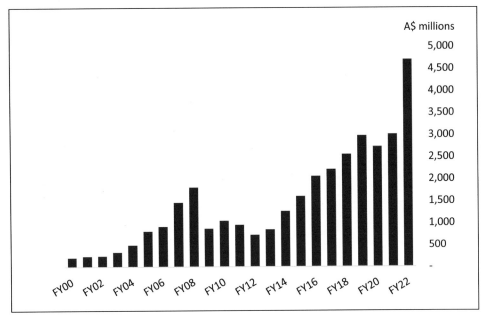

A chart showing Macquarie's annual profits from financial years 2000 to 2022.
Source: Macquarie Group.

Macquarie Group CEO Shemara Wikramanayake at the COP27 summit in 2022, on a panel including Mike Bloomberg and Simon Stiell, executive secretary of the United Nations Framework Convention on Climate Change. Source: Macquarie Group.

Australian equivalent to Macquarie at the time, said it would bid A\$7 billion.[14] The two institutions, who until this point had largely stayed out of one another's way, traded bids and counter-bids.[15] 'It was a bit like going to an auction of a house in a really hot market,' says Robert Dunlop, who worked on the deal. 'We really knew what it was worth and we knew the risks. But Babcocks were really keen to get the assets and we reached our maximum.'[16]

In the end Alinta opted for Babcock & Brown because of higher confidence in the scrip component, meaning that part of the takeover would be paid for in Babcock shares. This would not prove to be the best call.

One person who cut their teeth on the Alinta process was Kate Vidgen, now Macquarie's global head of industrial transition and clean fuels. She has good reason for remembering it: she had had her first child just weeks before the first bid. 'There is a little bit of a legend of having a four-week-old baby in the bidroom,' she says. Vidgen's husband is Robert Dunlop: they were quite the team, advising on a complex deal and raising a baby simultaneously.

But she recalls how the sale concluded a long relationship between Macquarie and Alinta that went way back to when they were a small privatised entity, advising it on the acquisition of assets from Duke Energy, the later floating of those assets into another vehicle, and the acquisition of the Dampier to Bunbury natural gas pipeline, among many other things. All of that was rather obscured by Macquarie, however one views the circumstances, being removed by the board. 'We did a whole range of things and actually built up a really valuable business,' Vidgen says. 'And it was done in conjunction with the board and the management and a lot of stakeholders. There was a lot of press around it, but the reality was the board was keen for us to bid because they thought we could ensure there was maximum competition.'

And it worked, for Alinta. 'At the end of the day, the shareholders made a huge amount of money,' she says. 'It was a bit of a wild ride for us. But really, the people that were supposed to, benefited.'[17] And, by the time Babcock & Brown had gone under and Alinta's assets were up for grabs again in 2010, Macquarie was advising Alinta on its recapitalisation—as well as one of the bidding consortia.[18]

∎

Macquarie was shooting the lights out, and its people were getting very rich along the way.

Here are Macquarie's after-tax profit numbers in sequence from the 2002 to 2008 financial years: A$250 million, A$333 million, A$494 million, A$812 million, A$916 million, A$1.463 billion, A$1.803 billion. That's a sevenfold increase in six years, even when the starting point was itself a record.

Macquarie's annual reports always included the compensation arrangements of top staff and the executive committee, and from about 2005 they became the very first thing one turned to when they were released. That year, Allan Moss earned A$18.5 million, Clarke A$9.7 million, and four members of Exco topped A$10 million apiece.[19]

As profits soared, the pay went with it. Total remuneration—that is, short term and long term—earned Allan Moss A$33.5 million, Moore A$32.9 million and Bill Moss A$30.6 million in 2007.[20] This would be the peak for the time being,[21] but this was the period in which Macquarie's top earners firmly catapulted them into the tall poppies bracket.

At every press conference around a result, the questions would be the same. How can you justify earning this much money? How much is enough? It was around this time the bank's much-loathed but widespread external nickname—the Millionaires' Factory, or Millionaire Factory—began to seem woefully inadequate, underestimating the matter by at least one decimal place.

But there were good reasons for these numbers, because they always reflected money being made by the bank.

Macquarie's compensation structure went all the way back to David Clarke. Mark Johnson recalls that 'one of the very fundamental building blocks of where Macquarie is now' stemmed from Clarke's model, expanding an existing option scheme, in order to bring about a sense of staff ownership of Macquarie. 'Staff in Macquarie work like hell and are really good, because it's their bank,' he says. 'They actually own such a significant chunk of it that they think about it as their bank. Everyone's got a stake, and that stake is not short term.'

The model would be refined over time—Nicole Sorbara would steward the modern iteration after the global financial crisis—but throughout, two things have been central: compensation is linked to performance (which means profit, after expenses, not revenues as in some international peers), and the higher you get, the more you are locked in for the long term in order to receive the attendant rewards, which are skewed towards shares. 'This produces a mindset that is proprietorial and is different to many other financial institutions,' Johnson says.

Tony Berg, who was also instrumental in refining the early policies, says it comes down to a fundamental idea. A bank has a certain amount of capital invested in it by its shareholders, and they deserve a minimum rate of return for that. But returns above that are less to do with the capital those shareholders put in, and more to do with the people who have generated the profit. 'So they should get an increasing share of the surplus,' Berg says. 'That's how the profit share scheme got developed.'

From the outset, this proved to be not only a method of attracting talent but keeping the people who were already thriving. Johnson notes—and this remains true today—that people who left Macquarie didn't tend to go to competitors but instead went to do something different or start their own shop. 'And that's because people have got a stake in the business.'

When Moss took the top job, he was already imbued with the same ethos. 'The most critical aspect of Macquarie culture is that people very genuinely feel a sense of ownership of the businesses. There's a real understanding that if they help to grow a business they will actually benefit from that business.' The most important factor in their bonus will be the profitability of the business they are in, their contribution to that business, and then the profitability of the bank.

'Most of the people who were getting these bonuses had made a very material contribution,' Moss says. 'It wasn't like these guys had inherited the business from somebody who'd retired. Nicholas Moore built the infrastructure business. Andrew Downe built the commodities business. In that context, these bonuses were appropriate.' Moore was routinely paid almost as much as Moss, and occasionally more; Moss had no problem with it, in the same way that Shemara Wikramanayake is not apparently bothered that she was out-gunned to the tune of A\$10 million by Nick O'Kane in the 2022 financial year.[22]

Clarke, who was chair through these boom-era AGMs, is no longer around to ask, but the chairs who succeeded him—Kevin McCann and then Peter Warne—note that compensation paid by Macquarie to its executives rarely came up as an issue with shareholders.

'Even before regulators required it, Macquarie deferred payment from the profit pool and required it to be invested in Macquarie shares,' McCann says. 'While the remuneration for key management personnel was high compared with Australian companies, it was actually modest in comparison with remuneration paid by some of its global competitors.'

In his last few years as chairman Warne was involved in about 30 meetings with investors annually leading up to shareholder general meetings. He recalls remuneration being raised and discussed in just two of them, 'and the conversation rarely lasted more than two minutes.' He feels that Macquarie's ability to communicate what was happening with compensation improved over time. 'In the noughties we hadn't got the message through very clearly,' he says. 'And we put a lot of work into being able to demonstrate firstly, that it was pay for performance, and secondly, that we are in a global market with more than half of our people outside Australia.'

This second point is important, but was inevitably never going to resonate in Australia. Compensation at Macquarie felt outlandish because nothing else in Australia compared with it, but in US and European banks, figures like these were reasonably commonplace. Also, while Macquarie as an Australian institution had to disclose the performance of its top earners, the likes of UBS or Goldman Sachs didn't have to say what they were paying their top brass in Australia, because they weren't Australian institutions. Consequently, Macquarie stuck out like a sore thumb. It doesn't anymore, in an environment where digital entrepreneurs can become almost instant billionaires, which is one reason there's much less sniping now at the compensation of Wikramanayake or O'Kane compared to Moss and Moore.

Matthew Russell, in corporate communications in this time, remembers how senior executives wouldn't like it as the annual report publication date, usually on or just ahead of the AGM, rolled around and they steeled themselves for scrutiny of what they earned. 'It got to the point where Nicholas said: these are just like telephone numbers, and this is always going to be something that seems ridiculous from the perspective of ordinary Australians.' The best thing they could do was shift the announcement of compensation details to coincide with the results themselves, 'which was significant, because then you tied the figure back into the performance.'

Some would be irritated that their compensation had to be disclosed at all. Peter Costello, the treasurer of the time, had limited sympathy. 'I said, yeah, well I don't like the disclosure laws either, because my salary gets disclosed too,' he says. 'But unlike you it embarrasses me because it's so small.' Costello accepted Moore had a point that it wasn't fair Americans didn't have to disclose what they paid in Australia, making Macquarie salaries look out of step with anyone else. 'But what do you want me to do about it, Nicholas? Abolish the disclosure laws in Australia? Say that because Goldman doesn't have to disclose the salaries, Australians don't have to disclose theirs? It's not the real world.' As Costello said to another bank executive, not at Macquarie, 'you'll just have to cry into your millions at night.'

Some other perspectives of executives below the top level are interesting. Andrew Downe appeared in the top earners every year for at least a decade, but says that in terms of it being disclosed, 'I didn't really have a problem with that if people thought it was relevant information, mainly because of the way compensation worked at Macquarie. It is very much a performance-based remuneration, and if your performance is not good, you will not get paid. And the deferral has always been so long it's very hard for people to get away with burying a skeleton and hoping they're gone before it appears.'

Instead, Downe's concern is about what the scrutiny of profit and pay represents. 'I think the tall poppy thing is really sad,' he says. 'And it's sad because Macquarie is only tall in Australia. Once you get outside Australia, we're not particularly tall at all.'

Another interesting view comes from Oliver Yates, who feels that the structure used to be exceptional but may have deteriorated over the years.

Back in his time in financial packaging in the early days, he feels remuneration rewarded innovation. 'When you're doing the first deal or the first type of transaction or the first new asset, it's a lot more complex than doing the 16th airport or the 25th railroad,' he says. 'The first two or three are the most complex, but they tend to be smaller.'

That raises the question of correct reward, since those innovative early deals are not the ones that bring in the huge numbers. 'You should be paid more for the early deals that are harder to do, rather than the fat gorilla who says I'm sitting on a $10 billion fund, I should be paid all this money even though all I'm doing is cranking the wheel on acquisition number 95.' Early on, he says, Macquarie was very good at getting that balance right: at saying, could someone else have done that job?[23]

Nicholas Moore, who would oversee a further revamp of the model under his tenure, thinks the whole thing can be quantified.

'The culture of the organisation is the difference between the book value and the market cap,' he says. Shareholders' funds is about A$31.3 billion at the time of writing; the market cap, about A$70 billion. That's roughly A$40 billion of goodwill, created by about 19,000 staff, 'so there's a lot of goodwill per person. It's a way to put a financial value on that culture.'

He adds: 'The essence of Macquarie is the culture which allows people to develop opportunities within a strong balance sheet and risk management system.' The risk system prevents poor decisions, including poor risk-return outcomes, and the culture allows them 'to learn from both the successes and the inevitable disappointments. Opportunities for us are solving client problems, or more broadly meeting their needs, and our point of difference has to be how our people do this successfully—not just the people individually but more importantly how they work together, their shared culture.'

He estimates over 100,000 people have now worked at Macquarie within this system.

■

At the more junior levels of the organisation, young people who were drafted into Macquarie wouldn't quite know what had hit them. Those who were getting started in this era recall that they never worked so hard—or partied so hard.

The young candidate would arrive for an interview at 1 Martin Place and would be struck by the feeling of a five-star hotel lobby in the bank's reception. It was a construct of white marble and glass, of plush carpets and wealth, where a row of beautiful young women, immaculately dressed and groomed, would be sitting in dark suit and skirt ensembles behind a reception desk. Having navigated this grand arrival, the interviewee would sit distant from their inter-viewer across a table of absurd size—'it felt like Vladimir Putin's meeting table situation,' says one—and would then go through the three tests of the day: the infamous psychometric test, a literacy test and a numeracy test.

Every company says their culture is work hard, play hard. 'But nothing comes even remotely close to how hard they used to work and how hard they used to party at Macquarie,' says one employee from the research unit during this era. New arrivals were told that bankers' standard hours were 7 am to 7 pm, which sounds extreme from the outset, but rather undersells the typical hours of the time: 7 am to 11 pm was not uncommon, and during reporting season, all-nighters. One junior associate calculated that, assessed on an hourly basis, he was paid less than a McDonald's worker. It was true.

It didn't suit everyone. 'When a new associate came in, bankers would give them three months, the typical time it would take to break or make them,' says one. 'The bankers used to say if they could endure the first three months, they were in: they had what it took.' It wasn't just the hours; Macquarie wasn't a place where you could get by just by being at your desk all the time. Successful people were productive and efficient, with a can-do attitude, striving for more. 'There were a lot of brilliantly clever people there and everyone just wanted to do better.'

One recalls a colleague who would lament, while drunk on the contents of the booze fridge in the kitchen, that he had promised himself when his son was born that he would quit in a year so he could spend time with his family. But he was still there, and his son was now 15: he had somehow trapped himself in a life with three privately educated kids and a huge house to pay off where it was impossible ever to leave.

Macquarie tried to make sure that the incentives to leave the building were reduced. There were several well-stocked fridges in the kitchen—the one full of free booze was the biggest—and every week it was restocked, not just with beers and local wines but champagnes and international selections. The fridge was a thing of wonder: it had a sort of seductive back-lighting and a glass door so its contents could be seen without opening the door. It had a sign—'fridge opens at 12pm'—which was not always rigorously observed in an environment where people worked so long that an early morning could really be a late night.

'It was not uncommon to see bankers at their desks working with a beer in hand,' says one employee from this time. 'It was not considered unusual, just something they needed to do to take the edge off every now and then.'

The misogynistic culture of the industry and the era did not escape Macquarie. One woman who worked there recalls the hushed callout that would take place every Wednesday among the guys who wanted to have lunch together. 'It was an open secret that they'd go to Men's Gallery, the strip club across the road from work, for lunch every Wednesday.' The men had regular golf days too, which excluded women, who were left behind at work. 'I don't think any of the men, or heads of department, gave a thought to the women's position or how unfair and discriminatory it was.'

Some of this, while not unique to Macquarie, is deeply problematic by today's standards and wasn't much better even in the less enlightened boom years. There was a staff database that could be filtered by various different criteria, among them languages spoken. It became known that one male banker had amassed, with some effort, a list of all the women in his target market who worked at Macquarie, and then distributed it to his friends, who distributed it to their friends. 'The staff database was often used akin to a dating database,' says one woman who worked there. 'It had our names, photos, job titles, the division in which we worked, phone numbers, email addresses.'

If the place could be turbocharged by day, that was nothing compared to what happened at night. Security guards who did the rounds would regale people with tales of what they'd seen: people having sex in the shower or under their desks. One day a large stack of pornographic magazines was discovered in the ceiling above the disabled toilets.

No day was more eagerly awaited than White Envelope Day, when bonuses were awarded. The juniors would observe the bankers and their behaviour through the day. 'Their bonuses dictated what their next year looked like—new house, new car—but more so, it was about their worth, sacrifice and egos, and if it was recognised and rewarded by the size of their bonus,' says one former junior. 'Everything they'd done and sacrificed over that past year was tied to that bonus.'

As if watching a sport, the juniors would see the bankers go into the head of department's offices one by one to receive their envelope.

'The whole day, people would be watching the door of that office, and more so, the bankers' faces,' one recalls. Some came out ecstatic, others angry, some poker-faced, some red-faced. There was little modesty or embarrassment about a big sum: a good bonus was to be boasted about. 'You always knew who got a million dollars plus,' says one. 'They weren't shy about sharing the news.' White Envelope Day was a write-off in terms of work, and one that nearby bars would plan for, getting extra staff in ready for the high-octane debauch that would follow.

Another big day was the AGM. Everyone finished early—which generally never happened—and got properly dressed up. It was the only time they could meet everyone else who worked at Macquarie, and at the more junior level served as something of a dating facility at the post-AGM parties.

Parties pervaded the whole place at that time. Each division would have them with reasonable frequency, and the organisers would try to outdo one another on where to have the next one and what to do. 'Expectations were high,' says one. 'They were Macquarie, which meant they were successful and only the best would do. It seemed like there was always an excuse for a party.' Bankers would cut loose with considerable flair and, more often than not, karaoke. Thousands of dollars of booze would be left abandoned on tables at the end of the night. They were held in five-star hotels, on yachts, in Luna Park. There were gifts, and more than decent ones too: a Tiffany keyring in a blue box for Christmas one year, then a silver Georg Jensen bowl in a red box with silk lining.

'There was just so much money everywhere,' says one who worked there in the 2000s. 'Down in the carpark there were the latest models of luxury cars. They all lived in money suburbs in the Eastern Suburbs or Lower North Shore.' People in their early 20s were being paid six figure salaries that would more than double in bonuses.

'A few bankers I knew used to, on a whim, fly out to places like Thailand on Friday after work, because they felt like eating Thai food from a particular restaurant.'

One day, to great excitement, Russell Crowe toured the building as he was going to play a banker in an upcoming movie, *A Good Year*. Half of Macquarie went to see it in order to see how they were portrayed. The verdict: he didn't get it.

■

By 2007 Allan Moss had been at the helm for fourteen years and was starting to reflect. 'I wasn't quite 60, but 60 was within sight,' he says. 'And I thought it was the right time in Nicholas's life. He was just coming up to 50, which I thought was a good age for him to become CEO.'

There was some unfinished business Moss felt obliged to deal with under his own watch, in particular the creation of a non-operating holding company (NOHC) structure.[24] Moore would have been quite capable of doing it himself but, just as he would delay his own departure ten years later in order to ensure that he rather than Shemara Wikramanayake faced the royal commission, Moss considered it his own responsibility.

Though arcane in its formulation, Project Jigsaw, as it was known internally, was an important step. At its heart was a growing problem: that the bank wanted to raise capital, but the investment bank 'was doing things that APRA [the Australian Prudential Regulation Authority] didn't want banks to do,' as Richard Sheppard, who was responsible for carrying out the project, recalls. So they set up a structure where a holding company would be created to own the investment bank, and then there would be a separate licensed bank.

'I regard that as a very important transaction,' Sheppard says. 'And it occurred in 2007, which was only a year or two before the global financial crisis. It turned out to be a pretty important milestone in that story as well.'

Not every decision or venture makes its way up the board, but this one certainly did. 'NOHC took an enormous amount of board and committee time,' recalls Catherine Livingstone, who served on the board for a decade until mid-2013. 'It was a significant initiative.'

In fact, the corporate restructure was much less drastic than it might have been. The 2007 annual report reveals that the board and management considered moving the whole enterprise overseas. 'Given the high and growing proportion of international income, the board thought it appropriate to consider the Bank's head office location.' The report concluded that Macquarie should, as the song and Qantas anthem has it, still call Australia home, for reasons of location, sources of income, regulatory environments, and the cost and complexity of relocation. But Macquarie did submit an application to the UK Financial Services Authority in July 2007, ostensibly to allow it to pursue growth there and in Europe and to provide a European passport for the banking businesses, and there may have been at least an option of using this as a change of domicile in the long term.[25]

In the end the NOHC went through in its more prosaic form, with the formal establishment of Macquarie Group Limited on 13 November 2007. It and Macquarie Bank became two separate external funding vehicles with segregated funding, capital and liquidity management arrangements, though both were and are regulated by the same institution, APRA.[26]

Moss could then think unencumbered about the future. 'Once we got that done, I started thinking about: is this a good time?,' he says. 'Either I leave now while I have enough energy to do something else, or I carry on to 65 and just retire, sit on the beach. To me, anything in between made no real sense.'

Moore had been the obvious person to take over for years. Andrew Downe had been equally successful in building the commodities and treasury group, in its various incarnations, and Bill Moss's success in reinventing the whole idea of property banking was exceptional. But neither ever appeared to be in the frame.[27]

What made Moore the stand-out candidate? 'It was performance,' says Allan Moss. 'He was just doing great deals from the moment he walked in the door. Very sensible, very professional, innovative, leading initially small teams. And the deals got done and they made money.' He shared Moss's innate understanding of risk and was in by far the largest part of the business: in the 2008 financial year, Macquarie Capital, as investment banking was now known, accounted for 58 per cent of group profits.

So the date was set; 23 May 2008 would be the date of Moss's retirement and Moore's succession. Michael Carapiet, Moore's long-time wingman (or attack dog, as some who got on the wrong side of them put it), became head of Macquarie Capital, another succession that had been obvious for years. Moss had done fifteen years at the top.

There were gathering clouds in the world economy. Bear Stearns had failed in March 2008, the word subprime had entered the popular lexicon, and a crisis was developing in mortgage funding. 'Global mortgage securitization markets have been effectively closed for the past six months,' the 2008 annual report said. Before Moss departed, Macquarie slashed its mortgage origination in Australia, exited it completely in the USA, and suffered a write-down of A$293 million on holdings in its real estate investments as the global REIT market began to fail.

Still, those mortgage businesses represented less than 1 per cent of Macquarie's total operating profit that year. Macquarie, seeing more challenging times ahead as credit markets began to lock up from about August 2007, had trebled its level of liquid assets in a year to

A\$18.3 billion.[28] 'The future availability of term funding markets to market participants, including Macquarie, will be of critical importance,' the bank told investors,[29] warning that Macquarie might need to 'consider a reduction in term assets.'

So there was a sense of good times coming to an end, of risks to be navigated and of battening down the hatches in preparation. But nobody, including Macquarie, had any sense of what was about to happen. History will probably judge Allan Moss's departure as among the most well-timed in the history of banking—and Moore's timing as the worst.

Chapter 10

THE GFC

Here's what would happen when a journalist interviewed Nicholas Moore during his time as chief executive.

The reporter would arrive primed with information and questions, determined to structure the time to cover all necessary ground, and perhaps to reveal some element of the man's private nature that had hitherto remained hidden from public view.

The pleasantries would be fine: he would be polite and interested. And then, after the first question was boldly asked, something odd would happen.

It was as if, through some mighty effort of interior will, he had slowed his heartbeat. Several seconds would pass in silence as he digested the question, plenty enough time for the journalist to fear they had asked something crushingly stupid. And then the answer would come, as if from a financial sage who happened to be in the middle of a program of transcendental meditation, an iceberg with an IQ of 200.

The answer would contain no ums or ers, no deviations or subplots. It would be precise. And the journalist would emerge at the end of the allotted time, thinking: that man said absolutely nothing he didn't intend to say at the outset, not one single surplus word.

One had to admire the discipline and technique. Moore was not rude, aggressive nor unfriendly, but anyone—banker or media— who has been in a meeting with him will speak of a sense of edgy glacial terror at being wrong-footed or unprepared. Executives say the worst thing one could hear from him in such a meeting was a sentence prefaced with: 'Well, I'm just a humble accountant, but . . .'

Moore wasn't really like this as a straight-shooting banker on the way up, nor since stepping down as leader in 2018. But he adopted this careful, fastidious manner as chief executive for good reason. He inherited the institution at the worst imaginable time and, having stewarded it through the storm intact, would change a great deal about it—starting with the noise.

■

Many of the bank's senior executives had been getting increasingly restive for at least a year before what we now call the global financial crisis—the GFC—really kicked off in 2008.

Nick Minogue was eight years into his term as head of the Risk Management Group when credit markets began locking up in 2007. An articulate and trusted figure with a dry wit, he had spent the past decade trying to instil in everyone an interest in and appreciation of risk management. There was a custom in the 1990s and 2000s to have an annual presentation from each of the group heads. 'I would try to make sure that the risk presentation was more interesting than anybody else's,' he says. 'I'd have to say there wasn't a lot of competition.' He got Opera Australia involved for one of them, arranged fireworks for a Harry Potter theme on another occasion, found some Star Trek props at a third.

Similarly, there was an introduction for new staff called Camp Macquarie,[1] carried out largely by group heads. One year, for this, Minogue invented a trading game based around Nick Leeson, whose errant trading had blown up Barings in 1994, in order to demonstrate how random profits could appear to be the result of great skill.

He recalls a subset of an asset class in the USA, around federal guaranteed student loans, starting to fall apart in early 2007. 'And I couldn't see where the process would stop,' he says. 'Once you look into that particular abyss, it is very frightening. Really frightening.'

Why? 'It's the liquidity underpinnings of the entire western economy. The whole idea of being able to trade all the time—if you take this away, everything looks pretty bleak. The question then becomes: if successive asset classes fail in this way, and nobody will trade them, where does that leave banks? You ultimately end up with a run on every bank.'

Minogue had seen the future.

Suitably alarmed by this revelation, he had gone to see Allan Moss, and presented to him the idea that it was worth explaining his fears to the local regulators. Moss advised against it—'and I'm sure he was right, it would have spooked them entirely'—and for the time being they set about bolstering liquidity to be ready for whatever came next.

But Moss, too, was certainly aware of trouble ahead. Peter Warne, who had just joined the board in 2007, recalls Moss standing up at a board meeting in August that year warning about the forthcoming economic downturn 'which was going to be the worst in his view since the depression of the 1890s. And I thought: people failed to mention that in the interview process.'

Indeed, not everyone thinks the timing of Moss's departure was entirely motivated by it just being the right time to go. 'There is no doubt in most people's minds Allan gave Nicholas a hospital pass,' says Earl Evans, a former Macquarie private wealth figure who now runs Shaw and Partners.[2] 'Allan was way ahead, he could see what was happening.'

By early 2008 debt markets were in trouble, and had been for half a year, but the equity markets were still going through the roof, a contradiction that suggested one side of the market had its outlook wrong.

Bankers have some curious barometers for these things. Michael Carapiet remembers going to a meeting with Goldman Sachs one morning in February in New York—'massive building, lifts the size of your house'—and arriving at the main floor, where he noticed that his was the only coat in the cupboard for guests. 'I thought, you've got to be kidding. This is Goldman Sachs and there's no one in the meeting rooms on a Tuesday morning at 8.30? This is bad.' He came back and told Moore, who said: 'I think you're panicking, Carras.' He replied: 'Remember that thing that only the paranoid survive?'

Greg Ward, as CFO, was troubled too. 'I certainly had the perspective that the market was tremendously highly valued,' he remembers. 'Credit spreads were so thin that your money was virtually free.' He remembers being in the USA where bankers explained new credit products to him, highly leveraged and apparently elevating impaired loans to the level of triple-A tranches through securitisation. He couldn't see how they would work, and was also increasingly aware of the same US institutions saying they were on alert about funding markets.

Macquarie—and this would be crucial—had always been less leveraged than most banks, although the satellite funds were a different story. Many banks were highly geared, which would bring several of them unstuck in the months that followed. 'But because we were relatively small, we didn't really think of ourselves as a bank,' says Ward. 'So our liquidity policy was to borrow long and lend short, while the banks were borrowing short and lending long,' the classic model of taking deposits and lending them out for up to 30 years as mortgages. 'We were the other way around.'

This meant, in theory, that in a liquidity crunch, Macquarie would be able to wind down the funding at the same pace that debt rolled off, which—again in theory—would ultimately leave Macquarie in surplus no matter what happened. 'It might be smaller, but you'll still have a balance sheet, and it was designed that way in our liquidity policy.'

The trips of Ward and others to the USA made them realise that this might not be enough. 'We decided to build a fortress-like balance sheet on top of what we already had, because there would be extraordinary buying opportunities if there was market disruption,' Ward says. He was by parts amused and annoyed by the popular comment of the time that the shutting down of the commercial paper market, which was beginning to happen in the USA through 2007, had never happened before. 'Well, yes it has, and that's what caused BT to be for sale. This has been in our modelling and our liquidity policy is engineered so that it could happen again. So how could you be surprised that it has?'

In the financial year that included the GFC, Macquarie raised A\$21.5 billion of term funding. At one point they raised A\$9 billion in a single facility, 'which meant that we had so much funding, we were never that bothered,' Ward says.

'Never that bothered' is putting a seriously brave spin on what happened next.

Nicholas Moore, who would inherit this grim situation pretty much as soon as he became CEO in May 2008, was well aware of the preparation the bank had made for worst-case scenarios, and the practice of extending and broadening the bank's long-term funding would continue throughout his time. 'We used to say, if the markets closed, if we had not even one dollar of new money coming in the door, we could keep running the business and there would never be a period of insolvency where people would be asking for money that we didn't have.'

In this, he aligns with Ward's view that Macquarie's position was anathema to the established theory of banking where you take deposits and have the central bank as a backstop if the whole thing unravels. 'But for us, we never believed we were in that happy position. So we always had to have funding all the way through.

'We would ask ourselves: what is the worst-case outcome?' That would include short-term funding drying up, deposits being called. 'We would need cash to meet these outflows. Similarly, we need to assess what will happen to the assets on our balance sheet. How much can they fall in value and how liquid will they be in challenging times?'

But this fastidious planning missed one thing: it was all well and good for an institution to be in proper shape, but what happens when the entire system falls apart? What happens when the abiding emotion in the markets is fear and distrust, where nobody cares about your funding mix or your public numbers because nobody's listening?

■

If Macquarie really did know what was coming, it puts an even less palatable spin on perhaps the bank's least edifying ever deal: the float of BrisConnections, which was put together to design, construct, operate, maintain and finance the Airport Link toll road in Brisbane.

When this deal plunged 60 per cent on debut on 31 July 2008, that was only the start of its troubles. The deal represented all of the worst things about Macquarie's boom-era model of the decade, and it was the last time they would ever appear in such scale. Huge leverage? Check (a A$4.8 billion project funded by A$3.2 billion of debt and gearing of about 65 per cent. Worse, in this case BrisConnections borrowed against future instalment payments, which brings us to our next point). Unnecessarily elaborate structure for retail? Check (each stapled security was sold at A$1 but came with an obligation to pay two separate further instalments of A$1 per share.) High fees? Check ($110 million[3]).

Institutions promptly fled, Macquarie itself among them, dumping stock and avoiding a commitment to make a further A$120 million of instalment payments. By March 2009, 80 per cent of the float was in retail hands and the securities had fallen from A$1 to A$0.1 cents, the lowest possible tradeable price. Worse still, some retail buyers then started buying in, failing to understand the obligations to make the two subsequent A$1 payments were still intact; one, a floppy-haired IT professional called Nicholas Bolton, would end up in court after buying 47 million of these units, for an outlay of just under A$48,000, thus bringing an obligation of A$94 million of debt he was unsurprisingly unable to pay.[4] He was not alone: many failed to understand that the BrisConnections five-letter Australian Securities Exchange (ASX) code, BCSCA, meant it was a partly paid unit.

Worse, years later it would emerge that Macquarie had allowed some of its wealthy customers to pull out of the float when it became clear it was going to tank. More than A$20 million of BrisConnections shares were handed back by only a select group of clients to Macquarie stockbrokers before they began to trade.[5] As for the road itself, it would eventually go into receivership with A$3.1 billion of debt in February 2013.

■

On the day Lehman Brothers went under on Monday 15 September 2008,[6] widely considered the start of the true horrors of the GFC,

Minogue happened to be in New York. What did he do? 'I walked around and looked at the ticker tape above the Lehman building' on Times Square, he says. 'Wow.' Macquarie didn't have any significant exposure, just some trading lines, but it was clear something monumental was happening. 'It was a very, very torrid time.'

Minogue, the senior person in New York that day, pulled together an impromptu presentation for all North American staff by video-conference, 'basically running through why you should be clear that Macquarie is not really threatened by the sort of things that you can see. This is what we have prepared ourselves for, and it's far worse than what's happening now.'

Minogue was presenting a reassuring face to deeply worried people, but he knew he was in the eye of an extraordinary storm.

In Australia, Moore quickly set up a war room of sorts. He asked Robin Bishop to help him manage cash, funding and liquidity. 'I probably spent six months in Sydney doing that with him closely and developed a deep appreciation for his capability,' Bishop says. Tim Joyce, now head of Macquarie Capital for Asia-Pacific, was drafted into the working group as Robin's second in command. 'We created a little office,' Joyce says. 'Sort of a bid room on Nicholas's floor in 1 Martin Place. It was a pretty intense period, because both Robin and I lived in Melbourne.' Not for the next few months they didn't: it was just as well that Macquarie's building shared premises with the Westin Hotel.

Helen Nugent was on the board at the time.[7] 'We said, what do we do if this persists further?' she recalls. They drew up lists of assets, worked out what could be done to prune the cost base. They would, with remarkable haste, turn the discussion to: how can we take advantage of this? But we'll come back to that.

Everyone who worked with Moore during this time considers his performance quite remarkably calm under extreme pressure, the more so since he'd just sat down in the CEO chair. 'Nicholas showed extraordinary leadership in that time and was calm, methodical, decisive and consistent, leading the organisation through the decisions that had to be made,' says Catherine Livingstone, who was on the board at the time. 'That's not to understate [the] amount of work and the very long hours. But the leadership was really important, actually very impressive.'

It would swiftly be tested. The Lehman collapse had led to an uncomfortable truth: the markets seemed to be more worried about Macquarie (and its doomed peer, Babcock & Brown) than anyone else.

Macquarie had been on an absolute tear, reaching what would turn out to be the highest point for the next ten years when it closed at A$97.10 per share on 18 May 2007. It had been steadily drifting down, though roughly in step with the broader market, through early 2008 and had been trading in the 40s in early September. Then when Lehman went, Macquarie fell from A$43.28 on the Friday before the bankruptcy announcement, 12 September, to A$25.62 the following Thursday, 18 September.

Worse, the credit markets seemed to be doubting the quality of Macquarie's paper. Bank debt is roughly divided into two camps, senior and subordinated, which refers ultimately to the priority investors get if something goes wrong and things need to be repaid. The spread on debt—measured in basis points, each of which equate to one one-hundredth of a percentage point—increases in times of stress, meaning that at a wider spread, a bank has to pay more to get investors to buy its debt. In the week after Lehman fell, Macquarie's senior debt went to 320 basis points, far wider than usual.

The sensitivity internally at Macquarie rapidly became clear when journalist Adele Ferguson wrote a piece that week,[8] partly about the credit spread numbers, and partly about a research report from respected banking analyst Brett Le Mesurier of Wilson HTM.

Le Mesurier had calculated that over the next year Macquarie could potentially need to refinance A$45 billion[9] of funding. Ferguson wrote: 'While most of it will be relatively easy, more than A$5 billion could prove difficult to get away at a decent price and decent length of time.'

The same day, Macquarie made an announcement that the article was 'false and inconsistent with information provided to the market by the Group.' Macquarie went into detail about its funding position, saying it had liquid assets of more than A$20 billion, but did not go into the debt figure; Greg Ward told the *Australian Financial Review* that day that it was more like A$25 billion[10] (the difference, as explained in the footnotes, is principally that Le Mesurier had also considered the possibility of deposits being withdrawn during a crisis of confidence, severely affecting the funding position).

The Australian Securities and Investments Commission, ASIC, then published a statement of its own the same day, saying it was investigating allegations of false rumours linked to market manipulation, and that Macquarie Group was one of the affected companies. 'Pushing false rumours designed to harm a company, such as by forcing a share price down, is illegal,' it wrote. But Le Mesurier told ASIC he'd based his analysis on Macquarie's own disclosures. The matter was dropped without action, but not before both he and Ferguson had been hammered in the press.[11] Around that time, UBS also had ASIC trawling through its Macquarie research, but to no avail.

The incidents were symptomatic of a growing mood of paranoia and distrust in the industry. The phrase 'rumortraging' had entered the industry, and the sense of sinister intent at a time of extreme uncertainty prompted ASIC to ban naked short selling on the Friday of that week, 19 September, with a requirement for disclosure of covered short selling.[12] The regulator spent the weekend considering the position and looking at what was happening in other markets,[13] and banned covered short selling too on the Sunday, 21 September.

There has been much discussion about Macquarie lobbying ASIC and government to make this change. Catherine Livingstone recalls: 'I'm sure there were many people and organisations trying to convince ASIC on that Sunday, and no doubt Macquarie was among them.'

For its part, both regulator and government have always said the decision was about much more than any one individual institution. Former Australian Treasurer Wayne Swan tells us: 'I can absolutely say that the one-off decisions on short selling, they weren't driven by Macquarie. The whole world was acting . . . I went and saw the bloke who ran the New York Stock Exchange and he was against short selling. And he was a Reagan Republican. It defies me to understand to this very day why anyone could allow something like naked short selling.' About Moore, he adds: 'I've got no memory of Nicholas Moore being either difficult or abrasive.'

Nobody in their right mind really thought Ferguson was trying to extort some sort of shorting scam; journalists frankly don't have that much money. But back in New York, a noted short seller *was* causing considerable trouble for Macquarie. This was Jim Chanos, the founder of a US investment adviser called Kynikos Associates focused on short selling (Kynikos is modern Greek for 'cynic'), who had made his name by correctly predicting the collapse of Enron and shorting it right up until its 2001 bankruptcy.

Chanos had been hitting Macquarie for some time, puzzled by the frequency with which the bank (or rather its funds, although he never made the distinction) seemed to be the highest bidder on many of the infrastructure assets it approached. He was particularly vexed by the Indiana Toll Road—which, in fairness, did go bankrupt.

A prominent guest on the CNBC *Squawk Box* program, Chanos depicted Macquarie as relying on on-selling assets to its own funds, over-paying to get assets, and hiding debt and leverage. In the end Greg Ward wrote to Chanos,[14] not for the first time, in an open letter taking on many of the American's contentions. (This letter did reveal that the average gearing level of Macquarie's investment banking funds was 58 per cent, and property funds 48 per cent; it's symptomatic of the time that this was intended to be reassuring.)

Chanos was a thorn in Macquarie's side at a difficult time. 'His thesis was just wrong,' Ward says now. 'But don't let the facts get in the road of a story, because it sounds convincing: here's another investment bank that's relying on leverage, and that's what the others did, and they fell by the wayside so this has to be next.' The problem was, in that environment, it chimed with the surrounding sense of fear. 'Without looking at the balance sheet, that sounds plausible,' Ward says. 'But we were a regulated bank, which was pretty different to those institutions. The leverage ratio at Lehmans versus our leverage was like this.' He spreads his hands so wide they leave the shot of the Zoom call.

There was a lot to support Ward's contention; importantly Macquarie (then) had no proprietary trading book of the like that Lehman Brothers and other US investment banks had. 'We had none of those sorts of exposures,' he says. 'We weren't a prime broker. It's just apples and oranges.' Plus, it was built on a risk management approach that dated back to Macquarie's foundation. The bank had, after all, just concluded a fifteen-year stretch with a chief executive who made his whole name building a risk management division.

But the problem—and really it was a very hard problem to deal with—was that no amount of preparation could deal with rumours that prompted people either to pull out of the stock or, worse, pull credit lines.

Another term that entered the public lexicon during the GFC was credit default swap (CDS),[15] which came to be seen as a key indicator of financial collapse. These, in particular, really did appear to be suggesting the worst: CDS spreads on Macquarie's subordinated debt went from 200 basis points to 1800 basis points, implying that the market felt Macquarie was becoming more likely to collapse.

And it is very hard to argue with an unemotional number like a market spread. 'There is a risk that it does become a self-fulfilling prophecy,' says Ralph Norris, who was CEO of the Commonwealth Bank at the time of the GFC, and involved in meetings at the highest level with regulators and the Reserve Bank through the crisis. 'If you have your credit default swaps at such a level where it causes the market to doubt, your share price sinks and you're in a situation where people take the view that where there's smoke there's fire. If these things go from being seen as a possibility to a likelihood, you've got to be able to manage that situation very well to retain that confidence in the organisation.' Norris believes Moore handled the situation extremely well.

Today, Ward blames the immaturity of the CDS market, creating movements that were amplified and did not reflect reality. But this was the tone of the time.

Moore and Ward will argue until they are blue in the face that Macquarie was never at risk, that its funding position was secure, that they didn't need a government guarantee in order to survive. Logically, they are correct. But there is, to this day, a school of thought, including among people who have served at the highest level of the bank, that the bank could have been brought to its knees just by the idea, by the withdrawal of credit lines.

Kevin McCann, the lead independent director, was the acting chairman at the time; David Clarke was battling cancer and a six-month leave of absence was disclosed to the ASX on 28 November.[16]

'They were very, very challenging days,' McCann says, from the severe shorting of Macquarie shares to the manipulation of opaque credit default swaps, creating doubt about Macquarie's creditworthiness.

'We also had a situation where some counterparties would not deal with Macquarie.' If a bank is trading in commodities or futures on an exchange, it is customary to post cash collateral as security for completion of the trade. 'While Macquarie had cash available to post collateral, some leading global banks still declined to deal with us.'

That year, 2008, the International Monetary Fund (IMF)/World Bank annual meeting in Washington DC happened to fall right in the middle of the crisis, over the weekend of 11 October.

Moore was there. 'For at least eighteen months, liquidity and confidence had been drying up,' says Moore. 'The crisis of confidence peaked that weekend. This was the time that the governments of the world acted, I believe correctly, because otherwise Monday would be very challenging for the financial markets.[17]

'We wouldn't have been down, by the way, just to be clear,' he insists today. 'We did have term funding in place, we were fine. But if all your counterparties fail, it's not much of a world you are surviving.'

The Australian government had been watching events around the world and preparing to react. Ireland had been the first of the world's banks to guarantee all bank deposits on 21 September, and many others had followed. Australia did so on 12 October. In line with other state interventions around the world, this bestowed Australia's AAA rating on the debt of any bank that borrowed under the scheme, including Macquarie.

At this point it became exceptionally useful that Macquarie had gone to the non-operating holding company structure the previous year, because it meant that Macquarie was, unarguably, a bank; had it taken another approach and ditched the banking part in order to just focus on the investment banking activities, there might have been a whole different outcome. As it was, Macquarie was just as eligible for relief as any other bank in Australia.

'We were no different from any other financial services organisation, not just in Australia but in the world, over that weekend,'
Moore says. 'We were better placed than any of them as we didn't
have the same level of short-term funding. But it would have been a
catastrophe for everybody if everybody else had collapsed. It would
have been a very dark world.'

Moore therefore gives short shrift to those who say Macquarie
was bailed out by the state as if it was some kind of special treatment.

It is, indeed, common to hear people say that Macquarie was
saved by the government guarantee, and it certainly did provide a
psychological floor and bring some sense of stability to the markets.
But the truth is—and this tends to be forgotten—Macquarie's plight
actually got worse *after* the government guarantee was put in place.
Macquarie's share price would not reach its crisis low close of A\$15.75
until 2 March the following year.[18]

This, in McCann's recollection was the worst moment. 'If you are a
bank whose shares are in freefall, and your CDS are being manipulated
and some counterparties will not deal with you, the outlook was grim,'
he says. 'Yet, this occurred despite Macquarie operating profitably and
when most of its funding was long to medium term debt.'

It didn't help that Babcock & Brown, which had become dubbed
a mini-Macquarie despite a very different balance sheet position,
collapsed around this time.[19] Another enterprise with similarities to
Macquarie in its infrastructure and property investment focus, Allco
Financial Group, had also gone into freefall.[20] None of this helped sentiment towards Macquarie despite a stronger balance sheet position.

There are few people in the world with a more useful perspective
on this than Peter Yates, who had spent fifteen years at Macquarie
from 1985, knowing the place intimately, and who at this point of the
GFC was running Allco Equity Partners, a cashbox within the broader
Allco group. 'Banks are only at risk if they have a liquidity problem:

an asset and liability mismatch, or a negative cash flow,' says Yates. And this was the difference between the three enterprises. 'Allco had a terrible mismatch. Babcock had a bad mismatch. Macquarie did not: Allan Moss understood risk.' Also, unlike the other two, Macquarie had a banking licence, so any mismatch would be under the scrutiny of the Australian Prudential Regulation Authority (APRA).

But if that was obvious to Yates in the eye of the storm, it wasn't obvious to the market, which wasn't listening.

It was also clear that people who wanted to short Macquarie weren't being put off by the fact that ASIC had banned it. There were over-the-counter derivatives like forward sales agreements that could have the same effect. Also, some analysts were still not convinced by the bank's turnaround story: Jonathan Mott at UBS, for example, was still writing in March that a 'significant and prolonged' fall in the value of the listed satellite funds, particularly Macquarie Infrastructure Fund and Macquarie Airports, would require impairment charges for Macquarie itself of A$1.5 billion. This was a legitimate concern: even if the mother ship was fundamentally fine, what responsibility did it owe to its plummeting satellite funds, whose assets weren't on Macquarie Group's balance sheet but were nevertheless clearly connected? On 2 March Macquarie felt compelled to put out a release trying to reassure the market about the strength of those listed funds. The result: the share price just kept falling.

Some, even at the board level, wondered if one of the big banks would be told by the Reserve Bank, or APRA, or the government, to take Macquarie over. We know now that the idea was canvassed in meetings at the Reserve Bank of Australia, with the Commonwealth Bank the likeliest candidate. 'There were some discussions with the RBA in that regard,' says one who was close to the talks. 'But never a point where we had substantive discussions.' Both BankWest and Suncorp would instead become a greater focus for the Reserve Bank, and the government guarantee seemed to draw a line under any idea of a threat to Macquarie's independence.

Then something changed in early March 2009. Sentiment seemed to turn, and by 6 April the share price had doubled from that low, crossing the A$30 mark. On 1 May, the bank successfully priced an A$540 million capital raising in the domestic and international capital markets through an institutional private placement at A$27 per share. Ward said that day the placement, in conjunction with other capital initiatives, would give Macquarie an A$4.1 billion buffer of capital in excess of minimum regulatory requirements. Separately, all ordinary shareholders were given the opportunity to participate in a share purchase plan.

In McCann's recollection, 'the successful capital raising pretty much put the GFC behind us.'

■

Once it was clear that Macquarie was going to survive, attention turned to a problem that had become very clear: nobody really understood what Macquarie actually was.

'Shareholders knew that we were a company where earnings grew every year. Not all of them fully understood the business,' Moore says now. 'When the GFC happened and the share price fell, we needed to explain the business to the investment community, and indeed our own people.'

Macquarie had been a black box. People don't mind a black box when it's producing great profits year after year. In a bad year, they wonder what's inside.

'In 2008 it was shoot first, ask questions later,' Moore says. 'We had to create a very clear narrative about who we were. And that wasn't at all clear.'

This was evident in some of the efforts to box Macquarie into an obvious comparative description in the boom years. People used to call it the Goldman Sachs of Australia, 'which was not appropriate given our business mix,' Moore says, but that was a lot better than the occasional description of being the Lehman Brothers of Australia. Neither was accurate, but Macquarie simply had no natural comparison anywhere in the world, so it was little surprise that when it really mattered, investors found they couldn't easily get their heads around what it was.

'So therefore, it was very important to articulate something that was just understandable, and repeatable,' Moore says. 'So we had to break our business down into bits that people could understand, and put them into a context people could understand, with a cultural and risk management overlay that people could understand.'

Much of this work would fall to Stuart Green, who was head of investor relations at the time. 'That was an interesting time,' he says with crisp understatement. 'This was a once in a hundred year event.'

In some respects, Macquarie's interim results announcement for the half-year to 30 September 2008, presented on 18 November, was well-timed, because it allowed the group to demonstrate an important truth that everyone seemed to be forgetting: Macquarie was still profitable. Its profit of A$604 million for the half-year was well down,[21] but it was still nowhere near a loss. In fact, it would remain profitable for the whole financial year.

'The 101 of business is thou shalt be profitable,' says Nicholas Moore. 'And we were profitable all the way through. It's true our profit halved. But in the circumstances, it was understandable and outperformed most of the global industry.'

The interim result also allowed Macquarie to hammer home a few important truths: that it had capital of A$10.3 billion, which was A$3.3 billion more than regulation required; that it had cash and liquid assets of A$26.3 billion, compared to short-term wholesale issued paper outstanding of A$18.9 billion; that it had raised A$7.8 billion of term funding in a year and also that it had a plan to unwind assets to the tune of A$15 billion of initiatives. By this stage it had announced it was selling its unloved Italian mortgage business (to this day, people still tend to shudder when they say 'Italian mortgages' at Macquarie) and an investment lending business, in addition to the commitment earlier in the year to wind back Australian mortgages and stop originating US ones.[22]

But if anything, the result cemented the sense that people just didn't understand Macquarie: that it was too complicated and opaque. 'So the main focus became making Macquarie easier to understand,' says Green. 'When people understand, they feel more confident making decisions about investing or not investing in a business. People were nervous about the markets at the time, so the more we could help explain Macquarie, we felt the better it was going to be.'

Like McCann, Green remembers March 2009, not September or October 2008, as being the worst, the real trough in Macquarie's valuation. Today, he remembers the turning point as being nothing that Macquarie did, but a reassuring memo from Citigroup.[23] But the rally that followed, and the May fundraising, was enormously important, and the increased capital became a key part of the story to tell. 'We went on roadshows, and we just explained who we were and what we did,' says Green. The share price would almost quadruple in the eighteen months from that March low.[24]

Moore found himself distilling the bank to what it was really about. 'We tried to explain ourselves as simply and accurately as possible, avoiding clichés,' he says. 'It needed to be a consistent story and we needed to be disciplined when communicating, internally and externally.'

■

In the trenches, the bankers were, for once, not focused so much on making a buck as protecting what they had, and working through a laundry list of things that had worked just fine in the good times but no longer did. 'The attitude was, how do you eat an elephant? One bite at a time,' says Michael Carapiet. 'It was pointless trying to solve every problem immediately because you just couldn't do it. You had to get through day by day.'

Attempts to present a business-as-usual ethos would sometimes appear tone-deaf. In November 2008 the *Sunday Telegraph* reported that Macquarie had splashed out between A$500,000 and A$750,000 on a Christmas party, hiring Cockatoo Island on Sydney Harbour and booking the award-winning dance act The Presets. 'While other companies cancel or downgrade their end-of-year bashes as 2008 ends in financial disarray, the so-called millionaire factory spared no expense,' the paper said. Macquarie called the figures 'massively inaccurate' but still, a lesson was learned: Michael Carapiet, who recalls the party in question was for Peter Maher's Banking and Financial Services division, had canned any idea for Macquarie's investment banking arm to have a Christmas party of its own. 'None of the senior executives in the investment bank were really in the mood for it,' he says.

One immediate problem brought into sharp relief by the GFC was Macquarie's many funds, which had been built with considerable leverage: as Ward had disclosed in his rebuttal of Jim Chanos, an average of 58 per cent in the investment banking (chiefly infrastructure) funds going into the crisis.

In those days Macquarie used to produce a quarterly report on its specialist funds, usually over 100 pages long, and the September 2008 report[25] is something of a museum piece, a snapshot of a time that was about to end. (Indeed, it was the last such quarterly update ever produced.) The table of contents listing the individual funds ran to two pages and 33 separate fund families, from Africa Funds[26] to the Retirement Villages Group.[27] On 30 September that year, as the tempest raged, Macquarie had A$239 billion in assets under management through these funds and there was scarcely a part of the world they didn't touch: Mexico, Taiwan, Tanzania, Slovakia.[28]

In some respects the picture is similar today—when last disclosed, Macquarie had A$795.60 billion[29] in assets under management—but the big difference is how many of these things were listed. Macquarie had nine listed funds over five stock exchanges in Australia, Canada, the USA, South Korea and Singapore, with A$17 billion of market capitalisation between them.[30] Today only two, in Korea and Mexico, remain.

The underlying assets of infrastructure funds were generally in reasonably good shape: they provided essential services to communities, making them resilient in terms of cash flows. The problem was the changing nature of the debt markets to deal with their gearing, and the fact that the listed markets were ascribing far less value to the listed funds than they should theoretically have been worth.

Most of the businesses had begun to see trouble coming through 2008 and started to act accordingly.[31] The property funds also slimmed down.[32] Some fared better than others. Macquarie Airports had announced a sale of its stakes in Brussels and Copenhagen Airports for A$1.5 billion in August 2008,[33] a month before the world turned to custard, in order to fund a A$1 billion share buy-back and to deleverage the company. That looked very smart, given it had just reported a half-year net loss of A$274 million, but guess who the buyer was? Macquarie European Infrastructure Fund 3.

Elsewhere, the funds had been refinancing. In the year to 30 September 2008, funds under the Macquarie Capital umbrella raised A$17 billion.[34]

The work gradually moved from pre-emptive strikes to firefighting as the crisis unfolded. There was a lot at stake, although perhaps not quite as much as would be suggested by the noise around all these publicly held vehicles with a lot of panicking retail investors in them: 21 per cent of Macquarie's operating income in the six months to 30 September 2008 was derived from specialist funds. Gradually, the contribution of listed funds to group income diminished, and was at about 5% by the end of the 2009 financial year on 31 March 2009.

Ultimately, though, the end was in sight for listed funds. There is a chart in that 2008 document that allows one to identify the precise moment when the model jumped the shark. It plots an index of the accumulated performance of the listed specialist funds against the MSCI World index, from 1995 onwards. The *annus miserabilis*, 2002, would prove to be a blip; from then to the end of 2006 the listed funds would soar upwards while the MSCI, in Aussie dollar terms at least, drifted sideways. And then it peaked, and by September 2008 was falling hard, describing the summit of a mountain in the chart, a mountain the funds were rapidly descending.

In a broadly encouraging ASX statement on 2 March 2009, in which Macquarie outlined the various sales and refinancings at the funds, the bank noted the considerable gap between the valuation of the assets in the fund and the valuation the stock market was suggesting. They were throwing everything at the problem—asset sales, debt refinancing, security buybacks, capital returns—but it was increasingly clear what many had known for some time: the listed markets were just the wrong place for these assets to be.

One by one, in the months and years that followed, the funds would be wound down, sold, taken private and generally removed from the listed markets. March 2009 brought a bid for Macquarie Communications Infrastructure Group by old friends in Canada,

CPPIB.[36] June came with an agreement to internalise the management of Macquarie Leisure Trust Group.[37]

For Kerrie Mather and the Macquarie Airports team, the news came in July 2009 that the management would be internalised into the mother ship.[38] 'Our airports came through the GFC in good shape,' she says now, 'but following the move away from Macquarie, it was a good opportunity to consider whether it was a good time to sell some of the smaller investments.' MAp Airports, as the internalised division was known, bought progressively larger stakes in Sydney Airport with the proceeds of those sales, buying out the stakes of partners like Ferrovial over a period of years. Mather led a corporate restructuring to make Sydney Airport itself the listed entity, and became CEO of Sydney Airport in 2011; two years later Macquarie sold its cornerstone stake in MAp Airports, which by then was something of a relief, in that it removed any fear investors might have that Macquarie might plan to take that vehicle private. 'The fact that they sold removed an overhang and created liquidity for shareholders.'

For the unlisted funds that remained, it was clear leverage could not remain at the boisterous levels of the early 2000s. 'It came down, is the short answer,' says Leigh Harrison, head of real assets for Macquarie Asset Management. 'There were a lot of lessons learned across all sectors during the GFC about the behaviour and performance of different companies. One of the lessons was that some very good businesses can struggle when they don't have time to trade through cycles, and leverage can be a catalyst for short-term outcomes that they can't trade through.'

■

Then Macquarie set about doing something it had never really had to do before: firing people.[39]

Nicole Sorbara was promoted to executive director in 2008 and was asked to step in as head of HR to cover a maternity leave; the three months she was meant to do it for became three years. 'I guess if there's ever a time to be a head of HR at an investment bank, it is during a financial crisis,' she says.

Macquarie had just never fired people, except on a piecemeal basis when they didn't fit. Allan Moss had always liked to use a slide that showed the correlation between people and profit: hire more good people, make more money, simple as that. 'So it was a massive cultural change for the organisation for us to get our head around the idea of needing to let people go,' Sorbara says. As we'll discuss in the next chapter, she was doing so at the same time as trying to integrate the incoming staff of five new acquisitions at the same time.

Several senior figures took this change badly. 'For the first time in my life, I had to let a lot of people go, and I hated it,' says Carapiet. 'Because we'd always hired people. I had to make some difficult calls and I found that very hard.'

Carapiet, in fact, was one of several senior people who found this a turning point for their relationship with the bank. 'Then I realised I didn't want to do it anymore. I realised that if you're going to head it up, this is something you're going to have to do more than once. I'd done it once and I didn't want to do it again.' He would not formally retire until July 2011, but this was where he lost heart.

Similarly, Charles Wheeler, who had joined the bank in 1987 and came up through the bank's renowned structured finance team before relocating to New York in 2007, never quite got past the GFC. 'It was just utter misery,' he says. 'Macquarie had always had this culture of picking people up and carrying them forward when they fell down.' Failing to succeed.

'But I feel we pivoted through the global financial crisis.' He felt the media saw competitors firing staff, pushing Macquarie to do the same, and it buckled.

He had to lose people who'd worked for him for eight years, and people who'd just arrived from Australia two months earlier. 'It was horrible, really, really, horrible. And I just felt like the whole culture of the organisation changed at that moment.'

There's a palpable sense of betrayal in the way Wheeler, who had been among the most proud and admiring of the Macquarie culture, talks about this time. 'The thing that really upset me was there was no: let's sit down and see what creative solutions there might be.' Wheeler says he would have worked without pay for years if it would have saved the team; he was on the cusp of building a renewable energy business that it would take Macquarie many years to return to, by which time Wheeler had set up his own shop, Greenbacker Capital, to do it himself. 'We weren't really consulted. You just had to get rid of people. It was just so demoralising that I can't even put words around it.'

Wheeler then spent the next eighteen months stuck being the chairman of a property investment that had gone sour in the USA, Spirit Finance, taking him away from his intended focus on renewables. After that he'd had enough, and left.

Asia seemed to be hit particularly hard by redundancies. For Andrew Low, then head of Asia, it was the first time in his career he had ever known people to be laid off. 'There was always a little bit of hiring and firing, moving people out who weren't quite right for the business,' he says. 'But the GFC was the first time where we actually had quotas: you've got to lose so many people.

'That was quite wrenching for a lot of people globally, because we had really known nothing but growth.'

Shemara Wikramanayake was among those who had to learn this tough new skill. 'Look, I only had to do that once in the global financial crisis, because typically our business is growing and it's people-led and you're backing them,' she says now. 'But the whole asset management industry then had more headcount than the base of business could support.'

She had been advised by someone from Citigroup: you've never been through this before, so if you're going to do it, go early and go deep, so you don't have to keep chipping away and hurt morale. That would give those you'd let go the best chance of finding new roles. 'But for me it was one of the toughest things, to take away the livelihoods of people.'

Chapter 11

DON'T WASTE A GOOD CRISIS

Among the many Macquarie mantras, up there with Loose–Tight and Fail to Succeed, Bias to Yes and Freedom within Boundaries, is this one: Don't Waste a Good Crisis.

As crises go, there had never been one quite on the scale of the GFC. As we've seen, it took some navigating. But once it became clear that Macquarie was going to survive the crisis intact and independent, attention turned to a new directive: what can we buy?

It is a sign of Macquarie's enduring gumption that there was significant overlap between crisis and opportunism. One of the most significant acquisitions in Macquarie's history, Constellation Energy, was announced a month *before* Macquarie's A\$15-a-share low, as the bank's counterparties poised their fingers over the eject button and everyone from the receptionists to the board wondered what would come next.

But the purchase does support Moore and Ward's contention that they were never seriously worried about the group's viability, given that, the whole way through the crisis, they were preparing to buy the casualties of it at bargain prices.

The USA was the heart of the crisis, and also the heart of the bargain-hunting that followed it. Two deals here would prove pivotal to Macquarie's fortunes: Constellation Energy, announced in February 2009,[1] and Delaware Investments, announced that August.[2]

The first of them came in the commodities business, and it's time to understand that group and its people a little better.

■

Andrew Downe was employee number 139 when he joined back in 1985, a time when you knew and could name every person in the organisation and when it was still navigating its way to independence from Hill Samuel.

Downe is not nearly celebrated enough in the Macquarie story, partly because of a quieter and more introverted, media-shy temperament than some of the Macquarie Capital and asset management stars, and partly because commodities and global markets have nothing like as much noise around them as investment banking. It's not just Macquarie: the world is full of disgruntled markets bankers quietly pointing out that their earnings drive the bank while big-shot investment bankers get all the plaudits. But Downe put in over 30 years of effort to build what is, at the time of writing, the most profitable group of the whole enterprise.[3]

Not that Downe complained about it: he seemed to like it that way. He started under Tony Berg's leadership, initially in the futures division, before working across areas including bullion and commodities, which had been built by early leading lights of Hill Samuel such as Clive Carroll[4] as the markets evolved for derivatives around wool, agricultural commodities, gold and then financial instruments.

'We did a lot of stuff in Australia from first principles,' Carroll remembers. 'It was trailblazing.' Carroll's successor Ray Hall continued the growth trajectory.[5]

Downe gradually worked his way up the rungs through bullion, currencies, interest rates, principal derivatives and the rest of the markets matrix, learning as he went. 'So, for example, bullion was interesting, but it wasn't just about bullion. It was about currencies, it was about interest rates, funding, the balance sheet,' he says. 'Gold was like one tiny piece of the puzzle, and you were taught to understand the whole puzzle of what was going on, not confine yourself to one very special little piece of it and assume everything else around it is what other people told you.'

He learned early on to challenge assumptions, to find things out for himself, and the value of figuring that out before anyone else did. 'If you came up with something new, you had six months before everybody had it. We were pretty fast on innovation, because we had to be. If you just do the same as last year, you are accepting that you are dying.'

He learned, too, a particular way of thinking that characterises leaders in global markets businesses to this day. 'We started every day at minus two million dollars of expenses. So, what are you going to do to cover those costs?' Thus the day was mapped out with the urgency of making money from it.

At the same time, there was longer-term forward planning there: a push into commodities that 'was going to be a minimum three-year investment to get to first base. We got used to not underestimating how long it really took to establish yourself with a real competitive position. One of the jokes I would make is that we spent twenty years running around the world, starting with: how do you spell Macquarie?'[6]

The Bankers Trust acquisition in 1999 benefited the business considerably, giving it a fully formed agricultural commodities division among other things, but still in many areas Macquarie was happily below the radar, almost trying not to get noticed before they built critical mass.

'I really hate the tall poppy syndrome we have here in Australia, but it served one fantastic purpose for us, which was [an attitude of]: for God's sake, whatever you're doing, don't tell anyone and don't make a big noise about it because you'll get crushed [by a bigger competitor] if somebody finds out.' Is this why he gained a reputation for being secretive, never speaking to the press? 'Well, in some respects, yes, because what's in it for us?'

The other thing Bankers Trust brought was some balance sheet to the business, which raised a new possibility: going global. 'We'd been trying to go overseas without a balance sheet by doing joint ventures, which really sucks damn hard,' says Downe. 'But we had to do it because we didn't have any way to do it ourselves.' But the arrival of a decent balance sheet opened some new horizons.

At this point we meet Nick O'Kane, who had started out in 1995 on the foreign exchange desk, feeling the full glamour of Macquarie early on by being assigned to the graveyard shift of a 24-hour currency options trading desk out of Sydney. He then went to Malaysia, an experience that must have made the graveyard shift look appealing, because he was in a business providing foreign exchange and interest rate products to domestic Malaysian corporates at the exact point when their prime minister Mahathir Mohamed implemented currency controls during the Asian financial crisis in 1998, thus destroying that entire business. 'We wound down that book trade by trade, which was a good learning experience for me,' he says. 'I had to negotiate the exit of every trade that we had on the books.'

He then went to South Korea, experiencing the challenges of joint ventures in Macquarie's tie-up with Kookmin, and was then in London in the mid-2000s. By this stage Downe had been looking at the American energy market, in which Macquarie had no presence, but had been put off by Enron's dominance and success. That, as we all now know, was a mirage, and when Enron collapsed in 2001, Downe took a second look. 'We had a look over a few bits and pieces, but we were just too scared of any skeletons in the closet,' he says.

So they set about building a presence organically, which was always a reach from scratch—'we lost money in energy for at least the first three years when it was a basic cost centre,' Downe recalls—when an opportunity arose.

Cook Inlet had been formed in California in 1991. Cindy Khek, who is now Macquarie's co-head of North American power, gas and emissions out of Houston, was there from 1997, and remembers the early days, seeing the traders getting going at five in the morning in order to be able to serve the east coast time zones, navigating the challenges of technology so primitive that the physical process of moving natural gas molecules around was done by fax.

It was a client-driven shop with tight credit that, in turn, led to a strong risk management culture, which would prove attractive to Macquarie when the Australians came across it in 2005.[7]

David Hochberg, who today is head of Macquarie Commodities Trading, its physical oil trading business in Houston, was also at Cook. 'It was a niche player, a company that survived Enron and the other big companies that had fallen over,' among them his former employer, Aquila in Kansas City, which bailed out of wholesale energy and trading in 2002.[8] 'It was fun, a neat environment: everyone was young and working together,' he says. 'We challenged each other every day.' Cook had principals who were ready to exit in 2005, which Hochberg thinks was just the right time. 'When Macquarie bought us, it was a pretty big inflection point, because the talent of the company was outgrowing the opportunities at the company,' he says. 'None of us knew who Macquarie was at the time.'

Cook was, Downe says, one of those rare opportunities that arise sometimes—'it wasn't like we went looking for it'—that helped Macquarie move faster along a path it had already mapped.

To O'Kane, it was a real find in a fragmented marketplace. The disappearance of Enron and others, who were bringing balance sheet and not charging for it in a most un-Macquarie state of affairs, 'left a bit of a void for us to come in and bring some financial discipline. But it took a long time to find Cook: a company that had no legacy issues, with a risk culture we felt was consistent with ours.'

More to the point, Cook brought with it 400 contracts and some very talented people. O'Kane moved from London to Los Angeles to run the business. 'Who knew,' he says now, 'that sitting in Los Angeles was a whole bunch of 30-year-olds who turned out to be just unbelievable contributors to Macquarie Group.'

■

By the time of the GFC, the business—now called Macquarie Cook Energy—was making strides, notwithstanding the fact that their first four years of business had included two devastating hurricanes[9] with considerable impact on energy volatility even before the financial crisis kicked in. But then came the biggest opportunity yet.

On the other side of America, Constellation Energy had run into trouble. A Baltimore-based energy major whose legacy businesses dated back to 1960, by 2008 it had hit a liquidity crisis, sold itself to Berkshire Hathaway's MidAmerican Energy Holdings, and in November announced plans to sell its downstream gas trading operations, based in Houston.[10]

'Constellation was an interesting opportunity,' says O'Kane. 'They were a much bigger trading operation than we were: little old Macquarie Cook, as we called ourselves back then.' Cindy Khek remembers it feeling like 'a small fish trying to go after a big fish.'

The sale was a competitive process, which Macquarie rushed to insert itself into even as Sydney was grappling with the worst of the financial crisis at home. O'Kane was not unaware of this by any means, but thought: 'Wow, we're not going to get the chance to buy a business like this again, where we're not going to pay very much for it.'

Besides, this is a reminder that the direction of these things never came from the top, but from in the field; that hadn't changed no matter how apocalyptic the surrounding market circumstances. The energy business, and the deals that built it, 'were not something where Nicholas said you need to go and do this,' Downe says. 'This was something dreamed up at the coal face.'

Geographically it looked a good fit, with Cook most active on the west coast, and Constellation on the east coast and mid-central region. Culture-wise, it looked good too. Hochberg[11] remembers working with his new peer from the Constellation side, trying to align mark-to-markets so they would be consistent on the merged systems from day one; they went through 240 curves and everything was exactly the same, which gave the reassuring proof that they were approaching business in the same way.

'It wasn't that they were doing anything that we didn't already understand,' says O'Kane. 'They were just doing more of it. They had people with more experience, and who knew more than we did.' The contracts that came with them were fantastic, he says, but it was really about the hundred or so people. The deal was announced on 4 February 2009,[12] right in the teeth of the GFC.

The swoop moved Macquarie from niche to powerful. 'That deal completed their footprint in the lower 48 states,' says Ozzie Pagan, who joined Macquarie through the Constellation deal and now runs commodity finance for the Americas (he's also ex-Enron). 'Constellation was routinely in the top five of the largest physical traders of natural gas at that time.' The team that came remain vital today.

'What you find downstairs[13] is really the backbone of what used to be Constellation's natural gas trading platform.'

It must have been a challenge to imprint the distinctive Macquarie culture on two separate American enterprises[14] and bring them all into a collective.[15] But it worked: the power and natural gas businesses grew in tandem, sharing information and expertise, and then together they built a physical oil trading group. There wasn't much overlap. 'Slowly, over the next probably three to four years, those different parts of Macquarie and Cook and Constellation became integrated, and were largely organised the way you see them today,' says Pagan.

Today Moore considers the Constellation acquisition one of the most significant deals of his time, and a classic Macquarie story. The fact that they could do it at all was in some sense a vindication of years of risk management discipline.

'In practice, almost all institutions get caught up with this boom-bust cycle,' he says. 'We have a long-term history of buying businesses where people had bought in the good times and sold in the bad times.' In Moore's case, that went way back to Security Pacific in the nineties. 'So the ability to just stay in the space and not go boom, bust, boom, bust is just really powerful.'

Powerful enough to buy things when everyone else is selling. 'So even though it might not have been great profits back in 2009, 2010, we made money in those years,' Moore says. 'And if you're making money, you still get shareholder support, you still get debt market support, and therefore you can still do stuff.'

Before we leave commodities for the moment, it's perhaps instructive to learn about the deals that aren't done, the products that are ignored. Andrew Downe says Macquarie's planning and culture 'is perhaps best illustrated by what we didn't do.' In his case, he highlights credit derivatives: he says he ran around Wall Street interviewing people before eventually concluding they wouldn't do it, for two reasons.

One was that there was a very limited circle of people who understood the business, 'and so to think that Macquarie could attract the best people in that area was dreaming.' The other was that it had a mark-to-model system, rather than mark-to-market,[16] which is what every other business did, meaning that on any given day there was an independent valuation available for everything Macquarie did. So they stayed out.

O'Kane highlights water. Macquarie does own a water pipeline business in Oklahoma through the asset management side, but doesn't involve itself in water as a commodity. 'I just don't see how we would have value to add to the market,' he says. 'If you can't work out what you're bringing, I don't think you've got a business.'

The result is a Commodities and Global Markets (CGM) business that, by the time Downe stepped down in 2019,[17] was offering 140 products in 24 markets and yet still could claim to be selective and niche. We haven't even delved into the fixed income and currencies business run by Simon Wright, who has spent 30 years refining a business across foreign exchange, interest rates and structured credit;[18] or the asset finance business now found within CGM, representing decades of expertise on everything from aircraft leasing to shipping finance, helicopters and UK parking meters.

'Macquarie still has the advantage of being small enough to decide where it wants to fight,' Downe says now. 'Nobody says it has to do everything.'

■

Ben Bruck had been given a mandate: scour the world and find things to buy. On the plus side, there was plenty to look at. On the minus, many of them were on sale for the very good reason that they weren't worth owning.

Bruck was a long way into a 30-year career at Macquarie when the GFC hit, perhaps not the path he had expected when he studied biochemistry at university. He had worked through the risk management division, the market trading floors of the ASX (Australian Stock Exchange) and the Sydney Futures Exchange, and had risen to the top of the investment management business, eventually running it. Along the way he had made a name for taking Australia offshore, starting off with asset management joint ventures in Malaysia, South Africa, Taiwan and South Korea.

Even before the GFC, Bruck and his then-boss, Richard Sheppard, had decided the future of the business was overseas, 'but taking much more equity risk this time, rather than trying to do joint ventures.' They'd also decided that the best opportunities would be in developed markets. 'That's where all the money was.'

Bruck hired a man called Michael Walsh who had just come out of one of Macquarie's most trusted proving grounds, the Harvard MBA program, and then they started looking. But then the financial world blew up. 'And so we switched gears,' says Bruck. 'Very quickly.'

The two of them decided to focus on northern hemisphere financial institutions, since they were in the most profound state of crisis. 'And most of them owned an asset manager,' Bruck says. 'They were starting to land into their own liquidity problems and urgently needed to raise money.' Many of them—banks, insurers—were in the Troubled Asset Relief Program.[19]

Bruck asked Walsh to identify all the top 500 banks and insurers around the world with asset management subsidiaries, and together they tried to figure out which had a good business they might want to sell. There were a lot of them: of the 500, about 400 had asset management arms and 300 would probably at least be open to a conversation.

'And we literally cold called, warm called or met with all of them,' Bruck says. 'We just went through the entire list.' They formed a chart with axes of how desirable something was and how actionable it was, and established a few names that scored highly on both—the hot zone, as Bruck called it. Once a name was considered a target, it got a code-name, generally a fruit variety that had some vague link to the target. It's hazy now, but Bruck clearly remembers a walnut.

By this stage Nicholas Moore had restructured divisions to start to consolidate the asset management businesses within Macquarie, initially around public listed securities and called them Macquarie Funds Group,[20] with Shemara Wikramanayake in charge. Bruck brought his chart to both of them, and showed them the names in the hot zone, most of which were in the USA because of the size of the market and sheer scale and violence of the disruption under way there at the time. 'Ben said to me: this is a once in a lifetime chance now to get a position in the biggest capital market in the world,' Wikramanayake recalls. 'There's a big pay to play cost in being in that equities and fixed income asset business: you need operating plat-forms, you need legal, compliance, distribution for the high volumes of daily transactions. It's very different to the private markets.

'So whether you manage A\$2 billion of assets or A\$100 billion you need the same expense base, and this was our chance to get A\$100 billion of assets to cover the fixed costs of that expense base.'

One of the names in Bruck's hot zone was Delaware Investments.

Delaware was a storied name in American asset management, dating from 1929, founded by a Philadelphian admiral who thought any significant enterprise should be named after a ship or a body of water. The Delaware River, which passes Philadelphia, is a particu-larly revered waterway in American history—George Washington crossed it in order to attack the British on Christmas Day 1776[21]—and so the name was settled.

In later years it became the first asset management firm in America to be put into a private equity structure, and was then bought by a US life insurance company called Lincoln Financial Group. 'We were known as a large cap value shop, who focused on dividends and stability,' says Patrick Coyne, who joined Delaware in 1990 and was its president at the time Macquarie appeared on the scene. In the 2000s, when being a dividend value shop while everyone's head was being turned by the tech boom was not really the best place to be, they increased their fixed income team, and thus they became pretty close to a full-service shop with few major gaps.

The GFC hit Lincoln much more than it did Delaware. Lincoln took money from the federal government and would be among the first to pay it back, but in the meantime had short-term financing problems when there was little liquidity in the market. 'We were probably the most liquid or marketable business unit at the time,' says Coyne, and so Lincoln decided to sell Delaware. Coyne insisted on being closely involved in selecting the bidders.

Macquarie became aware and expressed an interest. (Bids in which someone else came to Macquarie and told them an asset was for sale got a different code-name, which is why Delaware, rather than being referred to as some gladioli or grapefruit, got the more glamorous name of Project Superbowl). The frame narrowed to two bidders, Macquarie and a private equity shop, with a UK fund manager also in the frame.[22]

Macquarie had advantages from Delaware's point of view: entering the USA pretty much from scratch in terms of public funds, there was little overlap in products. 'So they wanted everything kit and caboodle,' says Coyne.[23] 'That was a big concern of mine: I wanted to make sure that we could essentially keep the firm intact, because we were on a really nice trajectory.'

Macquarie, meanwhile, was still chasing multiple targets at once. There was a day when Bruck and Wikramanayake had to engage in two critical presentations simultaneously, one in New York with an insurer selling its asset management business, and the other in Philadelphia with Delaware and Lincoln. Wikramanayake had, by now, been dispatched to the USA by Moore; she and Bruck would bounce up and down between the two cities on the train, presenting and negotiating. Delaware, which 'came down to the wire,' according to Bruck, was the better fit. The deal was announced on 19 August 2009 (details in footnotes[24]).

Delaware employed 580 people; that's more than had ultimately come across in the BT deal in 1999. This was, on many metrics, Macquarie's biggest ever deal and largest investment.

The transition from Delaware to Macquarie was inevitably not to everyone's tastes. Since Macquarie had no brand name in American mutual funds, Delaware's name was the more powerful. 'You can't really buy United States culture, flip the switch and make it a part of Macquarie culture, there's going to be a lot of pushback,' says Coyne. 'I made that fairly clear. During my tenure a big part of that was holding that [transition] off as long as I could, because I didn't think it would be beneficial to growing the asset management business. I always said, no disrespect, but your brand will not bring us more money here in the United States.'

Macquarie agreed at first, and did not change the overall name from Delaware to Macquarie until Coyne was replaced by Shawn Lytle in 2015, a period in which the head of equities, general counsel and chief operating officer also departed. This is the point at which Delaware truly became Macquarie. 'It had been moving that way, but that was when we really accelerated things,' says Lytle.

Along the way to that moment were four years of small frustrations and cultural friction, from expenses to profit share models to Macquarie's idea of competing teams, before the business was truly absorbed.

But none of these challenges change a simple fact about the Delaware deal. At a stroke it transformed Macquarie into a mainstream, public-facing asset manager in the biggest capital market in the world. 'The reason the Delaware Investments acquisition was so important is the simple fact that 25 per cent of the world's wealth sits with US individuals, predominantly invested with funds or ETFs [exchange-traded funds] or separate accounts,' says Lytle. 'It is a significant market Macquarie was not exposed to.

'I want to build a first-class brand in the US where everybody knows how to pronounce our name.'

There were other deals besides. On the exact same day that the Delaware deal was announced, Macquarie also said it had set up two funds to invest in infrastructure businesses in China in a joint venture with China Everbright, each contributing US$100 million to funds that would aim to raise US$1.5 billion in aggregate.[25] Throughout 2009 Macquarie would buy Fox-Pitt Kelton Cochran Caronia Waller, a mergers and acquisitions investment bank, for US$130 million;[26] Tristone Capital Global, an energy advisory group; and several businesses of Sal Oppenheim.[27] The Canadian retail broker Blackmont would be added to the fold, while the Corporate and Asset Finance business would acquire a A$1 billion portfolio of auto loans and leases from Ford Credit Australia.

'The project of trying to find bank and insurance company divestitures probably went on for five years,' says Bruck, 'but its focus moved from the USA over the Atlantic to Europe.' There would be some successes here—an example was ValueInvest Asset Management in Luxembourg[28]—but nothing quite so transformational as Delaware. 'We got some small businesses but we never got the couple of biggies that we really wanted,' says Bruck. Macquarie was outbid on Robeco, was in the mix for Dexia, and lost out on Scottish Widows and Pioneer. One deal they couldn't get over the line was a

Kansas City-based fund manager called Waddell & Reed. No matter: they got it a few years later instead, not long after Bruck retired.

They would not all work out. Fox-Pitt Kelton and Sal Oppenheim are remembered as duds today, and Blackmont didn't work out. But they still speak to an essential Macquarie message: that if you're there with capital in the bad times, you'll get generational opportunities.

Greg Ward remembers: 'As much as we were doing all the work with the market and shareholders to assure them of our funding, I was spending just as much of my time on new acquisitions and businesses,' he says. 'As one of the guys internally said: this is the best buying opportunity of our lifetime. And we didn't want to miss out on that.

'And as much as wanted to settle the nerves of everyone that thought we'd be the next Lehmans, we never stopped thinking about the opportunities.'

■

Meanwhile, at home, there was plenty to keep the bank occupied.

One of the most controversial decisions the bank took in the immediate aftermath of the GFC was to seed a new business under Ben Brazil. The business itself—a lending operation within the Corporate and Asset Finance Group, and more specifically a combination of lending directly to low-rated companies and buying their existing loans in the secondary market[29]—was not especially contentious. It was the funds that it was investing that were in question.

The person behind this new business was Ben Brazil, who has the rare accolade of picking up a nickname based on his intelligence even in a place where everyone has an absurd IQ. Ben the Brains, a Queenslander and the son of a successful farmer,[30] had started in corporate advisory in 1994, swiftly moving to Nicholas Moore's Project and Structured Finance team, for a time in New York and

Europe. His mind is greatly admired, even if a mischievous few think there's more than one reason for the nickname. 'He is very, very smart,' says one former colleague of the nickname. 'But then again, he does look quite a lot like Brains from *Thunderbirds*.'

An interview with Brazil is an uncomfortable affair: pauses of a full minute are not uncommon while he frowns over the precise wording of a brief answer. But Brazil does volunteer one anecdote that shows his strong relationship with Moore, as well as what he admired about Macquarie.

It relates to the acquisition of Copenhagen Airport in 2004–05. Macquarie had acquired a shareholding below the disclosure threshold, and wanted to buy more after a cap on maximum shareholdings was removed. 'The appropriate protocol was to go and introduce ourselves to government in order to explain,' he says. 'I was relatively young and junior at that juncture. I asked Nicholas if I could get him to join.' They discussed the logistical challenges of getting to Copenhagen from Sydney and then Moore stopped and told him: 'You set up the meeting and I'll be there.'

Macquarie would go on to be controlling shareholder of the airport in what was considered one of the infrastructure group's best investments. 'But the point is,' Brazil says, 'an employee who experiences that level of support will act very differently to an employee who, in most global peers, learns (more implicitly than explicitly) that they really don't matter.'

Brazil left Macquarie for a time, working with the Packer family; James Packer called asset finance veteran Stephen Cook to ask his opinion, and told him: 'Any guy that can be called Brains at Macquarie must be so smart I'd better recruit him.' A planned private equity operation for the Packers was stymied by the GFC, and in 2008 Brazil called Moore asking to come back. 'Ben's a great guy and he was very good at doing business,' says Moore.

Moore wanted Brazil to join the Corporate and Asset Finance team, or CAF, which to that point was chiefly about things like lease financing for equipment, cars or aviation, with a modest lending business. It was in this lending part that Brazil would work.

The opportunity was that credit spreads had shot out to unprecedented highs during the financial crisis, and there was an opportunity for smart and attentive people to make money from it. Brazil doesn't really want to speak about that business, given the noise it generated, preferring instead to defer to public statements in annual reports and investor presentations. He did speak at an operational briefing in 2016, saying: 'It was a very opportune time to establish a business such as ours, and we made the most of that in 2009'.

So Moore explains it. 'Margins blow out in tight times, and they come in in times like now,' he says [this interview took place in April 2022, at a reasonably calm time in world credit markets]. 'And what Macquarie traditionally does is, we do more on the lending side when margins are like that. At a certain point we'll say the business isn't worth it and we will do something else. But when margins blow, we will be a beneficiary of it. Back then, it was good for debt returns.'

Moore is correct to say that this business existed prior to Brazil's return, but it's telling that investor presentations in later years about CAF Lending tend to start their charts in 2009:[31] there's no question Brazil was presiding over something that, if not entirely new, was certainly intended to expand dramatically.[32]

CAF, at this stage, conflated two quite different businesses, lending and leasing, but the fact that operating lease income was down 40 per cent year on year while CAF's total profit quadrupled tells you something about what was going on behind the scenes.[33] That year's results presentation referred to 'significant growth in corporate lending activities in CAF'.[34]

In the years to come CAF Lending would be carved out as a distinct arm of the business, and Brazil would build a high yield and distressed debt investment business that by early 2016 had invested A$33 billion[35] in 500 high yield loan exposures around the world, with a book that at any given time hovered between about A$9 billion and A$12 billion. If one considered them as a pooled fund, they would have been equivalent to some of the biggest high yield investors in the world, like BlackRock or Fidelity.

By February 2012 Brazil would be made co-head of CAF alongside Garry Farrell,[36] and in 2014, by which time his title was head of CAF Lending, he would join the Exco. That put his compensation into the public domain: A$10.675 million total short- and long-term compensation in the 2015 financial year, then A$15 million, $16.8 million, $16.94 million and $11.5 million in the year of his departure, financial 2020.[37] (His departure also speaks to another key Macquarie theme: don't be emotional about a business that has run its course. When the market opportunity Brazil had exploited reached its natural end, they just shut the business down.) 'I think the commitment to change if the market or circumstances change has been one of the hallmarks of Macquarie,' says Robin Bishop. 'One of the things that's been consistent for 53 years is being prepared to start new businesses and get out of old businesses that are no longer profitable or able to offer products that are valuable to clients.'

So far, so Macquarie. But where was this money coming from?

The wholesale funding guarantee had given Macquarie unfettered access to the debt markets using the government's AAA rating, a much easier and cheaper matter than funding under Macquarie's A rating. This didn't come free—Macquarie paid an annual fee to the government of around A$200 million for the privilege[38]—but by borrowing at this relatively cheap rate and putting the money into high-yielding assets like these, Macquarie was able to earn huge spreads above its own cost of funding. Macquarie raised about A$25 billion of government-guaranteed paper through 2009 alone[39] before stopping using the guarantee in August that year.

The recognition that large sums of government-guaranteed paper had been used to enrich Macquarie, rather than the intended purpose of fortifying the banking system and allowing it to continue to function for the benefit of society and the economy, did not go down terribly well either with government or the press. *The Sydney Morning Herald* led a feature on Brazil in 2010 with this: 'His name is Ben Brazil and he is the banker using your AAA-taxpayer credit rating to make millions for Macquarie Group and fuel the bonuses of its bankers.'

Wayne Swan, the Australian Treasurer at the time the facility was announced, says now: 'The whole world was melting down; we were watching what was going on overseas. We didn't want our banks to fall over. And we weren't doing favours for any individual bank.'

The Macquarie argument in response to all of this is threefold: one, they didn't raise any more money under the guarantee scheme than usual;[40] two, that all money is fungible and it's pointless trying to put it in boxes according to how or where it is used; and three, that they paid the government for the privilege of using the guarantee.

To take the first of these, Moore argues: 'As a simple statement of fact, our balance sheet shrunk over the period, it didn't grow. And the loan assets, the area where Ben was working, actually shrunk as well over the period.

'So the idea that this [guarantee] allowed a new source of business, it didn't. The point of the government guarantee was to allow banks to continue to do business. And was there good business to be done after the GFC for anybody who was in our business, the answer is yes, of course there was. But it wasn't like this was some free kick.'

Stuart Green makes the second point. 'Money is fungible. You don't put money in jars.' Money was also coming in, he says, from selling Italian mortgages and margin lending; his point is, who's to say which money Brazil was using? 'There were a lot of people saying the government guarantee money was raised and given to Ben. But financial institutions can't work that way.' He also points out that at any given time, Brazil's book peaked at around A$12 billion, which was less than the A$15 billion raised from asset and business exits. 'Now, you can no more link the A$12 [billion] of the peak in that book and the government guarantee, than you can link the A$12 and the A$15 from asset sales.'

This is fair enough, so far as it goes, but it's also fair to argue that Brazil would not have been able to deploy such a significant book of capital without the bank raising funds in the international markets, and doing so benefited from the government guarantee. The only question that really matters, to be blunt, is whether you think that's taking the piss.

■

The Cash Management Trust (CMT), as we have learned, had been a reliable golden goose for Macquarie since its inception. In the financial crisis, it would deliver once again.

By early 2010, the CMT had A$9.5 billion under management,[41] which was a handy chunk of funding to have on hand at a time when banks needed it more than ever, but was starting to decline: the effect of the government guarantee on retail deposits was that people were abandoning trusts for bank accounts, a process that could already be seen well under way in the USA. Since the CMT was a trust, a plan was made to switch it all into an on-balance sheet cash management account (CMA) Macquarie had set up in 2008.

Announcing it to the ASX on 4 March, Macquarie presented it as reflecting 'current market conditions and retail investor preferences', which it was. But moving those funds under the government guarantee was also useful for Macquarie. 'It was done at a time of a strategic inflection point for Macquarie, and it boosted the balance sheet significantly,' says Peter Maher, who was in charge of the division at the time, which was now called Banking and Financial Services after absorbing the Banking and Securitisation Group in February 2008. 'And that provided an opportunity for some of the really smart investment bankers to take that money and make a lot of money out of it. The name Ben Brazil just happens to come to mind.'

It was not straightforward, though. Irene O'Brien, who ran communications for the division, recalls a Friday evening meeting with several top brass from the retail division trying to work out if they could get the CMA covered by the government guarantee, because it fed into wrap accounts, which brought technical complexity. They decided it could be done but that it needed a unitholders' meeting, which required a two-thirds majority.

'It was a couple of months to make that work,' she says. 'And we needed to get a guarantee from the government that the government guarantee would cover that particular account.' Because, if they said no, that they wouldn't cover it because it was a different structure, 'then what was the point? You'd still be in the same boat that you were in, and money would still be bleeding out the back door.'

Eventually they got their assurance: a guarantee of a guarantee, a sort of guarantee squared. 'I remember the day of the vote,' says Maher. 'We had it in the old Entertainment Centre.' They won, with over 97 per cent of the vote.[42] 'It was a pivotal change.'

■

July 2010 brought another restructuring, this one more significant than a few name changes.

The biggest was that Macquarie Capital Funds would merge with Macquarie Funds Group,[43] basically putting every different bit of asset management under one roof with total assets under management of A$306 billion. Shemara Wikramanayake, who had been responsible for integrating three funds and funds-based structured product businesses to create Macquarie Funds Group in 2008 and was then instrumental with Ben Bruck in the Delaware acquisition, would run the merged group. The new MFG was among the top 50 asset managers in the world with 1800 staff in nineteen countries.[44]

Wikramanayake's path to the top was increasingly clear from this moment on.

As Macquarie gradually shifted its shape to deal with this strange new post-crisis world, there was one more thing to revise: pay.

Nicole Sorbara, who had become executive director in 2008 and head of HR through the course of the crisis, was responsible for a restructure of the bank's remuneration arrangements. 'While the principles are still long-held and have been a key part of the success of the organisation, it was still a major change,' Sorbara says.

Sorbara had started this process in late 2008, only to find that changes in the Australian tax laws through the Corporations Act 'ended our scheme and we had to spend a lot of time getting that back on track'. But the essence of it, announced in the 2009 results review, was this: for executive directors, the amount of profit share they were paid out in cash would be reduced, and the amount retained would increase, with the retained profit share invested in a combination of Macquarie shares and equity in Macquarie's managed funds. The vesting and payout schedule for that was pushed out, to three to seven years, and clawback provisions were added.[45]

The idea behind all of this was to lock in staff, and in particular executives, for the long term, and to align their compensation even more directly with their contribution and the success of the business. (That work continues but is being tweaked: the 2022 annual report showed a further revision[46] with the vesting period for granted shares to key executives being shortened by two years. The amounts retained under Macquarie's profit share structure are also being trimmed by up to 10 per cent.[47])

The earlier changes required approval at the 2009 AGM, which they easily received. After all, it was in keeping with the basic ideas of linking people and pay to performance that David Clarke had championed all those years ago.

One assumes he approved, but the sad truth was that Clarke was now terminally ill. He had resumed his duties as chairman on 31 August 2009, relieving Kevin McCann who had been acting chair from August 2008, through the worst of the crisis. But at the 2010 AGM, held at the Sheraton on the Park on 30 July that year, it was clear that Clarke's return was temporary and in some respects symbolic. He was present, seated between company secretary Dennis Leong and non-executive director Helen Nugent, but not active. 'We are delighted that David could join us today but in view of his programmed radiotherapy treatment, it has been decided that I chair today's meeting,' McCann said.[48] Clarke was re-elected as a director.[49]

Though the end was clearly not far away, it was of some relief that Clarke had lived to see Macquarie revived. That AGM presented the results for the 2010 financial year, in which profits had topped a billion like the old days: A$1.05 billion, up 21 per cent year on year, at a return on equity of 10 per cent with A$326 billion under management. It was the 40th anniversary of Macquarie's inception, and not only had it defied rumours of its impending demise to be around to celebrate it, it had set about reinventing itself and was growing afresh.

Clarke formally resigned as chairman on 17 March 2011 and died just three weeks later, on 8 April.

The 2011 annual report is filled with tributes to Clarke and what he helped create. He joined an organisation of twelve people and left it with a staff of 15,500 operating out of 70 offices in 28 countries. A *Vale* included several of his quotes, of which the most simple stand out. 'You have to have a clear idea of what you want to do. And you must find the best people to help you do it.' 'I knew that if we were doing the basics right, we would grow well and we would become big.' 'Don't accept anything. Question everything. That's always been very much part of the culture at Macquarie.'

The *Vale* talked about his philanthropy and involvement with the Salvation Army, Opera Australia and Social Ventures Australia; Clarke had set up the Hill Samuel Charitable Fund in 1978, made sure Macquarie had a philanthropic arm at launch, and chaired it for 26 years. By the time he died it had contributed A$145 million. 'I was always taught by my parents and grandparents that if you are successful in life, you have an obligation to give back.'

At the time of writing the Alex Harvey-chaired Macquarie Group Foundation had contributed more than A$520 million to help drive social change at the local community level. In Macquarie's 2022 year, A$44 million was contributed to more than 2300 non-profit organisations.

In February 2022, Macquarie outlined a one-time A$20 million additional Foundation allocation to expand its Social Impact Investing pilot. That followed an initiative during Macquarie's 50th anniversary year around a A$50 million grant program, split between five winning organisations that will each receive A$10 million over five years.

The Foundation's activities cover Macquarie Sports, which was established by foreign exchange employee Guy Reynolds, and the

Macquarie Group Collection, an art collection that was the brain-child of Tony Berg but set up by Julian Beaumont.

The art collection supports emerging Australian artists through the purchase and display of their works. 'We based the collection on artists who were young, emerging and full of promise, with only a few exceptions to the rule,' Beaumont says. The collection houses works by artists including Cressida Campbell and Tim Maguire.[50]

Macquarie Sports offers scholarships to young athletes and has provided sporting opportunities to more than 200,000 children across Australia.

'Shemara, Alex, Mary Reemst,[51] they've all shown up for Foundation events, where it's staff-driven in particular, because it really matters to staff to show that they're really, genuinely interested,' head of the Macquarie Foundation Lisa George says. 'This matters to us as an organisation.'

Chapter 12

AUSTRALIAN ROADTRIP

JOYCE MOULLAKIS

It may seem a little odd beginning this plane, train and road trip at a bustling construction site 40 kilometres south of Perth, Australia's fourth-largest city by population size.

We find ourselves in the Kwinana Industrial Area, at a site that has multiple cranes in operation, cladding being foisted onto a large building frame and trucks circling about. There are two ramps on either side of the large building structure where Australia will house what is being dubbed as its first thermal utility-scale waste-to-energy facility.

When it's up and running the project will use moving-grate technology to thermally treat waste, converting the energy generated into steam to produce electricity. Rubbish in this era of sustainability and emissions reduction is turning into a lucrative business and Macquarie obviously views it as treasure over junk.

Environmentalists will be closely watching how this technology evolves as mismanaged projects are being linked to unhealthy emissions[1] and dioxins being released into the air.

This waste-to-energy site is not far from the city of Kwinana[2] on the traditional lands of the Nyoongar people, where two earlier attempts at European settlement largely failed before an oil refinery would finally see an industrial hub developed. That harkens back to the 1950s when the Western Australian government forged an agreement with a company now known as BP to construct the refinery, with the state to build infrastructure and housing for employees.

As the huge task of decarbonisation takes shape globally, enter Macquarie and several partners including DIF Capital Partners who are seeking to get the waste-to-energy facility operational. At the time of writing the project is already behind schedule, though, given construction was meant to be complete by the end of 2021.

The concept of converting waste to energy makes some sense and it's happening in other parts of the world too, with Europe leading the charge.

The initial 2018 announcement says the A$698 million Kwinana project[3] aims to eventually feed 36 megawatts of baseload energy to the power grid. If that occurs it will supply the electricity needs of more than 50,000 households. Macquarie and its partners estimate the facility will see 400,000 tonnes of household, commercial and industrial waste diverted from Western Australian landfill annually, amounting to a quarter of Perth's post-recycling rubbish.

The plant will also be able to process commercial, industrial, construction and demolition waste. The project is being co-developed, with other parties involved including Acciona and Veolia.

Macquarie and the Dutch Infrastructure Fund are providing A$275 million of equity finance, while a group of financiers and Australia's Clean Energy Finance Corporation are tipping in A$400 million in debt finance for the facility. The Australian government's Renewable Energy Agency is providing a A$23 million grant.

It's an area Macquarie is prioritising internationally. Macquarie—via investment capital and finance—has backed more than 30 waste and bioenergy projects globally.[4] In the UK, Green Investment Group is playing a large role in this, which you'll read more about later. In Australia, Macquarie's infrastructure funds and its co-investors even acquired listed rubbish collection firm BINGO Industries in 2021 as part of a push into the sector.

Just a hop, skip and a jump from the Kwinana waste-to-energy facility we encounter Macquarie again. Still in the Kwinana Industrial Area, close to the Indian Ocean coastline where idle flare stacks and large circular oil storage tanks litter the somewhat desolate landscape, a lot of work is being done to prepare for the production of green hydrogen. The tall metal flare stacks were once used for gas combustion so that burning happens at the top of the stack further away from ground level.

The broader industrial precinct houses companies that are also sizeable emitters, hence making it an attractive destination for hydrogen production. Aluminium giant Alcoa has a Kwinana Alumina Refinery for example, and Wesfarmers' chemicals, energy and fertilisers division has a manufacturing plant close by.

In a shock move amid the COVID-19 panic, BP announced in late 2020 that it would stop fuel production at its long-standing Kwinana refinery.[5] It had employed 400 permanent staff and 250 contractors, so the decision had far-reaching implications for the community.

Not too long after, though, and BP hand-in-hand with Macquarie Capital started figuring out an alternative use for the expansive site. It's a stark example of the transition taking place in energy markets in many parts of the world. At the time of writing, BP and Macquarie are conducting two feasibility studies including for a renewable fuels plant and the production of green hydrogen at its Kwinana refinery.[6]

The hydrogen hub will include installation of an electrolyser—a system that uses electric energy to convert water into hydrogen and oxygen—that is likely in excess of 75 megawatts, hydrogen storage, compression and truck loading facilities. BP's head of trading and shipping Nick Shaw expresses optimism in the plans and the ability to draw on existing refinery infrastructure and skills.

'Kwinana has some of the best engineers and some of the greatest knowledge on how to handle really dangerous things like hydrogen,' he says. 'While hydrogen is new to the energy world, Kwinana was making hydrogen for 75 years.

'The muscle memory that goes with that, the learning, the skills of our staff to understand how to effectively manufacture it and be able to safely handle it; we really want to retain that.'

Shaw highlights existing infrastructure at the refinery including a weighbridge on the way in, a wastewater facility and the fact that it's gated, that will expedite the hydrogen project.[7]

The renewable fuels project is aiming to produce a cleaner substitute for diesel and a sustainable aviation fuel. On the vexed issue, though, of whether BP's various proposed energy projects—in partnership with Macquarie—will be able to employ as many people as the refinery did previously, Shaw says: 'We are at reasonably early stages on our full aspiration, but we would hope that with the right project, which we think this is, and with the right support from government, it could be an employer that is equivalent to what we had previously.'

Before the road trip resumes its itinerary, it would be remiss not to mention another bigger project that involves BP and Macquarie, among other partners.

If the road trip were to head 1250 kilometres north into Western Australia's mineral-heavy Pilbara region, we would arrive at the massive US$36 billion Asian Renewable Energy Hub (AREH). The 26-gigawatt project is one of the largest planned hydrogen and renewable energy projects globally, and the 6500 square kilometre site covers an area ten times that of Singapore.[8]

BP is the largest shareholder in the AREH at 40.5 per cent, while InterContinental Energy, CWP Global, Macquarie Capital and Macquarie's Green Investment Group are also investors. Before the hub got going in its current form there was an assessment around going straight to export by utilising an under-sea cable from the project to Singapore.

'We didn't think it was feasible,' Macquarie's critical minerals and energy chairman Robert Dunlop says. 'For these sorts of projects to get up you do need to have a domestic basis before you go to export. We see the site of AREH to be very important for the mining sector up here. All of those parties are very keen to decarbonise.'[9]

The idea is that the combined solar and wind power generating capacity of the hub would produce 1.6 million tonnes of green hydrogen or nine million tonnes of green ammonia annually. But the huge project still has some hoops to jump through. It is contingent on Australian government approval, which was not forthcoming—in 2021—because of the hub's expected detrimental impact on birdlife in the area.

■

Traversing due east almost 2700 kilometres across the vast Nullarbor Plain we arrive in Adelaide, known as the city of churches, and the capital of South Australia.

In this state Macquarie is also omnipresent via a string of assets including its ownership of Land Services SA and three citrus orchards in the Riverland region.

The orchards—which in 2021 were plagued by a fruit fly outbreak—were acquired when Macquarie took over Vitalharvest and continued leasing the orchards to listed fruit and vegetable producer Costa Group. That means there aren't any suited-up bankers tending to the orchards!

Macquarie has been steadily building up its land and farming interests, predominantly in Australia and Brazil where it now invests in and operates 4.7 million hectares of farmland producing things like red meat, grains and oil seeds. It is the sixth largest agricultural landholder in Australia with 5.7 million hectares trailing the likes of Crown Point Pastoral, Australian Agricultural Company and Gina Rinehart's Hancock Agriculture and S Kidman & Co, according to the *AgJournal* publication.[10]

AgJournal has Macquarie as the second-largest investor in Australian farmland ranked by dollar value, with investments amounting to A$2.5 billion. That figure covers assets including the Paraway Pastoral business and Viridis Ag. In first spot is Canada's PSP Investments with Australian farmland valued at A$5 billion.

Macquarie's head of agriculture Liz O'Leary says the group is closely assessing its growth options and ways to reduce emissions in farming and adopt more data and newer practices.

'It is just about using data and information to make really precise decisions that drive production, drive productivity and they give us the opportunity to really dial up performance on good farms.

'Then the big question for us is how do we fix the busted ones and those that are most heavily impacted by environmental conditions? This is where—not universally but in certain parts of the world and Australia—the emergence of environmental markets, be they carbon and biodiversity, give us a huge opportunity to rethink what a farm plan looks like.'[11]

Macquarie has in the past dabbled in agricultural assets and getting investors access to quirkier asset classes, particularly if the tax and return metrics were favourable. Take Macquarie Forestry

Investment 2004, where investors got an investment in the trees as well as the land they were grown on.[12]

Investors got exposure to Tasmanian blue gums that were on a Victorian plantation and had an off-take agreement from a pulpwood exporter.[13]

Back to Adelaide, though, and we end up on Grenfell Street, which is close to an array of cafes, eateries and the Rundle Mall shopping district. From the exterior it's a tired looking Land Services building with red brick and panelling flanking the windows. There is slightly more character on the inside with open spaces, cafes and a sandstone feature wall.

It's here the state's land titles registry and services operate, a function that was privatised to boost South Australia's budget coffers in 2017. This building was home to one of Australia's last shouting rooms where land transfers and property settlements happened in person, and all in a small room where loud voices were required to ensure the list of transfers was studiously seen to.

A consortium of Macquarie Infrastructure and Real Assets and Canada's Public Sector Pension Investment Board paid A$1.6 billion to secure the rights to oversee and manage the registry and services unit for 40 years.[14] This transaction had a twist in that the registry had a valuations office attached to it, which needed additional due diligence by the buyers. That spurred a deal associate to track down outside research and ring around academics because there weren't comparable Australian deals for Macquarie to draw from as it sought about putting together a binding offer.

These infrastructure-style assets are hard fought over by pension funds and other investors for their steady returns. That partly reflects that Australians are obsessed with residential property ownership, given house prices have dramatically increased over the past two decades helped by policy settings and population growth.

■

The next leg of this long and winding road trip takes us south, into the state of Victoria and the Moorabool Shire. Lal Lal Wind Farms is close to the highlands towns of Ballan and Yendon and where we visit is a twenty-minute drive to Ballarat, which was historically a gold mining town.

It's rather ironic that we arrive at the wind farm on a very still day. That helps the temperature outside, though, given the brisk Victorian autumn at the time of the visit. The grass is still very green from all the rain in early 2022 as we make our way to one of the Lal Lal sites, closer to Yendon, where 38 turbines of a total of 60 are situated.[15] The turbines with their slicing blades have a commanding presence even from the road as they tower above us, only moving intermittently. We turn onto the site, passing a shearing shed displaying solar panels on the left and a power substation on the right. An important component of a wind farm is, of course, having facilities on site and connectivity close by to feed into the energy grid.

This part of the Lal Lal Wind Farms has two landowners, the largest being Wen Qingnan, the Chinese magnate behind Tianyu Wool. He acquired the expansive sheep-grazing property from sixth generation farmer Geoff Fisken in 2014,[16] and draws on the estate to produce fine merino wool that often eventually ends up with designer labels.

Lal Lal Wind Farms is a 220-megawatt development[17] utilising turbines that each tower about 161 metres from hub centre to the ground. As we drive around the Yendon site past sheep quietly grazing, we notice it's rather hilly terrain for a wind farm. We wonder—still donning our hard hats—how markedly that impacted construction of the site and getting cabling installed underground?

A met mast out on its own is pointed out which is a reference point for the turbines and is constantly feeding data and statistics back to the office. It was set up years ahead of the turbines to gather data on the viability of the area for the wind farm. Interestingly, the turbines are programmed to minimise down time and tilt towards the wind, all backed by complex mechanics and hydraulics. Peeping inside the turbines there is a fire extinguisher and a lift that takes technicians about 93 metres up the turbine, where there are four sections and a platform at each deck. You need to have completed specific training to make that journey—and technicians use lifting bags to carry their tools up—so for now we stay firmly planted on the ground.

The turbines also need protection from lightning strikes, which is built into the 20-metre zone around the base of the turbine. That's not to say lightning can't do damage, as it did here in 2019 when a turbine blade broke and crashed to the ground. Off in the distance you can just spot Wen Qingnan's homestead and its sprightly green roof.

Lal Lal Wind Farms is owned 40 per cent apiece by Northleaf Capital Partners and InfraRed Capital Partners, while Macquarie owns the other 20 per cent. The latter two owners are reportedly in the process of selling their stakes to Igneo Infrastructure Partners.[18] It hasn't always been a smooth ride for the Lal Lal owners. There was initially some community angst in relation to the sites. It appears relations are now cordial and after initially meeting monthly, a local community group now meets quarterly to get updates or discuss any concerns. The site also has a bird and bat management plan that leads to reporting of dead animals found due to the turbine blades.

The other section of Lal Lal has three landowners and is referred to as the Elaine site. If we had more time we could also venture to other Macquarie-linked assets including the Murra Warra Wind Farm[19] in north-western Victoria, which aims to have 99 turbines in operation. That project sits on farmland used for sheep grazing and cropping.

As the offshore wind opportunity finally gets going in Australia,[20] amid an energy supply crunch and debate about the pace of renewables development, Macquarie is also there. It is among a small group of firms separately examining feasibility for the nation's first batch of projects. Namely, for Macquarie that involves a potential 1-gigawatt local offshore wind project off Victoria's Bass Coast.

■

In Macquarie's home state of New South Wales, this road trip can't go past a project occurring right on the company's doorstep in Martin Place, the heart of the central business district.

As we walk through this part of the city's financial district—about 100 metres from the headquarters of the nation's central bank—it appears the construction zone is a source of frustration, noise and an eyesore, as cordoned off areas block large parts of the walkway.

Macquarie is on the hook for the Martin Place integrated train station development[21] and to assist it appointed Lendlease as the design and construction contractor. It's a sweeping project that has seen 51 anchors installed beneath 50 Martin Place to ensure the sandstone is secure, while more than 25 Olympic swimming pool-sized loads of crushed rock have been removed as part of the excavation. Tunnelling underneath 50 Martin Place was completed in late 2021, and at the time of writing underground station platforms were constructed and several escalators had just been installed.

All of this action relates to an agreement formed between the NSW government and Macquarie in 2018 for a brand spanking new Martin Place metro station as part of a new commercial, retail and public precinct. Included in these extensive plans are that one of the new buildings, at 1 Elizabeth Street, will be Macquarie's new global headquarters.

So just how did Macquarie get involved? Well, it's an interesting story that illustrates the company's ability to quickly seize on any manner of opportunity. As Macquarie Capital's joint boss in Australia and New Zealand John Pickhaver recalls, the metro project, after a previous incarnation was shelved, came to Macquarie's attention when then NSW transport secretary Rod Staples rang Nicholas Moore. It was just a courtesy call to warn him of the disruption and noise that would be occurring as part of the plan.

'That conversation led us ultimately to put an unsolicited proposal to develop the station for the government and offer value share,' he says. 'It was actually a great example of when you can bring all those skills to bear, have an idea like Nicholas did for this and actually have the expertise to hand to deliver it. We went and hired lots of other people, and we're going to pull in resources from Lendlease and get other people involved. But it's that idea generation.'[22]

It didn't hurt Macquarie's prospects that Pickhaver had done postgraduate study examining heritage buildings that had rail tunnels built beneath them, basically to assess if the construction would cause damage. Strangely, despite supply chain disruptions and the lockdowns that gripped Sydney in 2020 and 2021, the new Martin Place precinct is at this stage on track to hit its scheduled completion in 2024. Pickhaver's role is changing at the time of writing as he heads to the USA to take up a new role running the infrastructure and energy capital business.

■

Next we grab a train from central station to Sydney's Olympic Park—which hosted many events for the 2000 Olympic Games but has since

morphed into a burgeoning residential precinct after being identified by the state's government as a priority growth area.

Here we visit the Scarlet Pavilions apartment complex, which
was developed by property group Mirvac and includes ten specialist
disability units to house residents with disabilities and another as
an office for on-call carers. Macquarie has partnered with Summer
Housing—a not-for-profit sister organisation to the Summer Foundation—on this project.

It's an impressive start to the visit: the entrance to the complex
is wired to allow the main door to be activated via a barcode on a
wheelchair and that gives the resident priority access to the lift. The
letterboxes for the disability residents—who are spread out over
multiple floors—are the right height for those in wheelchairs. One
of these apartments will house an Australian Paralympian, who had
not yet moved in.

We learn that Macquarie started investing in this sector in 2018
after about two years of due diligence[23] and recognising a chronic
undersupply of housing for those with extreme functional impairment or very high support needs. That issue means there are
currently almost 4000 disabled people under 65 in Australia living in
residential aged care due to a lack of options for accommodation.[24]
Private capital fed into the sector from Macquarie and others—
including Australian Unity, Conscious Investment Management and
Lighthouse Infrastructure—plays a role in funding, building and
refurbishing specialist disability housing.

But it's not just a social good and impact investing pursuit for
Macquarie since, where there are shortages and high demand,
investment returns can be attractive. Investor returns are specified
by the National Disability Insurance Agency in a price guide and are
expected to be 11.6 per cent pre-tax, which includes yield and capital
growth in the property.

It's also a sector the federal government is supporting with annual funding of A$700 million. But the model and funding decisions have been hindered by delays and just A$204 million of that was allocated to participant plans in 2021.[25]

Essentially, under the specialist disability accommodation model tenants enter into leases with the accommodation provider and contribute rent that is topped up by Australia's National Disability Insurance Scheme.

To the untrained eye the apartment looks like a regular new flat. But when you peer closer there are a host of differences starting with a bench that can be height adjusted. There is also a duress button and a two-hour back-up battery supply of power should the complex's power fail, for example. The technology set up also appears cutting edge with a large control box, hidden away in a cupboard, that looks after things like lights, blinds and temperature control via voice control and a chosen device. There are three flat monitors on the wall that are touch screen to allow things like opening of the front door and calling for carers.

The carers are stationed in another apartment onsite (aptly named the concierge) with support available 24 hours. In the model pursued by Macquarie and Summer Housing that support is provided by a different, independent organisation and funded by the National Disability Insurance Scheme. Macquarie's asset management arm at the time of writing holds a portfolio of 230 apartments or 239 dwellings in total when houses are included. Specialist disability accommodation backed by Macquarie spans the capital cities of all mainland Australian states as well as the Gold Coast and Sunshine Coast in Queensland.[26]

The apartments are made to a template, but there is a lot of scope for customisation depending on the person's disability. Macquarie's executive director overseeing these investments, Ben Barry, says

Macquarie started out making the capital outlay via its balance sheet and has just ruled off a fund from investors raising A$350 million to continue its push in the sector.

'Once Macquarie understood the investment it committed and began investing at scale, accepting that if government support for the policy disappears there is a risk to the investment.' When asked about any specific incidents that Barry may have encountered in disability housing he says there was a failure of multiple lifts in a dwelling in 2021, but it was handled well with no injuries or loss of life reported.

■

Heading north on the Pacific Motorway, or M1, from Sydney to Newcastle and to a completely different asset that Macquarie is involved in. That's Newcastle Port—which recorded its first commercial shipment in 1799—and is embedded in the city's mining and industrial history.

The port handles some 4697 ship movements and 166 million tonnes of cargo annually.

On the day we visit, torrential rain on Australia's east coast has left the water filled with debris and very murky. The volatile weather experienced in Australia in the months before and during our visit saw the port closely monitoring low-lying areas and putting flood mitigation measures in place. There are still signs of plenty of activity during our visit as bulk carriers including Taiwanese vessel *Taipower Prosperity VII* and Panama's *United Sapphire* navigate the port's waters. Scattered around the port are well-known Australian company names including Orica, Aurizon and Infrabuild.

Newcastle Port is equally owned by The Infrastructure Fund, which is managed by Macquarie Asset Management, and China Merchants Port Holdings Company. As coal use is scaled back and production of greener or less-emission intensive forms of energy is ramped up, the port is also attempting to get involved in the transition.

It has put a 2040 Masterplan[27] in place creating a blueprint for a broader diversification strategy that included plans for a new deep-water container terminal, bulk terminal for commodities such as fuel and wheat, an automotive so-called roll-on roll-off or 'Ro-Ro' hub and a cruise ship terminal—the last of these being scrapped when the state government withdrew funding.

At the time of writing, there was some consternation about the port's new deep-water container terminal plan, given questions about whether the federal government had shelved an announcement worth A\$250 million to the project. Port of Newcastle also plays a part in Macquarie's push into green hydrogen. The Port of Newcastle Green Hydrogen Hub Project in April 2022 received a further A\$41 million in government funding, on top of an earlier A\$100 million funding for hydrogen readiness.[28] The hub—which is subject to a feasibility study—is being managed as a joint venture between Macquarie Capital and Macquarie's Green Investment Group.

The attractiveness of the port for such a hub is associated with its access to domestic and export infrastructure and renewable energy, and also where it is located relative to potential sources of demand for green hydrogen. The feasibility study is examining things like green hydrogen mobility, bunkering technology and infrastructure and industrial uses.

The idea is in its first phase to have an electrolyser of at least 40 megawatts that over time could increase to a capacity of more than 1 gigawatt. The funding announcement positions Port of Newcastle as an important site to establish a hydrogen hub, with connectivity to domestic and export infrastructure, proximate demand and access to renewable energy. By 2025, it's envisaged that phase one of the hydrogen hub will be complete.

'We started early and that gives us credibility,' says Port of Newcastle CEO Craig Carmody of the group's diversification and environmental, social and governance plans.[29]

■

From the port we head north along the New South Wales coast, bypassing popular tourist spots including Byron Bay to end up in what is meant to be the sunny state of Queensland. But again, our visit was poorly timed, with not a lot of sunshine and more than ample amounts of rain causing flood warnings in some parts of the state.

The first stop is Gold Coast Airport—which includes domestic and international terminals—where the entrance is marked by a grey, orange, blue and green sign and plenty of palm trees line the drive in.

It's much the same as any other small regional airport, including the bellowing sound of a plane overhead approaching. But there is a hive of activity adjacent to the somewhat dated terminal, where an extension is taking place to add fourteen new outlets including a café and bar that has a menu curated by local chef Matt Jefferson.[30]

However, when we visit in May 2022 work is still under way and the brand-new building is cordoned off by white and blue mesh, with Lendlease signage clearly visible. Progress appears to have been made as we can see panelling, electrical work, laid concrete and of course, given the tropical theme, a further smattering of planted palm trees.

Why are we here? The Infrastructure Fund, which is part of the Macquarie stable, is a shareholder of an entity called Queensland Airports, which owns the Gold Coast, Townsville, Mount Isa and Longreach airports. Other shareholders include State Street Australia, likely as a custodian, Perron Investments and former Macquarie CEO Allan Moss.

So Macquarie still has a presence in the airport sector.[31]

Inside the existing Gold Coast Airport terminal are the requisite ingredients for air travel including the current era's COVID-19 testing clinic and a visitor information centre. We are impressed by a dog-petting area, where therapy dogs are employed to 'help alleviate the stress that can be associated with travelling'.

The last stop in this tour is quite a distance north-west from Gold Coast Airport and was meant to be the landmark and sprawling cotton farm Cubbie Station. But the drenching rain throughout this trip stymied the on-the-ground visit to the huge 80,600-hectare property that has captivated Australians and at times created controversy and backlash against water usage, rights and irrigation.

We were looking forward to seeing the white fluffy cotton—a crop that requires large amounts of water to thrive—up close as it is harvested during autumn, the season the visit was slated to occur. Cubbie is, after all, Australia's largest cotton producer.

An agricultural fund managed by Macquarie in early 2022 acquired a 51 per cent stake in Cubbie, which delivered it 100 per cent ownership of the historic property.[32] Macquarie bought the controlling holding from debt-laden Chinese textile firm Shandong Ruyi, after earlier snapping up a 49 per cent interest in 2019 to satisfy an undertaking to the Foreign Investment Review Board,[33] a move sparked by concerns about Chinese and other foreign firms owning vast quantities of Australian agricultural land.

The abundance of rain in 2022 is extremely positive for cotton producers including Cubbie, and as a flow-on of that, the conditions help boost the prices for those selling cotton farms in Australia, despite logistical issues around getting people to-and-from work. As Cubbie's website says: 'The project is integrated into the flood plain to allow the passage of flood waters and the project is a closed system.'

Despite controversy in the past, Macquarie's head of agriculture Liz O'Leary says the group wants to protect the ecosystem at Cubbie and is taking a long-term view.

'When it is appropriate to farm to the max, farm to the max and generate income. When there is an abundance of water, let's maximise it for high quality production and for community benefit. But when there's not, let's acknowledge that the first flush after a dry period, you're not going to grow a crop anyway.'

Updates on Cubbie's website show that no cotton or other crops—including wheat, sorghum, sunflowers, barley, chickpeas and corn—were harvested in 2019, the end of a severe multi-year drought. The last time Cubbie took any water from the river system was in 2017 when it drew fourteen gigalitres, or about 9 per cent of what passed through the nearby town of St George.

As Australia has often endured droughts, water licences and allocations can create a lot of controversy in regional towns and communities where the pressure is more acute. With some 19,000 hectares of the Cubbie property being irrigated cropping fields, Cubbie's water usage has frequently been in the crosshairs of criticism from farmers.

When the 2019 purchase of the Cubbie stake was announced by Macquarie, the owners committed to supporting the Northern Murray Darling Basin with a voluntary contribution of up to ten gigalitres to the Culgoa River and Lower Balonne intersecting streams. At the time, Ruyi and Macquarie said the contribution would 'increase the volume of water in the river at critical times and help deliver a range of community and environmental outcomes'.

This trip underscores the point that Macquarie's presence goes much further than pure infrastructure assets and deal-making in Australia. The company is prepared to look at all sorts of acquisitions, often with partners, as long as the potential returns are juicy enough and stack up against the risk Macquarie is prepared to take.

Chapter 13

SELLING THE MESSAGE AMID CONTROVERSY

The term 'annuity-style businesses', now firmly entrenched in the Macquarie lexicon, emerged as Nicholas Moore realised pushing further into divisions less reliant on wild market swings would help diversify the company and shield it better in the face of another financial crisis. It was the 2012 half-year results,[1] handed down by Moore in October 2011, where these terms became a clear part of Macquarie's investor language and its quest to better explain its model and future growth objectives.

After a period of workshopping, two distinct buckets emerged. The market-facing businesses—which were leveraged to volatility and financial markets—were the classic investment banking businesses. They included Macquarie Securities, Macquarie Capital and Fixed Income Currencies and Commodities.

The other bucket was the annuity-style businesses, which typically provided more reliable growth and earnings every year and included Macquarie Funds, Corporate and Asset Finance (CAF) and Banking and Financial Services (BFS).

Macquarie was reinventing itself once again. It would prove a long-term project for Moore and his lieutenants to get the message across and shed light on how the company was positioning for the future, and they felt it would also assist investors and research analysts to more accurately value Macquarie.

'You've got one hour to explain yourself and you can't give them [investors] a black box,' Moore says. 'So we invested a lot of time and thought to explaining ourselves in a simple, accurate way, and making sure we told it consistently, internally and externally.'

Initially the pitch about the two buckets of businesses also helped explain what was dragging Macquarie's profits lower, amid fluctuating financial markets and a still-difficult operating climate.[2]

The marked shift to more stable income streams was again part and parcel of Macquarie's ethos of evolving, seeking out opportunities and rapidly repositioning when required.

'Evolution has been a fundamental tenet of Macquarie's business. Staff have always been empowered to explore ideas and develop business opportunities within strict risk management disciplines,' the 2012 annual report[3] said.

Macquarie's corporate motto would evolve too. Its code of conduct would be refined to reflect three principles: opportunity, accountability and integrity.[4]

■

Around 2012, the re-opening and normalisation of funding markets saw Macquarie spot an opportunity to re-start its operations in mortgage lending and attempt again to become a force in Australia's highly concentrated retail banking sector. After all, the Banking and Financial Services (BFS) arm was in the annuities-style earnings bucket and home loans were a profitable business. The BFS division was formed in 2008 when the Banking and Securitisation Group was merged with the Financial Services Group.

The seizing up of funding markets during the GFC had seen Macquarie shut the door to any new Australian home loans, and it closed down its US, Canadian and Italian mortgage businesses. The company retained its existing Australian portfolio of loans and that made it somewhat easier to recommence lending when the climate became more favourable.

By this stage in the 2012 financial year, the cash management account had amassed about A$16 billion and customer deposits totalled A$28.6 billion.[5] That gave the BFS division enough scope and liquidity, alongside external funding sources, to get back into home loans. This time Macquarie would also lean on its balance sheet to fund mortgages rather than solely using securitisation.

One way of ramping up its operations was to partner in 2012 with home loans stalwart and celebrity businessman Mark Bouris,[6] who was best known for selling non-bank lender Wizard Home Loans for a bumper A$500 million price in 2004.[7]

Bouris—who also had a multi-season stint as a *Celebrity Apprentice* and *The Apprentice* host on television station Channel Nine in Australia—knew Macquarie mortgage operatives well. That helped in being able to secure their backing for his newish wealth and mortgage venture Yellow Brick Road.

Macquarie's involvement was in addition to Nine Entertainment Co, owner of Channel Nine, which also got involved as Bouris still had a close relationship with the company. Those ties had their origins in the formative Wizard days when hard-nosed then-proprietor Kerry Packer was convinced by Bouris to tip in A$25 million.

The Wizard sale reportedly saw the Packer family more than double its money on its initial Wizard investment. 'As a shareholder in Wizard PBL (Publishing and Broadcasting Limited) did very well backing Mark,' billionaire James Packer[8] said in an emailed statement to one of the authors in 2018.[9]

Macquarie became a Yellow Brick Road partner, equity holder, mortgage funder and home loan white-labeller in 2012. What followed were mammoth marketing efforts by Bouris in the early years to talk up the company's prospects, particularly with Macquarie's backing, including the potential to become a fifth pillar to rival Australia's major banks.

Those claims were later played down by Moore since Bouris's flamboyant style differed to that of Macquarie, which had—and still has—a preference for letting results speak for themselves.

As Macquarie was stepping up its Australian mortgage operations it also emerged with stakes in a spate of other companies that had an exposure to home loan broking, including aggregators Connective, Perth-based AFG and online broking group firm Lendi. The latter—which in 2021 merged with Aussie Home Loans[10]—is the only mortgage broking holding that remains in Macquarie's portfolio now that its focus has shifted to organically growing its own mortgages.

It's no coincidence that Bouris's company names—Wizard and Yellow Brick Road—both drew on popular children's movie *The Wizard of Oz*. But this time round Bouris was finding it immensely challenging to turn a profit and get traction with Yellow Brick Road, despite drawing on the success of Wizard.

Yellow Brick Road posted its maiden annual profit in 2017, but swung into the red again the following year. By September 2018, Macquarie had lost all patience and offloaded its remaining stake in Yellow Brick Road, parting ways and drawing a line under the failed foray with Bouris.[11]

■

One of the curiosities of the last ten years has been why Asia has become an apparently diminished force in the global Macquarie context.

It didn't use to be this way. Macquarie bought the old Barings business from ING Securities with considerable pride in 2004, gaining a ten-market brokerage and research platform that made Macquarie Securities a serious force for a time, in a deal so good we understand ING actually paid Macquarie to take it.

A bright era of equity capital markets activity followed. In 2010 Macquarie appeared as joint sponsor, joint books and joint lead on the US$22 billion IPO for Agricultural Bank of China,[12] one of the most significant deals ever from the country. Andrew Low, who was head of Asia from 2004 to 2010, recalls that time as an era of rapid year-to-year growth in deal number and size.[13]

In Chapter 6 we saw the South Korean business rise, flourish and then shrink, though it's still unarguably a success. As recently as 2010, Macquarie was talking about itself as an Asia-Pacific business. But then something seemed to change.

Asia's operating income was overtaken by the Americas in the second half of the 2010 financial year, and by Europe in the first half of 2012.[14] In the half-year to March 2022, the Americas generated more than nine times as much income as Asia, and Europe, the Middle East and Africa (EMEA) almost three times as much.[15]

More people continue to be employed in Asia than any other bloc bar Australia,[16] but its contribution to overall operating income has been steadily declining since Macquarie first set foot outside Australia.

What's happening here? There are a few explanations, the most obvious of which is that the Americas has just grown extraordinarily quickly and is supercharged by a surely unsustainable contribution from commodities and global markets (as is EMEA). It's also been bolstered by major acquisitions such as Delaware. But that's not the whole answer, as Asia hasn't really grown in absolute terms either: its income in, say, the second half of 2011 was higher, in Australian dollars, than the first half of 2022.[17]

Another reason is that Asia's contribution to the group isn't always reflected in its earnings numbers. Asia is a terrific source of capital given the growth of sovereign wealth and pension funds in the region, but Macquarie often helps take that money elsewhere. Only A\$40 billion of Macquarie's A\$795.6 billion in assets under management are in Asia as at 31 March 2022.[18] 'Asia has become our most important source of capital, but most of that capital is exported right around the world,' says Ben Way. 'Macquarie's biggest private market investors are based in North Asia,' he adds.

Also, although CGM (Commodities and Global Markets) has an important commodities trading hub in Singapore and a long-standing relationship with the city state—Andrew Downe still speaks with respect about the Monetary Authority of Singapore's relationship with Macquarie—it's not automatic that trades will be booked there.[19]

There are structural reasons too. The economics of being a bookrunner on China-related deals in particular are not what they were. After his time at the Asia helm, 'the Hong Kong market later changed, the share of ECM [equity capital market] wallet that international firms have relative to domestic firms has changed, and there was massive fee compression,'[20] Andrew Low says. Macquarie no longer chases these low-fee capital markets trades, nor does it have much of the research presence it once had. Equities trading and corporate finance, once the engine of the Asia businesses and the biggest footprint in terms of revenue-generating bankers, have faded in tandem.

But beyond that, Asia is complex, and it's not always automatic that a vast population means good business. 'There's a lot of people who get on whiteboards and go, okay, GDP growth on one axis, population on another, and say therefore if I sell this amount of products per person I'll make a lot of money,' Way says. 'But getting market entry, working with partners, navigating the culture, even having a product that's culturally simpatico with that group of people is a very complex algorithm to solve. And you've got to solve it country by country.'

Ben Bruck, who built his career in Asia and who says the relative financial underperformance of Asia 'used to bug me a lot,' thinks this last point is the key one. 'It was very hard to break into markets in Asia with the discipline that the Macquarie model imposed upon us,' he says.[21]

The clearest example of this logic in action is the relative paucity of the bank's activity in the biggest of all Asian markets, and the second-largest economy in the world: China.

When one of the authors asked Shemara Wikramanayake about exposure to China geopolitical tension, she actually highlighted the relatively small exposure to Asian financial markets, noting that 'Asia is 7 per cent and China is a smaller portion of that.' This was presented as a good thing.[22] Considering Macquarie has been active in China since 1995, has been on some of the nation's largest IPOs, handled truly innovative landmarks such as the Dalian Wanda deal[23] and has built numerous property and infrastructure funds, this is at first glance surprising.

But perhaps it shouldn't be when you think it through. The environment being what it is in China—with its far-reaching and unpredictable regulation, geopolitical tension with Australia and the USA, a lockdown approach to COVID-19 now out of step with anywhere else on earth, intervention in local markets and a partly restricted currency—one can perhaps understand the Macquarie view, though it's never explicitly stated like this, that there are simply easier places to make a buck. If Macquarie stands for one skill above all others, it is the ability to price risk. One assumes it made the calculations for China through this lens and didn't much like the view.

Bob Carr, the former NSW premier who represented Macquarie in an ambassadorial role from 2005 to 2012, tells a revealing story about speaking with an official in China about toll roads. He remembers the official told him, in a candid moment: if one of these big roads we built is making a profit, we won't want to sell it. If it isn't, you won't want to buy it.

There's an important point behind the tongue-in-cheek remark. Macquarie, building a toll road anywhere, would want legally binding assurances, enforceable in the courts, that, for example, no competing non-tolled road would be opened on the same route. 'Now, can you get that sort of guarantee out of the Chinese system?' says Carr. 'The answer is no.'

Dealing with China requires the patience of a saint. 'We are thinking about China over the next 100 years,' says Way.[24]

But is Macquarie really thinking about China, or Asia, over the next 100 years? Many people, including several current and former executives, think that at various stages Macquarie's attitude has been too short-term for the cultural norms of Asia. We saw it in Korea with John Walker's arguments against the exiting of businesses. It's true elsewhere too. 'I think the Macquarie model is all about getting the medium term right, rather than the long term,' says Bruck. 'And in China and Japan you needed extraordinary levels of patience.'

Macquarie has, at times, tried to build those long-term views; one of the reasons Warwick Smith was hired from politics was for his China relationships. But he can see why Macquarie has wavered in its commitment. 'They took the view, and I think they are right, that the competition from Chinese-sponsored banks was going to be very large,' he says.[25]

So regardless of cultural norms and expectations, Macquarie has not hesitated to exit a business if it seems the right time to do so. China is no more or less sacred in that respect than any other market.

Still, when it comes to infrastructure, one thing is clear: Asia needs more of it than anywhere else. Macquarie said in 2022 that Asia required 54 per cent of total global investment and that the region needed US$41 trillion by 2040.[26]

Verena Lim, head of Asia, says the region 'will get bigger over time' in terms of its contribution to group income. 'Asia is still in the growth phase.'

Internal rate of return targets are slightly higher in Asia, in terms of target returns, than in Europe, the Middle East and Africa and the Americas, and both Lim and Frank Kwok, head of Macquarie Asset Management Real Assets for Asia-Pacific, believe it's important that Macquarie has outgrown the need to use joint venture and partnership structures to get in to markets, as it initially did with Everbright in China and the State Bank of India. 'We've evolved to be comfortable to take full control,' Kwok says. He is diplomatic about how those tie-ups went.[27]

'It's self-serving for me to say it, but I genuinely believe Asia is where the growth should continue to be,' Kwok says. He points out that while the Macquarie European Infrastructure Fund series is up to seven, Asia is only on its third vintage of regional fund strategies.[28]

■

In 2011, Macquarie's private wealth advisers were acing their competency exams and everything on the face of it seemed to be going swimmingly.

Macquarie's profit results for 2012[29]—ruled off on 31 March—flagged the Banking and Financial Services division would see higher earnings the following year, and in private wealth increased adviser numbers were expected to deliver improved profitability for Australia and Canada. But behind the scenes there was a storm brewing. Regulators were circling the private wealth business within BFS after conducting a mystery shopper exercise and also receiving a tip-off about extremely lax record keeping and poor business practices.

The private wealth division housed advisers—across retail stockbrokers and financial planners—giving investors access to financial advice, trading and investment products and platforms.

The business had gained a national footprint aided by a series of Macquarie acquisitions.[30]

While everything seemed fine at the grass-roots, those running BFS knew the Australian Securities and Investments Commission (ASIC) had made contact with Macquarie in 2011 about allegations against its private wealth unit, via then commissioner Peter Kell and his team. The shocking findings were then briskly taken to the executive committee and the board, but in an odd chain of events Macquarie initially found no evidence of non-compliance. That came after an examination of paperwork in the private wealth unit, the findings of which didn't seem congruent with what ASIC was alleging.

It was a Mexican standoff of sorts for a while, but as often turns out regulators tend to eventually get an outcome. In this instance ASIC wasn't backing down and persisted with its engagement with Macquarie, to the point that Moore felt more due diligence was required. He sent in a team on a weekend to scour the paperwork and conduct deep analysis at an individual financial adviser and stockbroker level.

The results of the operation were eye-opening and triggered a change of position at Macquarie. It was reported to the board that there were deficiencies in the firm meeting its obligations. 'I'll never forget Nicholas contacting us all to say, actually, what ASIC is saying is correct. And it's got to be fixed,' a board member at that time recalls.

Macquarie had fallen well short of the regulatory developments required, largely stemming from its interpretation around implementing the *Financial Services Reform Act 2001*. The legislation included a transition period for the industry and came into effect in early 2004. Macquarie had clearly missed the mark on the implementation.

'ASIC had done reviews as they were mystery shopping a number of times, as they did with all major licensees. They pinpointed a number of advisers primarily who were involved in options and some of the more complicated strategies who were basically not doing the right thing,' BFS boss Peter Maher recalls. 'It would be great to think that we could have had a conversation about it and talked that through, including appropriate remediation, but they proceeded with the enforceable undertaking.'

After a lot of back and forward with ASIC's executives the regulator in January 2013 slapped Macquarie with a court enforceable undertaking (EU)[31] for a string of compliance failures and shoddy practices within the private wealth arm. The company—under the EU—was compelled to fix a long list of deficiencies dating back to 2008.

ASIC's chairman Greg Medcraft said at the time the regulator's surveillance found Macquarie 'fell significantly' short, prompting ASIC to take action.

The ASIC statement showed the issues were rife within the Macquarie wealth unit, an embarrassing stain on an organisation known for its hands-on approach to risk management. Even worse, the regulator had identified the problems rather than Macquarie self-reporting.

It would serve as a wake-up call that sent shudders through Macquarie. Among the issues uncovered were poor client records, a lack of detail in financial advice documentation, deficiencies in supporting paperwork to justify advice given, and customer files not containing mandatory statements of advice. There was also often not enough evidence to prove how an investor was classified as sophisticated—meeting a series of income or asset tests—which meant they could be marketed far more complex products and services.

As part of the EU, Macquarie appointed KPMG as an independent expert to provide updates to the regulator on deliverables under the clean-up program.[32] At one stage Greg Ward—who was appointed to run BFS and steer Macquarie through the compliance mess—and his team would meet with ASIC almost weekly to update them on progress.

The revelations also prompted a purge of senior staff and advisers linked to the saga, although some were steered to retire. It seemed Macquarie was keen to swiftly clean up the mess and move on from the embarrassment, but it remains debatable whether the right people took the bullet over those compliance shortcomings.

Before the regulatory action Macquarie had about 440 advisers and brokers in the unit; as at the time of writing, and following an overhaul of the model to focus solely on high-net-worth customers, it has 125 bankers. Macquarie moved to a more private-banking style model in 2019, meaning its staff would earn a salary and bonus and ceasing the practice of revenue sharing. The commission-based pay structure—which saw advisers and brokers earn a percentage of revenue they wrote—was scrapped at Macquarie[33] in the wash-up of the Royal Commission into Misconduct in the Banking, Superannuation and Financial Services Industry (the Hayne Royal Commission) but also due to issues raised in David Murray's earlier Financial System Inquiry.[34]

Later it would be revealed by Fairfax Media that a large cohort of Macquarie advisers and brokers were cheating on their competency exams, using readily available cheat sheets—called internally the

Penske file—to copy answers. The file got its name from the *Seinfeld* episode in which George Costanza notoriously claims he is working on the Penske documents while not doing anything at all.

Advisers and brokers canvassed by the authors said the file was readily available via the executive assistant of a manager in the private wealth unit and was widely used. Oddly, when news stories of the controversial file emerged in 2014 Macquarie denied its existence, prompting *The Sydney Morning Herald* to publish some of its contents.[35] The graphic accompanying the story even showed handwritten notes on the Kaplan exam warning which multiple choice questions were incorrect.

Several advisers, brokers and managers said that while Macquarie appeared to blame the rank-and-file advisers and management of the unit, the fact earlier risk audits didn't pick up on systemic issues in compliance pointed to risk executives being deficient in their duties.

Earl Evans says: 'The reality of it was the risk management group just weren't doing their job.'

Darrell Seeto, who has worked at firms including Citigroup and Ord Minnett, and Macquarie at that time, notes: 'Macquarie actually allowed all of its advisers to operate under their so-called risk and compliance policy, which at the time was known to be a Macquarie ethos of "loose but tight" because ultimately the bank was driven by profit. Macquarie Bank has been dubbed the "millionaires' factory".

'They had risk and compliance but they were actually loose or flexible when compared to your JPMorgans of the world, your Goldman Sachs, your Citigroup.'

On the Penske file's widespread use another former adviser says: 'Most of the managers there did their exam off the Penske file. They were handing it around to everybody.'

There had been an inkling ahead of the ASIC engagement that the private wealth business needed to become more professional.

Peter Maher had hired Eric Schimpf, a Merrill Lynch managing director, in 2010 to help steer better standards and processes within private wealth, but when the proverbial hit the fan not long after both would leave Macquarie in the wake of the enforceable undertaking.

Maher went into bat for Schimpf trying to explain he was part of the solution not the problem, but the board wanted scalps and Macquarie parted ways with Schimpf in 2013.[36] After a short time in purgatory, Schimpf landed on his feet though, returning to Merrill Lynch and at the time of writing was head of its Pacific Coast unit, among other roles. 'At the time, we'd already made moves to increase the quality of the overall advice business by bringing in Eric Schimpf, from Merrill Lynch,' Maher says. 'Merrills were a global leader in the advice business.'[37]

Maher was also soon to exit,[38] announcing his retirement from Macquarie in May 2013, even as the Banking and Financial Services division posted a record result for that financial year.

Ward would appoint executive director Bill Marynissen in the futures business and integrity office to help steer the private wealth clean-up, despite his limited experience in the area. Marynissen essentially replaced Schimpf at the helm of private wealth, and responsibility for compliance in that area was shifted and centralised at a group level.

Consultants at Deloitte came in to examine the culture within private wealth and lodged a disturbing report with the company in May 2013. The high-octane sales and commission-focused culture had led to an array of issues within the division.

Later, when asked about the Deloitte report, Moore would tell the Hayne Royal Commission in 2018: 'It's a pretty clear story of . . . a lack of control, a lack of challenge. I think one of the expressions used is freedom without boundaries,' he said.

Seeking to allay concerns from customers around the EU, Macquarie took the decision to write to more than 160,000 customers asking they come forward for a review of the advice or services provided by the private wealth business. It was a mammoth task.

Despite those efforts, the regulatory spotlight on Macquarie didn't end after the EU drew to a close in 2015, with ASIC forcing a twelve-month program of further work.[39] That included continued reporting to the regulator, via KPMG.

The dramatic reshaping of the private wealth business during this time was another example of Macquarie's about-turn in an area of the industry it was finding difficult—both from a relative returns and reputation perspective. It was a notable downsizing in private wealth that ensued and only accelerated in 2019 as adviser commissions were axed. Scores of advisers were exited by Macquarie or poached by rivals during the upheaval.[40]

The EU also wasn't the first time Macquarie had run afoul of ASIC; the collapse of Storm Financial in 2009 also entangled the bank, which had provided margin loans or mortgages to many customers that ended up wearing heavy investment losses. Commonwealth Bank and Bank of Queensland were also caught up in the investment scheme's controversy.[41]

Storm had been providing templated investment advice urging customers tip large amounts into index funds, using a method referred to by the regulator as 'double gearing'. It involved customers taking a mortgage and a margin loan to buy units in index funds and paying fees to Storm. In many cases the strategy represented inappropriate advice to customers who were retired or approaching retirement and were gearing to excessive levels.[42]

Under a revised settlement, following ASIC intervention in the Full Federal Court seeking a greater sum, Macquarie agreed to pay A$82.5 million by way of compensation to customers and costs. The GFC, coupled with the Storm ordeal, saw Macquarie exit margin lending via a sale of its loan portfolio to Bendigo and Adelaide Bank.[43]

The private wealth EU, although damaging to Macquarie's reputation, was fortuitous in its timing, as Macquarie had to address the
damning compliance and training shortcomings well in advance of
the landmark Hayne Royal Commission into Australia's banking
sector.

'The enforceable undertaking was a blessing in disguise, to be
quite frank,' former Macquarie chairman Peter Warne says. 'Once
we'd been made aware of and discovered what the issues were in
MPW [Macquarie Private Wealth], we responded very seriously in
terms of changing all our internal processes, changing the management, spending a lot of money on systems, and then had a huge team
working on the remediation with our clients.'

Ward had put his proposed transformation plan for the broader
BFS division to the board, including the extensive but staggered
clean-up of private wealth. It spanned the reduction in headcount,
changing processes and updating technology so that advisers and
brokers were more closely monitored.

Moore says while Banking and Financial Services was a small part
of Macquarie's profit at the time the EU 'was a traumatic event'.

'We had to go through our retail area root and branch and go
through all the people, procedures, processes, go through it from the
top down and say, does this match the legislation today?

'And it was traumatic for many people, but it was obviously absolutely essential.'

At the Hayne Royal Commission, while giving testimony Moore
used his trademark measured tone to outline consequences linked
to the EU for those involved. They included being fired, not being
considered for promotion or in the case of a senior executive in the
area, a halving of his profit share. Moore outlined that those removed
from the business included advisers, managers, reviewers, and people
in the compliance function.

Meanwhile, Ward was conducting his overhaul, including getting the BFS division to build a modern digital bank that would in many respects leave behind any clunky legacy systems. He wanted the unit to think more like a technology company to tap into a better customer experience but also upgrade the core banking system that is at the heart of a bank's infrastructure.

Ward, flanked by his then corporate strategy man Ben Perham—who in 2016 moved up to oversee Macquarie's personal banking and mortgage business—also managed to recruit Spanish bank BBVA's head of technology for digital banking, Luis Uguina, in late 2014. That would bolster their efforts to become a technology-led player.

They were looking forward to what they thought a leading digital bank would look like in ten years' time and plotting how to get there. Faster mortgage turnaround times and efficiency in the process were top of mind. Today, Macquarie's growth in the mortgage market has been well and truly eclipsing that of the major Australian banks, seeing it account for about 4.8 per cent of the domestic home loan market, albeit from humble beginnings. At the time of writing, Macquarie also had among the fastest mortgage turnaround times, versus its main rivals, and was seeking to shake up the at-call deposit market with attractive interest rates.

■

Moore looked only slightly uncomfortable but remained calm and measured in fronting Kenneth Hayne and the banking royal commission[44] on 22 November 2018.[45] He was just days out from retiring from Macquarie after an announcement in July[46] that he was handing the baton to a trusted pair of hands in Wikramanayake.

Moore, wearing a suit and dark-blue patterned tie, kept composed at all times and only stumbled over his words briefly while giving an oath. In the front row of the viewing gallery—at the Family Court in central Sydney where this round of hearings was held—Macquarie's head of operations Nicole Sorbara and corporate affairs boss Paul Marriott sat in support. Scattered around them were aggrieved customers from a range of different banks and other institutions who wanted to see an adequate grilling of executives, after a spate of scandals exposed over the previous three years.

They included antiquated medical definitions used to avoid paying out life insurance policies, charging dead customers' accounts for financial advice and steering customers into products such as junk insurance with no value. Moore had a final task before retirement of fronting the commission, something he had volunteered to undertake because he had presided over the period under scrutiny. The commission had, however, already skewered and put in a pressure cooker major bank chief executives and chairmen and many of their senior managers.

When Hayne's final report landed with a thud in early 2019,[47] it wasn't long before it cost then-National Australia Bank chairman Ken Henry and CEO Andrew Thorburn their jobs. Hayne pinpointed the pair for not having learned from the lessons of NAB's many compliance failings.

Senior counsel assisting Rowena Orr and Michael Hodge—both senior barristers—put most royal commission attendees through their paces, peppering them with queries, questioning versions of events and accountability for a string of bank scandals.[48] Hodge would take Moore to task over the risk failings and consequences in Macquarie's private wealth arm but it was light questioning compared to other big names that took the stand. Specific probing on the behaviour of advisers and brokers and how many remained within the business was limited.

When asked if Macquarie's risk systems would now identify an issue without ASIC having to point it out, Moore replied: 'Absolutely.

As we said before, the failing was ... not having an appropriate second line of defence. Given it reported into the [Banking and Financial Services] business, sadly, it was not sufficiently objective to see the weaknesses.

'We do have a very clear second line of defence now across Macquarie.'[49]

Macquarie's remuneration model was also a subject of questioning given for executives it focused on having a large proportion of remuneration at risk via the profit share pool, which is also deferred over several years. Moore outlined key elements that fed into decisions on pay including financial performance, risk management and compliance, customer outcomes and leadership and professional conduct.

Commissioner Hayne prodded further on the pay side, perhaps in light of other big bank executives having less of their overall remuneration at risk, to ask about what other firms may take away from Macquarie's approach. 'Profit share is more powerful than bonus,' Moore said at the time, noting no cap on the overall pay a Macquarie executive could in theory earn.

'A deferral, I think, is very important, as we know decisions being made today have consequences over many years. And so making sure there is that alignment, over a period of time, I think is very important.

'That consciousness, we think, is the greatest safeguard we have in terms of the long-term health of the organisation and the client outcomes.'

Despite his somewhat easy passage at the royal commission, Moore had certainly prepared for all eventualities. Macquarie had kindly hired security guards to accompany him safely out of the building, through the questioning media throng, to a waiting car. Moore now says: 'When the royal commissioner looked at us, he could see that we were not perfect. We had had problems. But I think what he liked is the fact that we had identified the problems.

'We had highlighted what had gone wrong. We had moved forward with vigour, to settle the problems and to make sure going forward, our systems were really robust and strong, and weren't going to give rise to those problems again. It has been suggested that that was the message he wanted to give out to the world.'

■

Nicholas Moore's time at the helm of Macquarie—presiding over stellar 117 per cent growth in profit and a more than doubling in market capitalisation to $41.7 billion—was a remarkable feat given the GFC chaos that ensued in the early years of his tenure. He oversaw a sweeping overhaul of the Macquarie model during his time at the helm after helping to build many of the businesses, Macquarie Capital and Corporate and Asset Finance among them, that would be cornerstones of the group's earnings for many years.

Moore was also a key architect in building the infrastructure funds business and ramping up growth in funds and asset management globally as other investment banks grappled with the wash-up of the GFC. He had a knack for deep analysis around the broader macroeconomic themes that would help to drive infrastructure to become a huge asset class in its own right.

Precision and strong execution around the timing of acquisitions such as Delaware and Constellation were also hallmarks of his time at the top. Moore had morphed from being a humble accountant—to use his own words—into one of Australia's most astute bankers and CEOs. He took Allan Moss's push into global markets even further as well, gaining Macquarie kudos on the global stage.

In his final set of profit results, 67 per cent of Macquarie's income was derived from outside of Australia, while 60 per cent of earnings reflected annuity-style divisions and 40 per cent market-facing businesses.[50]

'The most creative person in my history at Macquarie was Nicholas by a long way. The whole infrastructure side was really Nicholas right when you really break it down. He had good people around him and lots of help,' Stephen Cook says of Moore. 'He was extremely lateral in his thinking.'

Robin Bishop says: 'It would be easy to think that Macquarie was just naturally going to grow like that. But the reality is Nicholas was the driving force behind the globalisation of Macquarie, the driving force behind the creation of the global infrastructure and funds business, the driving force behind the whole principal investing strategy.'

Others are less flattering: 'He thinks he's the smartest guy in the room and everyone wants something from him,' a former Macquarie banker says.

In Pamela Williams's book *Killing Fairfax*, James Packer gives a harsh assessment of Moore and Macquarie, who were working on one of four proposals for his media interests in 2006. In the end, Packer sold a 50 per cent stake in Nine Network, ACP Magazines and his interest in internet portal ninemsn to private equity firm CVC Asia Pacific for A$4.5 billion.

Packer had canned a Macquarie option for an IPO with high levels of gearing. 'My reality as I look back is that Macquarie did not give me good advice. I just don't trust Macquarie. I believe they solve for themselves, not their clients,' Packer said in the text.[51]

Moore's tenure was marred by several other regulatory blow-ups besides the EU. Given his background in tax, it may be coincidence or perhaps bad luck, that several of those included tax structures or loopholes that Macquarie took advantage of.

One of these was an Offshore Banking Units dispute with the Australian Taxation Office that lasted several years.[52]

Macquarie made use of a structure known as Offshore Banking Units (OBUs), which saw earnings taxed at 10 per cent rather than the prevailing Australian corporate rate of 30 per cent at the time. The regime was established to facilitate more expansion by Australia's banks outside their home market.

But for Macquarie the regime would cause consternation when the Australian Taxation Office (ATO) conducted retrospective audits of Macquarie's 2006, 2007 and 2008 financial years and issued amended assessments. The ATO was not satisfied with Macquarie's treatment of OBUs and closely scrutinised where it booked expenses and if a decision had been made to lower tax bills in Australia where corporate tax rates were higher.

The battle ended up in the legal system, with the Federal Court eventually dismissing Macquarie's application for an injunction to stop the issuance of amended assessments in the audit of the bank's offshore banking unit.

Tax treatment would again become a legal sticking point for Macquarie in 2018, when authorities in Germany launched a legal broadside at a practice many banks were employing to facilitate the double claiming of tax credits on dividends.

It was known as the 'cum-ex' tax strategy and was a form of dividend arbitrage.

Essentially, the controversy in Germany related to a period before changes in legislation in 2012 stopped a practice that allowed both holders of shares and those that bought stock from a short seller to claim tax credits on the same dividend payment.

Germany's public purse is estimated to have lost out €5.7 billion to the strategy—hence the legal action being pursued by German prosecutors and tax authorities against about 100 banks and a string of individuals.

Moore and his successor Wikramanayake were on the targeted suspects list at Macquarie, although the German action has proven protracted and slow moving. At the time of writing, no one from Macquarie had been formally interviewed by the German authorities over the allegations.

Macquarie's latest disclosures—in October 2022—on the German probe[53] included that it 'has progressed' in recent months, and that the company continued to respond to requests for information relating to the investigation of its historical activities. Macquarie also noted a number of civil claims against it.[54]

Macquarie has previously said the total amount at issue is not considered to be material for the group.

Initially Macquarie also outlined that the German legal matters primarily related to its lending to investment funds in 2011, with the funds then facilitating investor trading to benefit from dividend withholding tax credits. That means Macquarie wasn't pocketing any tax credits but its lending and short-selling activities mean it is firmly entangled in the mess.

Macquarie has said it disputed the claims and legal advice suggested it was 'acting lawfully'.

The legal matter harps back to the issue of financial institutions having a social licence to operate. While it appears the dividend tax practice was technically allowable in Germany during the disputed period, banks including Macquarie should have asked the question: Should we be facilitating this? The Australian banks' social licence to operate was a hot topic during the Hayne Royal Commission, as evidence tendered showed many were engaging in underhanded or negligent behaviour to boost profits, including charging fees to dead people or selling junk products to vulnerable consumers. The royal commission triggered a spate of regulatory and legislative changes to clean up the industry. Australia's asset privatisation drive—think back to the selling off of Sydney Airport or Telstra—has also helped fan public distrust of the financial institutions that are often involved.

■

As the enforceable undertaking was taking up a lot of attention within Macquarie's risk and banking teams, elsewhere dealmakers were busily looking for lucrative fee-generating transactions.

The Corporate and Asset Finance division was on the hunt for deals and while they didn't all come off there were some marquee and notable transactions that did get across the line.

In aircraft leasing, Stephen Cook was keen to build on the 2010 purchase of more than 50 aircraft from International Lease Finance Corporation, a unit of American International Group that was bailed out by taxpayers during the GFC.[55]

Macquarie had two years later created a new European rail business on the back of a deal to acquire a rolling stock leasing business from Lloyds Banking Group. Then in early 2015, Macquarie agreed to buy a portfolio of 90 commercial passenger aircraft from AWAS Aviation Capital, owned by Guy Hands's Terra Firma and the Canada Pension Plan Investment Board. The planes were leased to 40 airlines and the transaction catapulted Macquarie to just outside the world's ten largest plane lessors.[56]

The deal was sealed and it was second time lucky—but this time round for a large chunk of AWAS—after losing out on the entire asset almost a decade earlier to Terra Firma. Macquarie had also missed out on other transactions in the aircraft sector, including some that were markedly larger. In late 2011, Macquarie had been involved in a joint bid in a high-profile auction being run on behalf of beleaguered Royal Bank of Scotland (RBS), which was seeking to shed its aircraft leasing division. The deal was part of a broader divestment spree under UK government ownership and the RBS aircraft business ended up being bought by Japan's Sumitomo Mitsui Financial Group for US$7.3 billion.[57]

In the same year as the AWAS portfolio buy was announced, Macquarie also turned up as the successful acquirer of the A$8.2

billion Esanda dealer finance portfolio from ANZ Banking Group.

It was a bumper period for transactions, and Macquarie seemed to have its deal mojo back. Of course, not all of the transactions sealed during this period would go to plan. On the dealer finance book, Macquarie agreed in late 2021 to sell the floorplan loan book operated by Banking and Financial Services to Sydney-based Allied Credit for about A$650 million.[58]

Macquarie tapped investors twice in 2015 to help fund the AWAS and Esanda transactions respectively. Around this time, Moore as the CEO had a delegated authority to sign off on deals of up to A$500 million, albeit with some exceptions, one Macquarie board director told the authors.

Increasingly, the Corporate and Asset Finance (CAF) division came to represent Macquarie's ability to find every last niche and exploit it. Are you familiar with Macquarie Rotorcraft Leasing, the helicopter leasing business? How about its position in UK parking meters? Or mining equipment? Or its position in commercial solar energy financing? We mention those four businesses to make a point. They were all part of that one group, CAF, and only really from half of that group, the bit that does asset financing.

Jennifer Coyle, now COO for the Americas, joined Macquarie after taking her own mining leasing business from Caterpillar Finance in Nashville and pitching to Garry Farrell to take it on, which he did in February 2011.

Mining finance is not like other CAF businesses.[59] Mongolia, where the team supplied trucks to the equipment dealer for the Oyu Tolgoi mine, presented different challenges: staff had to fly from Sydney and Perth to conduct a site inspection on 21 December, a temperature difference of 40°C above zero to 40°C below. 'I remember they made us heat seal signs on the side of the equipment to say Macquarie, with a phone number on it: "If found, please call John".

Still, the experience was illustrative: the new business took two years to make money, but she felt support rather than pressure. 'When you do take a leap people are willing to back you,' Coyle says—'within reason.'[60]

■

It wasn't just acquisitions that were keeping Macquarie's bankers busy during the 2010–2015 period. In 2014, the Australian government was seeking to privatise major health insurer Medibank Private and prestigious mandates were up for grabs. Bankers worth their salt know work for the Australian government comes with additional probity and a host of hoops to jump through for investment banks and typically slimmer fees.

But deals like this help in pitching for other government divestments—be they federal or state—and also look good in marketing documents to other companies.

In pitching for the Medibank work, the Macquarie team, led by Robin Bishop, were hoping to avoid media coverage or being spotted in Canberra hovering around or exiting the Department of Finance building where enthusiastic press photographers may be lurking.

'We were told to cover our faces with umbrellas, Robin was just caught out,' a member of the deal team recalls, noting a picture of Bishop that made the local newspapers. 'We were trying to keep a low profile. The experience during T3 [the federal government's sale of a third tranche of Telstra shares] was there was a photo of a line of 30 of us strolling through Canberra, so we were focused on not being in the press.'

Macquarie missed out on working on T3 for the government, with ABN Amro Rothschild, Goldman Sachs JBWere and UBS lining up as joint global coordinators and Macquarie even failing to get a guernsey as a co-lead manager or on the long list of banks in the institutional selling syndicate.[61]

Whatever Macquarie did during that Medibank pitch worked, despite the snaps of Bishop, and it was one of three banks selected by Treasury to work on the A\$5.7 billion float.[62] Goldman Sachs and Deutsche Bank rounded out the joint lead manager deal team that would work closely as the transaction got to its pointy end with then-Finance Minister Mathias Cormann to price the deal and get it away.[63]

Australian taxpayers, Medibank customers and participants in the broader health insurance market were closely watching the outcome. Medibank's initial public offering process exceeded the government's pricing expectations and rose 7 per cent on debut. At the time of writing, those that piled into the IPO remained in the black versus their initial investment.

On the divestment front, in late 2013 Macquarie's long-held and at times highly turbulent association and investment in Sydney Airport came to an end. Again, it was vintage Macquarie. The structure would see the company distribute A\$1.3 billion in Sydney Airport shares—or 18.4 per cent of the company—to its own shareholders[64] via a special distribution. That would see ties to Sydney Airport dating back to 2002 severed.

That transaction would help Macquarie side-step a large capital gains tax bill and also extinguish speculation that its bankers were seeking to orchestrate a takeover of Sydney Airport, so the company could vend its shares into an attractive deal. Macquarie had already been paid to cease managing Sydney Airport in 2009, as its model of clipping the fee ticket at every opportunity came unstuck in listed markets.

The distribution—which was overwhelmingly supported by Macquarie's investors—saw them receive one share in Sydney Airport for every Macquarie share owned. It was effectively Macquarie passing its stake in the airport to its investors along with other sweeteners like a special dividend. Stapled securities—where two or more securities are contractually put together and can't be sold separately—were used by Macquarie for the transaction. The company booked a A$228 million gain on the distribution.

Another landmark deal, Thames Water, discussed in the next chapter, was both a success and a magnet for a great deal of controversy. In its aftermath, Macquarie's corporate affairs team may have been hoping for a breather from the harsh criticism in the UK press. But that wasn't to be, as Macquarie already had its sights on the Green Investment Bank and its people were constantly scouring global markets for growth options across market-facing businesses and its annuity-style businesses.

Chapter 14

GOING GREEN

Forty-three kilometres off England's East Anglia coast stands a cluster of 102 wind turbines, spinning vigorously in the reliably brisk winds of the North Sea. Macquarie, through its Green Investment Group (GIG) arm,[1] owns 40 per cent of this farm, which can produce 714 megawatts of clean energy. That's enough to power 630,000 homes each year, almost twice as many as exist in the county of Suffolk[2] where the cables from these machines land on the mainland. Three more farms are under development nearby.

These turbines, standing like sentinels guarding the British coast, are symbolic of what renewable energy has become for Macquarie. Renewables and energy transition are Macquarie's most visible priority, the driving force of its modern infrastructure business. This drive has brought about a happy confluence: of the sense of doing some social and environmental good, a theme upon which CEO Shemara Wikramanayake is vocal; and making a lot of money out of an asset class that is custom-made to reward innovation and Macquarie's entrepreneurial fail-to-succeed ethos.

They're also representative because Macquarie's ownership of them takes place through a business that came about—or was certainly galvanised—by one of Macquarie's most important and sensitive ever acquisitions: the Green Investment Bank (GIB), launched by the UK government as a catalyst for renewable energy in 2012 and sold to Macquarie amid considerable noise and controversy in 2017. Macquarie's absorption by osmosis of this group, first into Macquarie Capital and then Macquarie Asset Management, requires it to digest a golden share, which invites vocal scrutiny from a panel of supervisory trustees established by the UK Parliament.

Renewables tell a story that begins with some experimental exposures to wind farms at the start of the new century and brings us to Wikramanayake rubbing shoulders with world leaders at the the United Nations Climate Change Conference COP26 climate summit, as a voice not only for the bank she leads but for private finance itself as an engine for climate transition and decarbonisation. It's not always been a smooth voyage: several of the bank's renewables pioneers have left along the way to start their own enterprises, dismayed either by pace, ambition or conflict. There are some who find a glib contradiction between the save-the-world statements of some of the bank's asset managers and a commodities book that is actively expanding in oil trading.

But this increasingly feels like Macquarie's future. It has over 30 gigawatts of renewable capacity under development across 240 projects[3] in 25 markets worldwide, from South African hydro[4] to Indian solar[5] and Polish onshore wind.[6] Over the years, renewables and ESG (environmental, social, governance) data have moved from occasional references in the annual report to long sections that dominate the page count, while the reports themselves have turned steadily, both figuratively and literally, green.[7] And whatever you choose to think about Macquarie's motivations (and it certainly still expects to make a profit out of all of this), the truth is Macquarie's can-do chutzpah is potentially an extremely powerful force for getting things done in an area that needs things to get done as a matter of civil survival.

■

While the Green Investment Bank acquisition in 2017 would be the most significant step in this process, it all begins considerably earlier. Europe is in all sorts of respects, from engineering to investment, a leader in renewable ideas, and it was here that Macquarie made its first serious forays into the asset class, both in its own right and through funds.

In December 2004 Macquarie launched a joint venture[8] with fellow Australian Novera Energy to acquire and operate renewable assets, originally in the UK and then Germany. Then Macquarie European Infrastructure Fund moved in, buying a portfolio of six wind power projects in France and Sweden in 2005, as well as a UK portfolio of biomass plants ('the chook-poop power station', as one executive fondly remembers it) and a stake in Yorkshire Wind.[9]

There was, originally, an economic and risk problem with investing in renewables. Daniel Wong, who would go on to co-head Macquarie Capital, remembers being involved in some of the earliest wind farms. 'They were operational, and tiny,' he says. 'And it was interesting, because our approach was that the funds don't want to do development because it's too risky, but by the time it gets to operational, the returns are too low for an infrastructure fund. So you can imagine, with that didactic approach, an infrastructure fund could have completely missed the entire renewables development side of the energy transition.'

It didn't, because Macquarie was able to combine the varied skills of its investment bank, asset management arm and the balance sheet.

Fairly quickly, and just as it had done with highways, Macquarie would move from buying established wind assets to being at the forefront of developing them, which had several advantages: they could drive development in the manner they wanted, they got far better economics from doing so, and could also exit at the right time into a hungry market.

'Our role at Macquarie Capital is typically at the front end of development,' says John Pickhaver, co-head of Macquarie Capital for Australia. (See Chapter 12 for more on the Australian renewables story.)

It was a simple transition to make, given Macquarie's experience in infrastructure dating back to the 1990s. Pickhaver, who cites AGL as an example of a client where Macquarie went from advising it on wind farms to even selling them one Macquarie had developed, says: 'These were projects that came out of our PPP experience, which we had been doing for twenty years, putting it all together.

'We had that ability to see the pieces, put them together and get it to financial close.'[10]

Then gradually, over time, as Macquarie came to understand the assets better, they would move earlier and earlier in the process. 'There's a bit more risk early on, but we understood those risks,' Pickhaver says. 'If you started earlier in the development cycle, you needed a higher return.' For that, they needed expertise, and around the world they started hiring engineers and other professionals. Macquarie looked at everything the ecosystem required: not just the physical wind farms but transmission, storage, electrification, everything that has to go along with power generation for it to make any sense.

All over the world, Macquarie was beginning to see opportunity in renewables. In 2006 a group called Fremantle Energy Holdings was founded in Austin, Texas, which in partnership with Macquarie Capital would go on to create a pipeline of solar and wind projects.[11]

The Fremantle business hosted meetings on global renewables in Austin. Lachlan Creswell, who today is head of the Green Investment Group for Australia and New Zealand, recalls being at these meetings with other leading lights in the renewable idea such as Oliver Yates, David Roseman and Ian Learmonth. Creswell remembers that as a landmark for global connectivity among the businesses in which it became clear that everyone's individual dabbling in renewables added up to a considerable expertise.

'There was a realisation that we were doing a lot of advisory work in Europe, but if we had actually invested money with the developers who we were advising, it would have been a far better use of our resources,' Creswell says. 'We wouldn't just have been earning dollars for the time that we were risking, we would have generated a far greater return by having some capital alongside.'

Creswell spent an early part of his 20-year career at the bank in Mexico, having suggested, in typical Macquarie style, that he should go and set up there and see what could be done. 'It was an experience of wearing out a lot of boot leather,' he recalls, but led to them raising their first Mexican infrastructure fund[12] in around eighteen months, and much of the initial interest was in renewables.

'Firstly, it was an area where we could be competitive in a way that was more independent of local partnerships than the PPP space,' he says. 'And with renewable energy, 70 per cent of the cost base is things that you can bring in on a ship and purchase from international suppliers.' A year after the fund's 2010 launch, it was part of a consortium to buy the owners of a 396-megawatt wind energy project on the Isthmus of Tehuantepec in Oaxaca, which is—and this was the sort of tantalising nugget of information you discover all the time when you write about Macquarie—one of the windiest places in the world.[13]

Europe would be the driving force. Mark Dooley, who today is the global head of the Green Investment Group, joined from ABN Amro in 2005, where he had been running a broader European infrastructure projects business, which was initially his mandate at Macquarie too. But increasingly, his path took him more and more towards renewables, initially through the transmission assets that support the offshore wind sector. By around 2010, he felt, transmission activities gave way to rapidly growing momentum in solar, offshore wind and waste to energy.

Perhaps most importantly, European governments were getting involved in a big way. 'Here was this new asset class that was getting lots of policy support. It required huge volumes of investment.' It also featured more modest levels of gearing than existed in other infrastructure assets because of the risk profile; 50 to 80 per cent gearing levels became more common than the 90 per cent often seen in PPPs, Dooley says.

'It meant the equity cheque where we play was bigger,' he says. 'There was much more meaningful volume and it was a very appealing draw into the space. It took over my radar screen completely over the first half of the last decade.'

■

In 2012, the UK government established the Green Investment Bank (GIB) in order to try to get private investment to take part in the green economy. The UK had already made climate change commitments, and to reach them, it needed an enterprise to provide public money to wind farms and bioenergy projects while encouraging private capital to do likewise.

It made progress, but by June 2015 the government had concluded that it could not afford to make further public investment into GIB and that it would consider selling the bank into private ownership. 'It was always our intention that GIB should mobilise maximum private investment in the green economy,' said Sajid Javid, a former Chase Manhattan and Deutsche banker with a background in global credit trading[14] who by now was Secretary of State for Business, Innovation and Skills.[15] 'This reflects our policy aim of getting the market to work in tackling green policy challenges. Bringing private ownership directly into GIB is part of this aim and a natural next step for the company now it has proved itself a successful commercial enterprise.'[16]

It was a controversial idea, on many counts. Why would this state-backed entity throw in the towel of its independence so quickly? Could it really be counted upon to continue to invest in renewables, and specifically renewables in the UK, if it was absorbed into some bank or other private sector actor?

Stephen Moir was building out the corporate affairs and government relations function at GIB when the sale was mooted, and would later join Macquarie and become the regional head of corporate affairs for Europe, the Middle East and Africa (EMEA). He still remembers being there when Javid met Lord Smith of Kelvin, GIB's independent chair, framed by a portrait of Margaret Thatcher, to make the case. At that point the government was advancing plans to privatise a number of state assets, with GIB first on the slate because it was expected to be easy. 'That turned out to be far from the experience,' says Moir, and other plans were subsequently shelved.

'It was only a few years in and some people felt fundamentally it was too soon,' Moir recalls.

But there were arguments for selling. 'When they set it up it was very precise,' says Dooley. 'They identified a couple of sub-sectors of renewables where they thought the private markets needed an accelerant, and GIB was pointed at that.' Offshore wind was the best example, and the most obvious success story in UK renewables: it is today one of the world's largest offshore wind markets, with more than 10 gigawatts of cumulative installed capacity across 38 sites.[17]

'But by 2015, the private markets were pumping along quite nicely, and it was starting to become noticeable that many private players like ourselves were competing with the GIB,' Dooley says. 'And that is not what they were there to do. They were there for additionality.' There was an emerging feeling that it had done its job and there was not a policy intervention case for it to be owned by the government using taxpayers' money.

'They got it right,' Dooley says.

Once it was clear that the government was ready to sell, Macquarie swiftly entered the frame. 'When people don't want things,' like BT, or Security Pacific, or Delaware, or Constellation, 'that's something naturally we're interested in, if it's in our space,' says Nicholas Moore. 'We think we are good stewards of public assets. Our history with infrastructure, up until that time, was all about being a good steward of public assets. And our credibility in the UK was very high, so we sat down with the UK government.'

The process took more than two years from Javid's June 2015 statement to complete the sale, far longer than planned, and not helped by the considerable distraction of the UK's Brexit referendum in June 2016. Another point of deep discussion was the structural idea of a golden share, which would be owned by the government and would require the GIB, once sold, to remain under continuous monitoring by an independent group. But by late that year Macquarie had emerged as one of two realistic bidders,[18] and then the fun really started.

'People were very proud of the GIB, a policy intervention in a field people really care about,' says Dooley. 'So people were sensitive, and being an Australian investment bank wasn't necessarily the most winning opening line in terms of winning over all stakeholders.'

Part of this had nothing much to do with Macquarie. 'The privatisation was heavily criticised before Macquarie's name entered the frame, and whoever became the lead bidder was going to carry that opposition,' says Moir: 'Opposition in principle to privatisation, rather than specifically to them as an owner.

'People projected their worst fears of privatisation onto Macquarie.'

But there was a part of the objection that very much was Macquarie, or at least what it represented. 'The great concern was we would get this thing, dismantle it and it would disappear somehow,' says Dooley. 'That wasn't our intention. We thought it could be additive and multiplicative to what we already had in the space. The people who were there,' a team of people in London and Edinburgh, 'looked a bit like us: a mix of people with financing backgrounds and people with niche hard asset skills.

'We liked their assets, we thought renewables was already one of the best stories going in Mac Cap, and we thought it would be a great inflection point.'

But the problem was the sheer number of voices rising in objection. By early 2017, with Macquarie clearly the preferred bidder, *The Guardian* was able to quote politicians from every single major political party uniquely aligned on one thing: that GIB shouldn't be sold to Macquarie.[19]

Vince Cable of the Liberal Democrats was particularly vocal, as was Green party leader Caroline Lucas and a former Conservative minister, Gregory Barker (even though it was a Conservative government, under Theresa May, that was doing the selling). Greenpeace had launched a freedom of information request which it felt demonstrated that Macquarie could, if it wanted to, still invest in fossil fuels through GIB despite the special share.[20] And Macquarie's old friend Richard Branson was also speaking out against the idea of selling the whole group. 'It is only just getting started,' he said.[21]

David Fass, who was head of EMEA at the time, says 'I spent, I think, 75 days on Whitehall that year, meeting with dozens of MPs from every single party in every different constituency, explaining to them who we were, what we were about, why we wanted to do this and what our views were about renewable energy going forward.' What did they want to know? 'I think they feared we were getting a great deal. We were going to sell everything that we bought from them and fire all the people and make a lot of money and then run around and tell our shareholders how smart we are. I think that's what they were afraid of.'

And there was a phrase that kept appearing in newspaper articles at the time: Vampire Kangaroo.[22] This was a regurgitation of an article in the *Sunday Times* from 2013,[23] and was itself of course a derivative of the famous *Rolling Stone* article calling Goldman Sachs a Vampire Squid.[24] And to understand what that was all about, and the challenge it was causing Macquarie as it inched towards the finish line with the UK government for Green Investment Bank in early 2017, we have to go back a bit.

■

Macquarie's European business, which we last met after the Cintra and Kvaerner deals in the early years of the new millennium, went from strength to strength in the years that followed.

The first time Macquarie broke down regional contributions was 2006, when Europe, Africa and the Middle East accounted for 34 per cent of international income and just under 17 per cent of overall income; EMEA, as the geographical grouping is now known, has varied between 20 and 29 per cent of overall income from 2016 to 2022.[25] That might not sound a huge change, but the overall pie has grown so much over that time. The 2006 figure equates to A\$680 million of income,[26] the 2022 one, A\$3.51 billion. A more than fivefold increase in fifteen years, a period that includes a global financial crisis and a global pandemic, is good going.

London, where Macquarie opened its first office outside Australia in 1989, has become one of its biggest locations[27] worldwide; increasingly, post-Brexit, the momentum now is across the European mainland.[28]

Over the years numerous assets came and went. Fiscal 2006 alone brought an airport in Denmark, a toll road network in France, tank storage businesses in Germany, gas and electricity networks in the Netherlands, directories businesses[29] in eight countries, two ferry services in the UK (plus a gas and electricity distribution business and a media services provider) and the Gdansk sea cargo port in Poland, a greenfield asset that Macquarie bankers tend to speak of with considerable pride and which brought several Australian super-annuation funds with it.

New funds came too for them to be placed in. By the 2011 financial year the three European infrastructure funds had raised €7.3 billion between them, fundraising was under way on a fourth, and the same techniques had been used for emerging market infrastructure funds in China, India, Mexico and Russia.

There was ample infrastructure advisory work too, particularly out of London. 'The scale of the UK PPP program was huge,' says Neil Arora, who worked in the team before moving to Singapore. 'We advised on schools, hospitals, police stations, firearm ranges.'

Nor was the story just about infrastructure:[30] Paul Plewman, who now has the title of head of EMEA, has spent much of the last twenty years building a commodities and global markets business for the region. It is somewhat overshadowed by the success in the Americas but still extremely powerful, the more so at the time of writing as war in Ukraine disrupts energy supply and prices.[31] 'Gas and power have become increasingly important for us,' says Plewman. 'There's a huge amount of client need for that, given what's happened in Europe.'

And in July 2007, Macquarie applied to the UK Financial Services Authority to establish a UK-incorporated banking entity, also providing a European passport for its banking businesses (which was stymied by the Brexit vote; Macquarie has since shut the London bank and opened one in Dublin instead, with a Paris branch. But that's a whole other story.[32]).

Along the way, Macquarie made one of its most publicly watched acquisitions ever—perhaps the most since Sydney Airport—when a consortium[33] it led bought Thames Water for £8 billion on 1 December 2006.

Macquarie was sufficiently proud of this to put it on the front of its 2007 annual report.[34] In the opening text it gave a grand account of the asset's scale, importance and history—all of which, in one sense or another, would prove problematic. 'Thames Water is the largest water and wastewater services company in the United Kingdom, serving eight million water and thirteen million wastewater customers across London and the Thames Valley,' it said on the inside front cover. 'The history of Thames Water dates back to the early 1600s when the privately funded New River, a 40 mile channel, was built to create London's water supply.'

And there it is. Thames Water touched the lives of a lot of people; in the nation's capital where the noise and attention is greatest; it is a truly essential piece of infrastructure conveying water, something people intuitively think they already own, or sewage, which they only think about at all when it's a problem; and it is very, very old.

There is probably no transaction or asset in the world where the opinion of Macquarie differs so dramatically from public perception of the job it did. Macquarie, which by the time it bought Thames Water had already digested another regulated UK water company called Southeast Water[35] as well as the Wales and the West gas distribution network, claims it did wonderful things with this precious, vital and thoroughly unromantic asset. 'After we bought it from RWE, we increased investment to more than a billion pounds of capital every year,' says Leigh Harrison, head of real assets for Macquarie Asset Management. 'That's £11 billion invested into the network during our ownership period. We reduced leakages by over 20 per cent while keeping customer bills flat.'

John Roberts says: 'When we went into Thames, we went in almost as zealots to change performance and culture ... I think Thames did unbelievably well in terms of increased service quality, though I know that's not always the public perception.' Neil Arora, in London at the time: 'What I saw was a genuine attempt to own and manage those assets properly, professionally, with integrity.' And Shemara Wikramanayake: 'Thames was a great asset for investors, and it delivered really good returns above investment case, but it also delivered to the community: the way we reduced leaks, all the capital investment and the upgrading.'

But the press view was rather different. That Vampire Kangaroo line in the Sunday Times was just the most memorable remark. There is a BBC radio documentary, *Macquarie: The Tale of the River Bank*,[36] which is 38 minutes of the most withering criticism of the Australian bank, beginning with a trip down a stretch of the Thames at the River Marlow and this memorable exchange between journalist Michael Robinson and a local boat broker:

'We noticed quantities of foam ... blobs of foam coming down the river.'

'What colour?'

'Brown. It was affectionally known by the locals as crappucino.'

Other articles in the British press around this time referred to Macquarie's 'sprawling interests and ruthless profit taking' and 'heavily criticized ... for its asset-stripping ways.'[37]

So what led to the disconnect? There is a range of reasons, starting with the state Macquarie says the asset was in when it got hold of it. It's something of an achievement to have water shortages in a city as rainy as London, but that was the case when the Australians took charge. Previous owners RWE had previously claimed this was because of bombing damage caused to pipes during the Second World War, which, RWE being a German utility, was a cause of great merriment in the British tabloids.

Moore says Macquarie went in with the attitude: we're fixing all the leaks, and here's the money. None of this was straightforward or lacking in disruption. 'Remember, this is an ageing Victorian-era network with increasingly leaking pipes,' says Harrison. 'Thames Water is spread throughout Greater London, which is densely populated and very high profile.'

But there were three problems, one of which wasn't Macquarie's fault, two of which were.

One is that when someone's fixing a water pipe, all the public sees is a blocked road, not a company spending millions to replace pipes and reduce water shortages. It illustrates a truism of the infrastructure business: that it's boring and not newsworthy, until it is, and then you wish it was boring again.

This brings us to the two things that do fall on Macquarie. In March 2017, Thames Water was fined a record £20.3 million[38] after it admitted dumping 1.4 billion litres of raw sewage into the River Thames. Macquarie was out by then: it sold its final stake in Thames Water for £1.35 billion to Omers[39] and the Kuwait Investment Authority earlier in the same month.[40] But the dumps took place in 2013–14, very much on Macquarie's watch, an incident that Judge Francis Sheridan called 'a shocking and disgraceful state of affairs.' And just three months later, Thames Water was investigated by Ofwat for its 'unacceptable failure' to control leakages.[41]

The other issue was debt. Leaving aside all the gripping quotes about floating brown scum, what the BBC really got hold of was the fact that much of the debt Macquarie took on in order to finance the acquisition was then put on to Thames Water's books, meaning it effectively paid for its own takeover with money that could have been spent avoiding spillages and leaks. The BBC concluded that of £2.8 billion of debt Macquarie borrowed to finance the purchase in 2006, £2 billion was repaid through new loans raised by Thames Water through a subsidiary in the Cayman Islands. During Macquarie's eleven years in charge, the Financial Times concluded,[42] it received returns of between 15.5 per cent and 19 per cent annually, and in total paid itself and its investors £1.6 billion in dividends while Thames Water was loaded with £10.6 billion of debt and ran up a £260 million pension deficit while paying no corporation tax.

And this brings us to an inherent problem Macquarie had to navigate and learn from before it could take on Green Investment Bank. This sort of financing might well fly in the corporate world, and even in certain forms of infrastructure; loading some of the debt of acquisition on to the company being acquired is really nothing new. But, like it or not, infrastructure is emotional, and people have a closer connection to it than any other private enterprise even if, legally speaking, there is no difference. Water falls from the sky. People assume they own it.

In every infrastructure asset Macquarie has ever touched, its bankers have had to make this calculation: that it will be scrutinised as a steward and that its ecosystem of stakeholders is a lot bigger than simply the investors and the vendor. There is a broader question, certainly still alive and kicking in the UK, about the appropriateness of private sector ownership of truly vital assets like water and power utilities, though there's no avoiding the fact that there simply isn't the money in the UK state (nor most others) to keep infrastructure up to scratch through taxpayer funds.

Today, Macquarie tends to cite the lesson learned from Thames Water as not being anything about debt or financial engineering or service, but the ability to get on the front foot and tell their side of the story. Daniel Wong, who was closely involved in Thames Water and remains proud of what was achieved, thinks Macquarie had been influenced by its beatings from the Australian press in previous years, in particular over Sydney Airport. 'We had a default setting of keep your head below the parapet,' he says. Arora calls Macquarie 'camera-shy.'

Wikramanayake says: 'If there's a takeaway from Thames Water, it's the public nature of these assets and how social licence can be impacted by misunderstanding.'

So why do we mention all of this now? Two reasons. One was that the furore about Thames Water didn't really kick off at the time but instead just as the Green Investment Bank sale came into public view. That Vampire Kangaroo article was from 2013,[43] but only really started getting traction with the GIB bid throughout 2016, during Macquarie's final year of ownership of Thames Water (although the description was still in abundant usage when Macquarie, with characteristic thick skin, shrugged off past bad press and took a majority stake in Southern Water in 2021[44]). So the PR battle was entirely relevant to the Macquarie bid for GIB.

But the other was that Macquarie's painful lessons about stakeholder and community engagement through Thames Water would prove essential in its bid for, and conduct with, GIB. 'We have learned the lesson that you shouldn't let others narrate your own story,' says Moir.

■

On 18 August 2017, Macquarie announced it had completed the acquisition of Green Investment Bank for £2.3 billion.[45] Macquarie committed, among other things, to a target of leading £3 billion of investment in green energy projects over the next three years, to its supervision by the Green Purposes Company Trustee, and that the renamed Green Investment Group would be Macquarie's primary vehicle for green projects in the UK and Europe.[46]

Macquarie has drawn some criticism for compromising GIB's promised independence by folding it into Macquarie, first into Macquarie Capital and then in 2022 into Macquarie Asset Management. The idea was that Green Investment Bank, whatever it ended up being called, would be an independent entity with its own book of renewables business: to some, absorbing it into Macquarie erodes that independence and makes it no different from any other commercial enterprise.

But Moore presents the amalgamation as having strengthened GIB. 'Rather than putting [GIB] into Macquarie, we saw it more as putting our existing businesses into it to make it bigger,' Moore says. 'We added our own team, who had a long and successful renewable history, and our assets under development in the UK and around the world, to make it a much better Green Investment Group'.

Whatever the governance sensitivities, Macquarie cannot be accused of failing on its targets. The Green Purposes Company writes an annual letter as trustee to measure GIG's performance against its purposes, and noted in the 2020 letter that 'GIG will exceed its first three years commitment of £3 billion of new investment ... in the UK or Europe',[47] in fact achieving £2.3 billion of that in the 2020 financial year alone, over £2 billion of it in the UK. The trustees are not shy of challenging GIG, noting in the 2019 annual letter that it had concerns around transparency,[48] and calling on it to 'continue to evolve' in an increasingly crowded market in the 2021 letter. 'They're not backwards in writing down where they think we've gone in the wrong direction,' says Dooley. But the tone has generally been very positive. 'GIG appears to be having a positive influence over the wider Macquarie group in respect of their approach to green investment,'

GPC chair Trevor Hutchings[49] wrote in September 2021.[50] 'This is significant and welcome.'

As a consequence, says David Fass, 'our association with the UK government as a result of having done that transaction is 180 degrees from where it was ten years ago.'

Dooley calls the acquisition 'a great galvanising moment.' He and his team used to keep a running tally of how many times Moore used the word green in his speech at the AGM—'a valuable metric'—and whatever that number is, it's certainly grown further under Wikramanayake.

Daniel Wong recalls there being two camps in Macquarie when it came to GIB. One thought of it as £2.3 billion of balance sheet investments at a decent price that would probably grow: the straightforward camp, you might say. 'The other camp was: yes, we'll do all that, but we'll get a team, we'll get a brand, we'll get a connection with a company that was created by the UK as a public institution to drive a mission, and we'll have this whole network of activity that comes with it.' Wong was very much in the second camp, but does recall peers even in the same team who couldn't understand why Macquarie would bother buying a business full of people doing the same things they were already doing. There were some good assets—Galloper offshore wind farm, for example, and Race Banks[51]—but some just thought they should be put into Macquarie European Infrastructure Funds (MEIF) and that was the only appeal.

'Nicholas saw the potential platform value,' says Wong. 'And he said: it's not just a collection of assets, it's a real business.' From then on, the momentum existed to make the deal transformative.

A global green committee was created in order to ensure that all the businesses pulled together on green and ESG (environmental, social, governance) priorities: not just infrastructure, the obvious one, but commodities and global markets through its equipment leasing or emissions trading businesses, or even banking and financial services. 'There probably is a cross-group set of opportunities that we're not capitalising on because historically we tend to operate in our business groups,' says Miki Edelman in New York, who is on the committee (now renamed the Climate Solutions Task Force). 'So rather than being so vertical, it's designed to go horizontal.'

That all helped. 'But the biggest impact,' says Dooley, 'was that GIG as a unit was now across all of these different technologies.' There was a strong combined story to tell in offshore and onshore wind, carbon capture and other technologies across 25 markets. 'That was a snowball getting bigger and bigger.'

Asked for an example, he picks a partnership with TotalEnergies— 'big oil and gas have a huge role to play in the decades ahead with this transition'—in developing offshore wind in South Korea, with the distinction that rather than anchoring tower foundations into the sea bed, they want to put floating towers out there. 'We will pioneer commercial scale offshore floating wind with TotalEnergies in Korea.' The group is also backing numerous offshore wind projects around the UK, from the East Coast of England to the west of Scotland's Orkney Islands. All told Macquarie has a 15-gigawatt renewables development pipeline in EMEA and plans to grow it; GIG has expanded from the UK to 25 new markets, twelve in EMEA, since its acquisition.

But where the combination of Macquarie attitudes and the greater social need should be best is in newer technologies, not yet saturated but requiring a willingness to take calculated risk. This is what the GIG's supervisory trustees are most keen to see progress: the stuff that's not yet established. Ultimately, Macquarie's credibility as an owner and steward will depend on this.

'One of the great things about Macquarie is it's good at new things,' says Dooley. 'We find solutions for mature things, but we're also a very disciplined pioneer.'

It's never reckless. 'We drive each other nuts asking the what ifs and testing our way into new stuff,' he says. 'But if we've done all our work and it still looks good, we are happy to go into something new and be a pioneer. We don't need to point to ten other shops that have done it.' There's a financial reason for this too. 'As these markets mature, we want to balance between having a solution for maturing asset classes where margins can get squeezed, and also testing yourself against what's coming next.'

The two clearest examples of this are on battery development and hydrogen.[52]

One person who is instrumental in this transition is Kate Vidgen, GIG's global head of industrial transition and clean fuels, and a member of the Australian Clean Energy Regulator board. Vidgen was for years involved in Quadrant Energy, a business formed when Macquarie and Brookfield Asset Management led a deal to buy the Western Australian oil and gas assets of Apache Corporation for US$2.1 billion in 2014; the business was renamed Quadrant, Vidgen worked in it for four years, and then sold it to Santos four years later. Macquarie uses the deal as a case study of partnering with its own clients.[53]

When Vidgen wrapped that up, she asked to make hydrogen her priority. 'And to give Macquarie a lot of credit, they said: OK, go and find some hydrogen assets,' she says. 'They didn't even blink an eyelid, what was quite amazing, because I had a number of people externally at that time describe it as a science experiment.'[54]

A proprietary fund called Pathway already existed to invest in longer-dated investments such as hydrogen; building on those early efforts, Vidgen and her team have spent four years developing a business plan that has now evolved to cover all renewable fuels and initial transition technologies. Now, she says, 'we can see the J curve coming', the point at which interest and investment in the sector begin to levitate.

You can see the evidence already. Wikramanayake argues that Australia could make itself a global centre for green hydrogen.[55] It is working with BP to consider a green hydrogen project at the UK company's former oil refinery site in Kwinana, Western Australia (see Chapter 12).[56] 'They've got a fantastic site, great infrastructure,' says Vidgen. 'We're going to put an electrolyser there to really try to decarbonise all the surrounding industry.'

And globally,[57] GIG has set up a joint venture with Netherlands-based chemicals maker Nobian, which will run that company's green energy spin-off, the Hydrogen Chemistry Company. It comes with a pipeline of electrolysis projects that will use renewable energy to make green hydrogen. GIG has also signed a memorandum of understanding with ExxonMobil and SGN to use carbon capture at Exxon's complex in Southampton in order to create a blue hydrogen hub to service British power needs, and is building an industrial-scale green hydrogen production plant on the island of Flotta in the Orkney Islands with TotalEnergies and Renewable Infrastructure Development Group.[58]

A key to success in new areas, Vidgen says, is partnership. 'As soon as you say to someone: I want to be in everything, and I want the whole pie, they won't talk to you,' she says. 'We're open to saying: we're really flexible, we can mix and match solutions with partners. It's a much more successful strategy than trying to put your arms around the whole thing.'

Gradually GIG has developed new portfolio companies as plat-forms for expansion in specific areas. Blueleaf Energy, for example, specialises in renewable energy in the Asia-Pacific, particularly solar. Another is Corio, a specialist offshore wind business, and a third is Cero Generation, a specialist solar energy company active in Europe. There are more in the works.

The 2022 movement of GIG from the investment banking to the asset management arm of Macquarie reflects a change in strategy reflected by the formation of companies like that, Dooley says. In MacCap, 'we were expected to recycle the balance sheet and make merchant banking type returns through the fairly short term,' he says. 'Now we're going to a place where our LPs, our clients, want us to deliver outcomes across a long span of time. That's a big shift.'

■

An equally significant shift has been in the voice of the chief executive. It's not as if Moore was blind to the opportunities in renewables: it was under his watch that the GIB acquisition took place. But he was not particularly vocal about climate change in anything other than a Macquarie context.

The clearest sense of a change in this approach came in the vital COP26 climate change summit in Glasgow in October 2021. Perhaps the most high-powered climate conference ever attempted, it was impeded by COVID-19 travel restrictions and, from the Australian perspective, a certain governmental ambivalence; one might now argue that then Prime Minister Scott Morrison's refusal to engage with the action plan that came with the event is part of the reason he is no longer Prime Minister Scott Morrison. Instead, Australia's effective leader on the UN climate change stage appeared to be Macquarie CEO Shemara Wikramanayake.[59]

In fact, Wikramanayake appeared to be a voice not only for Australia but the potential of private sector finance to be an agent of climate transition. The difference between her approach and Moore's is that she's not just speaking for the bank, with an exhausting range of public roles including some linked to the United Nations and the Global Commission on Adaptation.[60]

Wikramanayake herself visibly recoils at any attempt to depict her as any kind of figurehead. Many leaders do this—'It's not about me, it's about the team'—and rather fewer actually mean it, but

Wikramanayake genuinely seems like she would rather nail her foot to the floor than talk about individual leadership. 'You'll find this answer frustrating,' she says, before describing half a dozen key members of the team across the world who were instrumental in Macquarie's ESG journey. She's vocal on the problem—how to effectively transition from carbon emissions to new solutions, with a realistic transition path for legacy pollutants 'to gradually glide path over, instead of precipitously shifting when we don't have all of the solutions'—but she's uncomfortable as an icon for that idea.

'I'm spokesperson for everyone, so if someone has to represent us on the Glasgow Financial Alliance for Net Zero or at COP26 I'll be the figurehead,' she eventually says with some reluctance, before going through the list of people who were representing their businesses in Glasgow with her, among them O'Kane, Dooley and Plewman. 'I may be fronting and doing a range of meetings. But to get to what Macquarie does takes the 20,000 people that we have.'

Others, though, do see her in a leadership position whether she likes it or not. Ben Way: 'I was really proud of the role we played at COP26. And I was particularly proud of Shemara's leadership: it was almost like Macquarie's global breakout performance. I've never seen someone work harder than Shem did during that period.' He recalls her meeting the Queen one evening and being seated next to Boris Johnson at a limited-invitation dinner the next. 'Shemara ensured we have a voice in trying to solve a global existential crisis. That's a remarkable story for a business that's only 50 years old.'

Janet Dietrich, who leads energy transition in the CGM (Commodities and Global Markets) business in Houston, adds: 'It's been hugely important. The first thing is, it's really meaningful to her, and to her family. She's a very genuine, a very real person.'

One thing Wikramanayake is not touchy-feely about at all is when the subject is raised of whether CGM must one day exit the trading of fossil fuels, particularly oil, in order to match its business lines with its ESG credentials. As we saw in our US roadtrip, Macquarie has actively sought to increase its gas and oil trading business through the operations it acquired from Cargill in Minneapolis and Calgary. Surprisingly, although Macquarie has committed to end lending exposure to coal past 2024, it still has a small coal trading business.

The argument against Macquarie here is that the trading of fossil fuel products is damaging even if the bank is not directly involved in financing the projects that get those products out of the ground. Advancing this argument, the supercharged profits Macquarie has made from commodities trading in recent years stand at odds with its supposed green credentials.

But Wikramanayake, who has committed to reaching net zero operational emissions for Macquarie by 2025 and is working with asset management clients to manage portfolios towards a 2040 global net zero emissions target, is firm when this argument is made.

'We're shooting ourselves in the foot if we try to say we're going to get off gas tomorrow in 2022, because we do not have baseload renewable energy to replace it,' she says. 'So, if we want to get back to living like cave people, let's do that. But if we want to be intelligent and considered let's think about how we develop firming solutions.' She says 20 per cent of global energy capacity is now wind and solar, 'which is wonderful, it's competitive in price, but it's intermittent. So we need storage or some sort of low emission firming.

'There are people on our planet today that are living very difficult lives, whose nations want to lift their living standards through the consumption of energy,' she adds. 'And we can't in the developed world sit here and say: we emitted all the carbon that's in the world now to get to comfortable lifestyles, and you can just stay where you are because we've emitted enough now for the whole global community and population.'

In the CGM businesses themselves, people tend to choose their words carefully. 'As someone who's leading one of the oil businesses, we are committed to this business,' says David Hochberg in Houston. 'We're trying to help our clients understand how to transition. We spend a lot of time talking about zero carbon. We could still be in the oil business, but it could look very different five years or two years from now depending upon what the market needs.'

Janet Dietrich, working on the same floor in Houston, is responsible for helping clients make the energy transition. 'It's a 24/7 opportunity right now,' she says. 'It's a differentiator for Macquarie already.'

But Nick O'Kane, the one most directly involved in this question as head of CGM, gives the clearest answer when asked if he can foresee a time when his business won't be able to handle oil. 'At some point in the future, I think the answer obviously has to be yes,' he says. He agrees with Wikramanayake that the world is in a transition phase in which, for the moment, it does require oil, and most certainly natural gas. But he adds: 'In CGM we're extremely well placed to help our customers to transition because some of them have a pretty material carbon footprint. And if they want to stay in existence, they've got to change.'

Certainly that remaining coal exposure looks not only incongruous but ugly, and will remain that way until it rolls off the books. But what of solutions in the trading businesses?

One would expect Macquarie to want to be on the right side of any uptake in carbon trading, an idea that has been stubbornly resistant to critical mass. O'Kane says Macquarie has set up a global carbon team of 10–15 people from London over the twelve months prior to our May 2022 interview; there is an emissions trading desk in Houston. Plewman reports a 'growing and hiring' carbon business in Europe, which not only trades but invests in projects such as cookstoves in Africa to generate carbon credits to on-sell to clients.

'Pricing carbon is an important factor in terms of ensuring that the transition happens in an orderly fashion,' says O'Kane. 'We're investing in growing that.'

In the meantime, Macquarie continues to tilt towards the renewable opportunity. In the first two weeks of June 2022 alone, as we draft this chapter, GIG and its subsidiaries have committed to a hybrid onshore wind and solar project in Brazil,[61] a 2.5-gigawatt wind farm off the coast of Victoria,[62] five Brazilian offshore wind projects worth 5 gigawatts,[63] and a partnership with Bluestone Energy to develop 2 gigawatts of UK battery storage projects.[64]

It's like roads and airports in the 2000s: momentum, innovation and money. Macquarie wants to make a fortune in this space, and that will be its priority and principal motivation. But this time, it can also be aligned with something advantageous to the planet.

Chapter 15

SMASHING THE GLASS CEILING

Quietly spoken, just a tad over five feet tall and of Sri Lankan heritage, she's the polar opposite of what one imagines of an investment banker who has risen to the highest echelons of Macquarie. In fact, Shemara Wikramanayake—or Shem to those close to her—is right at the top of Macquarie after being elevated to CEO in 2018.

Her intellect, sharp mind and deal-making prowess are coupled with a friendly and unassuming style,[1] that set her apart early in her Macquarie career.

A self-described maths geek, she had as a child aspired to be a pilot, astronaut or even a James Bond-type international spy. Wikramanayake's deep sense of adventure, resilience and capacity for navigating difficult situations was instilled in her early, as her family uprooted their lives and moved away from Sri Lanka.[2]

At just three months old she was sent to Sri Lanka from London to live with her grandparents for a year; then, when she was eight, the family moved permanently in the other direction to England to build a new life. That was reportedly due to political controversy that had engulfed the family, particularly her grandfather, who was a barrister.[3]

The England move saw the family face a period of financial hardship, prompting Wikramanayake's immediate family to move homes several times, which meant changes of schools and friends. When she was thirteen, the family adjusted course and migrated to Australia, where her father would find work as a doctor. It was an experience that would test the mettle of any child, but Wikramanayake saw it as an opportunity to gain important life skills and it didn't deter her from thinking big about the future.

'I looked on it as an opportunity, possibly from natural reliance. I was able to quickly accept that I could do nothing about peripatetic circumstances, but I appreciated that I still had choices and things I could control including my attitude,' she told a Chief Executive Women (CEW) event in 2020.[4]

That mindset would eventually prepare her well for the cut-and-thrust world of investment banking, but interestingly after some thought she shied away from applying for a Macquarie trading role during her university years as others, including Richard Jenkins, had done. Wikramanayake completed degrees in commerce and law at the University of New South Wales and worked stints at an accounting firm before joining prominent Sydney law firm Blake Dawson Waldron.

But something in her professional life was missing. Wikramanayake sought out advice about a career change to financial services—where she could put her maths brain to use. Eventually, after ruling out private equity and stockbroking, she connected with Macquarie executive directors Robin Crawford and John Rendle.

She found her fit and joined Macquarie in May 1987 in the Corporate Services division, just months before the crash eviscerated financial markets.

'I remember, leading into the crash, we were doing a lot of equity capital markets IPO business, because markets were very buoyant,' Wikramanayake says. 'With the stock market crashes, asset prices fell a lot so we moved to doing M&A [mergers and acquisitions] work. We responded to the needs of our clients.'

Over the next three decades at Macquarie, her career would see her live and work in Sydney, Melbourne, Auckland, Wellington, Hong Kong, Kuala Lumpur, London, New York and Boston. Wikramanayake is credited with setting up and leading Macquarie Capital's advisory offices in New Zealand, Malaysia and Hong Kong and spearheading the firm's infrastructure operations in the USA and Canada.[5]

In her early years working on deals Alastair Lucas is among those credited for recognising her talent and getting her involved in a wide range of transactions and mandates. As Wikramanayake forged her way in the Corporate Services division, she became known for being highly analytical and a good listener, with the ability to win the confidence of clients via a no nonsense and human approach.

'Her greatest strength in the early days of her career was the ability to take complex problems and deconstruct them into manageable smaller issues,' a former colleague says.

Ben Bruck, who worked closely with Wikramanayake within the asset management unit, says: 'She's got an elephantine memory, a fine sense of risk and can connect authentically with just a bamboozling number of people.'[6]

But challenges did present themselves in those early years.

On a complex deal in Melbourne, Wikramanayake told the CEW event that a client questioned her colleagues about whether a 'very young looking, brown-skinned female' would be able to get the job done. Wikramanayake was none the wiser about those views and got on with the task at hand, but by the end of the transaction the same client was thanking her for teaching him about 'irrational prejudice'.

By this stage the Macquarie Melbourne office had splintered somewhat between the old guard of bankers at one end and the upcoming crop of mid-level bankers (helping to mentor junior staff) at the other. Peter Yates recalls the younger bankers dubbing themselves 'The Oasis' group in the office, a clear demarcation from the older clan. It was certainly a tight-knit group as the likes of Wikramanayake, the Yates brothers, Richard Price, Michael Burn, Tim Burke and others still to this day meet for dinner annually.

'Because it was an L-shaped office Alastair Lucas would come down our end and complain that he couldn't find a brain cell down there. And we actually said, no we're The Oasis away from the sea of boredom and backwardness,' Peter Yates says.

At times, though, it wasn't 100 per cent safe to be going about your deal-making in 'The Oasis'. Oliver Yates remembers a rather competitive game of indoor office cricket that ended up with Wikramanayake taking a ball to the head, and him annoying two future Macquarie CEOs in one batting stroke.

'She was in the same office and Nicholas was bowling, and I was the junior guy and clobbered Shemara in the head,' Oliver Yates says. 'Nicholas made me go down and get some flowers and give them to Shemara.'

Also while in Melbourne making a name on the deal-making scene, the course of Wikramanayake's personal life would forever change. Hill Samuel used to host an annual banker exchange to transfer a talented person Down Under, while the Australian business would likewise send a bright person to London. In 1993, Oxford-educated Ed Gilmartin was sent on the exchange and was meant to be heading to Sydney, which was experiencing a lull in takeover activity relative to Melbourne. That triggered a change in plans and Gilmartin was shipped to Melbourne instead, there working on a number of key transactions before heading to Sydney and helping Simon Hannes on the RTZ-CRA deal for Macquarie.

While in Melbourne, the Englishman's desk was fairly close to that of Wikramanayake's workstation, and that's how she came about meeting her future husband. They share two children and Gilmartin later left Macquarie to take on the primary parenting responsibilities.[7]

Wikramanayake's career went from strength to strength at Macquarie including working in a prudential role filtering and conducting detailed-risk assessments of principal transactions for the firm. That was a key position that saw Wikramanayake report to Nicholas Moore, and she and younger colleague Grant Smith— now head of infrastructure for asset management in Australia—were stationed close to his office.

As a trusted and highly capable pair of hands, Moore made it a habit of throwing Wikramanayake into somewhat challenging positions at Macquarie. She was later tasked with going to the USA to ramp up the infrastructure business there, as Moore saw it as a market primed for potential growth and opportunity.

'In terms of potential for the group back then, in the Macquarie Capital group, that [the USA] was obviously the most important place and so I asked her to do that, and she did it, and she did it well,' Moore says of Wikramanayake.

'Shemara is an exceptional individual: talented, hard-working, very empathetic, great values and very effective,' Moore says. 'We have a lot of talented, hard-working people at Macquarie, and some, like Shemara, are particularly effective at getting things done.'

Wikramanayake recalls being pushed by Moore to take on the US opportunity.

'He said we really need this done with our infrastructure funds in the US, we've got this half-billion balance sheet position, it's not getting launched to investors. You've got to get over there. And three weeks later, I was living in the US with my young family and doing the work on the infra funds,' she says.

When Moore took the CEO reins in 2008, it was trusted lieutenant Wikramanayake who was soon appointed to run the newly formed asset management division, seen as a future growth engine in a tumultuous period for financial markets.

'Shemara took on every new role with enthusiasm, won the confidence of her new team and clients, and was able to grow it successfully,' Moore says. 'Business is never without its challenges and she has been able to meet and overcome them consistently.'

Wikramanayake wasn't particularly enamoured of taking over the fixed income and equities business, which she knew little about, but immersed herself in the project at a particularly busy time. 'There was a period of five years of just head down, trying to get the public asset manager streamlined, the Delaware acquisition to global scale, a whole lot of things that went on with repositioning that business. Then the infrastructure funds came into it. I said to everyone at the beginning [in 2008], in five years, we're going to make a billion dollars (from initially effectively nothing), just to give them something to work towards. But we did make more than the billion after five years,' she recalls. The team had delivered.

Similarly to Moore, Wikramanayake has shied away from the limelight and carefully avoided courting a media profile. Those at Macquarie that crossed paths with her over her time running asset management said her leadership style was inclusive and Wikramanayake made sure to gauge and hear the views of as many people as possible before making important decisions.

But she was also tough when required.

'In addition to being a hard taskmaster and questioner she was, and is, very supportive of just doing new things,' says Ani Satchcroft, a senior managing director in Macquarie's asset management unit.

■

As soon as Moore took the helm the Macquarie board had started thinking about the next round of succession planning, despite the pressure the global financial crisis was exerting.

Then-chairman Peter Warne says planning for Moore's replacement more or less started immediately. 'Probably since Nicholas took the job,' Warne says of the process, noting Wikramanayake was always a serious contender. 'She was running the biggest division and very profitably and having had her experience around the whole organisation, multiple businesses, multiple countries, she was always on the list from day one or two. There might have been things we'd encourage Nicholas to get her to do.'

That was about making sure CEO candidates for the next round had filled out any gaps in their experience or style to ensure the firm had a string of serious candidates to choose from when the time came for a baton change.

Catherine Livingstone says the long tenures of most executives who have come up through the ranks gives the board an edge in the succession planning process. 'It's that longevity in the business which is key to succession considerations,' she notes. 'There's plenty of time to observe people and understand their strengths and weaknesses.'

Macquarie's 2022 annual report put the average tenure of the group's key management personnel at 22 years,[8] a staggering figure that perhaps reflects the ability of the profit share model to retain and align staff. Many in the top echelon of Macquarie have also had a raft of different roles during their time, often spanning different parts of the world.

Moore was always based in Australia, but travelled often. Under his rein, Macquarie changed course and stepped up the focus on annuity-style businesses with Moore notching up a decade in the hot seat as he methodically steered the group out of the GFC abyss. By this stage Wikramanayake had been told she was on Moore's and the board's broad succession list, but she didn't expect a changeover would happen in 2018.

'When Nicholas said he was going I have to say, I was surprised. I imagine others would have been as well.'

Others had also believed Moore would stay on to celebrate Macquarie's 50th anniversary in 2019 before hanging up his company boots. After an action-packed decade, though, Moore had decided to retire from Macquarie, setting the wheels in motion for execution of the succession plan.

'It wasn't really until he came and said to me, I've basically decided to retire, these are the reasons I'm retiring, which as I say, initially, it was all about, oh my goodness, Nicholas is going, how are we going to cover for a whole lot of stuff Nicholas does?

'Then, he said to me, well I'm thinking you should take over and go away and think about it for a very, very short time, because I need to tell the board. And I didn't really have time to think about it.

'Then I'm talking to the board, and they're saying, what are you going to do with the business?'

Whatever Wikramanayake presented to the board that fateful day and in subsequent discussions secured her the coveted spot as Macquarie's next CEO.[9] The changeover was managed smoothly— despite investors demanding to hear from their new leader at the 2018 annual general meeting (the day the news became public)—with Moore staying almost five months to help with the transition.

That included fronting the Hayne Royal Commission and flanking his successor at investor meetings as she learned the CEO ropes. By this stage former Reserve Bank Governor Glenn Stevens had knocked back other offers and in 2017 took a seat on Macquarie's board, setting up options for Warne's eventual replacement as chairman, which took place in May 2022.[10]

■

Early in Wikramanayake's tenure she did have a raft of executive departures to contend with, which spurred some anxiety among investors, but that didn't last particularly long. Well-known names were lightening their responsibilities or departing the Macquarie mother ship, and new fresh faces were joining the executive committee. Andrew Downe stepped away from leading Commodities and Global Markets in March 2019, but continued to run cash equities globally and CGM in Asia.[11] This saw Nick O'Kane promoted to group head, following what Macquarie cited was a two-year transition period in anticipation of the changeover.

Ben Brazil, aka Brains, became chairman of Corporate and Asset Finance (CAF) Principal Finance and left Macquarie in August 2019, a move that saw Florian Herold elevated to group head CAF Principal Finance. Tim Bishop retired from Macquarie in mid-2019 after the Macquarie Capital[12] division had delivered what was then a record profit. Daniel Wong and Michael Silverton then took over as joint co-heads of Macquarie Capital. Wong would later part ways with Macquarie in early 2022 to run the European operations of Stonepeak, founded by his former colleagues, leaving Silverton as the sole boss of Macquarie Capital.

Wikramanayake replaced herself at the helm of Macquarie Asset Management with company stalwart Martin Stanley in 2018, who was succeeded by Ben Way in 2021. The retirement of Mary Reemst in 2021 saw Stuart Green take the reins as head of Macquarie Bank. Wikramanayake also presided over the 2019 banner year for Macquarie, as the group celebrated its 50th anniversary. And what a jam-packed half-century it had been. The milestone was celebrated with a host of events, one of which was a panel discussion including all the surviving prior CEOs alongside Wikramanayake.

It was titled 'The shoulders of giants' and senior staff were given rare insights to the early years at Hill Samuel Australia, the deregulatory environment, and a smattering of old photos including the obligatory male sideburns to set the scene. Johnson and Berg discussed the earlier years and Moss and Moore took carriage of more recent times, and there were plenty of references to the foundational building blocks that shaped the place.

Johnson told the group: 'We put in place excellence as the standard for recruiting and for the delivery of all our services. Believe it or not, this was a slightly novel strategy for recruiting in Australia!' He went on to say that excellence was 'gender and colour blind', remarking that when Helen Brown led the credit unit in the 1980s it was not a remarkable occurrence for the firm.

The theme of that event was drawn from Sir Isaac Newton's sage quote from 1675: 'If I have seen further, it is by standing upon the shoulders of giants.' The messages that were revisited that day at Macquarie's anniversary event had certainly made their impression on a young Wikramanayake, who still lives and breathes the culture. She is a staunch believer in the bottom-up ethos and allowing Macquarie to empower people to find business opportunities, but with the right levels of accountability.

There is a tendency, both inside Macquarie and in the broader industry, to fall a little bit in love with the *idea* of Wikramanayake: the very fact of her advancement and success is a cause for everyone to pat themselves on the back because it says something pleasing about an otherwise white and male-dominated world.

Not everything about that attitude is positive. It masks the failings of a still hopelessly undiversified sector, it patronises Wikramanayake and it also clouds clear assessment of her skills and performance.

The diversity question is problematic at Macquarie, given gender representation of females in senior levels of investment banks and asset managers is universally poor.

But those statistics, and having a diverse universe of employees more generally, are topics that are gradually being addressed.

'There is a gender issue in our whole industry, because we only have in the industry 10 per cent to 12 per cent female representation at senior levels, and our executive director representation is only 17 per cent, albeit up significantly in recent years,' Wikramanayake says.

'But I think one of the challenges is as well, our industry is not attracting females at the entry level. We have one-third female applicants, and here we are 35 years on, females are still not opting to do this. We're doing a lot of work trying at the entry level, to persuade females that this industry actually can be really fun.'

While Wikramanayake says she didn't encounter any bias against her at Macquarie and found it was a meritocracy, some women canvassed by the authors did find it difficult to juggle their career and parenting duties.

Others had a much more positive experience. One senior Macquarie manager told us after having her third child she told Moore she was resigning, but he convinced her instead to take extended leave. She returned after two years and remains in a senior position today. Wikramanayake also had time away from Macquarie, taking a one-year sabbatical and during that time setting up a scholarship to help disadvantaged children in Africa and South America finish their schooling and access tertiary education or vocational training in countries including Australia.

Macquarie's board—when you include Wikramanayake—has more female directors than men, a feat few listed Australian companies can boast.[13] The group's ten-member prestigious executive committee, though, has just three women.[14] While the numbers present mixed results, Wikramanayake is mindful of the benefits of having a diverse workforce.

'All these things we do, I always say they're smart business, not just good for the community but good for the business. Because if we are attracting talent from all different parts of the community, that's in our interest because we want to get the best people from everywhere and not have any roadblocks,' she says.

Wikramanayake is also front and centre of Macquarie's latest code of conduct, released in November 2021.[15] She has carved her own legacy at Macquarie, including her leadership on issues such as climate change and capitalising on the notable business opportunity around that.

But there are critics of Wikramanayake's style and approach, including those who believe she is the kind of CEO that will build on the existing structure in a measured fashion, although shy away from transformational deals or big shifts in Macquarie's strategic direction. One former executive says: 'She has a different approach I believe to Nicholas, who was into options and lots of different things. I think the risk for Macquarie is it's eliminating options.'

He suggests some of that related to the firm's scale, although if Macquarie had more appetite for risk and growth in differing areas of private markets its market capitalisation could be double its current value.

Another says: 'A lot of people talk about Steve Jobs as part of the Apple DNA, and now Tim Cook runs it and it's lost that magic. I'm going to somewhat controversially say that Nicholas had more Steve Jobs in him and Shemara's probably more of a Tim Cook.'

Among changes to Macquarie's structure under Wikramanayake was the dismantling of the Corporate and Asset Finance unit as a standalone division.[16] The restructure saw CAF Principal Finance subsumed into Macquarie Capital, where the idea was to bring together all of the group's principal investing activity. Meanwhile, CAF Transportation Finance joined Macquarie Asset Management as the AirFinance business also evolved into a different beast. Garry Farrell retired from Macquarie alongside these divisional changes.

In hindsight it may represent one of the best-timed deals ahead of the pandemic, considering what started to grip global aviation markets in 2020. Macquarie in December 2019 agreed to sell a 25 per cent stake in its plane leasing unit to industry Australian superannuation fund giant Sunsuper.[17] That transaction followed Dutch pension fund PGGM snapping up a 25 per cent holding a bit over six months earlier, cutting Macquarie's exposure by half as the COVID-19 pandemic grounded all but essential air travel. It was a timely deal, not by design, but it worked in Macquarie's favour.

As panic started to filter through the business community in early 2020, Sunsuper operatives were looking at any available options to delay the transaction's closure. They made a call to Macquarie to request a postponement, but were politely told the deal was too far progressed to make any timeline change.

Another strategic decision by Wikramanayake saw the Green Investment Bank moved to sit within Macquarie Asset Management in 2022, as a way of giving investors more access to the huge decarbonisation theme. But first there was a deadly global pandemic to navigate.

■

Due to Macquarie's extensive global operations and the havoc COVID-19 inflicted on cities, hospitals and businesses in 2020 and 2021, the company had to move quickly to mobilise its pandemic crisis response. Group operations boss Nicole Sorbara led the crisis team around monitoring the health response and outcomes across markets and the sweeping shift to remote working.

That crisis team met weekly at the various peaks during the pandemic and at the time of writing had scaled those meetings back to monthly. 'While we have a very coordinated global approach, the actual execution of it is regional,' Sorbara says.[18]

As employees bunkered down at home, lines of communication and connectedness also needed to be maintained and Wikramanayake was again front and centre.

The Corporate Operations Group had conducted thorough analysis around the health issues and government directives around the world, and decided 98 per cent of Macquarie's staff had to make the shift to working from home. Wikramanayake provided input around the messaging and communication, but rapid-fire actions were required as cities around the world were being locked down.

'Here's a script, get on the video, tell everyone they're going home,' she recalls being instructed. 'We've got the technology; we think we can support them to keep doing what they do. I just had to trust them. Because they were doing deep work, we had a crisis management team that was meeting constantly, they were sharing data with us.'

As the pandemic wore on and there were further waves of infection, Wikramanayake came up with her own initiative of conducting video focus groups with younger and mid-level employees, to maintain her engagement with staff.[19]

As well as keeping staff safe in cities ravaged by COVID-19 there were other data and logistical issues to deal with too. With the pandemic came a greater risk of data breaches, leakages and security incidents, but Simon Wright says his division fared well in spite of the challenges. 'We had fewer risk breaches, we had fewer issues. It was quite extraordinary, and the technology worked.'

Macquarie also had to step up its efforts to help customers navigate choppy financial markets and, in some cases, shore up their balance sheets as the COVID-19 drama unfolded.

The equity and debt capital markets teams were in constant contact with customers and each other as companies figured out how to wade through the unprecedented events. Liquidity and debt management were priorities, particularly across industries that saw sharp declines in activity and therefore income due to the pandemic.

Macquarie—sometimes alongside other banks and advisers—in Australia helped raise capital for companies including outdoor advertising agency oOh!media, travel agency Flight Centre, IDP Education and National Australia Bank.[20]

■

During the pandemic Macquarie's appetite for acquisitions actually increased, a reminder of how the group looks to seize upon market disruption. In early December 2020, Macquarie would again look to beef up its asset and investment management business by snapping up New York-listed Waddell & Reed for US$1.7 billion.[21] The transaction included Macquarie hiving off Waddell & Reed's wealth business to LPL Financial Holdings for US$300 million plus excess net assets.

Through its subsidiaries, Waddell & Reed had provided investment and wealth management services through the USA since 1937. When the deal was completed the acquisition added US$78.6 billion under management to Macquarie's books. But there were pertinent questions being asked about the transaction.

In a report at the time of the announced acquisition Jonathan Mott, then a UBS analyst, said while the purchase would be accretive to Macquarie's earnings there were challenges in buying a business experiencing outflows. 'Waddell & Reed's revenue and funds under management have been in decline for several years. We believe that buying asset management businesses in outflow and attempting to achieve synergies is rarely successful.

'Further, it will be difficult for the market to benchmark the success of this acquisition as once integrated into Macquarie, tracking its funds under management, revenue and synergies will not be disclosed.'

Macquarie's global head of public investments, Shawn Lytle, says Waddell & Reed fits a strategy to fill business gaps following the Delaware purchase, and sees the group on its way to completing a mission to build a specialist active firm. 'When we looked at our line-up a number of years ago we saw strengths, but also gaps we needed to fill,' he says.

These have included small-cap growth teams in New York, global growth out of San Diego and global value in Luxembourg. Waddell & Reed offered capabilities in growth equities—both large and mid-capitalisation stocks—as well as sector specialisations in science and technology, and a presence in US high yield fixed income. The acquisition also resulted in a strategic partnership with the LPL wealth management network, and 'it was a good cultural fit,' Lytle adds.

With deals such as this, a lot of people also need to be shown the door and in this instance the transaction also included a real estate challenge in Kansas City that appears in our US road trip (Chapter 7). But this is modern asset management: as much scale as possible on one expensive platform in order to drive margins.[22] The business still has gaps, notably in ESG (environmental, social, governance) sustainability investing, quant investing, fixed income and investment grade credit. It would be no surprise to see Lytle and Wikramanayake preside over more acquisitions in this area.[23]

Just under a year after the Waddell & Reed acquisition was completed, Macquarie ruled off another US purchase that would add US$3.5 billion in assets under management. That reflected Central Park Group LLC,[24] an independent alternative investment advisory firm.

Closer to head office, Macquarie was also scoping out potential acquisitions. Macquarie tapped investors to raise A$2.8 billion in capital in late 2021 to help turbocharge business growth and pursue acquisitions. After weighing a bid for AMP in its entirety or buying separate divisions in the three years prior,[25] Macquarie in 2021 agreed to acquire the Australian wealth group's global equities and fixed income unit. That transaction was sealed after Macquarie in 2018 recused itself from being inside AMP's tent and conducting a strategic review of assets and a possible sale of the entire company, alongside UBS, when it realised it may be a better option to bid for all or parts of the wealth group. These acquisitions combined have added to Macquarie's heft in the industry. Macquarie's assets under management had swelled to A$795.6 billion[26] at the time of writing and the milestone of cracking A$1 trillion—as long as there isn't a sustained share market rout—must be in its sights.

The company has also pushed further into digital and technology assets to take advantage of the sweeping digitisation theme that only accelerated during the COVID-19 turmoil. Digital infrastructure[27] is a vast frontier and Macquarie is vying to become a formidable player in the space.

Macquarie's Asian infrastructure fund, for example, acquired a majority stake in Australian data centre firm AirTrunk in 2020, and two years later the company outlined plans to build a new hyperscale data centre in West Tokyo. Macquarie also formed a partnership and made an equity investment in California-based Prime Data Centers, invested in UK rural superfast broadband business Voneus, and in Spain closed the acquisition of MasMovil's Fibre-to-the-Home network. In listed Australian markets, Macquarie partnered with

Aware Super to complete an acquisition of telecommunications group Vocus in 2021.

Ani Satchcroft says Macquarie doesn't pursue these digital infrastructure opportunities from a standing start.

'We like to have things on our radar for a long period of time, get comfortable with them, socialise them, make sure we've had time just to think about any sort of things that could go wrong or would make it more attractive before we actually approach.

'With both AirTrunk and Vocus we had a thematic view that digital infrastructure was important.'

The sharp sell-off in the technology sector in 2022 hasn't dented Macquarie's resolve to take a long-term position in the digitisation trend.

■

As 2020 drew to a close, Macquarie's bankers had a reason to smile. A tiny A$10.5 million initial investment in 2011 into a data analytics and software player called Nuix was generating a lot of excitement among fund managers looking for the next hot Australian IPO.

An IPO issue price of A$5.31 was locked in, delivering Macquarie juicy sale proceeds in the order of A$564 million for the selldown of 76 per cent of its stake to a 30 per cent holding. The trading debut saw the stock close up a whopping 51 per cent, and it rallied as high as A$11.16 in the months following.

But it wasn't long before the wheels were starting to fall off 2020's hottest Australian IPO, as Nuix missed earnings forecasts and became mired in controversy with revelations of poor executive conduct. At the time of writing, Nuix's shares were changing hands at A$0.72 and as we go to print a Federal Court case is ongoing as former CEO Eddie Sheedy pursues the company over whether his options were subject to a stock split that occurred in 2016. Nuix claims arrangements made with Sheedy didn't entitle him to the stock split.

Nuix's failure to meet its earnings targets and serious questions raised about its accounts prompted the separate exits of the CEO and CFO. The latter was investigated by authorities over alleged insider trading, but no action was pursued.

Macquarie's Daniel Phillips—who founded the group's technology venture capital investment arm—stepped off the Nuix board in 2022, although he was chairman between 2018 and November 2020. He and David Standen were involved in Nuix for years and backed management to take the company public. In June 2022, the duo separately fronted the Federal Court to answer curly questions about Sheedy's options, as the case got under way. Standen, in particular, who flew in from Switzerland to take the stand in the hearing, looked uncomfortable giving evidence about Sheedy's options package and documentation.

It was in September 2022 that the Australian Securities and Investments Commission (ASIC) catapulted Nuix back into the headlines by starting Federal Court action for alleged continuous disclosure breaches and misleading or deceptive conduct. The regulator also alleges Nuix's directors—including Phillips[28]—breached their duties by failing to take 'reasonable steps to prevent Nuix from making misleading statements and breaching its continuous disclosure obligations.'

The whole torrid Nuix saga spurred investigative reporting about the company that uncovered that Nuix co-founder Tony Castagna had spent a year in jail for tax avoidance and money laundering before having his conviction overturned.

Despite the constant controversy swirling around Nuix, Wikramanayake stands by the investment. 'We're still a 30 per cent shareholder, we believe in the business, we're there and committed.[29]

We're a customer,' she says, referring to Nuix's natural language processing systems, which draw on machine learning and other technology.

The thorny topic of Nuix also triggered some questions at Macquarie's annual general meeting in 2021. Then-chairman Peter Warne said Macquarie had conducted an audit of the Nuix IPO.[30] 'We've done a full review of that and there have been no corners cut . . . In the actual IPO process, nothing has come out that is beyond our normal standard. In relation to the investment itself, that's something else that we'll be looking at over time.'

Just months before that meeting, Macquarie was being hit from another angle, this time by the banking regulator. The group's banking division was dealt a A\$500 million capital charge and threatened with further action, after the Australian Prudential Regulation Authority (APRA) uncovered unacceptable 'multiple material breaches' of prudential and reporting standards.[31]

It was a terrible look for a company that prided itself on its prudent management of risk. But APRA didn't hold back in its assessment of the matter. 'For one of the country's largest financial institutions to have committed breaches of this nature is disappointing and unacceptable,' APRA deputy chairman John Lonsdale said at the time.

The issues APRA identified had pay implications for Macquarie's executives in 2021, cutting performance share allocations and imposing further conditions on the release of part of their retained profit share.

To cap off a challenging compliance period, the securities and conduct regulator in 2022 kicked off Federal Court action against Macquarie's banking arm for not adequately monitoring and controlling transactions. They related to customers' cash management accounts and transactions spanning almost four years to January 2020.[32] The proceedings allege that the impact on Macquarie's customers includes A$2.9 million in unauthorised withdrawals by convicted former financial adviser, Ross Andrew Hopkins.

■

Despite the reputational issues Macquarie has endured in recent years, the record profits keep rolling in. For the twelve months ended 31 March 2022, Macquarie beat market expectations and posted a bumper A$4.7 billion result, underscored by a higher commodities revenue across gas, power, agriculture and oil, and buoyant levels of hedging activity during market volatility.

Wikramanayake was typically cautious with Macquarie's guidance for the 2023 year at the 2022 AGM, sidestepping any quantifiable estimates for the period ahead. But investors and analysts are attuned to this cycle of Macquarie steering clear of guidance early in its year, before providing more clarity typically sometime after its July AGM.

Citigroup analyst Brendan Sproules believes Macquarie confronts headwinds in its commodities and markets unit, given the challenging external environment. 'We think commodities revenues [will] decline from a peak of A$3.6 billion in full-year 2023 . . . Despite the ongoing war in Ukraine, we think hedging and trading opportunities subside as economic growth slows,' he said in October 2022.

But Macquarie bull and Jefferies analyst Brian Johnson says the group has plenty of long-term earnings levers to pull, particularly in the green energy sector.

'The Green Investment Group is the next iteration of the infrastructure model and it's nowhere near reflected in the current share price. With Shemara they've doubled down on their commitment to climate change.

'The courage to actually harvest the existing opportunities is pretty profound. Macquarie's success all comes down to that remuneration structure, because most banks may think on a three-year horizon. Macquarie generally thinks on a 20-year horizon.'

Johnson's analysis out to 2050 shows that total renewables investment is estimated to reach US$92–173 trillion, so given a point in between of say US$120 trillion geared at 50 per cent in 2050 he reckons the global pool of renewables sits at around US$60 trillion. If Macquarie Asset Management holds its 10 per cent share in this market its A$13 billion in energy assets under management would swell to US$6 trillion by 2050.

Johnson does outline, however, that a slowdown in capital velocity is a risk for Macquarie, if it becomes more difficult to complete transactions that would dent performance fees and hinder asset sales.

Wikramanayake is certainly taking a long-term view of Macquarie's prospects and also credits the remuneration structure— carefully crafted and put in place by David Clarke many decades earlier, with some tweaks along the way—with creating a strong overarching framework. 'That remuneration mechanism is really important, because people are sharing in the upside and downside and [are] aligned over the long term,' she says.

But can Macquarie really continue to be innovative and nimble in finding opportunities as it swells in size? Can entrepreneurialism thrive within a markedly larger organisation? It's in the company's DNA and something the leadership at Macquarie will be fighting to retain as the company traverses the next decade.

Wikramanayake certainly doesn't think Macquarie is of a size that makes retaining the essence of the group difficult. 'I don't think we're big at all. We may have a market cap of A$70 billion, JPMorgan I think they're US$350 billion. They have several hundred thousand people. Organisations preserve their cultures.

'Microsoft has more people; Google has more people. We do patient adjacent growth; we don't go and do some big new thing and a big new country with 5000 new people. Everything has been small patient growth, we bring on new teams, and we give them a little bit of capital, and we double down and double down. This allows us to grow while preserving our core cultural approach.'

Wikramanayake has strapped in for the journey and Macquarie's next leg of growth, with her commitment to Macquarie unwavering.

Wikramanayake's fondness of maths is evident today in her investment entities that are aptly called Aljebra Pty Ltd, Aljebra Superannuation Fund and Aljebra Investment Trust. That is where she houses some of her 1,088,094 Macquarie shares valued at about A\$193.7 million at the time of writing, excluding restricted and performance share units.

If you think that's a large holding, then you're right!

Mirroring Moore's approach to his Macquarie stock, Wikramanayake has never sold a share in the company she now leads. The 2022 annual report counts Moore as the nineteenth-largest investor in Macquarie at 748,709 shares, or 0.2 per cent of the company, trailing Wikramanayake who sits a couple of spots ahead of him, based on her most recent director filing.

'It's part of my alignment. While I'm working here, I need to be committed to the organisation, and I also need to be aligned with our investors and other stakeholders,' she says. 'I don't view it as a financial asset.'

EPILOGUE

Macquarie has passed its half-century with a number of records intact. Never a single year without delivering a profit, through the 1987 crash, the GFC and the COVID-19 pandemic. Never an external hire for a chief executive. Only six year-on-year declines in net profit in 53 years.[1]

Shemara Wikramanayake presides over a machine. Sometimes it's a bit of a Heath Robinson machine, with weird cogs and gears and odd bits sticking out of the side and internal workings that most of us could never hope to fathom, but it's a machine that largely works, efficiently and relentlessly. Aside from the slings and arrows of markets and geopolitics beyond its control, it's hard to imagine what can stop it from growing like this indefinitely.

Looking forward five years or a decade, one can be certain Macquarie will look markedly different again. The reinvention and evolution theme runs through the company's veins, forging to new frontiers or exiting businesses that are no longer as lucrative as they once were. One former Macquarie executive says that, during his time, an analysis of group income showed that at any given time, 40 per cent of the businesses did not exist five years earlier. That staggering figure is a Macquarie hallmark, and makes the firm stand out on the global stage.

'One of the key characteristics of Macquarie is that the external environment constantly changes,' says Wikramanayake, 'and the best way to be nimble and respond to this is to empower everyone on the ground to move very quickly and adapt fast to the needs and opportunities of their local communities.

'It's like a Darwinian evolutionary principle that you need to facilitate constant, small variations over time if you want to evolve and survive.

'I'm not going to sit here in the centre and say: in five years we will look like this. Even more so in ten years: I have no idea.

'There's 18,000 people on the ground in diverse locations with very diverse skills who will have a much better idea.'

Renewables illustrate her point. Macquarie made its first investments in the sector in the early 2000s. They account for 10 per cent of income in 2022 and that number will no doubt rise, while more traditional commodities and energy sources—today a much larger proportion of earnings—will likely decline.

The many cogs and gears within Macquarie make it hard to predict which ideas will emerge as the next big earnings winners. But you can be sure Macquarie's senior bankers—and the junior rank and file who are on the way up—will be weighing scenarios, cutting and dicing the numbers, and assessing where the money is going to come from. Some will be cash cows. Some will be controversial. Some will fall flat.

It's happening right now. As you read this, Macquarie is cornering the market in transfer factoring—lending funds to football clubs ahead of expected income—across European football leagues.

The book of Macquarie clients now includes Crystal Palace and Leicester City.[2]

Macquarie is, though, a machine that faces questions. Here are a few of them.

First, Macquarie has been built on entrepreneurial zest and a culture of management that empowers the individual on the ground rather than the grand design. This has worked. It has worked for more than half a century. But can it continue to work at such scale? With every passing year, it's not just the profits that increase but the headcount, the geographical scope, the range of operations. Of necessity, the person on the ground is a greater distance from the top in a larger enterprise than a small one.

There are older departed executives who doubt that Macquarie is still, truly, a place where one can fail to succeed, where one has freedom within boundaries, where the bank has your back if you get things wrong on the way to getting things right. None of them doubt Wikramanayake's performance: they look at the results and the share price and the dividend and they raise a glass (none of these guys have sold all their shares; to some of them it would seem an act of craven disloyalty, and economically stupid). But they do doubt whether a place this big can ever be as nimble as it was.

This brings us to a second question. It's a question that finds its expression in the windswept towers of Hudson Yards in New York, where Stonepeak has been built by former Macquarie executives and continues to take many of its brightest minds.[3] It arises in Singapore's One George Street building overlooking the Singapore River and the bars of Boat Quay, where Equis and a team of Macquarie alumni made themselves very wealthy indeed[4] in renewable infrastructure. It arises in London's Mayfair, in roughly equal proximity to the Royal Academy of Arts and a Bentley dealership, where star Ben Brazil now plies his trade at FitzWalter Capital. And further up Melbourne's

Collins Street from Macquarie's offices, where Robin Bishop now jointly runs private equity house BGH Capital as founding partner.

Just look around Sydney, littered with firms set up by Macquarie alumni. Where better place to start than the Governor Macquarie Tower, head office of Grant Samuel? Or Macquarie Street, where advisory firm Gresham Partners was co-founded by former Macquarie executive director James Graham?

Phil Cave's Anchorage Capital Partners resides on George Street, not far from fund manager Loftus Peak, while infrastructure manager Palisade Investment Partners is closer to the bustling Martin Place financial district. Also in the CBD are alternative investment management firm ROC Partners,[5] which was spun out of Macquarie in a management buy-out in 2014, and not-for-profit impact investing firm Social Ventures Australia.[6]

That question is: what could Macquarie have been had it been able to keep these people? Andrew Downe expresses it clearly. 'Macquarie has been a fantastic story,' he says. 'But it could have been way better, and way bigger. And the reason I say that is because of the number of good people we lost.'

Macquarie bankers tend not to go to the competition; headhunters moan about how hard it is to prise people from Macquarie to obvious rivals. It's not like UBS, which has proven to be the source of much of the staff of start-up Barrenjoey, or CLSA, which was raided when Jefferies set up in Australia.[7] What they *do* do, though, is set up their own firm, attracted by the idea of being small and nimble again.

So should Macquarie have done what, say, Blackstone tends to do, and provide seed capital to those who depart so they stay invested in the success of those they have trained? One former employee speaks of 'a slightly cultish element to leaving Macquarie under Nicholas' that prevented this.

The other perspective is that when people go, they're gone and there's no point perpetuating the misery with a stop-gap position. 'We have an institutionalised model,' says Michael Silverton. 'And that has benefits we protect.'

'I don't want people working here who don't want to work here,' Silverton says. 'In the short term reactively, you might think: how can we remain attached to this? But ripping the band aid off and moving on' is the better approach, he says.[8]

'Our tendency has been to just focus on what we're doing. If we're not going to do it, then someone else can do it, but don't get caught halfway in the middle.'

Macquarie has an extensive alumni network of about 100,000 people, and Simon McKeon views that as a huge asset to the organisation, given it can tap its networks on deals or other opportunities.

'I keep saying one of the biggest assets on the Macquarie balance sheet that doesn't get recorded, is the fact that the Macquarie alumni, certainly in this country, is everywhere. There's hardly a door that can't be opened,' he says.

A third question. In an environment where so much power in financial services has shifted towards private equity, ought Macquarie to be a private vehicle itself? Macquarie's listing has been essential for the access it brought to public markets and the mechanism for staff to engage in its success. But today, private capital is a vast and plentiful source in a way that it never was when Macquarie listed in the 1990s. Not everyone thinks Macquarie still needs the short-term lens of half-year reporting[9] and AGMs; that it could be, in effect, one of the world's great hedge funds, working for the long term without scrutiny.

Similarly, with every passing year, the question inevitably arises whether Macquarie is still truly an Australian institution and that Sydney is the appropriate place to call home. In the 2022 financial year Macquarie earned almost twice as much from the Americas as from Australia.[10] Already the global head of Macquarie Capital is in New York, and the head of the public side of Macquarie Asset Management is in Philadelphia,[11] while in the biggest group by income—Commodities and Global Markets—the Americas contributed almost three times the income that Australia did, and EMEA (Europe, the Middle East and Africa) two and a half times.[12]

Wikramanayake tends to give short shrift to any idea of moving when the subject is raised on results briefing calls.[13] Most Macquarie shareholders, both retail and institutional, are in Australia, as are its regulators and its listing, which isn't to say that a secondary listing could not be easily achieved. Also, the outsized contribution of the Americas had a lot to do with the power and gas business dynamics in that market, and it won't be this way every year.

Wikramanayake is herself an internationalist, having worked in nine offices in six countries, and most, but not all, of her obvious lieutenants are too. Leaving aside Silverton, who is in the USA, CGM head (and most obvious heir apparent) Nick O'Kane made his career in Houston, Los Angeles and, before that, London, Seoul and Kuala Lumpur; Ben Way, head of Macquarie Asset Management, has spent most of his professional career in various places in Asia; Alex Harvey, the CFO, was head of Asia; only Greg Ward, Nicole Sorbara and Stuart Green (who is himself British by birth) have had entirely Australia-focused careers.

But Wikramanayake is quick to point out that Nicholas Moore spent his entire professional life based in Sydney, albeit with a lot of travelling, and didn't do too badly in the organisation because of it. 'That's just my story,' she says. 'People pursue what plays to their passion and their strength. I have loved living all over the world, immersing myself in other cultures, being in the early stage in the trenches of building businesses in different markets. But you don't have to do that. You can have all sorts of careers inside Macquarie.'

As for the idea of going private, it seems unlikely now: Macquarie's market capitalisation peaked above A$80 billion in late 2021,[14] a mighty sum to take off the market, and the staff compensation mechanisms make a liquid method of reward essential. It would be more problematic if shareholders were pushing for short-term domestic gains as they tend to do with Australia's Big Four banks, but in practice most instos, and probably most retail investors, have long since accepted that Macquarie's earned the right to do what it wants to do in its own way and at its own pace.

Macquarie's board will need to be mindful, however, not to erode the important foundations set in the 1970s that have given the firm an edge. The entrepreneurial spirit of the place. Altering the key tenets that have helped frame Macquarie's culture could have consequences. For example, will the incoming change to the remuneration structure—that sees deferral periods for key executives cut from seven years to five years—have an impact?

Another question is: what have we learned about Macquarie's relationship with Australia? Twenty years ago it was the ultimate tall poppy, with its outsized compensation and its noise and its preposterous deal-making and layers of fees. One senses less of that now: executive pay is no longer so out of step with the rest of Australia in an era of digital billionaires, Wikramanayake presents a believable image of corporate engagement and environmental care, and generally people don't seem to find banks as inherently evil as they did in the GFC or through Australia's royal commission (or if they do, they've aimed more of their ire at the Big Four).

But there is still a curious duality about Macquarie's engagement with the people of its home market. It is a subject of envy and sometimes resentment, but it is also a national champion in a challenging world. 'I think Australia can take pride in the fact that this entrepreneurial and innovative financial institution has been enormously successful and taken its model to the world,' says Peter Costello.

'Along the way, has it pushed the boundaries? Yes. Has it been a model citizen at all times? Well I'm not saying that. But I'm pleased it's still here. I'll say we, Australia, would have been worse if we didn't have Macquarie.'

The importance of having an Australian corporate flagbearer in the global marketplace, particularly from banking, can't be overstated. Australia's four major retail banks have largely retreated from their offshore operations, notwithstanding ANZ's reasonable presence in Asia. And given the long list of Australian companies that have failed in their attempts to go global—think National Australia Bank or Wesfarmers, which have suffered from serious missteps in their attempts—Macquarie's success in this regard should be celebrated.

Macquarie's broader success can be traced back to the sturdy foundations that were laid in the formative Hill Samuel Australia days by a small group of smart bankers that had the foresight to build something well and that would last. Stan Owens, David Clarke, Mark Johnson and Tony Berg put those foundations in place in a thoughtful and meaningful way, which has enriched shareholders and staff. The underlying principles they built the firm around still endure today, despite some tweaks. Macquarie employees account for about 5 per cent of the company's shareholder register, a decent chunk of skin in the game.

A final question: what can we all learn from Macquarie, as businesses, as people? The secret sauce of Macquarie, for all its bells and whistles and angles and elbows, is really quite simple. Back people to take a chance on building new things, but have an iron grip on risk as you do it. Don't bet the farm on any one idea. Understand what you want to do, and study it until your knowledge of that niche is watertight. Test it. Articulate it. Then go and do it until you get it right.

There are other things in the mix: a preoccupation with assessing risk, understanding worst-case scenarios as well as the upside, taking calculated smaller bets, compensation structures that marry the employee to the firm and the culture for the very long run. But that backing of clever people is, in essence, what has made Macquarie the success that it is today, that has turned A\$31 billion of shareholder funds into many times that in market value plus a sea of healthy dividends through a business made entirely of brainpower and ideas. You can call them ruthless and profit-hungry. You can bemoan the brain drain they have created for a nation's brightest minds. But what you really can't do is doubt their success.

ACKNOWLEDGEMENTS

When we told Macquarie we were writing this book in late 2021, we don't imagine management or the communications team were thrilled. We knew that they could, had they chosen to do so, have made life extremely difficult, not only by blocking access to existing staff, but by leaning on Macquarie's vast and influential alumni not to speak to us.

That is not the approach they chose to take, and we are glad. In fact, Macquarie provided considerable access to its people and did not push back against direct on-the-record quotation, making for a more revealing and transparent book. Independently, we reached out to dozens of former Macquarie staff, who were mostly extremely open. All told, we interviewed around 130 people in at least 10 countries, including many outside the company, such as politicians, investors, clients and peers all over the world.

While Macquarie has not endorsed this book, members of its corporate affairs team have greatly assisted us, including with archived materials, and several of its executives past and present gave their time in interviews. We appreciate all their effort.

Macquarie and the corporate affairs team did not get to see the text any sooner than any other reader, bar checking quotes from current staff and executives for accuracy.

We would like to thank all the people who gave us detailed interviews for the book, including the five living chief executives, Mark Johnson, Tony Berg, Allan Moss, Nicholas Moore and Shemara Wikramanayake. David Clarke's second wife Jane kindly provided materials that reflected his commitment to Macquarie and delved into his inner thoughts on the evolution of the place. A shout-out also to Stan Owens' family for helping fill some initial gaps in our research from the early Hill Samuel Australia days.

Too many others were involved to name, and not everyone who was interviewed wished to be quoted, but we are grateful to everyone for their time and knowledge.

Chris would like to thank his editor at Euromoney, Louise Bowman, for the considerable latitude she gave him to work on this book while still being Asia editor throughout. It would not have been possible without her generous support.

Chris would also like to thank his family—wife Kathryn, children Chyna and Quinn, and helper Elma—for all of their support and tolerance, with much of this being written and researched while all of us were sharing the same space in the late stages of the COVID-19 pandemic. He would also like to place on record that his dog Cheddar was no help at all.

Joyce would like to thank her editors at *The Australian,* including Eric Johnston, Kylar Loussikian, Amber Plum and Chris Dore, for their support and for providing the flexibility to step away from her round to devote several months to compiling this book.

She would also like to thank her parents for their guidance and husband-to-be Jesse for his unwavering support and assistance through the many stressful days in meeting book deadlines. Pepi,

Joyce's dog, was a welcome guest in the study, bar the odd barking fit!

We would like to pass on a special thanks to the team at Allen & Unwin, in particular Elizabeth Weiss, who backed the idea from the outset, and Courtney Lick, who toiled over putting the book together. Working with them has been a pleasure and an education.

A heartful thanks also to Don Argus, John Symond, Steve Harker and Clive Horwood for reading our manuscript.

A final note on this book and how it worked with two authors: it is a joint publication written and researched by both of us, with some interviews conducted together and some individually, but clearly with each of us pursuing particular themes. Broadly speaking, Joyce wrote more on Australia (particularly the early and later years, including Shemara Wikramanayake's reign) and Chris more on international operations and the 1990s–2000s, with each providing input into the other's sections. But we opted only to byline the two roadtrip chapters as very individual pieces of writing.

Macquarie is an institution with 53 years of history and a global footprint, meaning we could have written much more but were constrained in our word count. All-in-all it was a combined effort and an immense project, but certainly an enjoyable and rewarding one.

GLOSSARY OF ACRONYMS AND ABBREVIATIONS

ABC Australian Broadcasting Corporation

AEP Allco Equity Partners

AFR Australian Financial Review

AGM Annual General Meeting

APRA Australian Prudential Regulation Authority

AREH Asian Renewable Energy Hub

ASC Australian Securities Commission

ASIC Australian Securities and Investments Commission

ASX Australian Stock Exchange (until 2006); Australian Securities Exchange (2006 onwards).

ATO Australian Taxation Office

BCIMC British Columbia Investment Management Corporation

BFS Banking and Financial Services

BHP Broken Hill Proprietary

BT/BTIB Bankers Trust/Bankers Trust Investment Bank

CAF Corporate and Asset Finance

CBD central business district

CDO collateralised debt obligation

CDPQ Caisse de dépôt et placement du Québec

CDS credit default swap
CEW Chief Executive Women
CFO chief financial officer
CGM Commodities and Global Markets
CMA cash management account
CMT Cash Management Trust
COO chief operating officer
CPI consumer price index
CPU central processing unit
DCM debt capital markets
EBITDA earnings before interest, taxes, depreciation, and amortisation
ECM equity capital markets
EMEA Europe, the Middle East and Africa
ESG environmental, social, governance
ETF exchange-traded funds
EU enforceable undertaking
FBO fixed base operations
FIBRA Fideicomiso de Inversion en Bienes Raices (a Mexican real estate investment trust)
FSHD facioscapulohumeral muscular dystrophy
FSS Financial Supervisory Service (in South Korea)
GFC global financial crisis
GIB Green Investment Bank
GIG Green Investment Group
HR human resources
IMF International Monetary Fund
IPO initial public offering
IPTA Industrial Property Trust of Australia
IT information technology
ITA Infrastructure Trust of Australia
KOSPI Korea Composite Stock Price Index
LNG liquefied natural gas
LSE London Stock Exchange
M&A mergers and acquisitions
MAIF Macquarie Asia Infrastructure Fund

MAM Macquarie Asset Management

MAp Macquarie Airports

MCIG Macquarie Communications Infrastructure Group

MCW Macquarie CountryWide Trust

MEAP Macquarie Essential Assets Partnership

MEIF Macquarie European Infrastructure Funds

MEL Macquarie Equities Limited

MFG Macquarie Funds Group

MIC Macquarie Infrastructure Corporation

MIG Macquarie Infrastructure Group

MIP Macquarie Infrastructure Partners

MIRA Macquarie Infrastructure and Real Assets

MKIF Macquarie Korea Infrastructure Fund

MPW Macquarie Private Wealth

NAB National Australia Bank

NOHC non-operating holding company

NSW New South Wales

OECD Organisation for Economic Co-operation and Development

OBU offshore banking units

OTPP Ontario Teachers' Pension Plan

PBL Publishing and Broadcasting Limited

PPP public–private partnership

PR public relations

QC Queen's Counsel

RBA Reserve Bank of Australia

RBS Royal Bank of Scotland

REIT real estate investment trust

S&P Standard and Poor's

SARS Severe acute respiratory syndrome

SEATS Stock Exchange Automated Trading System

TARP Troubled Asset Relief Program

TMT technology, media, and telecom

VP vice-president

WTC World Trade Center

NOTES

There is a lot to say about Macquarie—more than there was room to accommodate in this print edition. We compiled 25,000 words of additional notes. Some of this material relates to sourcing, or precise legal titles and additional numbers, but it also includes whole other stories, quotes, anecdotes and people.

To allow for the maximum book length and to accommodate as much of this additional material as possible, we have hosted these notes on a dedicated website, www.millionairesfactorynotes.com, which you can access by scanning the QR code below.

Perhaps you may wish to read this with both the book and the site open on your phone, a far easier way to view the notes as they arise than flipping back and forward in a book.

INDEX

Entries in bold indicate main entries on a subject.

Macquarie Communications Infrastructure
    Group (MCIG) 157, 199, 261
Macquarie Cook Energy 271
Macquarie Essential Assets Partnership
    (MEAP) 152
Macquarie European Infrastructure Fund
    (MEIF) I, III 151, 157–8
Macquarie Forestry Investment 296–7
Macquarie Foundation/ Macquarie Group
    Foundation xiv, 289–90
Macquarie Funds Group 276, 287
Macquarie Global Property Advisers 91
Macquarie Group Collection 290
Macquarie Group Limited
    establishment 237
Macquarie Infrastructure and Real
    Assets 163, 297
Macquarie Infrastructure
    Corporation 162, 167
Macquarie Infrastructure Group 97, 141,
    143, 148, 173, 200, endnote
Macquarie Infrastructure Partners 157,
    163, 173–4, 184
Macquarie Korea Infrastructure Fund
    (MKIF) 132, 134, 205
Macquarie Leisure Trust Group 262
Macquarie name 39–41
Macquarie Prologis 91
Macquarie Property Trust 87
Macquarie Rotorcraft Leasing 333
Macquarie Securities 309, 313
Macquarie Sports 289–90
Macquarie: The Tale of the River Bank 349
Maguire, Tim 290
Maher Container Terminal 179–81
Maher, Peter 190, **206–9**, 259, 286, 319, 322
Malaysia 89, 126, 269, 275, 365
Marriott, Paul 326
Marshall, Gerald 185–6
Martin Place (1) **102–3,** 190, 197, 232, 247
Martin Place (50)/Integrated Train Station
    development 300–1
Martin Place (60) 3, 5, 9
Martin, Vic 21
Marynissen, Bill 322

MasMovil 379
Mason, Peter 195
Mather, Kerrie 105, **193–201,** 262
May, Theresa 345
McCann, Kevin 228**, 252–6**, 258, 288
McEncroe, Frank 10
McKeon, Simon 47–8, 100, 391
McKinsey & Co 52–55, 58
McMeckan, Jim 72–3, 77
McNabb, Warren 151
McNeill, James 46–7
Meares Michell Elders 13–14
Medallist 93–4
Medcraft, Greg 319
Medibank Private 334–5
Melbourne and Metropolitan Board of
    Works Superannuation Scheme 38
Melbourne City Link 82
Mendelawitz, David 122
Merrill Lynch 27, 322
Mexico 205, 260, 341, 347
Michigan Electric Transmission 174
MidAmerican Energy Holdings 271
Midlands Expressway, UK 149, 214
Miller, Jim 141, 151
Minchin, Nick 197
Mineral Securities 2
mining finance 333
Minogue, Nick 117–18, 241–2, 247
Mirvac 302
Mission Energy 77
Mitsubishi Bank 32
Mohamed, Mahathir 269
Moir, Stephen 343–5, 342
Moldan, Anton 184–5
money market 12, 17, 26, 52–3
Mongolia 333
Monier 4, 23
Moore, Nicholas
    arrival and Financial Packaging
        Division 62, 71, 79–82, 280
    BT 99–103
    CEO 75, 238–9, 240–1, 244–8, 257, 276,
        281–4, 301, 312, 328–30, 333, 373,
        392
    compensation 226, 228–31, 385